Holy Cow St. Louis!

Mike Mitchell

Holy Cow St. Louis!
Radio's Best Days,
Harry Caray's Best Years
Mike Mitchell

Mike Mitchell

Copyright © 2023 Mike Mitchell
All rights reserved.
ISBN-13: 979-8-218-15940-5
mikemitchellbooks.com

Harry Caray promotional photograph taken in 1955. Edward Goldberger/D'Arcy Advertising Agency. Photo courtesy of the Missouri Historical Society, St. Louis.

Table of Contents

Acknowledgments	vi
Introduction	viii
St. Louis, 1944	1
Harry Carabina	23
Radio Daze	36
Dizzy at the Mic	46
Bombers, Flyers, Stretch, and Gabby	72
The Rookies of '45, The Battles of '46	95
Biggie's Boys and The Man	121
Ticker Talk, a Death Threat, and a Sale	138
Mavericks and Exiles	152
A One-Team Town	186
Good Night, Skip	204
Hello Jack, Milo and Joe	212
Listening to Harry	238
Out With Harry	258
Here Comes The King	269
"My Kinda Guy's Gotta Get Fired"	286
The Summer of '69	297
Did He or Didn't He?	310
Welcome Home, Harry	327
Appendix	351

Acknowledgments

The book in your hands is the result of nearly three years of research and writing, an outcome not possible without the contributions of the following people. The peerless Mark Tomasik, the great Cardinals historian and blogger at RetroSimba.com, read every word and offered thoughtful insight and guidance. So did Joan Mitchell, who began this endeavor as my girlfriend and is now my wife. My better half is a far better editor than I can ever hope to be. Any improvements in the pages to come are largely based on their feedback. Any mistakes are mine.

Ron Jacober graciously recounted the day Harry Caray's contract was not renewed, longtime Indiana University broadcaster Don Fischer offered his childhood memories of listening to Harry, and retired Oakland A's equipment trainer Steve Vucinich recalled his encounters with Harry in Caray's post-St. Louis years. A big thanks to Kevin Uhrhan at Wilson Sporting Goods for coordinating the latter two interviews. I'm forever grateful to Nick and Malon Argint, who welcomed me into their home and shared memories and pictures – never before published – of a young Harry and his parents.

Speaking of pictures, the one of Harry on the front cover comes courtesy of the Missouri Historical Society, St. Louis. It was taken in 1955 by photographer Edward Goldberger just after Caray and the Cardinals moved to KMOX radio. Work on the cover was enhanced at 99Designs. I wish to thank Lauren Sallwasser at the Historical Society for her assistance in supplying additional photos you will find inside.

Frank Absher, the Executive Director of the St. Louis Media History Foundation, is always a great resource and consistently generous with his time. Frank supplied the photo of Harry on the back cover and others that provide context to his early St. Louis years.

I am indebted to Amanda Bahr-Evola, Assistant Director and Head of Special Collections, and the staff at the St. Louis Public Library. The Alfred Fleishman Papers at the library are filled with Caray stories, writings and correspondence, as well as countless corporate memos that flew between Fleishman-Hillard and Anheuser-Busch regarding Harry's words and behavior. Poring over the collection gives a reader insight into corporate attitudes about Caray's broadcasts. Any surprise at Harry's dismissal in 1969 is replaced by a new thought: How did he last as long as he did?

Holy Cow St. Louis!

Work on this book began long before the Cardinals named Chip Caray as their new television broadcaster. His grandfather, a consummate entertainer, always had great timing. I hope this book finds a bit of the Caray Karma and is read for years to come. If Chip can make it to 2045 with the Cardinals, the year he and I both turn 80, baseball fans will celebrate the 100th anniversary of a Caray in the broadcast booth. Fingers crossed.

There are two audiences for this book. I was three days shy of turning four when Harry discovered he was no longer the broadcaster for St. Louis Cardinals baseball. People my age (I'm 57) and younger have no memory of listening to Harry's early play-by-play calls at Sportsman's Park or Busch Stadium (I and II). I hope to inform, surprise and delight those whose recollections of Caray are confined to his days of cable television broadcasts in Chicago. Long before his time in the Windy City, Harry called St. Louis home for nearly six decades and spent a quarter-century rooting for and describing the local teams. It's a legacy worth remembering and celebrating.

The other audience for this book is those whose earliest memories are listening to Harry and Cardinals baseball – people like my old high school coach, Terry Glenzy. "Coach T" attended his first major league game at Sportsman's Park in 1950. He was eight years old. He fondly recalls listening to Harry and his broadcast partners – Gabby Street and "Stretch" Miller – on the Griesedieck Brothers radio network.

To paraphrase a saying coined by another St. Louis brewery and Harry employer – this book's for you.

Mike Mitchell
March 2023

Introduction

It is one of the most iconic moments in major league history and a legendary moment for baseball broadcasting. With their playoff series tied at a game apiece, New York outfielder and third baseman Bobby Thomson hit a game-winning home run in the bottom of the ninth inning at the Polo Grounds off Brooklyn pitcher Ralph Branca to propel the Giants to the 1951 World Series. "The Giants win the pennant!" broadcaster Russ Hodges repeatedly thundered into his radio microphone.

That highlight, accompanied by Hodges' voice, has been endlessly played for generations of sports fans over the past seven decades. Far fewer realize that sitting just inches away from Hodges and describing the event for listeners back in St. Louis that October day was Harry Caray. "We ended up putting Caray in the same booth with us," Hodges later recalled for his autobiography, "hanging a blanket between his microphone and ours."[1]

Harry loved to tell the story about that extraordinary day. In 1966, Dick Kaegel of *The Sporting News* wrote that Caray called it his "greatest radio thrill."[2] Harry described the event to a group of Midwest sports editors five years later. "Hodges taped the game and you've all heard the tape played over and over again. (Actually, Hodges didn't tape it, but a baseball fan did.)[3] I didn't tape mine, but it was my greatest sports thrill. I'll never forget it," he said.[4] Caray gave a more detailed response to *Newsday* in 1985. "When Thomson hit the ball, I called it as I always call a home run. I said, 'It might be, it could be, it is' but I could hardly get it all out because it was a line drive that went out there so quickly. I said almost the same thing as Russ but not with the enthusiasm he did because it wasn't our team. I did say 'the Giants have won the pennant, holy cow,' the term I used long before a certain guy in New York [Phil Rizzuto] became identified with it."[5]

With the game over, Hodges needed interviews from the winning locker room. Here's where the story gets a little murky. Decades after the event, Caray added a postscript to the 1985 interview not found in the earlier accounts. According to Harry, Hodges departed the broadcast booth and turned over his New York audience to the St. Louis broadcaster. "For about five minutes, I was talking to people in both New York and the Midwest, rehashing the thing like Mickey the Mope. Hodges came back on after five minutes – he must have flew – with interviews from the Giants' clubhouse," Caray recalled.

But that's not how Hodges remembered it. His crowded booth that day also included Pittsburgh broadcaster Bob Prince and Pirates first baseman Ralph Kiner, the National League home run champion for 1951. Neither man was there to work, just in town to watch the deciding playoff game. Hodges remembered Prince when he got up to walk out. "I turned and shoved the hot mike into his face, and he started talking," he recalled. When Hodges reached the winning locker room, the broadcaster vividly remembered how Prince turned it over to his colleague. "The Giants won the pennant," Prince said, "but remember – Ralph Kiner is still the home run champion of the National League – and now – Russ Hodges." The Giants broadcaster described Prince's introduction as "a masterpiece of hometown loyalty."

Given Hodges' specific recollection of Prince's words and the fact that he recorded his memory far closer to the original event (he published his autobiography in 1963), his account seems the more credible of the two. Elements of both may be factual. Maybe Prince ended up sharing the microphone with Caray until Hodges was ready. Either way, the incident fits a pattern seen throughout Harry's life. Caray loved to describe an event and make it just a little more fabulous. (Harry never had any trouble defending these embellishments. When broadcaster Monte Moore once protested that Caray's words to a reporter weren't true, Harry replied, "Hey, kid, I'm just trying to get us some ink."[6])

But here's where the story from 1951 takes a second twist. Regardless of who spoke after Hodges, everything about this Forrest Gump-like serendipitous moment – a cramped booth separated by a blanket, the stunning game-winning home run, the confusing postgame scramble – made for a remarkable story. Harry reveled in telling it for decades. And yet, when it came to writing his autobiography – published just four years after his detailed description to *Newsday* – the account is nowhere to be found. Caray's "greatest thrill," a moment he would never forget, didn't merit a single mention.

And here we see another side of Harry. A man prone to embellishment and exaggeration could also downplay, minimize, or completely omit details. "The straight dope is missing," a *Chicago Tribune* reviewer wrote of the Caray autobiography. "Harry chose to dummy up on a lot more than he told."[7]

"I simply do not remember a lot of names, dates and places," Caray confessed early in the book, an acknowledgment that he would not, or could not, revisit details of what he viewed as a difficult childhood. It seems Caray loved to tell stories, but the one he most struggled with was his own.

In that respect, one is reminded of another iconic figure in baseball history whose life stories blended fact and fiction. He, too, had a challenging childhood, spending years in an orphanage. And like Harry, stories regarding Babe Ruth get magnified and inflated over time. When Caray died in 1998, the broadcaster drew comparisons to the Bambino. "Harry Caray was Babe Ruth at the microphone," said sportscaster Jon Miller. "He was larger than life."

Ruth and Caray shared another trait. Fans flocked to them. "We used to train in St. Petersburg in the spring with the Cardinals, and I'd go to dinner with Harry," recalled longtime Mets broadcaster Lindsey Nelson. "I'd be ignored – He'd be mobbed by people from the Midwest. I was absolutely amazed. I'd never seen anything like it. Nobody had, I think, the kind of following Harry did when he was with the Cardinals – they totally idolized him."

Players knew him, too. Harry was as well known to major leaguers of the 1940s and 50s – "I get a kick out of that Harry Caray, the St. Louis broadcaster," Jackie Robinson once said – as he was to athletes of the 1980s and 90s.[8] Coming up in the Chicago Cubs farm system, Mark Grace once had dinner with Caray in Peoria, Illinois. "It was like Muhammad Ali. Whether you loved or hated Ali, you watched Ali. That's an icon. That's a legend."

Harry's fans included future big league players, umpires, and coaches. A young Lou Brock not only listened to Harry but learned from him as well. "Listening to the radio made you use your imagination," he said. "Harry Caray taught me how to hit. He would describe the way the big-league players stood in there to bat and we would emulate it."[9]

Long before his career as an American League umpire, Durwood Merrill was a child in rural Oklahoma in a house with no running water and battery-powered electricity. The wind would charge the battery during the day. Radio provided entertainment at night. "It was the St. Louis Cardinals and Harry Caray doing the play-by-play," he recalled for his autobiography.[10]

Longtime major-league coach Dan Radison grew up in Columbia, Illinois, across the Mississippi River from St. Louis. "I can't explain to you what it was like to listen to Harry Caray on the radio at [the age of] five. It was the most exciting part of my day. I couldn't wait for the games to start."[11]

Neither could Harry. He brought a fan-like enthusiasm to his broadcasts because that is how he always viewed himself, just a rooter in the stands who happened to have a microphone. "I've often thought that if you gave the microphone to a fan, he'd sound a lot like me," Caray believed. They were bartenders, taxi drivers and post office workers. "My people," Harry called them.

Caray's habit of name-dropping conversations with famous guests at the ballpark or mentioning the hometowns of out-of-state visitors always irritated a vocal minority of fans. They would fire off letters of complaint, pleading with Harry to stop. He never did. He knew his fanbase.

"In St. Louis itself, opinion was divided on Caray, say fifty-fifty," believed columnist and Caray critic Bob Broeg. But outside the city? "That's the difference. There, it was like ninety-five to five – Harry was a god."

Harry repaid his rural fans across the Midwest and South by showering them with attention. In his St. Louis days, there was almost nothing Caray wouldn't do; nowhere he wouldn't go. He went to a baseball party in Mason City, Iowa, paid tribute to athletes with the Jaycees in Jasper, Indiana, addressed the tri-state traffic club in Joplin, Missouri. He broadcast high school football games, judged beauty contests, and spread the gospel of Cardinals baseball from Tulsa, Oklahoma to Omaha, Nebraska. One year, he joined a group of players on a postseason barnstorming tour. As the public address announcer, Harry could be seen and heard introducing players in places such as Tamaroa, Illinois and Columbia, Tennessee. He drove to Paducah, Kentucky on an off-day in 1951 to broadcast three innings of a minor-league game. His hosts presented him with a Kentucky ham. That same year, city officials in Blytheville, Arkansas sent Caray nine rabbits' feet to "break the jinx the Dodgers have over our Cardinals." When the talismans failed to produce the desired results, the police chief had an explanation. "Caray didn't distribute the rabbits' feet to the Cardinal players Friday night; that's what happened," said Chief John Foster. "They'll still break the jinx."

Caray had boundless confidence: "I knew I was popular from the first day I ever broadcast." And called games with a distinctive voice: "He sounds like a guy who got hit in the throat with a shovel and never recovered," is how a Chicago writer described it.[12]

The colorblind Caray would arrive at the park in interesting and occasionally arresting hues and shades. He'd greet fans, talk baseball, and sell beer; first for Griesedieck and later for Anheuser-Busch. He would add additional beverage sponsors to his resume in Chicago, but regardless of who paid him, he never lost his enthusiasm for the product. "How do they make it so good," he would say, "and sell it so cheap."

On sweltering summer days in St. Louis, Harry would strip to his underwear in the booth with a stack of paperwork on one side and a fish net for foul balls on the other.[13] One afternoon, a foul ball off the bat of Ken Boyer sailed into the broadcast booth. When Caray tried to catch it, the stack of papers flew into the stands and on the field. Time had to be called as players and umpires helped retrieve the records.[14]

It wouldn't be the last time players and umpires paused to consider the actions of Caray. Harry's unfiltered criticisms spared no one connected to the game. If a player made a poor play, an umpire made a bad call, or a manager made a decision that he disagreed with, he let his audience know exactly what he thought, consequences be damned. "A broadcaster has to maintain his integrity and if he steps on someone's toes, too bad," he once said. (His critics claimed his biting commentary only went so far. "Caray could be very tough on anybody who didn't sign the checks," said Broeg.)

Eddie Dyer complained bitterly about what he viewed as Caray's "second guessing." When the Cardinals manager stepped down after the 1950 season, the club asked Caray not to attend the news conference, fearing an incident between the two men. Harry's relationship with a later Cardinals manager was no better. Caray once stated in a radio editorial that hiring Eddie Stanky was the "darkest day in Cardinal history."[15]

Harry's words could leave scars that lasted for years. Tony La Russa was a rookie manager in Chicago when Caray called White Sox games. Like Dyer and Stanky, La Russa had a strained relationship with the broadcaster. Sixteen years after Harry's death, a reporter asked Tony if the two men ever reconciled. "Hell no," he replied. "Harry liked to pick on lambs, and I was a lamb."[16]

"We kept tabs on his broadcasts," acknowledged Cardinals outfielder Curt Flood. "If our stock was down, we needed to know it. Whoever among our pitchers was not working on a particular day was sure to be in the clubhouse, listening to Harry's spiel."

Players kept tabs because they knew Harry's words could influence fans, turning applause and approval into taunts and jeers. Caray's bashing of Boyer was so frequent it became a running joke among the players. Bob Gibson would loudly count to three from the dugout as Boyer was introduced from the on-deck circle. "On three, the boos would start heaping down from the upper deck," said Gibson.

Caray's penchant for occasionally turning against one of his team's players was deemed "reverse rooting" by columnist Jack Craig. "Getting away with this is the personification of power," he wrote.

Whenever someone called Caray a "homer," he pointed to the brutal takedowns, condemnations and disparagements he would periodically deliver. "If I'm a 'homer,' how come my job is in jeopardy at the end of almost every season because the owner, general manager, field manager or the players are mad at me?" he asked.

Baseball author Bill James agreed with Caray. "People confuse 'objectivity' with 'neutralism,'" James contended. Caray "is criticized for not being objective, which is preposterous; he is the most objective baseball announcer I ever witnessed."[17]

*****

After publishing *Mr. Rickey's Redbirds* in 2020, I searched for a new story to tell. I quickly settled on a narrative centered around Caray's time in St. Louis. Harry's career began when radio ruled the airwaves, multiple newspapers published daily in the city, and St. Louis featured two major league teams. I was also struck by the similarities in the careers of Branch Rickey and Harry Caray.

One may think twice about comparing the thrice-married Caray, who loved a late-night cocktail, with Rickey, a teetotaling Prohibitionist who married his high school sweetheart and stayed with her for the rest of his life. But both men spent more time with the Cardinals than any other franchise, yet are best known today for accomplishments and behavior elsewhere.

Rickey either managed or ran the Cardinals' front office from 1917 to 1942, but gained his largest fame from his eight seasons with the Brooklyn Dodgers. Caray called Cardinals baseball for a quarter-century but is recognized today as the man who sang during the seventh-inning stretch on summer afternoons at Wrigley Field.

Upset about being relieved of his managerial duties by owner Sam Breadon, Rickey threatened to sell his stock in the team. Hurt and angry after being informed of Gussie Busch's decision not to renew his contract, Caray threatened to sell his stock in the brewery. Rickey followed through. Caray changed his mind.

At the end of his career, Rickey returned to St. Louis and joined Caray as an employee of Anheuser-Busch. Both men played a role in a controversy that saw manager Johnny Keane leave after a World Series championship. Rickey was suspected of whispering in Busch's ear to hire Leo Durocher. Caray drove Durocher to his interview with the Cardinals president.

As a talent assessment and development pioneer, Rickey's Cardinals controlled the largest farm system the game has ever seen. Even without the signing of Jackie Robinson, he deserved a place in the Hall of Fame. Bob Costas made a similar point about Caray. "If he had retired in 1970 after the Cardinals let him go, he already would have earned a spot in the broadcaster's wing of the Baseball Hall of Fame. He was that good just on his pure merits."

Rickey's last conscious moments came in 1965 on a November Saturday in Columbia, Missouri. He attended a University of Missouri football game against Oklahoma in the afternoon and was inducted into the Missouri Sports Hall of Fame that evening. He collapsed during his speech and never recovered, dying a few weeks later. Caray's last days played out in a similar fashion. Having dinner with his wife, he rose to acknowledge grateful fans but quickly collapsed and was never seen in public again.

Caray's downfall with the Cardinals began on a November Saturday in Columbia, three years after Rickey's passing. Caray broadcast a University of Missouri football game against Oklahoma State and returned to St. Louis that evening. Crossing the street on the way to a late-night tryst, he was struck by an automobile, an accident that set in motion a chain of events that led to his dismissal the following October.

At the 1965 ceremony where Rickey spoke, Caray served as master of ceremonies. (An *Associated Press* photo from that evening shows Rickey at the dais with Caray – sans glasses – standing behind him.) Harry had just completed his twenty-first season calling Cardinals baseball and had long before asserted himself as the franchise's most controversial and best-known personality. Rickey had once been the team's most influential voice. This metaphorical passing of the torch had evolved over decades, with Caray and Cardinal fans there every step of the way.

When the World Series champion 1926 Cardinals returned for a celebration a quarter-century later, Caray introduced and greeted them on the field. When the star of that team, Rogers Hornsby, was fired as manager of the Browns in 1952, Caray gave him a sympathetic ear and a forum to address his grievances. When the 1931 Cardinals returned for their day of honor three decades later, Caray interviewed Pepper Martin, who recalled his wild throws from third base. "I did knock out the back of a lot of chairs," Martin admitted.[18]

The 1934 Cardinals featured Dizzy Dean, a hero on the pitching mound, and later the most popular broadcaster in St. Louis until Harry came along. Even Dean, no shrinking violet on the mound or behind a microphone, was surprised at the ferocity of a Caray broadcast. In the booth next to Harry, Dizzy once heard Caray turn a routine play into a drama-filled moment. "Are we broadcasting the same game?" Dean wondered.

It was Harry's turn to be surprised when the broadcaster interviewed Enos Slaughter about the great Cardinals teams of the early 1940s. The former outfielder waxed so long and enthusiastically that "it was one of the few times Harry has lost a verbal battle on the air," noted a columnist. Harry "had a tough time getting the microphone back from Enos to change the subject."[19]

The player Caray talked about endlessly was Stan Musial. Caray called Musial his "biggest hero," consistently praising Stan the Man throughout his career and beyond. "Musial was one of the few players who appreciated what the game did for him," Harry believed. After Stan retired, baseball needed a new commissioner. Caray recommended Musial for the role.[20]

Holy Cow St. Louis!

The two first met in 1946 when Stan returned after missing a year for military service. The GI Generation came home to packed ballparks and overwhelming ticket requests from former foxhole buddies. "I got phone calls from everybody but General Eisenhower," remembered Cardinals catcher Joe Garagiola. Baseball in St. Louis meant a game every day at Sportsman's Park. As the western outpost for both leagues, road trips meant extended train travel, spirited card games, and improvised music. Cardinals trainer Doc Weaver would play the mandolin "while Musial beat coat hangers on a chair."[21]

Given that he ended his career calling Cubs games on cable television, it's easy to forget these humbler beginnings of Harry's professional life. His time in the booth began a year earlier with Adolf Hitler still ruling Germany and American troops fighting in Europe and the Pacific. He was heard but not seen over a small radio network that featured games of both the Browns and Cardinals.

Born just months before the beginning of World War I, Harry's life spanned nearly the entire length of the twentieth century. He was alive for every Cardinals pennant-winning club of the 1900s. The man who interviewed Hornsby and Martin also broadcast games involving everyone from Terry Moore and Red Schoendienst to Willie McGee and Ozzie Smith. And while games involving the latter two came long after he left St. Louis, Caray never forgot his hometown and its ballplayers.

One night at his Chicago restaurant, Harry entertained a group of former Cardinals, including Tim McCarver, Musial and Schoendienst. When country music singer Tanya Tucker walked into the dining room, Harry talked her into joining him at the bar for a duet. Harry and Tanya sang "Take Me Out to the Ballgame" while Stan joined in on his harmonica.[22] On another night, Harry's guest list included Musial and Schoendienst, as well as Jack Buck, Mike Shannon and Whitey Herzog. "You can take the boy out of St. Louis, but you can't take St. Louis out of the boy," declared the *Chicago Tribune*.

Near the end of his career, Harry was asked about his greatest day in baseball. And here we get insight into a moment that Caray recalled with crystal clear clarity. It's a moment that cuts across time and geography. It involves St. Louis and Chicago, the Cardinals and Cubs, his favorite player, and a long-gone era. It's also a tribute to the people Harry embraced from his earliest days as a broadcaster.

Here's Harry in the 1990s talking about a moment from the 1950s regarding a player signed by Rickey's Cardinals of the 1930s.

"My greatest day in baseball? That would be easy; it would have to be the day that Stan Musial got his 3,000th hit. Not so much because I was there but because what took place was something that could never be recreated and will probably never happen again." That event took place in Chicago against the Cubs. What stood out to Harry was the train trip home.

"We got to the first stop, and the entire railroad platform was full of people who had come out to see Stan Musial. When you think about it, it was truly amazing — they were fairly small towns, and it seemed like the entire community must have been out there." It was the first of about ten stops along the way.

"I think it was around the third stop that he pulled out his mouth harp and started playing songs for them. And that's the way it went at every stop until we got to St. Louis. All these people in these small towns just came out to honor Stan because he'd just gotten his 3,000th hit," Caray recalled. "I think it's my greatest day because it's something that will never happen again. I mean, nowadays, why would all these people come out to a railroad station? They'd probably just stay home and watch it on TV or listen to it on the radio."[23]

St. Louis native Ed Moose was among those who grew up listening to Harry. "Educated by the Jesuits and the St. Louis Cardinals," Moose's first job was as an usher at Sportsman's Park. He later became a reporter for the *Post-Dispatch*. "He owned the town," Moose said of Caray. "He knew everybody. Anytime you went out with Harry, it was a three-ring circus."[24]

After leaving St. Louis, Moose became a co-owner of San Francisco's legendary Washington Square Bar & Grill. (*Sports Illustrated's* Ron Fimrite wrote a book about the saloon.)[25] Caray was a frequent patron on West Coast trips. After Harry's passing, Moose fondly recalled the St. Louis of his youth. "The three most interesting guys I knew in baseball were Branch Rickey, Bill Veeck, and Harry Caray, with Dizzy Dean thrown in for good luck," he said.[26]

In the pages to come, you will meet these men and many others who shaped the baseball and media landscape of St. Louis during the last century. Rickey made his major-league debut for the Browns, managed both the Browns and Cardinals, and beginning in the 1920s, helped shape the first World Series championship teams in St. Louis history. Dean developed into a baseball legend for the Gashouse Gang Cardinals of the 1930s and began a successful broadcasting career in the city in the 1940s. Veeck bought and later sold the St. Louis Browns in the 1950s.

All three would leave the city for greener pastures and greater acclaim. Rickey's passion and skill set enabled him to break baseball's color barrier with the Brooklyn Dodgers. Dean's knack for creative language made him a national television star for CBS. Veeck took his marketing genius to Chicago.

Holy Cow St. Louis!

But St. Louis still had Harry. For twenty-five years, he dominated the airwaves, commanded our attention, sparked interest, and generated controversy.

This is the story of how *Mr. Rickey's Redbirds* became – *Holy Cow St. Louis!* – Harry Caray's Cardinals.

---

[1] Hodges, Russ and Hirshberg, Al. *My Giants*. Doubleday & Company, Inc. 1963. It was a murderer's row of broadcasters in the Polo Grounds broadcast booth on October 3, 1951. Hodges and Ernie Harwell alternated between television and radio for the Giants (Hodges did the first three and last three innings on radio; the middle three on television.) Harwell's television call has been lost to history. "To this day, only Mrs. Harwell and I know that I did maybe the most famous call of all time," he said years later. Over in the Dodgers booth, Red Barber described the home run for his Brooklyn audience. The Dodgers three-man broadcast crew featured Connie Desmond and a young Vin Scully who was relieved that Barber made the call. "Then [age 23] it would have been too much for me," Scully later said. Smith, Curt. *Pull Up a Chair: The Vin Scully Story*. Potomac Books, Inc. 2009. In the Giants radio booth, Hodges had already invited Pittsburgh broadcaster Bob Prince and Pirates first baseman (and later broadcaster) Ralph Kiner to sit with him when he got the news that a St. Louis radio station (Hodges wrote that it was KMOX, but it was actually WIL) requested a spot for Caray. Even though all the booths were taken, Hodges accommodated the request. "I told them not to worry – we'd do something." Harwell wrote in his autobiography that the Mutual and Liberty Networks also carried the game, making a total of six networks (five radio plus television) in the park that day.

[2] *The Sporting News,* July 2, 1966.

[3] Using a tape recorder, Lawrence Goldberg held up a microphone to a radio speaker. He called Hodges the day after the game and gave him the tape. "It's been copied hundreds of times," said Hodges, "and whenever I feel down or blue, I turn it on."

[4] *Journal and Courier* (Lafayette, Indiana), May 25, 1971.

[5] *Newsday*, October 4, 1985.

[6] *Oakland Tribune*, April 6, 1980.

[7] *Chicago Tribune*, March 10, 1989.

[8] *The Call-Leader* (Elwood, Indiana), September 5, 1951. The newspaper cites the *Dodgers Line Drives* newsletter as its source. Robinson's comments came in the stretch run of the 1951 season. "We'll stay at the top of this league like the Yankees did in theirs. I get a kick out of that Harry Caray, the St. Louis broadcaster, saying that his fans should get out to see the Dodgers now, because they'd never be this good again."

[9] *St. Louis Post-Dispatch*, July 31, 1994.

[10] Merrill, Durwood with Jim Dent. *You're Out and You're Ugly, Too! Confessions of an Umpire with Attitude*. St. Martin's Press. 1998.

[11] Wolfe, Rich and Castle, George. *I Remember Harry Caray*. Sports Publishing, Inc. 1988.

[12] *Boston Globe*, July 22, 1984.

[13] Caray later credited Gabby Street, his first broadcast partner, for the fish net. "Gabby … would always go after foul balls when we were up in the booth. One day I said, 'We ought to have a net up here.' The next day there were five or six nets delivered up to the booth and I've been using it ever since." *The Journal Times* (Racine, Wisconsin), October 15, 1978.

[14] *St. Louis Globe-Democrat*, July 5, 1961.

[15] *Alfred Fleishman Papers, 1926-2002*. Housed at the St. Louis Public Library, St. Louis, Mo. Caray's editorial was broadcast on November 8, 1955. Fleishman sent a transcript of Caray's words to Anheuser-Busch executive Richard (Dick) Meyer six days later. Here is the quote in context. "Actually, it was not Stanky's fault. Whoever brought him in originally will have to bear the brunt within his own conscience, because that was the darkest day in Cardinal history."

[16] *Chicago Tribune*, July 27, 2014. "I just didn't think he was a good manager then, and I don't think he's a good manager now," Caray said of La Russa in 1984. "He was learning to manage in the major leagues." *Boston Globe*, June 22, 1984.

[17] James, Bill. *This Time Let's Not Eat The Bones: Bill James Without the Numbers*. Villard Books. 1984.

[18] *The Sporting News*, August 16, 1961.

[19] *Journal-Herald* (Dayton, Ohio), September 18, 1968. The columnist was Ritter Collett.

[20] "I've got enough jobs already," Musial said when informed of Caray's comments. "Don't get me involved in any more." *Miami Herald*, August 7, 1964.

[21] Vecsey, George (editor). *The Way It Was: Great Sports Events From the Past*. McGraw-Hill Book Company. 1974.

[22] *Chicago Tribune*, July 30, 1993.

[23] *My Greatest Day in Baseball, 1946-1997. Baseball Legends Recount Their Epic Moments*. As told to Bob McCullough. Taylor Publishing Company. 1998.

[24] *Chicago Tribune*, February 27, 1998.

[25] Fimrite published his book in the 1980s: *The Square: The Story of a Saloon*. Years before opening the Washington Square Bar & Grill in San Francisco, Moose and co-owner Sam Dietsch met at the Golden Eagle bar in St. Louis. *San Francisco Examiner*, June 27, 1982. The *Examiner's* Stephanie Salter called Washington Square "a public club for journalists, novelists, movie moguls, lawyers, investment types, visiting celebrities and jocks and their fans." The restaurant had its own softball team, Les Laupins Savages. "The brainchild of *Sports Illustrated* writer Ron Fimrite and the Square's original co-owner Ed Moose, the team played games in Paris, London, Ireland, New York and L.A. before I gave up the mantle of official scorekeeper," wrote Salter. "Later squads traveled to Hawaii and Moscow and finagled permission to play in such hallowed baseball shrines as Fenway Park." Ibid, March 23, 2000.

[26] *Chicago Tribune*, February 27, 1998.

Holy Cow St. Louis!

St. Louis, 1944

The city had never seen anything like it. When the American League St. Louis Browns clinched the pennant on the last day of the 1944 regular season, it meant the World Series would be an all-St. Louis adventure. The largest crowd to ever see a Browns game, 37,815, had poured into Sportsman's Park on Sunday, October 1 to witness the historic occasion. Before 1944, every franchise in baseball except the Browns had made at least one postseason appearance. Fans of the American League club that had called St. Louis home since 1902 could now anticipate a clash against a team they knew well. Like the name of the movie starring Judy Garland that debuted the same year, *Meet Me in St. Louis* now took on new meaning. The Browns would face the Cardinals, the team they shared Sportsman's Park with every year from April to September.

Their October duel was possible because of the Browns' accomplishments in their final regular-season series, a four-game sweep of the New York Yankees. When New York's Oscar Grimes fouled out to St. Louis first baseman George McQuinn to end the game on Sunday, a 5-2 Browns victory, fans politely stood and applauded. Then the public address announcer spoke. "Totals on the game...for the American League champion St. Louis Browns." The acknowledgment was all it took. Reality sunk in and the ballpark erupted. Fans sprayed confetti, rang cowbells, hugged and kissed. As word spread around the city, so did the celebrations in area taverns and neighborhoods, where some locals took the time to tie tin cans and washtubs to the backs of cars as horns blared and informal parades popped up. Still, the celebration was muted. Fans "realized soberly that 'there's a war on,'" noted the *St. Louis Star-Times*. "It was Sunday and most places were closed."

World War II had changed everything, including the fate of the Browns. The team would have called Los Angeles home for the 1944 season but for events of a few years earlier. Browns general manager Bill DeWitt Sr. had gone so far as to coordinate a travel schedule for teams to take trains from Chicago to the West Coast. League approval of the plan to relocate the Browns to California was set for Monday, December 8, 1941, the day after the Japanese attacked Pearl Harbor. The plan was scrapped.

A franchise that once drew 80,000 fans for an entire season (1935), and a few years later compiled a record of 43-111 (1939), the Browns were perhaps the most mocked franchise in baseball. "First in shoes, first in booze, and last in the American League," went a popular saying. From 1926 to 1943, eighteen straight seasons, the Browns finished last in league attendance. "The fans don't dare boo us," one player told a teammate during that dismal stretch. "We outnumber them." In the 1944 film, *Going My Way*, Bing Crosby won an Academy Award for his portrayal of Father Charles "Chuck" O'Malley, an East St. Louis priest who is transferred to a New York City church. He wore a Browns jacket in one scene. "That's the outfit to wear in a cellar," remarked another character.[1]

With a league-best record of 89-65 (a game ahead of the Detroit Tigers, who lost their finale), the Browns had swapped punch lines for newfound respect. The Browns have a "grand chance" to beat the Cardinals, Yankees manager Joe McCarthy told reporters. He wasn't the only one who believed in the team. With eight weeks to go in the season, Browns super fan Herbert "Zutty" Foerstel stopped shaving. The "Mayor of the Bleachers" at Sportsman's Park, Foerstel had vowed not to shave until the Browns won the pennant. With his goal accomplished, Browns owner Don Barnes convinced him to extend the deadline. "Zutty, you've hexed the rest of the teams with your whiskers," Barnes told him. "Leave them go for another week, and hex the Cards, too, while you're at it."[2]

In the coming days, he would be joined in the stands by an equally colorful character rooting for the opposite side. Mary Ott was known as "The Horse Lady." In a booming voice that could be heard throughout the park, she would neigh her disapproval of opponents and umpires alike from her seventh-row box seat to the right of home plate. "I like scientific rooting, something that helps the boys and makes the other guys sore," she once explained. "I figure I can knock a lot of pitchers out of the box in three innings."[3]

Ott's team, the Cardinals, had ended their regular season in New York against the Giants. On the train ride back to St. Louis, Cardinals manager Billy Southworth congratulated the American League champs. "I know the Browns deserve the pennant, and I'm really glad they won." A radio reporter told Southworth, "The Cards ought to whip the Browns four straight."

"Don't talk like that," Southworth responded. "After all, the Browns are the best-balanced team in the American League, regardless of what the Eastern critics think of them." While Southworth was diplomatic in his discussions about his opponent, some of his players were more blunt in their comments to reporters. "I think we'll beat the hell out of the Browns," said Pepper Martin, the former Gashouse Gang ringleader who had come out of retirement to rejoin the Cardinals in 1944.

Holy Cow St. Louis!

The season and franchise history of the National League champions stood in sharp contrast to their American League rival. The two teams shared a park and many former Cardinals either played for or managed the Browns through the years.[4] But any similarities end there. The Cardinals were making their third straight appearance in the World Series and eighth since 1926. The 1944 club won 91 of its first 121 games and finished August with an 18.5-game lead. Despite a September stretch where they lost 11 of 14 games, their lead was never threatened. The Cardinals clinched the pennant on September 21 and finished the season with a record of 105-49, the third straight year the club had won at least that many, and 14.5 games better than second-place Pittsburgh.

Postseason baseball was now old hat for the Cardinals and their fans. It showed. When the team pulled into Union Station late Monday afternoon, only a few diehards bothered to show up to greet the players. It marked only the third time the Cardinals had clinched the pennant on the road and the first time since 1928. When Rogers Hornsby's 1926 team arrived home from New York, a near riot erupted on the streets of St. Louis. The 1944 welcoming crew featured "six high school girls, looking for autographs" and "two high school boys, looking for heroes." With the Cardinals out of uniform and indistinguishable from the rest of the crowd, the girls didn't get any autographs and the boys didn't get many looks at their heroes.[5]

On the Monday the Cardinals returned home, St. Louis Mayor Aloys Kaufmann proclaimed October second through the ninth "St. Louis Baseball Week." Schools canceled classes and a federal grand jury recessed for the week. Arriving from the East Coast with the team were National League president Ford Frick, various baseball executives, umpires, and members of the media. The city's hotels were soon full. The president of the St. Louis hotel association, J.C. Meacham, attempted to accommodate guests by contacting facilities in East St. Louis and Belleville, Illinois and out west in St. Charles, Missouri. No luck. Those places were sold out as well.

Seventy-four-year-old Nelson Thomas, from Multnomah County, Oregon, traveled halfway across the country to see his first World Series. Local residents had chipped in $500 to make his dream come true. But he arrived without a hotel reservation or a ticket. A Portland, Oregon newspaper publisher talked the Hotel Statler into giving him a room and located a ticket for the first game. "I'm so excited, I don't know what to say," Thomas told reporters.

Lines began forming outside Sportsman's Park a day before the opener. They came from places as far away as Milwaukee, Chicago, Fort Sill, Oklahoma, and Buffalo, New York (likely arriving on trains since wartime gas rationing prevented long-distance car trips). They slept on boxes, chairs, and the concrete sidewalk. Some brought sleeping bags. One man offered collapsible chairs for rent. The cost was fifty cents.

If they brought along a radio, they could tune in to France Laux on KMOX previewing the World Series with former Cardinal great Hornsby and Browns legend George Sisler, along with Taylor Spink, the publisher of *The Sporting News*. Radio station KSD was part of a national network of 92 stations that would broadcast the games and a daily post-game show. After each contest, fans could hear sportswriter Grantland Rice and *Post-Dispatch* columnist J. Roy Stockton react to the outcome and interview managers Sewell and Southworth. Over on radio station KXOK, a young broadcaster aired his show each night at 5:45 p.m. On Monday, he interviewed Browns pitcher Denny Galehouse and outfielder Chet Laabs, the hitting hero of the Sunday finale. The KXOK host wasn't nearly as well-known as Laux or Stockton. That would soon change.

The two managers spent Tuesday giving their clubs one final workout before the start of play. Back in St. Louis on leave from his army base in San Antonio, Texas, Enos Slaughter joined the Cardinals and practiced with his old teammates. The outfielder hadn't played with St. Louis since the 1942 season. Because of military service, he wouldn't return to the team until 1946. Another member of the 1942 squad, Frank Crespi, was home on furlough in the fall of 1944. He, too, had plans to reconnect with his old teammates. The St. Louis native arrived at the family home on Hodiamont Avenue only to be greeted by his mother holding a telegram. Frank's brother, private first class Angelo Crespi, had been missing in Italy since September 14.[6] The war was never far from anyone's mind.

Inside the offices at Sportsman's Park, Browns GM DeWitt and staff worked feverishly to complete the mailing of tickets. Because of time constraints, the Browns had to order 34,500 tickets weeks before (with no guarantee they would even need them). They arrived on Saturday. Each block of tickets provided admission to the three contests in which the Browns served as the home team (Games 3,4, and 5).[7]

In an age where the telephone and typewriter were sophisticated pieces of office equipment, handling such a volume of requests in such a short period proved daunting. "As each request for tickets came to the office, we made a 3 by 5 card and numbered it the same as the letter," DeWitt explained. Season ticket holders came first. Everyone else was on a first-come, first-serve basis. Every ticket was delivered via registered mail. The tickets cost the Browns $1,500 to print and another $4,000 to distribute. Demand was heavy. The Cardinals estimated they had 18,000 unfilled ticket requests. DeWitt believed the total for the Browns was similar.[8] In addition to cashier's checks, many envelopes contained congratulatory notes. One especially caught DeWitt's eye. "Thank heaven," it read, "we will no more hear, 'What's the matter with the Browns?'"

With praise also came complaints. The Cardinals would later be upset over the seats their wives were assigned for games when the Browns controlled the tickets, a controversy that would play out over the week to come. Meanwhile, a potentially awkward situation between the managers was settled before the first pitch was thrown.

Because the Browns and Cardinals were never home at the same time, managers Sewell and Southworth shared an apartment on Lindell Boulevard[9] The Browns finished the season with sixteen home games. Sewell and his wife had been at the apartment since the middle of September. He hoped to invite his mother from Alabama to experience World Series baseball. On the Saturday before the Browns clinched the pennant, an anxious Sewell wired Southworth in New York. Southworth called him the next morning. "I don't want to go into any ifs with you," the Cardinals manager told him. "The Browns are going to win the pennant, so you go right ahead. I have rooms available at a hotel, and I'll just move in there when we return home."[10]

The dilemma highlighted a unique aspect of the 1944 World Series. St. Louis became the only city outside Chicago and New York to host the entire event. For the first time since the 1922 World Series, when both the New York Giants and Yankees called the Polo Grounds home, all games would be played in a single ballpark.[11]

A stadium and living quarters for the managers weren't the only two things the teams shared. As batboy, Bobby Scanlon did double duty for the Browns and Cardinals. Both teams voted him a piece of the World Series money. (He got $500 from each team.) For the Fall Classic, Scanlon served as the batboy for the designated home team.

With money and living arrangements settled, the only drama left for the managers was deciding who would be their starting pitchers for Game 1. Following the Browns' Tuesday workout at Sportsman's Park, Sewell announced Denny Galehouse would make the start. Later that day, Southworth selected Mort Cooper as his starter. Sewell's choice was a surprise; the selection of Cooper was not. The Cardinals ace had gone 22-7 in the regular season, his third straight twenty-win season. Sewell was expected to name Nels Potter, a nineteen-game winner for the Browns, as his starter. Instead, he picked Galehouse, who finished the season with a 9-10 record. Both starting pitchers, though, were emblematic of the choices and challenges baseball faced during the war.

*****

Cooper was nowhere to be found when the Cardinals reported for spring training. He was holding out for more money, insisting on a $5,500 raise.[12] Cooper's demand was considered bad form in the middle of a war. "I do not think it makes very good reading for persons who have their boys on the fighting fronts," remarked owner Sam Breadon.

The war was often invoked as a reason – or an excuse – to justify a particular behavior. Players would complain to Cardinals traveling secretary Leo Ward about uncomfortably warm railroad cars that forced them to open windows, often leaving them covered in soot. "Well, the war's on," Ward would tell them. "You can't do any better." After voting Ward a full share of the World Series money in 1942 and 1943, the players exacted their revenge by voting him just a half share in 1944.[13]

By this time, the armed forces had claimed more than 300 major league and approximately 3,000 minor league players. The vacuum had teams scrambling to find talent. Players who wouldn't have received a second glance in peacetime suddenly found themselves coveted by teams at the highest level of organized baseball.

Sig Jakucki pitched for the Browns in 1936, going 0-3, with an 8.71 ERA. The team sent him back to the minor leagues. He quit the professional ranks and began playing semi-pro ball in Texas. He worked as a painter and paperhanger during the week, played baseball and got drunk on the weekends. He was once described as having "a $100,000 arm and a million-dollar thirst."[14] He drank heavily, smoked constantly, and fought repeatedly. "Jakucki used to spit on your shoes and dare you to do something about it," said Browns backup catcher Joe Schultz. Thanks to high blood pressure, he was also 4-F (ineligible to be drafted, a description that fit more than a dozen members of the Browns). Eight seasons after his last appearance in a Browns uniform, the club gave the 35-year-old another chance. Jakucki predicted in March he'd win 12-15 games. He won 13 for the American League champs, including the pennant-clinching victory in the final regular season game.

Galehouse, Sewell's pick to start Game 1, had wartime work at a Goodyear aircraft factory in Akron, Ohio. Reluctant to leave his job and expose himself to the draft, he pitched for the team on weekends. "On Saturday, I'd get an overnight train to wherever the Browns were playing," Galehouse remembered. "I'd get there at 7:30 or 8:00 o'clock in the morning. I'd have breakfast and go to the ballpark; there wasn't any place else to go. We always had Sunday doubleheaders. I'd pitch the first game and then I'd leave and take the train and go back home."[15]

Struggling to stay in shape during the week, he eventually decided he needed to make a full-time commitment to baseball, or not play at all. Told by his draft board that he likely wouldn't need to take a physical until after the season ended, Galehouse quit his job and became a full-time baseball player.

Bolstered by DeWitt's acquisitions, Sewell's leadership ("I just talked pennant to them all year long"), and a red-hot start to the season, the Browns began to believe they could do it. "We won the first nine games, a record," remembered second baseman Don Gutteridge. "And the guys said, 'Hey, this is fun, let's do it.' That changed the whole season."[16]

*****

When the gates opened for the first game of the 1944 World Series, Blake Harper, the man who ran the concessions at Sportsman's Park, made sure to have an equal number of Browns and Cardinals pennants for sale. During the fifteen years he had been in charge of food, beverage, and memorabilia, the number of concessions at the park had grown from two to 70. No detail escaped his eye. Hot dogs had to be soaked in pineapple juice for days before placing them on the grill, a soda should have just the right amount of ice, and the words "soft drink" were never to be used. Name the brand, he would tell his workers. "That makes people thirstier," he believed.[17] Harper supervised a staff of more than 300 during the regular season. For the Fall Classic, he added another 200 workers. For the week, his crews served up hotdogs by the thousands, peanuts by the ton, and cases and cases of beer and soda.

The abundance of supplies and the eagerness at which they were snapped up by the tens of thousands of visitors who arrived at Sportsman's Park reflected a secret about the war years not many wanted to say out loud. All things considered, Americans on the home front had it pretty good. London endured the blitz, the Nazis occupied Paris for years, and Jews across the continent saw their businesses and homes seized and their families shipped off to die in concentration camps. The theaters of war were far-away places, the nations of Europe and the islands of the Pacific. While nearly sixteen million Americans served in the armed forces during the conflict, the vast majority of U.S. citizens' only experience with bloodshed and combat came from reading newspapers, watching newsreels, and listening to radio reports.

The Great Depression of the 1930s was gone. With millions of able-bodied men now in the military, the unemployment rate fell from 14.6 percent in 1940 to 1.2 percent in 1944. Fueled largely by huge government spending on the war, the economy boomed in the early 1940s. As measured by Gross Domestic Product (GDP), the economy grew 17.7 percent in 1941, 18.9 percent in 1942, and 17 percent in 1943.

With wartime restrictions in place (e.g., after 1942, American manufacturers didn't produce any new cars until 1946), people had money to spend, but not as many things available to purchase. The Office of Price Administration estimated the United States generated $130 billion of consumer income in 1943, with just $77 billion of goods to buy. With options limited, people increasingly turned to movies and sports for escape.

"Business is booming throughout the sports world," wrote *Star-Times* columnist Sid Keener in March of 1944. "Pari-mutual betting is establishing records at race tracks this winter. Even Oaklawn, down at Hot Springs, Arkansas, has set new highs for betting and profits. Basketball, boxing, wrestling, hockey, and other winter sports are packing 'em in this season. Why not baseball?"[18]

The columnist proposed to DeWitt that his Browns could draw 450,000 fans in the upcoming season. The comment "almost caused DeWitt to fall out of his chair," Keener recorded. "It has been many years since the Browns played to 400,000 at Sportsman's Park," said the club executive. In fact, the Browns drew 508,644 fans in the regular season, the highest total to see the team play since 1924, and the first time the Browns had outdrawn the Cardinals since 1925. "Why, this is a Browns' town," Lil Musial, Stan's wife, said during the World Series.

Bill Stocksick remembered when St. Louis truly was a Browns' town. He first joined the Sportsman's Park grounds crew in 1905, the beginning of five straight seasons in which the Browns outdrew the Cardinals (the teams played in separate parks at the time). The Browns' attendance of 618,947 in 1908 exceeded that of the Cardinals by more than 400,000. Part of Stocksick's duties in the early days was filling kegs full of water and oatmeal and placing them near the players' benches. The concoction was thought to prevent cramps during the summertime heat. The grass was cut with a 24-inch hand mower. After the Cardinals joined the Browns in playing at the intersection of Grand and Dodier in 1920, Stocksick spent so much time at the park that he began living there.

Two teams in one park meant someone played on the field nearly every day for six straight months. The constant assault on the dirt and grass caused endless headaches for Stocksick, who rose to the rank of grounds crew superintendent. Every April, the conditions on the field would be perfect. "The grass is a mid-summer's green, sparkling with the freshness of spring," columnist Keener wrote one April. Every fall, it would be an absolute mess. "The infield was as bald as Andy Gump's head," wrote columnist Bob Burnes one October, a reference to a popular newspaper comic strip character.

Stocksick did what he could to keep the field in shape. One year, he invited a groundskeeper consultant from Cleveland to suggest changes. Hummocks (small knolls or mounds) were removed around the infield and molding sand was swapped out for plain river sand. To reduce the hardness of the infield, Stocksick had it plowed and lowered in 1936 (an exercise he would repeat in 1947). To prepare for a season, he'd navigate the field on his hands and knees with a magnifying glass, looking for pebbles in the infield dirt. But nothing he did could prevent the brutal St. Louis summers. "When we get these hot summers here it is almost impossible to keep the grass alive," Stocksick said.[19] The "Sportsman's Park turf," sportswriter Bob Broeg recalled years later, was "never so weary-looking from two teams' use than in '44."

*****

None of that mattered to the more than 30,000 fans who filed into Sportsman's Park for the first game of the World Series. Morning rain had given way to a cool, cloudless day with bright sun and a light breeze. The city's police chief and 88 uniformed officers were on duty to help with traffic and crowd control. Other city officials noted 60 additional streetcars would be made available to handle post-game traffic and called on taxicab operators to load their vehicles to capacity to and from the park. Regulators with the Office of Price Administration circled nearby parking lots, looking for license plates that could indicate possible misuse of gasoline rations.[20]

Once inside the park, many fans purchased a scorecard for ten cents, complete with the day's starting lineup.[21] The idea of having a pre-printed lineup inside the scorecard was the brainchild of Eddie Browning. The first owner of the Browns, Robert Hedges, had awarded Browning the scorecard concession business when he arrived in 1902. "Browning proceeded to give St. Louis baseball fans the most accurate program in baseball," the *Globe-Democrat* once noted.[22] More than four decades later, Browning still had the business. Every morning, he would call the managers of both teams to get the lineups, which would then be reproduced on scorecards featuring up-to-date batting averages, also a first. St. Louis proudly claimed their scorecards were purchased by a greater proportion of attendees than any other ballpark in the country.

Wearing a bow tie and a straw hat, the nattily-attired Browning wouldn't wait for the business to come to him. With a stack of programs under one arm, he'd call attention to his product. He liked to hang out between home plate and first base when he wasn't busy selling. "It is a pleasant occupation," Browning said. "Living out of doors all the time keeps me healthy."[23]

The man charged with keeping the Cardinals healthy did his business under the stands. Frankie Frisch once described Dr. Harrison J. "Bucko" Weaver as "chief morale officer, director of entertainment and club mother."[24] During ballgames, he'd cast a spell on an opposing batter, baserunner, or pitcher by clenching his fist against his forehead, extending his index and little fingers, and staring down the opponent he wanted to hex. A "whammy" became a "double whammy" when he applied the trick with both hands.

Weaver kept a phonograph in the Cardinals dressing room, where he liked to play upbeat tunes like the Notre Dame fight song and the "Battle Hymn of the Republic." His players, many from rural areas in the South, preferred mountain music and sadder melodies. In 1942, a Harry James' arrangement of the hillbilly song, "Pass the Biscuits, Mirandy," became so worn out from daily play, the disc had to be retired. Two years later, another hillbilly song, "The Chill on the Hill Tonight," was playing when a reporter visited him before Game 1. "All these boys from the mountains want mountain music and wherever we go, they play 'Past the Grave at Midnight,' and 'Wasted Tears,' and stuff like that," said Weaver. "Depressing, that's what it is." The reporter's visit with the Cardinals trainer was interrupted by an urgent request from outfielder Deb Garms. "Hey Doc," he cried, "where is my pants?"

The Cardinals were an experienced, loose bunch of players. Fourteen of the 22 members had World Series experience, led by Pepper Martin, on a postseason roster for the fourth time. He walked into the clubhouse that morning wearing a five-gallon hat.[25] No player on the Browns had ever played in a Fall Classic.

Out on the field, the first sightings of Cardinals players at 11:50 a.m. brought "cheers and a few boos" from the fans. Many locals weren't sure how to respond to a Series featuring both of the city's teams. Unlike Chicago, which divided northside Cubs fans from southside White Sox supporters, or New York, where separate boroughs housed the Dodgers, Giants, and Yankees, no geographic division existed in St. Louis. Undoubtedly, many fans viewed the Browns, with their undistinguished history, as a sentimental favorite. But an editorial cartoon in the *Star-Times* captured the attitude of many. It pictured a player wearing a St. Louis uniform with a crown on his head, wearing an oversized glove leaping for a World Series baseball. "We Win," it read.

*****

Commissioner Landis didn't make it to the World Series for the first time in his career. Hired by baseball owners in the wake of the Black Sox Scandal, the autocratic Landis had ruled the game since 1921. Feeling ill, the 78-year-old Landis remained at his Chicago home. Baseball dignitaries who did make it to

Holy Cow St. Louis!

St. Louis included many with ties to local history. Leo Durocher, Frankie Frisch, Gabby Street, and Jim Bottomley had all managed and played the game and between the four of them, had a connection to every single pennant-winning team of the Cardinals of the 1920s and 30s. Durocher captained the 1934 Gashouse Gang Cardinals. His double-play partner was Frisch, who also managed the club. Frisch had played for Street, the Cardinals skipper who won a pennant in 1930 and a World Series in 1931. Bottomley also played for Street on both of those teams, and together with Frisch, was a member of the 1928 Cardinals squad that lost a World Series to the Yankees. Bottomley played for the Cardinals' first championship club in 1926 and later managed the Browns for a portion of a season.

Non-baseball VIPs were few and far between. The most prominent appeared on the field at 1:30 p.m., thirty minutes before the start of the game. Ohio governor John Bricker was photographed standing between managers Sewell and Southworth. That a governor of Ohio was in Missouri for a game between two St. Louis teams spoke to the other major domestic event happening in the fall of 1944. It was a presidential election year, and Bricker was running as the vice-presidential candidate for the Republican Party. The man at the top of the GOP ticket was Thomas Dewey. He opposed President Roosevelt, who was shooting for an unprecedented fourth consecutive term. Roosevelt's running mate would be in St. Louis for the second game of the Series. So would another man that Browns and Cardinals fans knew well. One was about to change baseball. The other was about to change the world.

*****

Branch Rickey and Harry Truman made for quite a pair. Both grew up in rural areas, toiled on farms, knew the value of hard work, were voracious readers and precocious children. But poor eyesight doomed Truman's bid to enter West Point. He didn't have a college degree. Rickey spent years in higher education, possessed diplomas from multiple colleges, including the University of Michigan, where he received his law degree. Truman was a bourbon-sipping Baptist and Democrat from Jackson County, Missouri. Rickey was a teetotaling Methodist and Republican from Scioto County, Ohio. Born less than three years apart in the 1880s, both men had served in the armed forces and knew the art of politics. They just practiced it in different fields.

Young Harry Truman was wearing glasses by age six and claimed to have read the Bible twice by the age of 12. He had a fascination for trains, a passion for the piano, and ran from fights. "To tell the truth, I was kind of a sissy."

When the United States entered World War I in 1917, Truman enlisted. At the age of thirty-three, he became the battery commander of a field artillery unit. Promoted to captain and sent to France in 1918, Truman and his unit saw combat action near the Swiss border.

When the war ended in November, Truman returned to the United States. He was a different man. "The change was astounding," wrote Truman biographer David McCullough. "He had new confidence in himself. He discovered he could lead men and he liked that better than anything he had done before."[26]

Truman ran the family farm before the war. Now back home again in Missouri, he started a business in Kansas City with a partner. He famously failed as the co-owner of a men's clothing store. Demand for silk shirts dried up when the country entered a depression following the war. The Pendergast family — the political machine that ran Kansas City politics — asked Truman to run for office. Elected as a county judge — an administrative job, not a legal position — he found his calling in politics. First elected as a United States Senator in 1934, Truman faced an uphill challenge in his re-election bid in 1940. It was in St. Louis that year that his political fortunes were forever changed.

Missouri Governor Lloyd Stark was considered the favorite to win the Democratic primary. Robert Hannegan was chairman of the Democratic City Central Committee of St. Louis and a Stark supporter. Influential and popular, Hannegan had been a football star at St. Louis University, and his father was once chief of detectives for the city. Two days before the primary, Hannegan switched allegiances and began backing Truman.[27] Hannegan's support was crucial to the outcome. Truman won the state by just 7,976 votes. The margin of difference in St. Louis was 8,411. With the Democratic nomination in hand, Truman then won comfortably in the fall, defeating his opponent in the general election by 44,000 votes.

Truman's victory in the 1940 Senate race changed the arc of history. Hannegan rode his influence to politically plum appointments. Over the years, he served as commissioner of Internal Revenue, chairman of the National Democratic Party and Postmaster General. But the bigger impact came from the life of the former farmer and failed haberdasher. A Truman loss in 1940 meant he wouldn't have been a sitting Senator in 1944. Without that status, he would have never been considered a possible running mate for Roosevelt.[28]

If the politician from Independence knew every square mile of Missouri, Rickey knew every square inch of Sportsman's Park. Everywhere he walked, there were reminders of his past. Scorecard concessionaire Browning was in his fourth year of business when Rickey debuted for the St. Louis Browns. Rickey's first year as a player was also the first year Stocksick started chalking the foul lines and raking the infield. A decade later, when Rickey was running the front office of the Browns, it was Stocksick who sent a teenage vendor up to the executive's office when he was looking for an assistant.[29] Bill DeWitt Sr. worked under Rickey with the Browns, and later with the Cardinals. When DeWitt and Don Barnes struck a deal to buy the Browns in 1936, Rickey brokered the sale.

Rickey was instrumental in getting concessionaire Harper to St. Louis. As a vice president for the Cardinals, Rickey first came in contact with Harper when he owned a minor league team in Fort Smith, Arkansas. The Cardinals bought Harper's franchise, an early signal that Rickey's team was serious about developing its own talent.

Rickey had known Cardinals trainer Weaver for years. Both men were Ohio Wesleyan alums. Rickey placed a call after the 1926 season, inviting Weaver to join the Cardinals. He'd been a part of the organization ever since. A year after Weaver joined the club, Mary Murphy was hired as a temporary secretary. Her position became permanent when she successfully transcribed several of Rickey's speeches from handwritten notes to typewritten pages. "That's just the person I'm looking for," said the Cardinals executive. When Rickey left St. Louis, he unsuccessfully tried to recruit both Weaver and Murphy to his new team.[30]

Murphy now typed primarily for the man who gave Rickey the financial wherewithal to expand the Cardinals' minor league system. Owner and president Breadon first got involved with the team as a small stockholder in 1917, the same year that Rickey left the Browns for the Cardinals. A New York native, Breadon had made his fortune in the automobile business. Three years after buying his first shares, Breadon became the team's president and soon accumulated the majority of stock. He quickly struck a deal with Browns owner Phil Ball to play in Sportsman's Park, allowing Breadon to sell the team's dilapidated structure at the intersection of Vandeventer and Natural Bridge Avenue. A sale to the St. Louis Board of Education netted the franchise $200,000.

This money allowed Rickey, the best talent evaluator in the game, to build a peerless pipeline. Critics hated it, calling it "Rickey's plantation," or "Rickey's chain gang," but eventually every other club adopted a similar structure. Over the years, it produced such talent as Bottomley, Dizzy Dean, Joe Medwick, and Johnny Mize. But a big farm system meant big expenses, including Rickey's base salary of $50,000 by the early 1940s plus a percentage of the money from any player he sold. With war looming, Breadon announced in 1941 that Rickey's contract wouldn't be renewed.[31] After the 1942 season, Rickey left for the Dodgers. A vice president in St. Louis became a president in Brooklyn, two titles that Truman would soon hold.

Just as Hannegan became instrumental to Truman's career, Rickey and Breadon are intertwined in the history of the Cardinals. This quartet of men, two Missouri natives and two longtime St. Louis residents, would make career-altering decisions in the next few years. One duo made consequential decisions in parallel. A single transaction permanently connected the other pair.

In the summer of 1945, Truman gave the green light to an atomic bomb that devastated two Japanese cities and ended World War II. Six days after the Japanese officially surrendered on the deck of the USS *Missouri*, Truman was back at a ballpark, throwing out the ceremonial first pitch in a game between the Browns and Senators. The following month, Rickey's Dodgers announced the signing of a black man to a baseball contract. In certain parts of America, the latter decision was far more controversial. Jackie Robinson, the man Rickey signed, broke baseball's color barrier when he debuted for the Brooklyn Dodgers in 1947. A year later, Truman moved to desegregate the military.

Riding baseball's postwar attendance boom, Breadon decided to cash out. When he sold the team after the 1947 season, Hannegan was one of the buyers. He left his position as Postmaster General to become president of the Cardinals. At a tribute dinner, Hannegan's former boss wired his congratulations to Breadon, a longtime Democrat. "Baseball is indebted to you for what you have done to keep it at a level of high integrity," President Truman told him. "Certainly all of us from Missouri owe you cheers for the Cardinals."

*****

Cheers came in abundance for the Browns in Game 1. "Browns' fans were in the majority," wrote Keener. "Even when the Cardinals threatened to score in the early innings, National League supporters were drowned out by the American League enthusiasts." The Browns only got two hits on the day, but one was a two-run home run by first baseman McQuinn. Galehouse, their formerly weekends-only starter, went the distance in defeating Cooper and the Cardinals.

Photographers captured McQuinn the next day sitting next to a smiling Truman. The Missouri Senator had arrived at Union Station and made it to Sportsman's Park in time to enjoy some pregame festivities. He told reporters he planned to be on hand for Games 2 and 3 before embarking on a 7,500-mile campaign tour that would see him head south to New Orleans, then out to the West Coast, before returning to the East. The entire trip would be made with train rides. Roosevelt had instructed him not to travel by airplane. It was important to keep one of them alive, an increasingly frail President told his running mate.[32]

Holy Cow St. Louis!

McQuinn's place in the second game's lineup moved from sixth to fifth as Sewell's team prepared to face a lefthander in Lanier. It was the Cardinals lineup that day that caught Rickey's attention. Cardinals manager Southworth had swapped out left fielder Danny Litwhiler, bothered by a knee injury, for Augie Bergamo. That detail provided an exclamation point to Rickey's influence on St. Louis baseball.

"In the second game when Bergamo started in left field instead of Litwhiler, you saw something that is without precedent," Rickey later told a Brooklyn reporter. "Every one of the nine Cardinal players who started a World Series game was a 100 percent product of the Cardinal system. And not one of the nine," added the perpetually frugal Rickey, "Bergamo, Hopp, Musial, Walker Cooper, Sanders, Kurowski, Marion, Verban and Lanier – received a bonus of as much as five cents when, as free agents, they entered the Cardinal chain."[33]

Rickey knew those details because he was responsible for bonuses when the players signed their contracts. His influence still towered over the franchise two years after leaving the Cardinals. His fingerprints were all over the opponents, as well. General manager DeWitt had been a Rickey acolyte for decades. His brother, Charley DeWitt, the Browns traveling secretary, had previously scouted for the Cardinals. Browns starting pitcher Potter had spent years in the Cardinals' minor league system and was once a minor league teammate of Lanier, his counterpart on the mound for Game 2. Browns second baseman Gutteridge had also once been a part of Mr. Rickey's Redbirds. In parts of five seasons with the Cardinals, Gutteridge had always played either third base or shortstop. Rickey had once told him he'd never be a second baseman in the big leagues. Gutteridge proved him wrong, becoming the Browns regular second baseman in 1943.

In addition to the homegrown Cardinals lineup, the ever-observant Rickey likely noticed something else about the events at Sportsman's Park that day. Black fans in St. Louis had long been restricted to seats in the pavilion or the bleachers. That changed in 1944. St. Louis was the last city in major league baseball to end segregated seating.

The Cardinals won the '44 World Series in six games. But it was Game 2 that really decided the matter. Because the Browns won Games 1 and 3, a victory in the second game would have meant a practically insurmountable 3-0 Series lead. It almost happened were it not for poor Browns' defense. The American League champions made four errors on the day. The game went to extra innings with the score tied at two. Both runs by the Cardinals were unearned. The National League champions won it in the bottom of the 11th inning on an RBI single by pinch-hitter Ken O'Dea.

For the Series, the Browns made ten errors to just one for the Cardinals. When relief pitcher Ted Wilks struck out pinch-hitter Mike Chartak to complete a 3-1 victory in Game 6, the Redbirds headed off the field to celebrate the fifth World Series title in franchise history. Second baseman Emil Verban had unfinished business. Still upset about the tickets given to his wife when the Browns were the home team (a pole blocked her view of the field), he sprinted over to the owner's box of the Browns. "Now, Mr. Barnes," Verban told him, "you're the one behind the post."[34] The indignities didn't end there. "If we had lost this Series to the Browns," Breadon told Barnes, "I'd have to leave town."

In a Series marked by a noticeable lack of offense, Verban stood out, hitting .412. The Cardinals scored just 16 runs for the entire six games. Only nine of them were earned. The Browns crossed the plate 12 times; half of those came in one game. Winning shares for the Cardinals came to $4,626 per player, while each American League champion received $2,744. It was the lowest payout since 1920. Ten percent of the players' money had to be invested in war bonds. It was even worse for the teams. Commissioner Landis decreed that fifty percent of their money had to be donated to war relief. "Jesus, here we are losing money, and for once we get a chance to make some money in the World Series, and we have to give half of it away," said Browns general manager DeWitt.

Despite the loss, the Browns held a party at the Chase Hotel that night. Jakucki showed up drunk with "dollar bills stuck in his shirt, in his buttonholes, his sleeves, on his ear. He must have had twenty or thirty dollar bills stuck all around," recalled Gutteridge. "He said, 'Now I'm in the money.'" Jakucki was found in a gutter in Illinois two days later, with not a penny on him. "He was broke and dirty, and somebody recognized him and cleaned him up and sent him home," Gutteridge said.[35]

The pitcher returned to the Browns the following season. Over a two-year period, Jakucki won 25 games and pitched a complete game in a World Series. The poster boy for what was possible during the war years had also increasingly alienated his manager with his belligerent behavior. Arriving at a train station for the beginning of a road trip in August of 1945, Jakucki showed up drunk and threatened Sewell and his coaches. The manager got in his compartment and locked the door. Traveling secretary DeWitt called the authorities. At the next stop, Jakucki was escorted off the train by police and suspended by the Browns. He never pitched in the big leagues again.

*****

The end of the 1944 Series pushed baseball off the front pages of the newspapers. Following the Cardinals' victory, the *Globe-Democrat* featured a page-one, seven-paragraph story by Bob Burnes with a straightforward headline: "Cards Win Fifth World Title." The afternoon *Post-Dispatch* dedicated its entire front page to war coverage. The banner headline in both papers regarded the surrounding of the German city of Aachen by American troops. Gas rationing prevented any parade or major civic celebration for the Cardinals. Even the clubhouse celebration seemed more sedate. "In those days, we didn't have champagne," Musial recalled. "And if we had, we wouldn't have sprayed it. We would have drunk it."[36] The city was also running out of tobacco. People in St. Louis "won't know what a cigarette looks like" by January 1, warned a sales manager at a tobacco company.[37] Most of the supply was going overseas. Supplies of cigars were in even worse shape. World Series crowds had accentuated the shortage.

Manager Southworth welcomed a steady stream of visitors offering congratulations. They included Barnes and Sewell of the Browns, American League president Will Harridge and a representative from the commissioner's office. He had one final visitor at his locker, Billy Southworth Jr., a Major in the Army Air Force. The younger Southworth had been playing minor league ball for Toronto when he enlisted after the 1940 season, becoming the first professional ballplayer to sign up for military service.

Southworth Jr. attended his first World Series since 1926, back when his father was an outfielder for the Cardinals.[38] The 27-year-old Southworth Jr. flew more than two dozen missions over Europe, wearing a Cardinals cap given to him by his father. His friends called him the "flying outfielder," and his plane became known as "Bad Check." It always came back.[39] It eventually became so shot up, Southworth was given command of another plane. His crew called this one "Winning Run." He received the Distinguished Flying Cross and the Air Medal with Oak Leaf Clusters. Described as a "handsome, husky man with black hair and a small, dark mustache," Major Southworth captivated Hollywood. Just months earlier, a movie producer had signed him to a motion picture contract scheduled to go into effect after the war.[40]

The day after the Southworth father and son reunion brought a reminder of the dangers faced by men who swapped a baseball uniform for military attire. Arthur Peters had served as the Cardinals batboy when the team beat the Yankees in 1942. He was inducted into the army early the next year. In October '44, the War Department notified his mother in St. Louis that Peters, now 24 years old, had been wounded in action in France.

That same month, a few prescient writers saw storm clouds on the horizon for the Cardinals. Despite winning 316 regular season games, three pennants, and two World Series titles in the past three seasons, the team had a few cracks below the surface. Under the headline, "Card Dynasty Falters," New York *Daily News* writer Jim McCulley observed that the Cardinals had curtailed their farm system, while Rickey's Dodgers had been furiously expanding their minor league operations. "It is logical to presume, then, that in a day not too distant, there will be a leveling off; a period when the scales will swing for a time in balance and then suddenly tip in favor of the Dodgers. In fact, the changeover may come with a crash more resounding than anyone suspects," McCulley wrote one week after the completion of the 1944 World Series.[41] Days later, a headline for a story in *The Sporting News* about Rickey's pursuit of the Cardinals read, "Wait Until '47!"[42]

November featured a victory party of a different sort. The winning ticket of Roosevelt and native son Truman carried Missouri and 35 other states and won an electoral college landslide, 432-99. Early the next morning, Republican candidate Dewey called Roosevelt to concede and congratulate the President. Truman never got such a call from Bricker, Dewey's running mate. He never forgot the slight.

Bricker later became a United States Senator. Truman saw him at a congressional reception. "Most of the Senators and Congressmen, I was glad to see, but there were [a] half dozen I'd rather have punched in the nose," he wrote in a letter to his mother and sister. "I told [wife] Bess if she'd trip up Bricker so he'd sprawl on the floor in front of us I'd give her the big diamond out of the scimitar the Crown Prince of Arabia gave me. It is about 5 carats. But she didn't have the nerve to do it. If she had, he'd been out sure enough."[43]

*****

Hollywood never did find out if Southworth Jr.'s talents could translate to the silver screen.[44] In February of 1945, the country lost a war hero. The Cardinals manager lost his son. Piloting a B-29 Bomber, Major Southworth and crew had made a brief stop at Mitchel Field on Long Island before departing for LaGuardia Field as part of a secret mission. Soon after, he radioed ground control that the left outboard engine had failed. He was coming in for an emergency landing. He overshot the airfield and crashed the plane in Flushing Bay. Five members of the crew survived. Five others, including Southworth, did not. Southworth's body wasn't recovered until August. His father took solace in the bottle. One of his players later recalled that anytime the club came to New York, manager Southworth would visit a park near the crash site and "drink and drink and drink."[45]

The new year brought death and change to the Cardinals, baseball, and the country.

Holy Cow St. Louis!

On April 12, America got a new leader. At his home in Warm Springs, Georgia, President Roosevelt collapsed from a cerebral hemorrhage and died a few hours later. Back in the nation's capital, Vice President Truman was summoned to the White House. Roosevelt's wife, Eleanor, broke the news to him. "Is there anything I can do for you?" Truman asked her. "Is there anything we can do for you?" she replied. "For you are the one in trouble now." Truman, so kept in the dark about Roosevelt's war plans that he didn't even know the Map Room in the White House existed, had been Vice President for 83 days.

On April 24, baseball got a new commissioner. Landis, the only commissioner baseball had ever had, died in November. Six months later, baseball owners narrowed the field of possible replacements to five. One of them was St. Louis native Hannegan, who received support from Browns owner Barnes, Cardinals owner Breadon, and Dodgers president Rickey.[46] But the owners ultimately coalesced around another man with extensive political connections, U.S. Senator and former Kentucky Governor A.B. "Happy" Chandler.

On April 21, Cardinals fans heard a new voice describing the action. On that date, the club welcomed the Cincinnati Reds to town for their home opener at Sportsman's Park. Fans could tune to radio station WIL, 1230 AM, to hear the new sportscaster and his broadcast partner, Gabby Street. A novice at major league play-by-play, the St. Louis native had left home a few years earlier to begin his radio career. He came back home with the expectation that he would be drafted. Poor eyesight kept him out of the military, ironic since his eyes would be the ones millions of St. Louis fans would come to depend on over the next quarter-century.

He left town as Harry Carabina. He returned home as Harry Caray.

---

[1] "The Browns annual report read like the lab report of a terminal patient," wrote author Bill Borst. "This was not a team, it was a disaster," *Los Angeles Times* columnist Jim Murray wrote in 1974.

[2] Herbert "Zutty" Foerstel was a drummer in the orchestra of radio station KSD. He estimated he saw "more than 66" of the Browns 77 home games in 1944. *St. Louis Post-Dispatch*, October 2, 1944.

[3] *Brooklyn Daily Eagle*, September 29, 1941. "Seventh row box seat…" *St. Louis Star-Times*, October 4, 1944.

[4] "Seventy players toiled for both St. Louis teams, almost all coming to the Browns after their careers with the Cardinals." Borst, Bill. *Still Last in the American League: The St. Louis Browns Revisited.* Altwerger and Mandel Publishing Co., Inc. 1992.

[5] *St. Louis Globe-Democrat*, October 3, 1944.

[6] *St. Louis Star-Times*, October 3, 1944. Crespi was killed in action in Italy on September 14. The War Department notified the Crespi family of the news on October 11.

[7] A grandstand block cost $18.75. Box seats for three games cost $22.50. Scalpers got three to five times that price on the streets.

[8] Ticket requests only applied to reserved seats. Each game day at 8:00 a.m., bleacher and pavilion seats would go on sale.

[9] When not in St. Louis, both Sewell and Southworth called Ohio home. Sewell lived in Akron, Southworth in Columbus. A profile of Sewell and wife Edna mentioned that "Mrs. Sewell would like to meet Mrs. Southworth someday but never has, as they are never in town at the same time." *St. Louis Post-Dispatch*, September 24, 1944.

[10] *St. Louis Post-Dispatch*, October 2, 1944. Other reports say Southworth found another apartment in the same building. Derrick Goold wrote that a coin flip decided the matter. Ibid, October 27, 2020. Goold's source was likely Hall of Fame Research Director Tim Wiles, who wrote about the Streetcar Series on its 50th anniversary.

[11] The experience of all games in a single stadium wouldn't be repeated until 2020, when the coronavirus pandemic forced the entire World Series to be played at Globe Life Field in Arlington, Texas.

[12] Cooper's holdout lasted only a few days. He signed for an estimated $15,000.

[13] Marshall, William. *Baseball's Pivotal Era, 1945-1951*. The University Press of Kentucky. 1999. *St. Louis Post-Dispatch,* October 22, 1944.

[14] *The Sporting News*, July 28, 1979.

[15] Mead, William B. *Even the Browns: Baseball During World War II*. Dover Publications, Inc. 1978, 1982.

[16] Ibid.

[17] *St. Louis Post-Dispatch*, October 1, 1944.

[18] *St. Louis Star-Times*, March 17, 1944.

[19] Ibid, March 15, 1938.

[20] "Most of the cars parked near the park bore Missouri license plates. The sprinkling of out-of-state cars were largely from Illinois and Indiana. Other out-of-town licenses noted were from Texas, Louisiana, Arkansas, Minnesota, Iowa, Kansas, and Oklahoma." *St. Louis Star-Times*, October 4, 1944.

[21] The price of scorecards had doubled from 1943. Inflation had come to the ballpark. "The cost of producing the scorecards and selling them has about doubled, and we felt justified in charging the same price the public pays in other ballparks," Breadon explained in a column. *St. Louis Post-Dispatch,* May 23, 1944.

[22] *St. Louis Globe-Democrat*, June 23, 1948.

[23] Ibid, September 25, 1927.

[24] *St. Louis Post-Dispatch*, August 14, 1962.

[25] Martin later told a reporter his contributions in the 1944 World Series consisted of being "batting practice pitcher and head cheerleader." After the Series, he retired for a second time. *New York Times, October 19, 1944.*

[26] McCullough, David. *Truman*. Simon & Schuster. 1992.

[27] "Why did Hannegan send out word to the ward bosses to drop Stark for Truman? The answer is not known," concluded a *Post-Dispatch* editorial. *St. Louis Post-Dispatch*, October 7, 1949.

[28] Ibid. "To a considerable extent, President Truman holds the highest office in the land because of incidents in which the late Robert E. Hannegan played a leading role."

[29] Charley DeWitt also took credit for recommending his brother to Rickey.

[30] Murphy's sister, Margaret, was a secretary for the Browns. She retired in September 1944 after working for the team for 28 years. *The Sporting News,* September 14, 1944.

[31] The rift between Breadon and Rickey wasn't strictly about money. "Breadon and Rickey, it is generally believed, have not seen eye to eye on policy matters for several years. When Billy Southworth succeeded Ray Blades as manager in June 1940, it was Breadon who made the shift. Rickey was not even consulted on the move." Ibid, October 8, 1942.

[32] McCullough, *Truman*. Henry Wallace was Roosevelt's Vice President in his third term, but the President wanted a new running mate for his fourth.

[33] *Brooklyn Daily Eagle*, October 11, 1944. Outfielders Litwhiler and Garms were the only two players on the roster not to come up through the Cardinals' minor league system.

[34] After the game, Barnes told Southworth, "You've got one louse on your ball club, Verban." Peterson, Richard, editor. *The St. Louis Baseball Reader*. University of Missouri Press. 2006. The Barnes-Verban tiff has as many quote variations as it does sources. In another version, Verban tells him, "Now, you get behind the post, you fathead!" Borst, Bill. *The Best of Seasons: The 1944 St. Louis Cardinals and St. Louis Browns.* McFarland. 1995.

[35] Golenbock, *The Spirit of St. Louis. A History of the St. Louis Cardinals and Browns.* Avon Books, Inc. 2000.

[36] *St. Louis Post-Dispatch,* October 23, 1985.

[37] Ibid, October 10, 1944.

[38] Southworth Jr. flew his bomber over Sportsman's Park during the second game of the 1942 World Series, giving his father the airman's salute by dipping the plane's wings. New York *Daily News*, February 17, 1945.

[39] *St. Louis Star-Times*, February 16, 1945.

[40] Southworth Jr. was signed by Hollywood producer Hunt Stromberg, who saw him at a boxing match in Los Angeles. The contract would start "when you return," Stromberg told him. "The eyes of the two men met. Each man knew the other was thinking of one word – 'if' – which neither would pronounce," wrote Whitney Martin in a story for the *Associated Press*. Stromberg was a former reporter and sports writer for the *St. Louis Times*.

[41] New York *Daily News*, October 15, 1944.

[42] *The Sporting News*, October 19, 1944.

[43] Ferrell, Robert H., editor. *Off the Record: The Private Papers of Harry S. Truman*. Harper & Row. 1980.
[44] Southworth would have been the next Clark Gable of the movie industry, Hollywood producer Stromberg told reporters when informed of his death.
[45] Daly, Jon. *Billy Southworth*. SABR.org research project.
[46] Columnist John Drebinger wrote that Browns president Barnes also had his eye on another candidate. "Barnes is believed to have started the boom for J. Edgar Hoover, FBI chief." *New York Times,* February 9, 1945.

Harry Carabina

He kept it a secret until the end. When Harry Caray died, *The New York Times* placed his age at 78. The newspaper was off by five years. Guessing Harry's age had been a journalistic parlor game for decades. Writers always suspected he wasn't telling the truth. He is "around 40," the *St. Louis Globe-Democrat* noted in 1957. (He was 43). "Estimates of Caray's age range from 73 to a more plausible 77," wrote Fred Mitchell in the *Chicago Tribune* in 1994. (He was 80). Even his wife didn't know (or wouldn't admit) the truth. Harry missed the first baseball games of his career in 1987 after suffering a stroke. Reporters wanted to know how a 67-year-old man could attempt a comeback. "You don't know him. He'll be back," predicted Dutchie Caray. "Besides, he's 70." (He was 73.)

Born Harry Christopher Carabina, he arrived on March 1, 1914 (not 1920, as the *Times* and other outlets later wrote). He was born in the city of Saint Louis, in a growing country of 48 states and 100 million people, in a world on the verge of one of its bloodiest conflicts. St. Louis had the fourth-largest population of any city in America in the early twentieth century. Only New York, Chicago, and Philadelphia claimed more residents than the 687,000 who called St. Louis home.[1]

Four months before Harry's birth, Henry Ford installed the first moving assembly line designed to mass-produce automobiles. But cars wouldn't be popular in America until the 1920s. Traveling any major distance meant riding the rails. "The 'Night Hawk' gives you a full evening here and lands you in St. Louis at the very beginning of the business day," read a 1914 newspaper ad for a rail line that left Kansas City nightly at 11:30 p.m. and arrived on the other side of the state at 8:00 a.m. the next morning.

It was a country dominated by men who had come of age in the previous century. In January, the police chief of Houston, Texas arrived at Union Station in St. Louis on his way to Chicago, guarding three million dollars in currency. He took the job for $500, about $2,000 less than an express company wanted for the same task. The police chief's only companions, according to one account, "were two revolvers of large caliber."

It was a city dominated in the summer by two bad baseball teams. On the day Harry was born, and as the Browns and Cardinals prepared to begin spring training, the *Globe-Democrat* printed a cartoon showing a group of baseball players diving into a hole. "Have members of both teams practice a running jump into a dark cellar – it will get them accustomed to their position in the coming pennant race," read the caption underneath. The previous season, the Cardinals lost 99 games. The Browns lost 96. Both teams finished in last place. Although a championship season was still over a decade away, better days weren't far off. The 1914 Cardinals improved dramatically, jumping to third place under manager Miller Huggins, who would go on to a Hall of Fame career in a different city. The 1914 Browns bumped up three notches in the standings under manager Branch Rickey, who would go on to a Hall of Fame career in a different role.

St. Louis was a city teeming with immigrants. At the beginning of the century, foreign-born residents, or their children, comprised 60 percent of the St. Louis population. Among those who left their native country behind for a better life in America were Harry's parents. Records show Christopher (or Christian) Carabina and the former Daisy Argint were born in Albania or Turkey.[2] Harry believed his father was Italian but claimed he never knew the man.

Like his offspring, the father had a flair for the dramatic and was prone to exaggeration. A front-page story in the *Globe-Democrat* in May 1913 heralded the couple's impending nuptials. The article, which appears to rely solely on Carabina's telling, describes the couple meeting as children in Bucharest, Romania. Carabina had been in the United States for twelve years and claimed to have amassed "a small fortune" in San Francisco. In St. Louis, he touted his connection to a downtown café. The night before the wedding, he flashed $150 in cash, spoke of a honeymoon to Chicago and New York, and maintained that his fiancé was a daughter of a Bucharest banker. Her wedding gown, trimmed with jewels, allegedly took six months to make.[3]

Carabina's description of the bride and his own resume punctures the enthusiastic picture he painted. Born Anastasia Argintaru, she was also known as Tasica and was called Daisy Argint after arriving in America in 1911. A dark-haired woman (as seen in her pictures), Daisy is described in the *Globe-Democrat* account as a "blonde beauty."[4] As far as that connection to a downtown café, Carabina was neither the owner nor the manager, but a waiter, based on the profession he listed in a 1912 city directory, the same occupation he would later list on his application to become a U.S. citizen.[5] Given the paucity of available information about the couple, we are left to guess what other liberties Carabina took with his anecdotes.

The marriage was over by May 1919. Here again, we see the ability of Carabina to shape the narrative. "Christ Carabina is tired of married life," begins the story in the *Westliche Post*, a German newspaper in St. Louis.[6] After the couple separated early in the month, Christ filed for divorce because his wife continued to baselessly accuse him of consorting with other women, he claimed in a petition. By making false claims to his employer, the Metropolitan Life Insurance Company, he alleged, she had him removed from his position.[7] Harry was five years old. (Christ's divorce petition was not granted. His wife was granted a divorce from him in January 1925 on the grounds of desertion.)[8]

Census information from 1920 reveals that Christ was living as a "roomer" on South Twelfth Street in St. Louis. According to family lore, Harry's father eventually returned to the old country and was killed in an automobile accident. Harry and his mother lived on LaSalle Street.[9] She was a garment worker in a factory.

Harry's mother would later marry again – to Sam Capuran – and the family moved to a home on Clayton Avenue. She died of pneumonia in April 1928 at the age of 37. Her obituary noted she was the "dear mother of Harry Capuran," who was 14 at the time.[10] It was a version of the story Harry never told. Over the years, he did tell reporters various accounts of his parents' lives. The same *Times* article that mentioned Harry was born in 1920 also claimed that his mother died when he was ten years old. That same day, the *Post-Dispatch* said he was eight when it happened. According to the *Washington Post*, both of his parents died by the time he was nine. "Harry's parents died when he was too young to remember them," wrote Richard Dozer in the *Chicago Tribune* in 1972.

In his autobiography, Harry admitted he had forgotten – or suppressed – large parts of his childhood. "The human mind has a mechanism that forces you – or enables you, as the case may be – to forget unpleasant experiences. With me, that mechanism has wiped out great parts of my early years," he wrote. "I simply do not remember a lot of names or dates or places."[11]

An accident as a teenager may have contributed to his memory loss. In January of 1928, Harry was riding in an automobile driven by his stepfather when it collided with another vehicle at the intersection of Grand and Choteau in St. Louis. According to one newspaper account, Harry suffered a fractured skull.[12] No additional details about his injuries are provided. It's another story Harry never told. (And one no previous writer or journalist ever has, either. It appears here in print for the first time since 1928.)

He had few words to say about Sam Capuran. "I didn't know my stepfather very well. He ran a restaurant, I think," Harry recalled years later. "He tried to keep me after my mother died, but that didn't work out."

He then moved in with his mother's brother and family at 1909 LaSalle Street. "Why I remember that address, I don't know," Harry said. (It was next door to where he had once lived with his mother.) But here, too, the picture is muddled by what he remembered or had forgotten. "Not long after I moved there, my uncle disappeared," Harry claimed. "He either deserted his family or died." According to their grandson, Nick Argint Jr., John and Doxie Argint separated sometime around 1940, more than a decade after Harry moved in with the family. (Doxie Argint's death certificate in 1959 lists her husband as deceased. In fact, he lived until 1963.)[13]

Harry remembered being raised by his aunt Doxie in a neighborhood he described over the years as a "slum" and a "ghetto." He once touted he was "the only guy who escaped the big house." But he had a different take when he returned to the area in the 1990s for a television documentary hosted by Bob Costas. While walking on the sidewalk outside his childhood home, Costas asked the man who claimed to be a former Golden Gloves champion, "Was this a rough neighborhood, did you get in your share of fights?"[14]

"No, I don't recall that at all," Caray said. "I can't remember any kind of fights. There [were] more friendships in those days." (Harry toured his old home but wouldn't let television cameras follow him inside.) The neighborhood did supply something that later became a staple of his broadcasts, the "Holy Cow!" home run calls. "Profanity was a common thing, so in order to refrain from it, I got in the habit of saying 'Holy Cow' instead of 'bullshit.'"

From there, Harry's childhood memories are few, the slivers of his past endlessly repeated to curious reporters, told in a boilerplate fashion with quotes almost identical from story to story. There was the motivational tale of the white flannel pants that everyone, except for Harry, wore at his grade school graduation. He couldn't afford a pair of white pants and was mocked by the other kids for wearing a pair of plain gray pants. "My heart was really breaking," Caray recalled. "But through the pain, through the tears, I made a solemn vow. Never again would I be unable to afford a pair of white pants."

A lending library sparked his curiosity and a lifelong love of reading. "We had a library on the corner of 18th and Choteau, and you could rent a book for a nickel. I sold papers and pocked 35 to 40 cents a day. Then I'd spend a dime for a chocolate-marshmallow sundae and invest in a book, and that's what occupied me through those summers as a kid."[15]

Harry found escape in books and sports. As a member of the Knothole Gang, he would spend his weekends at Sportsman's Park watching Browns and Cardinals games. From 1926, when Harry was 12, through 1934, when he was 20, the Cardinals won five pennants and three World Series titles. The 1926 title, the first in Cardinals history, sparked huge celebrations. The 1934 team, the legendary Gashouse Gang, provided diversion in the depths of the Great Depression. Babe Ruth hit three home runs in a single World Series game – twice. Each time it happened against the Cardinals in Sportsman's Park. Harry makes no mention of these teams or games in his autobiography.[16] The only mention of a player came in passing when he recounted walking onto the field after a game ended. "The biggest thrill was to take your place at home plate, pantomime a swing, sprint around first, slide into second, safe with a double, just like Rogers Hornsby." In high school in the early 1930s, he developed into a switch-hitting middle infielder. The Cardinals had their own switch-hitting second baseman at the time, future Hall of Famer Frankie Frisch. Did Harry model his game on Frisch? The record is silent. "I was a good baseball fan, not a great one," he once conceded.[17]

Young Carabina's favorite sports star wasn't Frisch, Hornsby or Ruth. Harry's hero wasn't even real. He was Frank Merriwell, a fictional star at Yale who excelled at sports "while solving mysteries and righting wrongs."[18] Reading books about Merriwell, Harry later recalled, "was probably how I developed my vocabulary, my interest in words, and perhaps even my desire and ability to communicate."

Harry remembered that desire to communicate being severely tested in his youth. He once told a story about how his wife would scold him for not attending church as often as he should. "She's right," he acknowledged. "But I tell her, that's where I spent a lot of my childhood. Where do you think I slept at night when I couldn't find any other place?"[19] The lack of a relationship with his parents and the sense of abandonment it spawned was "the one thing that really gnaws at me," he admitted late in life. Those deep-seated feelings manifested themselves every year at Christmas. "On Christmas Day, I have to be alone with my thoughts," he wrote. "For me, it's a melancholy time," Harry said about the time of year he always reflected on his upbringing. "I didn't have what everybody else had. I never had a mother or father around. No brothers or sisters. I never had the toys or gifts under the tree that other children had."[20]

Decades later, sitting in the Chicago restaurant named after him, Harry always wanted to be in the bar seat closest to the entrance. "He loved to be loved by the fans," said Dutchie. After his 1987 stroke, his wife began traveling with him on baseball road trips. He feared dying alone in a hotel room.

*****

The St. Louis of the 1920s featured bootleg alcohol, gang violence, silent movies, and segregated races. In 1916, St. Louis voters made it illegal for blacks and whites to move onto blocks with a majority of the other race.[21] Prohibition began in 1920 (the same year women got the right to vote), meaning the man who would someday be synonymous with beer and baseball likely didn't see a game with alcohol sales until he was at least 19.

The man who owned the Cardinals helped popularize the automobile in the city. Sam Breadon opened his Ford dealership in 1903. Four years later, Ford opened a sales office and stock department on Olive Street. In September 1914, the company opened a Model T plant on Forest Park Avenue. At its peak in the 1920s, 325 "Tin Lizzies" came off the assembly line daily. For many American families, the automobile came before the bathtub.[22] St. Louis was no exception. Home bathing in the city wasn't universally adopted until after World War II.[23]

The popularity of automobiles and the growth of telephones helped shrink time and distance. People began moving to the suburbs. Harry's family was part of the great migration. In 1930, he moved with the Argints and their four children to the St. Louis suburb of Webster Groves. In high school, he joined the Glee Club and played basketball in the winter and baseball in the spring.[24] One account noted Carabina's "speed and passing ability" on the hardwood. In another game, he scored three points. It doesn't sound impressive until you realize it was twenty percent of the team's output. Webster Groves defeated Wellston 15-14. Harry played AAU basketball with future Cardinals general manager Bing Devine. "I wasn't smart enough to think back then that he'd be a success in some field," Devine said years later. "But he had a strong voice and made himself heard and known." [25]

Harry claimed to be talented enough at baseball to draw a scholarship offer to the University of Alabama, but he turned it down because he couldn't afford room and board. In a pre-interstate highway America, St. Louis to Tuscaloosa was a difficult 500-mile drive. Perhaps a school closer to home showed some interest? If the question was ever asked of him, it doesn't appear the answer was recorded. "In his mind, he was damn good," remembered high school classmate Frank Fuchs Jr. "He was a wiry little guy, but a competitor. Even if you benched him, he'd be throwing every pitch, swinging every bat."[26]

He continued playing baseball after high school as a semi-pro player on the weekends. He took it seriously. "I didn't drink in those days. I wanted to be a big-league ballplayer." He told the *Boston Globe* he made $50 a game. "Do you realize how much $50 was then?"[27] To a television interviewer, he claimed he was paid $25 on Saturdays and $30 on Sundays to play on the sandlots of St. Louis. (He revised the figures down to $15 to $20 for his autobiography.) "I was a fine fielding second basemen who didn't hit much," he said. "I hit .100 righthanded and .100 lefthanded." Undeterred by his lack of hitting success,

Harry went to a tryout camp for the Cardinals. "They put a number on your back and you run and you throw and you hit – and you go home."[28]

After graduating from high school in 1932, he searched for work wherever he could find it. Was there ever a worse time in America to enter the workforce? By 1933, the unemployment rate in the country approached 25 percent. St. Louis officials put the local estimate at 35 percent, more than one in three people out of a job.[29] "I tended bar, waited tables, sold newspapers. I was a gofer, a flunky at a fight camp," he recalled. "Anything to make a few bucks to pay my way."

Despite his challenging upbringing, Harry moved comfortably in social circles beyond what he knew as a child. He married the former Dorothy Kunz in 1937. Her father, Dr. Valentine (Val) Kunz, studied at Washington University and was a dentist in St. Louis for more than 40 years. The marriage of Estelle Kunz, Dorothy's sister, made the Society News page of the *Globe-Democrat*. (Her husband, Dr. Ellsworth Westrup, was a longtime family physician in St. Louis.) Four years later, the now Estelle Westrup hosted a tea at her home where every guest was given a rose and a small scroll announcing Harry and Dorothy's engagement. They were married on Thanksgiving Eve. The Sunday *Globe-Democrat* featured a picture of the smiling couple.

The Kunz family made their home at 330 Chestnut Avenue in Webster Groves. The Argint family home was just around the corner, at 615 Selma Avenue.[30] Seven years after the move to the suburbs, Harry still lived with the Argints, a fact he confirmed years later. "All I had to do when I got married was move a few feet, from my aunt Doxie's house over to Dorothy's parents' place."

Internet real estate sites list the Selma Avenue home as being built in 1920, with a current (2023) value of more than a half-million dollars.[31] The ability of the Argints to relocate to a solidly middle-class suburban neighborhood at the beginning of the Great Depression suggests that, at least for a portion of his early years, Harry's lifestyle was likely more comfortable than he remembered.[32] "Unfortunately, Harry told his life story like he was broadcasting a baseball game," said Nick Argint Jr., whose father was one of John and Doxie's four children.[33] "My grandparents raised Harry from the time he was 14 or 15 [after the death of his mother]," Argint stated. "And he was loved," added Nick's wife, Malon, during an interview at the couple's home in Webster Groves.[34]

"He realized that he was living there, but he never felt that was really his family, his home," explained Dutchie.[35]

What Harry remembered, and never forgot, was the perpetual disappointment of father figures in his life. He believed his uncle, John Argint, had deserted his family. His relationship with his stepfather ended shortly after the death of his mother. He never really knew his birth father, but long after he left the United States, Christopher Carabina attempted to contact his son. "His father had gone back to the old country, and when he heard that Dad had become a success, he wrote him a letter," remembered Skip Caray. "Dad took the letter and threw it away, unopened."[36]

*****

By the time he married, Harry had found steady employment with the last job he ever had outside radio and television. He went to work for the Fred Medart Manufacturing Company, which made playground and school equipment.[37] A friend, Ray Higgins, worked as a sales manager for the company. Harry became his assistant, making $20 a week.

He spent his days writing letters, making phone calls and talking to customers about basketball backboards and school lockers. During the week, he'd listen to baseball games on the large, upright radio that sat in the living room of his in-laws. On weekends, whenever possible, he'd make his way down to Sportsman's Park, where he was captivated by the atmosphere of live big-league baseball. "There was the uncertainty, the anticipation, even the *smell* of being around a ballpark," he recalled years later. "It was a wonderful aroma that came from the ballpark and seemed to envelop the entire neighborhood."[38]

As a man who would later call Elvis Presley and Frank Sinatra friends, Harry viewed a baseball game as a theatrical performance, with the field as the stage and his bleacher seat as the balcony. "I don't subscribe to the theory that the game itself is enough to sustain the audience," he once explained to an interviewer. "I compare it to the theater. If the actor doesn't have a feel for the part he's playing, the play could flop even though it's a literary masterpiece."[39] A disconnect emerged between the games he watched and those he listened to on the radio. At the ballpark, "I felt that excitement; I experienced that thrill," he remembered. But back in Webster Groves, "what I heard was as dull and boring as the morning crop reports."[40]

Sensing an opportunity, he wrote a letter to Merle Jones, the general manager of radio station KMOX. Harry, around 25 at the time, decided he wanted to broadcast the games of the Cardinals and Browns. Never mind, as he freely admitted, "I didn't know anything about broadcasting. Nothing. I had never in my life seen a radio studio." The audacious plan came with a strategic twist. To make his missive stand out, Harry marked the letter PERSONAL and sent it to Jones' home address. "It was 825 South Skinker," he recalled. "The address changed my whole life."[41]

Jones read the letter and invited Harry to audition. The aspiring sportscaster didn't get a job at KMOX, but the radio general manager gave him a recommendation. Harry soon heard from a station in Joliet, Illinois that needed a sports and special events announcer. A broadcasting career was born and Harry had a story for the rest of his life.

He told a version of it to Bill Fleischman of the *Star-Times* in 1949, gave an expanded account to *Sports Illustrated's* Myron Cope in 1968, and recounted the tale to numerous reporters in Chicago for decades after he left St. Louis. But in the original version, first explained in a *Sporting News* article in 1946, it was Harry's wife who inspired him to act. "Harry, you could do better than that," Dorothy told him. "Why don't you try to get into radio?"[42] Three years later, he called her the "best fan I got. Never finds much wrong with the way I do things." Harry and Dorothy divorced in November 1949. Any references to his first wife's role in his broadcast beginnings ended with their marriage.

Regardless of who gets the credit, Harry's entry into the industry came at an opportune moment. Throughout the 1930s, many baseball owners operated under the assumption that the broadcasting of games dampened attendance. The Cardinals and Browns blocked broadcasts in 1934, a ban rescinded the following season.[43] Commissioner Landis launched an investigation into the impact of radio in 1936, an action that forced stations to pay for the privilege of carrying games the next year.[44] All three New York teams prevented radio broadcasts for years. But after 1938, Brooklyn president Larry MacPhail (who got his start in baseball working for Sam Breadon and Branch Rickey) decided to broadcast Dodgers games. The Giants and Yankees soon followed.[45] The two clubs jointly announced they had sold the advertising rights to three advertisers. "The tremendous cost of radio in the three New York parks precluded purchase by only one sponsor," explained *The Sporting News*. "As it is, the three rich companies which have bought the rights (General Mills, Vacuum Oil, and Proctor & Gamble) are going to spend something like a cool million around here this year, the first year for radio in the New York parks."[46] For the first time in 1939, all sixteen major league teams featured live radio broadcasts. There would be no turning back.[47]

That same year, a new technology emerged. "Major League Baseball Makes Its Radio Camera Debut," read a *New York Times* headline in August. The experimental television broadcast of a Dodgers-Reds doubleheader featured two cameras, one near the visitors' dugout and a second one behind the catcher. The NBC broadcast at Ebbets Field marked the network's second baseball telecast of the year. The first, a college game between Columbia and Princeton, occurred in May.

So by the time the young sales assistant wrote a letter to Merle Jones, sports television was beginning. Baseball on the radio was booming. Like all great entertainers, Harry Carabina had perfect timing.

---

[1] Officially recorded as 687,029 in the 1910 census.
[2] The 1920 census lists Daisy's place of birth as Albania. Her death certificate records her place of birth as Turkey (and that of her parents as well). There is similar contradictory information about Carabina with either Albania or Turkey listed depending on the source. Harry's father was also known as James. James Carabina is first listed in a St. Louis city directory in 1911, living at 1405 S. Pine with Costachi (John) Argintaru, Daisy's brother.
[3] *St. Louis Globe-Democrat*, May 25, 1913.
[4] Ibid. "She is a blonde beauty of pronounced [Romanian] type." She is referred to as "Tosica Argintarn" in the story, one of many spellings of the family's last name.
[5] *Gould's St. Louis Directory for 1912*. Carabina's address at the time was 1620A Olive. In 1914, the year Harry was born, his address is 614 N. 18th. The family moved to 1907 LaSalle Street in 1917. His occupation was listed as waiter when he applied for U.S. citizenship in 1918 according to Argint family research.
[6] Translation provided by the History and Genealogy Department of the St. Louis County Library.
[7] *Westliche Post*, May 13, 1919. Carabina is listed as an agent for Met Life in the 1919 Gould's Directory. The *Westliche Post* story says the couple reportedly married on May 27, 1913, a fact confirmed in an Ancestry.com search by Nick and Malon Argint. When she arrived in the United States in 1911, Anastasia (Daisy) was listed as a married woman on the ship's manifest. It is possible there were multiple wedding ceremonies.
[8] *St. Louis Post-Dispatch*, January 23, 1925.
[9] https://historicmissourians.shsmo.org/historicmissourians/name/c/caray/
[10] *St. Louis Globe-Democrat*, April 3, 1928.
[11] Caray, Harry with Bob Verdi. *Holy Cow!* Villard Books. 1989. "He never really liked to talk about his childhood, and so I never pushed it," Dutchie Caray later recalled.
[12] *St. Louis Star*, January 23, 1928. The story identifies his address as 6618 Clayton Avenue and his age as 14, more than a month before he would have turned that age if his birthday is correct. Sam Capuran suffered cuts and bruises and was charged with careless driving. Five years later, Sam Capuran of 517 ½ Market Street was fined $50 for violating liquor laws. *St. Louis Post-Dispatch,* April 28, 1933. The *Post-Dispatch* account of the car accident states that Harry suffered a "possible skull fracture." Ibid, January 23, 1928.
[13] John Argint was living in Seattle at the time of his death. His obituary mentions his four children, but not his wife. *St. Louis Post-Dispatch,* August 31, 1963. Similarly, Doxie Argint's obituary mentions her children but not her husband. Ibid, April 12, 1959. Missouri death certificates from 1910 to 1969 can be found online here. https://s1.sos.mo.gov/records/Archives/ArchivesMvc/DeathCertificates

14 "I'm a former Golden Gloves champ, you know. 126 pounds. Now, though, I'm a lover, not a fighter." *Chicago Tribune,* August 3, 1975.
15 Ibid, August 13, 1972.
16 Caray did write about Grover Cleveland Alexander's appearance in the seventh game of the 1926 World Series, but only in the context of a visit from President Reagan, who once played Alexander in a movie.
17 *St. Louis Post-Dispatch*, May 12, 1994.
18 https://en.wikipedia.org/wiki/Frank_Merriwell
19 *Chicago Tribune,* December 6, 1996. "I grew up ad-lib. I was an orphan but I was never in an orphan's home. I kept making it some way." *The Daily Journal/Scripps-Howard News Service*, March 22, 1985.
20 Caray, *Holy Cow!*
21 Lipsitz, George. *The Sidewalks of St. Louis: Places, People, and Politics in an American City.* University of Missouri Press. 1991.
22 Allen, Frederick Lewis. *Only Yesterday: An Informal History of the 1920s*. Harper & Row. 1931.
23 Lipsitz, *The Sidewalks of St. Louis*. The city of St. Louis didn't have a reliable water supply until 1904. One area of downtown featured 200 people for every bathtub. Between 1907 and 1930, the city built six major public baths and several smaller ones.
24 Before moving to Webster Groves, Harry attended Roosevelt High School.
25 *St. Louis Post-Dispatch*, February 19, 1998. "He was on a club with my cousin and several other athletes from Webster Groves High School. Through my cousin, I ended up on the team, too. Harry and I kind of sat on the bench together," Devine said. Wolfe and Castle, *I Remember Harry Caray*.
26 *Sports Illustrated*, October 7, 1968.
27 *Boston Globe*, June 22, 1984.
28 The tryout camp took place in Decatur, Illinois. "They took a good look at me, had me there a couple of days. But I just didn't have the physical skills – the arm, the speed, the eyesight – to play ball professionally," he wrote in his autobiography.
29 Ibid, October 25, 2014.
30 According to Nick Argint Jr., Val Kunz sold the Selma Avenue home to the Argints. Dr. Kunz had previously used a portion of the residence as a dentist's office. The home remained in the Argint family until well into the 21st century. Harry's grandmother, Anghelina Argint was living with the family when she passed away in 1931. The funeral was held at the Selma Avenue residence. *The News-Times* (Webster Groves), February 27, 1931.
31 Realtytrac.com. Google Maps places the distance between the two homes at 370 feet.
32 The 1940 census lists John Argint's occupation as a steward at a private club. He worked at Bevo Mill, a restaurant built in 1916 by August Busch Sr. At the time, the Anheuser-Busch brewery was manufacturing a non-alcoholic beer called Bevo. Argint's

grandson, Nick Argint Jr, told the author that his grandfather bought a Pierce-Arrow automobile from August Sr. and it was in that vehicle that a young Harry Caray learned to drive.

[33] Telephone interview with Nick Argint Jr., May 27, 2021. "Those stories about him moving from foster home to foster home? That's all bullshit," said Argint. He said the family was particularly upset about the 1968 *Sports Illustrated* profile of Harry where Myron Cope wrote that Caray was "passed around through foster homes" after his mother died. Argint remembers Caray as an adult attending events at the family home on Selma Avenue. "He'd drive over in a big blue Cadillac." According to Argint, all four of Harry's cousins - Nick Sr., Ted, Elizabeth, and Olga – attended Caray's funeral. He also recalled his aunt Elizabeth being close to Caray's daughter, Patricia.

[34] Interview with Nick and Malon Argint, January 3, 2023.

[35] *"Hello Again, Everybody"*: The Harry Caray Story. JLT Films. 2006. The documentary is available on YouTube.

[36] Ibid.

[37] Medart would later be involved in a price-fixing conspiracy lawsuit involving folding gymnasium bleachers at Illinois high schools in the 1960s. Medart had to pay $55,000 as part of the settlement. *Wall Street Journal*, June 16, 1964.

[38] Not everyone appreciated the scents and aromas arising from Sportsman's Park. "The neighborhood was strikingly shabby," wrote St. Louis native and author William B. Mead. "As we walked into the Knothole section in left field, the unswept grime crunched underfoot, and the park reeked of beer and other drippings. As one of the more egalitarian institutions in town, the Knothole Gang smelled pretty bad, too."

[39] Patterson, Ted. *The Golden Voices of Baseball*. Sports Publishing L.L.C. 2002.

[40] Caray, *Holy Cow!*

[41] Jones' home address was actually 725 South Skinker Blvd. *St. Louis Post-Dispatch*, September 19, 1943. His wife, Frances, worked for the Army Air Forces Aeronautical Chart Service during World War II, making maps and charts that assisted combat missions in Europe and the Pacific.

[42] *The Sporting News*, November 27, 1946.

[43] In April of 1934, the Cardinals and Browns announced the teams would allow radio stations to broadcast the score of games at the end of the third, sixth and ninth innings. *St. Louis Star-Times*, April 27, 1934. In the previous season, radio broadcasts were permitted on weekends only. Ibid, February 3, 1934.

[44] Patterson, *The Golden Voices of Baseball*. "Baseball men differ about the effect of radio on attendance," wrote Pat Robinson. "Some believe radio has made new fans in some cities such as Chicago. Others think radio hurt attendance in St. Louis." *Nashville Banner*, December 7, 1938.

[45] Listening to games in 1938 from his hospital bed convinced owner Jacob Ruppert that Yankee games should be broadcast. The ailing Ruppert died in January of 1939.

[46] *The Sporting News*, February 2, 1939.

[47] In 1938, the Pittsburgh Pirates successfully sued a local station that had been pirating the team's broadcasts. The decision helped solidify the broadcast rights of local teams. See https://theconversation.com/when-baseball-almost-banned-broadcasts-38150.

Radio Daze

Twenty-three-year-old Chicago native Bob Elson walked into the Chase Hotel in St. Louis one day in late 1927 and took the elevator to the top floor, home of radio station KWK. "I had never seen how broadcasts were made, so I decided on a lark to take the elevator up to see what was going on," Elson later recalled. "As things turned out it was the most important ride of my life."

Elson stepped off the elevator into a crowded lobby, full of dozens of men waiting to audition. He had stumbled into a broadcasting competition. "I saw about forty young men outside the studio and when I got there, a young lady said to me, 'Well, you're the last one today – good luck and don't be nervous." Like every other man that day, Elson was escorted to a booth and given a script to read. "I read some announcements and upon exiting was told I would be called if I were one of the three finalists." He received a call the next day, informing him he had made the cut. A group of local dignitaries, including the mayor, voted to eliminate one of the contestants, leaving Elson and one other as semi-finalists. The public picked the winner based on their performance in an evening broadcast. "I got the call the next day saying I'd won," said Elson, who, until that moment, had a different vocation in mind. "There went the career in medicine."[1]

The Chicago native soon made his way back to his hometown. Hired by WGN radio, Elson was broadcasting Cubs and White Sox games by 1931, and outside of a stint in the Navy in World War II, he described Chicago sports for the next four decades. Like so many broadcasters of this era, he crossed paths with Harry Caray on more than one occasion. When Elson left Chicago for Oakland, he replaced Caray as the voice of the A's. Caray assumed Elson's role calling White Sox baseball.

Both men could generate headlines not only for their broadcast descriptions, but for their interviews as well. Before a game with the Yankees in 1938, Elson asked New York outfielder Jake Powell what he did to stay in shape in the offseason. "Oh, that's easy," Powell replied. "I'm a policeman and I beat niggers over the head with my blackjack while I'm on the beat."[2] Elson immediately terminated the interview.[3] Commissioner Landis suspended Powell for ten days.

Holy Cow St. Louis!

Like the man he later swapped jobs with, Elson spent the early part of his career calling the home games of two baseball teams and spent the offseason broadcasting everything from football to hockey. "In those days, if you didn't work 80 hours a week, you were loafing," remembered Jack Brickhouse. When Elson signed up for the Navy in 1942, Brickhouse was tapped to replace him. When Brickhouse retired, the Cubs hired Caray to take his place.

In the late 1940s, St. Louis radio listeners could catch Caray on KXOK every afternoon at 5:45. At the same time on another local station, KSD, Elson presented his daily syndicated sports report. Caray became the summertime voice of St. Louis Cardinals baseball. One of Elson's jobs was calling Chicago Cardinals football in the fall. Caray became an institution in his hometown. When he left the Cardinals after the 1969 season, the move stunned the city. Elson "was the foundation of the Chicago baseball broadcasting fraternity," wrote author Curt Smith. When he departed after the 1970 season, the move "sent shockwaves through the Windy City."

Elson, known as "The Commander" since his days in the Navy, was honored by the Baseball Hall of Fame in 1979, receiving the Ford C. Frick Award for broadcasting excellence. Cooperstown honored Caray with the same award a decade later. One owed their big career break to a competition at KWK; the other to a letter addressed to an executive with KMOX. The unconventional methods by which the two men entered the industry may sound peculiar to a modern professional, but in the Wild West days of commercial radio, stories like these are quite common.

The most famous of the early baseball announcers, Graham McNamee, wanted to be an opera singer. He debuted as a baritone in New York City's Aeolian Hall in 1920. A few years later, he was serving on jury duty when he wandered into the studios of WEAF during a break. He decided to audition and was hired on the spot. By the fall of 1923, he was describing the World Series. He would go on to call a total of 12 World Series, in addition to such marquee events as championship boxing matches, Rose Bowl football, and the Indianapolis 500. The president of NBC was once asked to name the network's greatest asset. "Graham McNamee," he replied. By the time he died in 1942, a writer in *The New York Times* had noted that McNamee's voice "had been heard for more hours by more human ears than any voice in history."[4]

After graduating from law school at the University of Alabama in 1936, Mel Israel traveled to New York City, where he walked into the CBS building and asked to audition. The network granted his wish and offered him a part-time job. He had planned to return to Alabama and start practicing law. He never did. By 1939, he was calling baseball games in the city.[5] Israel's storied career with the Yankees would be bookended by two men who called St. Louis home.

When KMOX started broadcasting home games of the Browns and Cardinals, Garnett Marks was the man behind the microphone. His listeners didn't know the name. On the air, he went by "Rhino Bill," after the sponsor, Cupples Rhino Tire Stores. "Rhino Bill is a natural-born baseball announcer," wrote Harry La Mertha in the *Globe-Democrat.* "It is only necessary to go into a radio store or one of a dozen other kinds of stores, clubs, halls, or even along the street, to learn what radio means to baseball now." Fans couldn't get enough of Rhino Bill's calls in 1927, the first year of daily broadcasts from Sportsman's Park. "So realistic," wrote one female fan, "that we want to punch the umpire sometimes."[6]

His fan mail poured in from small towns all over the region. From 100 miles away in Vandalia, Missouri, J.O. Barrow spoke for many. "You will never know how the inland cities, teeming with rabid fans, appreciate your stuff." Others simply marveled at the sounds of the game. "We can hear'em hit the ball!" exclaimed Hub Griffith from Dent County, Missouri. After a car accident, one fan began listening to games from his hospital bed. He quickly became hooked. "While I recuperated, I used a radio and I listened to Rhino Bill give the plays," wrote P.K. Higgins. "I would have wrecked the place if they had taken my radio from me after that."

By August, Rhino Bill was gone. He hadn't been replaced but KMOX had changed advertisers. Marks was now "Otto Buick," in honor of the Vesper-Buick Auto Company. The following season, KMOX had a new sponsor and Marks had a new name. "Pierce Pennant" called the action. The Pierce Petroleum Corporation paid the bills. The company aggressively marketed the broadcasts, putting scoreboards on the side of its oil trucks with speakers on top. The company made these "traveling relay stations" available to non-profit organizations, group picnics and parties free of charge.[7]

Pennant was an appropriate name in 1928 as that is what the Cardinals delivered, their second in three years. Still using the pseudonym, Marks assisted Major Andrew White, the president of CBS, in calling World Series games that fall.

1929 saw the first major controversy over local radio rights to ballgames as it became increasingly obvious to broadcasters and baseball owners alike that the airwaves had value. Browns owner Phil Ball, who preferred no radio broadcasts at all, negotiated a deal with KMOX whereby the station had an exclusive arrangement with the American League team. KMOX paid the Browns $5,000 to broadcast their games, likely the first sports media rights deal in the city's history. Cardinals owner Sam Breadon, meanwhile, preferred an open-door policy. He allowed KMOX, KWK, and WIL (which later dropped the broadcasts mid-season) to call Cardinals games without a fee.

*****

By the end of the 1920s, the three stations that carried Cardinals games were fighting it out for local advertisers (station KSD was first on the air but focused on national programming). KMOX, which broadcast at 5,000 watts (and would soon go to 50,000), dominated the airwaves. The other two stations had weaker signals. When KWK sought to raise its strength to 5,000 watts, representatives from KMOX showed up at the hearing. Thanks to Thomas Patrick Convey, the two stations had a shared history.

Convey, a Chicago native, had arrived in the city in the mid-1920s and organized the St. Louis Radio Trade Association. He then helped put together the financing and construction of KMOX, which debuted in December 1925. He left the station after 18 months. "Too many bosses," he said.[8] He bought a small radio station, changed the call letters to KWK and moved its studios to the Chase Hotel. Convey helped a young Bob Elson get his start at WGN.

The owner doubled as the station's baseball announcer (just Thomas Patrick on the air). Like Marks, he developed a local following, with a signature call when the home team was trailing. "And the score," Convey would say, "Ohhh, that score!"[9] One of the first (perhaps *the* first in St. Louis) to re-create away games, Convey would invite fans to the Chase when the Cardinals were on the road. With 50 to 100 people gathered in the KWK studio, he'd call the action with the crowd supplying the cheers, the boos, and the yelling. Sponsors contributed to the atmosphere by distributing soft drinks and snacks.[10]

When the Browns and Ball announced their exclusive arrangement, Convey complained bitterly. But Ball, who traded players and fired front-office staff when challenged, wouldn't budge. It wouldn't be the last time KMOX and KWK battled it out that year over an exclusive arrangement. In July, two pilots from the Curtiss-Robertson Airplane Company landed at Lambert Field after setting a flight endurance record of 420 hours.[11] KMOX had contracted with the flight sponsors for "exclusive rights" to broadcast the event. Convey and KWK disagreed, taking the position that the flying field was public property. KWK had staff present when the plane landed. In the confusion that followed, one of the pilots began speaking into a KWK microphone. His message didn't last long. Someone cut the wire. KWK had a KMOX mechanic arrested. After a judge freed him, the mechanic sued KWK for $75,000. Convey's station responded by filing a lawsuit against KMOX for $100,000.[12]

The battles between the two stations spilled over into the next year as Convey maintained his station should be allowed to call Browns games. His persistence paid off. Ball changed his mind in 1930. Both the Browns and the Cardinals allowed KMOX and KWK to carry games free of charge (with no coverage on Saturdays, Sundays, or holidays). But both teams added language to the contract that announcers couldn't criticize umpires' rulings "or attempt in any way to bias the minds of listeners."[13]

With its powerful signal and the backing of CBS, KMOX would become the most popular outlet for Cardinals baseball in the 1930s. Its lead announcer would become a standard-bearer for the industry. It wouldn't be Convey, who died unexpectedly in 1934 at the age of 47.[14] It also wouldn't be Marks. His daughter, Marie, won the Miss Missouri contest in 1933 and represented the state at the Miss America Beauty Pageant in Atlantic City. (She was one of 18 semi-finalists but didn't win.)[15] A month later, she signed a film contract with Warner Brothers.[16] Marie and her parents soon moved to California. (Her first appearance was an uncredited role in the 1934 musical *Dames*.)

By 1936, Garnett Marks, who moved frequently, was doing radio in New York.[17] When the city's baseball teams lifted the embargo three years later, he and Arch McDonald were selected to broadcast Giants and Yankees games. Early in the season, Marks' work drew praise from a newspaper columnist. "The radio baseball men are uniformly good, but this column's pet is Garnett Marks," wrote Jimmy Powers in the *Daily News*.[18] "Garnett's voice, mannerisms, and general lingo are soothing to New York ears." Despite the promising start, Marks committed an almost unforgivable sin in broadcasting – he angered a sponsor. The sponsor was Ivory Soap, and when Marks referred to the product as "Ovary Soap" – twice – he was quickly fired.

The man who replaced Marks, Mel Israel, finished 1939 with his broadcast partner, but McDonald moved back to Washington D.C. for the 1940 season. Israel, who now went by a different last name on the air, became the lead announcer. Mel Allen spent the next twenty-five years as the voice of the Yankees.[19] When he was fired after the 1964 season, his replacement was another man with St. Louis roots, Joe Garagiola.

*****

Like Allen and McNamee, Elson and Caray, France Laux had a creative origin story that would be repeated through the years. But perhaps no baseball broadcaster got into the industry as quickly and unexpectedly as he did. In October of 1927, KVOO in Tulsa, Oklahoma prepared to re-create the first game of the World Series between the Pirates and Yankees. When the scheduled announcer became incapacitated, management scrambled to find a replacement. Station executive Fred Yates tracked down Laux on the streets of Bristow, Oklahoma, more than 30 miles away. "Can you broadcast a game?" asked Yates. "I don't know, but I'll try anything once. Why?" Laux replied. "Don't ask questions. Just jump in."[20]

Laux arrived at the studio with just 90 seconds to prepare. "What transpired over the next three hours was probably the greatest thing that ever happened to me," he remembered. Laux did so well with the broadcast that he started doing Oklahoma and Tulsa college football games. KMOX offered him a job in 1929. Laux recalled the moment he got the idea to apply to the St. Louis radio station. "I was listening to a wrestling match at two o'clock one morning and I decided to write KMOX to see if they had any openings."[21] The KMOX offer came over a telegraph. Laux replied with a phone call and was on a train bound for Missouri that evening.

Born in 1897, the Oklahoma native was a star athlete in high school. He served in the Army Air Force in World War I, then returned home and enrolled at Oklahoma City College, where he played halfback and right end. Laux later claimed to have played minor league baseball in Oilton, Oklahoma, once getting two hits in a game off Walter Johnson. "A wealthy oil man brought in several big leaguers to play," Laux told sportswriter Broeg. "Our second baseman that afternoon was a guy named Rogers Hornsby and you'll never guess who replaced me at first base after a few innings – George Sisler."[22]

In Bristow, Laux had an insurance agency and a real estate business. He also became a part-owner of a minor league team. When a neighboring team folded, Laux's club briefly had the services of a player named John Martin. "We liked young Martin and took him over, and he played with us until the entire league blew up in late August. We sold him to Greenville in the East Texas League for $300. I'd like to buy that young man's services today for $300, for he was none other than Pepper Martin of the Cardinals," Laux said in 1932.[23] Decades later, he added a postscript. "I found out later that because our league had blown up, I'd had no right to sell Pepper. He should have been declared a free agent."

Laux started his St. Louis radio career in March 1929 on a 30-day trial. He never left. His employer was soon confident enough in its young broadcaster that it began marketing his coverage of baseball games. "France is putting lots of pep into the games for the St. Louis fans this season over KMOX," read an ad that appeared in April. "In the early days at Sportsman's Park, there was no radio booth," Laux remembered. "The first two years I sat downstairs in the stands behind the screen and then, to escape inquisitive fans, moved to the edge of the upper deck."[24]

Over the next decade, men who broadcast games in St. Louis included Jim Alt, Allan Anthony, Cy Casper, Johnny Herrington, Neil Norman, Ray Schmidt, and Bob Thomas (Convey's son); names barely remembered or lost to history.[25] Only one name broke through to achieve lasting recognition. "The existence of France Laux as a real human person would have never occurred to us," wrote Dulcie Lawrence in the Minneapolis *Star Tribune* in 1977. "He was only a voice, omniscient, godly."[26]

Laux did every World Series over CBS from 1933 to 1938 and every All-Star Game from 1934 to 1941. At the 1934 All-Star Game in New York, he was behind the microphone when Carl Hubbell struck out five batters in a row. "That was the finest exhibition of pitching I ever witnessed and it was all the better because Hubbell was like me – just an old boy from Oklahoma." At the World Series that year in Detroit, he interviewed another native of the Sooner State, comedian and film star Will Rogers. "You don't know Judge Laux out in Oklahoma, do you?" Rogers asked him. "Just slightly," France replied. "He's only my dad."[27]

In St. Louis, Laux would do a "Dope from the Dugout" show before games, do nine innings of play-by-play, "Grandstand Managers" at the conclusion of every contest, then host his "Sports Review" show at night. He'd also tape a segment for the next morning where he would comment on "minor league, semi-pro, and town team baseball," as well as a capsule of the previous day's major league game.[28]

Broadcaster Buddy Blattner grew up in St. Louis and was a Laux fan. He never forgot seeing the announcer walk into Sportsman's Park one day. It was a simpler time. "I remember France Laux entering a ballpark and buying a scorecard, just as the fans did, and he did his broadcast from the card."[29] Another fan sent Laux one of his prized possessions, an oil painting of himself. The painting was done by an inmate at the Southern Illinois Penitentiary who had never met Laux; had never even seen him. He did the painting from a photograph.[30]

Laux had widespread appeal at a time when announcers were rewarded for just presenting the facts. "If you see men putting up gallows in center field and then see them lead me out to it and hang me on it, describe it into the microphone but don't question the justice of the hanging," Commissioner Landis once instructed. Landis controlled the announcers for the World Series and All-Star Games and Laux was one of his favorites. When he rewarded Laux with appearances at both events in 1934, he did so in a year in which the announcer did no regular-season St. Louis broadcasts due to the embargo imposed by the Browns and Cardinals.

Holy Cow St. Louis!

Two years later, *The Sporting News* praised his coverage of the 1936 World Series. "Without disparaging the efforts of others, the play-by-play accounts of France Laux ... stood out in the view of many listeners," noted the St. Louis-based publication. "Laux gave a matter-of-fact account of the play, supplying a true picture of the action, without growing excited or striving for dramatic effect."[31]

Laux admitted he always strove to be impartial in his broadcasts. "I've made it a policy from the beginning not to voice opinions or take sides," he said. "It's especially wise not to be partisan. You may be talking to people in Missouri, Illinois, Indiana, and Kentucky. Add'em all up and half of them may be for the Cubs or Reds and the other half for the Cardinals. They don't want a partisan account of what's happening."[32] (Broeg agreed with Laux's self-assessment. "He was impartial to the bone.")

That broadcasting style, so popular throughout the 1930s, began to resonate less and less with his listeners. A younger generation that had grown up on radio wanted more. When Caray described listening to games "as dull and boring as the morning crop reports" in his autobiography, he was referring to Laux. "When he [Laux] was young, he was pretty aloof, but he warmed up as he came to know St. Louis," recalled Broeg. "Remember, he came from the country, and it took him time to adjust. Eventually, he did that, but he still always spoke in a flat, metallic southern type of accent. It was accepted in the thirties, but later on, when competition hit him in the war years ... it was really quite a drawback."[33]

"He was good; he was the best then," said Blattner, remembering the Laux of his youth. "But things went by him." People thought he was "too old-timey," believed Broeg. "The truth was that when France had the field to himself, he could just *be* himself – there was no one to compare him with. Be a reporter, just tell the facts, and he could do that well. But when he had to entertain – jazz up the away re-creations or be flashy like his competitors ... he couldn't do it."

The first of his formidable competitors arrived in 1941 when Laux started broadcasting games over KXOK radio. (Under general manager Merle Jones – the man who gave Caray's career a boost – KMOX moved away from baseball. The station wouldn't return to the ballpark for live broadcasts until the 1950s.) The new man behind the mic had spent years in St. Louis and he knew the players well. He was raw, unfiltered, opinionated and controversial. Listeners never knew what he would say next. He later rose to national acclaim, but got his start doing Browns and Cardinals games. On the air, he would pitch beer, mangle names, tell stories, and belt out his favorite tune.

Fans just called him Dizzy.

[1] Patterson, *The Golden Voices of Baseball* and Smith, Curt. *Voices of the Game: The First Full-Scale Overview of Baseball Broadcasting, 1921 to Present*. Diamond Communications, Inc. 1987. Elson's comments to Patterson and Smith about his radio background directly contradict statements he made right after winning the contest when he told a reporter he previously worked at WAMD in Minneapolis as a program director. He also claimed to be a former soprano soloist in the Paulist Choir in Chicago and once sang for the French Red Cross during World War I. *St. Louis Globe-Democrat*, January 1, 1928. He was reportedly in St. Louis visiting a friend. Smith wrote that Elson was visiting billiards champion Willie Hoppe. Some reports allege Elson worked briefly for KWK before leaving for Chicago while Elson later said he never worked for the station. "I didn't want St. Louis anyway," he told Smith. Elson believed 1931 was his first year calling baseball, but he wasn't certain. "I think that's about the right date, but I can't remember." *Chicago Tribune*, August 3, 1969. Also see the sabr.org biography project. https://sabr.org/bioproj/person/bob-elson/

[2] McGregor, Robert Kuhn. *The Calculus of Color. The Integration of Baseball's American League*. McFarland & Company, Inc. 2015.

[3] The next day, the *Chicago Defender* published a statement from Elson that stated, in part, that "the remark of Mr. Powell was as offensive to me as it was to many of my good friends."

[4] *New York Times*, May 17, 1942.

[5] The Giants and Yankees reportedly offered the job to France Laux, but he turned them down to stay in St. Louis.

[6] *St. Louis Globe-Democrat*, June 12, 1927.

[7] Ibid, March 18, 1928.

[8] *St. Louis Post-Dispatch,* September 10, 1929.

[9] Ibid, March 12, 1969.

[10] *Tampa Bay Times*, June 1, 1975.

[11] "420 hours, 21 minutes, or 21 minutes more than 17 ½ days." The previous record was 246 hours, 43 minutes, and 32 seconds. The two pilots were Dale Jackson and Forest O'Brine. *St. Louis Star*, July 31, 1929.

[12] *St. Louis Post-Dispatch,* September 10, 1929.

[13] Ibid, January 15, 1930.

[14] In May of 1934, Convey was stricken with appendicitis. An operation at a local hospital revealed his appendix had burst and blood poisoning had already set in. He received a blood transfusion but died the next day. *St. Louis Post-Dispatch*, May 18, 1934.

[15] One article described her as "an ardent Cardinal baseball fan." *Southeast Missourian*, August 1, 1933.

[16] *St. Louis Globe-Democrat*, October 12, 1933. The Marks family was living at 5512 Delmar Blvd.

[17] Marie Marks "has gone to 14 schools in St. Louis, Hollywood, Chicago, and Cleveland." The family had previously lived in southern California when she was a child. Ibid. Also see https://missamerica1933.com/contestants/mo-marks.html

[18] New York *Daily News*, May 22, 1939. Later that year, Powers wrote, "Garnett Marks, our idea of a swell news and sports commentator, is in town again after a baseball stretch at Rochester." Ibid, December 6, 1939. By 1949, Marks was back in St. Louis and working at KWK. A story on the radio station noted he was a native St. Louisan and "was a singer of note before starting his announcing career." *St. Louis Globe-Democrat*, June 16, 1949.

[19] Allen was his middle name.

[20] Patterson, *The Golden Voices of Baseball*.

[21] Absher, Frank. "France Laux was St. Louis' sports voice," *St. Louis Journalism Review*. July-August 2009.

[22] *Post-Dispatch*, July 2, 1972.

[23] *The Sporting News,* January 14, 1932.

[24] Patterson, *The Golden Voices of Baseball*.

[25] Casper was an All-American halfback at Texas Christian University in 1933. He played professionally in Green Bay and Pittsburgh.

[26] *Star Tribune*, March 13, 1977.

[27] Laux introduced Gene Autry on radio in Oklahoma. "Gene was working as a telegraph operator in Chelsea, Oklahoma," remembered Laux. "Will Rogers had told him he ought to try singing on the radio." Patterson, *The Golden Voices of Baseball*.

[28] *The Sporting News*, June 2, 1938.

[29] *Kansas City Star*, April 6, 1969.

[30] *The Sporting News*, January 16, 1936.

[31] Ibid, October 8, 1936. *The Sporting News* later honored Laux with a trophy in a tribute dinner at the Hotel Jefferson in St. Louis carried by 113 radio stations across the country. Ibid, January 27, 1938.

[32] *St. Louis Post-Dispatch*, March 28, 1940.

[33] Smith, *Voices of the Game*.

Dizzy at the Mic

When Dizzy Dean died in July of 1974 at the age of 64, legendary college football coach Paul (Bear) Bryant and country music Hall of Fame member Roy Acuff attended the funeral.[1] Just weeks from resigning, President Richard Nixon felt compelled to issue a statement. "To my generation of Americans, Dizzy Dean will always be remembered as the blazing fastballer who led the Gashouse Gang of St. Louis to the pinnacle of baseball glory. To the young, Dizzy will also be remembered as the sportscaster who brought an extra touch of excitement and color to every game he covered. Dizzy Dean was indeed a man of all generations."

The man of all generations captured national attention as the lead announcer for the CBS "Game of the Week" in the 1950s and '60s. He quickly surpassed France Laux in popularity in the 1940s, broadcasting Browns and Cardinals games. He first soared to popularity pitching for the Cardinals in the 1930s, winning a World Series and a Most Valuable Player Award in 1934. Pitching and broadcasting were the focus of his career. He had plenty of sidelines.

Shortly after winning a World Series, he broke into the movie business. "Did a two-reel short for Paramount in '35," Dean recalled. "Did it at Ebbets Field in Brooklyn, and the Three Stooges, you remember them, was funny as all blazes. So was I."[2] That same year, he earned an estimated $30,000 or more advertising everything from Camel Cigarettes ("Camels never frazzle the nerves") to Grape Nuts Cereal. In 1937, his wife claimed he would make $40,000 that year just from radio appearances. By the time he retired from baseball in 1941, he had earned more than a quarter-million dollars, with nearly $100,000 of the total coming from appearances and endorsements. A movie studio approached him about doing a series of films. A three-year contract to make four Westerns a year would have paid Dean $75,000. He turned it down. "I just don't want any part of Hollywood," he said. While Dean wanted no part of Tinseltown, Hollywood was very interested in him. With Dan Dailey starring as Dean, *The Pride of St. Louis* debuted in 1952. With "Dan Dailey playing him in high gear and in accents that reek of the hills, he is an utterly fascinating blowhard, a delightfully entertaining clown, but also a warmly sentimental and genuinely ingratiating guy," noted a review in *The New York Times*.[3]

By this time, Dean had several properties in Texas, including a 300-acre ranch where he raised Hereford cattle.[4] In the 1930s, he owned a service station in Bradenton, Florida and once traded an autographed bat for a small piece of land from a Kansas oil prospector. Two years later, Dean received a telegram. "Your well came in today."[5] He later owned a carpet business in Arizona.[6] By the early 1960s, he was pulling down an estimated $100,000 a year from CBS calling baseball games. He was also a world-class golf hustler, with Yankees co-owner Dan Topping a favorite mark.[7] "I think he made enough from golf alone to last him the rest of his life," said his one-time broadcast partner Buddy Blattner. He spent the last years of his life living with his wife in Mississippi, where he had a charcoal briquet manufacturing company, and was so popular he once considered a run for governor.[8]

When he passed away following a heart attack, he was memorialized by writers coast to coast. "He was as vain as a movie star, as amiable as a dolphin," said *Los Angeles Times* columnist Jim Murray. "As a ballplayer, Dean was a natural phenomenon, like the Grand Canyon or the Great Barrier Reef," wrote *New York Times* columnist Red Smith. In the same newspaper, Joseph Durso called him "a folk hero who brought great turns to the English language," while David Condon in the *Chicago Tribune* believed him to be "one of the pioneer baseball announcers."

For a man who once golfed with President Eisenhower, dined with Henry Ford, and ad-libbed with Bob Hope on the comedian's radio show, it all began under far more humble circumstances.[9] "If it weren't for baseball," Dean once reflected, "I might still be picking cotton in Arkansas."

*****

For every fact about Dean's early life, another story challenges the narrative. He had three different birthplaces, three different birthdates, and two different names. "Them ain't lies; them's scoops," he once explained when asked why he gave different answers to different reporters. He often called himself Jerome Herman, but he was born Jay Hanna Dean in Lucas, Arkansas – not Holdenville, Oklahoma or Bond, Mississippi – in January of 1910.[10] His father claimed he was named after Gilded Age millionaire Jay Gould and Republican politician Mark Hanna.[11]

Dean once claimed a ninth-grade education on a job application.[12] But he often told, and writers loved to quote, a different version – that he quit school after the second grade. "And I didn't do so good," he would add, "in the first grade."[13]

He quit school to pick cotton. His father, a migrant sharecropper, moved often with sons Jay, Paul, and Elmer. Jay's mother, Alma, died of tuberculosis when he was seven. He had two older siblings who died in childhood. His father later married a woman who had three children of her own. The family traveled across Arkansas, Oklahoma, and Texas, planting crops and picking cotton for fifty cents a day.[14] On the move to the next farm field one day, Elmer was in one vehicle, the rest of the family in another. The first vehicle got through a railroad crossing before a train blocked the second. It took four years before the family reunited.[15] "It is impossible to accurately chart the Dean's family wanderings after Alma's death," wrote biographer Vince Staten.

Somewhere along the way, he started playing baseball in sandlots across the Southwest. He claimed to have pitched for the high school team in Spaulding, Oklahoma at the age of 12 (likely closer to 15). George Mayfield, an unofficial coach for the squad, remembered the young athlete. "Jay had a head of his own and he used it, and we had to coach him sometimes, but he was all right. He struck out a lot of men and he won just about every game he pitched," adding that Dean had "an arm that wouldn't quit."[16]

He quit working in the cotton fields to join the military. He lied about his age – claimed to be 18 when he was 16 – and joined the Army at Fort Sam Houston. He also played ball for Uncle Sam, getting a bonus in the process. "There, in the field artillery, I got my first pair of shoes," he remembered. He also got something else in the Army, the nickname he would carry for the rest of his life. "You dizzy son of a bitch," an exasperated sergeant once yelled at Dean for throwing freshly peeled potatoes at garbage can lids.[17] Dizzy would vex men of authority for years.

It was possible in the 1920s to buy your way out of the military. Dean's family arranged for his release, paying $120 to get him out of the service.[18] Dizzy took a job at a Texas utility company, the San Antonio Public Service Co., and began playing baseball for his employer's team. Records dug up decades later revealed that Dizzy applied to the company in the spring of 1929 under the name Jay Herman (a mix of the two names he frequently used), cited the U.S. Army as his only previous employer, and listed the man who gave him his nickname, Sgt. James Brought, as his only reference. On the application, likely the only one he ever filled out in his life, he stated that he was living in San Antonio with his father and brothers, was 18 years old (actually 19), and his trade was "mechanic."[19]

Riley Harris was a meter foreman and the manager of the company baseball team. "A lot of people will tell you that the Public Service Co. bought Dizzy Dean out of the Army. That just isn't a true story," he said in 1965. "The truth is Dean had already gotten out of the service when he came to us." Assigned to a crew revamping underground electric service in downtown San Antonio, Dean worked the night shift during the week and spent his weekends on the baseball diamond. He went 12-6, the worst record of the pitchers on the Public Service Utilities staff, but Harris always used Dizzy against the toughest opponents. "Dean would have pitched every game if I'd allowed him to," the manager recalled. "Regardless of who was supposed to pitch that day, Dean would start warming up."[20]

His abundant talent began to attract attention from major league scouts. It didn't take long for Don Curtis, a scout for the Cardinals, to make up his mind. "Curtis saw him pitch only one inning before blurting out that here was a man he wanted to sign," said Harris. But the manager wouldn't let it happen. At least not right away. Dean was under contract to his employer's team, and Harris wouldn't let him out of it until the season was over. Curtis watched Dean pitch a shutout to win the city championship. Dizzy's last game for the Utilities came on September 15 against the Cuban All-Stars. Following the game, Harris released Dean from his Public Service obligation. Curtis signed him to a contract with no bonus and a salary of $100 a month.[21] Dizzy Dean was now the property of the Cardinals.[22]

*****

In March of 1930, the club sent Dean to a camp in Houston. He later spent time at one in Shawnee, Oklahoma. The locations were home to two of eight minor league teams the St. Louis franchise now owned outright, a piece of Branch Rickey's grand vision to expand the talent available to the big league club.[23] Every spring, while current and potential major league players flocked to Florida, Rickey would hold additional camps around the country. Because the team always signed more players than spots available, the camps acted as an important filter to evaluate prospects, the raw material the Cardinals used to replace aging or more expensive talent or as trade chips to use in deals with other clubs. Rickey first met Dizzy that spring.

"One day, I went to Shawnee where we were having some seventy-five players work out," Rickey recalled. "I'd plant myself behind the batting cage and I could see as many as thirty-five pitchers in an afternoon. They'd work just one inning apiece." It wasn't long before someone whispered to Rickey, "Here he comes." Of the nearly three dozen pitchers the Cardinals executive saw that day, there was only one he was still telling stories about years later. "Dean walked onto the mound and fanned three men so quickly I still hadn't seen him," he remembered. "So I had him come back for another inning and no one even hit a foul ball as he fanned three more. Dean stalked off that field like a pouter pigeon, braggadocio personified."[24]

That night, in the hotel lobby, Dean introduced himself. "Hello, Branch, I'm Dizzy Dean." Not used to being addressed in such an informal manner, least of all by a bush-league rookie, Rickey decided to call his new acquaintance "Mr. Dean" and pretended he didn't remember seeing him pitch. "He began to get a little mad," Rickey remembered. Dean told him he was ready to join the big league club immediately, but the man in charge of the Cardinals minor league system thought he needed more seasoning. "But that was my introduction to Dizzy Dean. He called me 'Branch' and I called him 'Mr. Dean.' The odd thing is that he never addressed me other than 'Mr. Rickey' afterward."[25]

Over the years, the relationship between the two men would be one part executive-employee and another part parent-child. As Rickey had already discovered, Dean's personality featured a unique mix of conviction, immaturity, and naivete. Talented and temperamental, he could be exceptional, erratic, or just downright eccentric.

When the season began, the Cardinals sent Dean to their farm team in St. Joseph, Missouri. While playing for the Saints, he eventually set up residence in three different hotels. (He didn't realize he needed to check out.) When it came time to pay at the end of the month, he had the bills sent to business manager Oliver French. "Go ahead, Ollie," Dean told him. "Give it to'em." The debt was settled for pennies on the dollar. He didn't wash clothes; he bought new ones (typically with borrowed money). He was involved in three fights on the baseball field by the end of May. Two of them came in the same game. In a contest against Topeka, he had words with the opposing manager after a play in the sixth inning. Tension escalated and fists began flying, but the two were quickly separated. Dean then got into a second fight with an opposing player. It took two policemen to separate the pair. All three were banished from the park.[26]

He went 17-8 for St. Joseph before the Cardinals promoted him to their club in Houston. He won another eight games there and was on the mound at Sportsman's Park for the last game of the regular season. He beat the Pirates 3-1, pitching a complete game, with his manager calling him "the nearest thing to Walter Johnson I ever saw."[27] From St. Joseph to St. Louis in six months, with 26 combined wins along the way. It had been quite a ride. It was only beginning.

Worried about how Dean would behave in the offseason, the Cardinals sent him to live with French and his family in southeast Missouri. In the bootheel town of Charleston, he'd hang out at the local drug store, Ellis Confectionary, where he'd attempt to impress girls by buying them ice cream cones with hot checks. He fell in love with one of them, a 16-year-old, going so far as to send her a pair of silk pajamas for Christmas. Her parents sent them back. After one night out on the town, he checked into a local hotel, saying he was too tired to go home, even though the French residence was just a few blocks away. "Send the bill to Mr. French, my secretary," Dean told the clerk. French had Dizzy leave early for spring training. (Dean did the same thing to the Cardinals, racking up $2,700 in personal debt and charges to the team during spring training before Rickey put him on a $1-a-day budget.)[28]

Dean spent the entire 1931 season playing for the Cardinals farm team in Houston. Called up for good in 1932, he became close friends with Pepper Martin. The two men shared a love of practical jokes and stunts. They'd toss sneezing powder into ceiling fans, drop water balloons on unsuspecting victims, and surprise teammates with "hotfoots" (lighting someone's shoes on fire). On road trips, the pair would walk around hotels in carpenter overalls and suddenly announce they were starting repairs, to the shock of guests and staff alike. On one blazing hot day at Sportsman's Park, they started a fire on the field before a game and huddled around it, draping blankets over their shoulders. The antics caused endless stress for manager Frankie Frisch, who replaced Gabby Street in 1933. "I sure hope Frank manages the Cardinals forever," Dean once said. "I sure love to drive that Dutchman nuts."[29]

Dean would antagonize Rickey and owner Sam Breadon as well, by constantly threatening to quit and making endless demands for more money. At times, he'd do more than just talk. In June of 1932, with the team in Philadelphia, Dean announced on a Tuesday he was quitting and boarded a midnight train bound for St. Louis.[30] He didn't rejoin the club until the weekend. It took a three-hour meeting and a concession by the Cardinals to pay him $225 that had previously been deducted from his salary (and sent to his father) to get him to return.[31]

Dean would be contrite at the end of these episodes, apologize and get back to playing baseball. But he was never placated for long, complaining to any reporter who would listen that he was unappreciated and that the Cardinals, under Rickey and Breadon, were a cheap organization. Dean's insecurities and talents would soon be on bright display in a season that Cardinal fans would always remember. It would also be one Breadon would never forget.

*****

Two events in 1931 helped shape Dizzy's career and forever influenced his life. Signed by the same scout who signed Dizzy, Paul Dean started playing in the Cardinals minor league system, first in Houston, then Columbus, and finally in Springfield, where he spent most of the year.[32] Three years later, he would join his brother as a member of the St. Louis staff. Thanks to their magical 1934 season, "Me 'n' Paul" would forever be linked.

Dizzy married in 1931 after the Cardinals returned him to Houston early in the season. (Right after he arrived, the club sold Paul to the Columbus Red Birds.) It was a brief courtship. Dean arrived in early May.[33] By early June, their engagement made the newspapers. He wanted to get married at home plate before a game. She vetoed the idea. They were married in a church office. It was an early sign that the former Patricia Nash had considerable sway over the life of Jay Hanna Dean. Pat and Dizzy would remain married until the day he died.

Born and raised in Mississippi, Pat was working as a clerk at a shoe store in Houston when she met Dizzy.[34] Nearly four years older than her husband (she was one month shy of 25 when they married, he was 21), Pat became his defender, negotiator, and financial planner. From the very beginning, she took the long view. "A baseball player's life is short," she told a reporter. "Three big years. That's the record nine times out of ten." He made $3,000 his rookie year. She saved $1,800 of it. "I am determined Dizzy shall not end his career on a park bench," she told Marguerite Martyn of the *Post-Dispatch* at the beginning of the 1934 World Series. "I want to take what we get and salt it down in Government bonds. I simply won't allow it to be thrown away."

She also spoke of his upbringing in ways he never would. "When I first knew him, he had no affection at all. Nobody had ever done for him. He had been dragged up, not raised up." The family settled in San Antonio when Dizzy was in the Army. Fred Ankenman, president of the Cardinals team in Houston, once drove to San Antonio to have Dizzy's father sign a contract. "I could hardly believe that Mr. Dean could be living in such a terrible place. I took a few minutes to look the place over. I looked through the windows of the three small rooms and inside, they were in such an unkempt state," Ankenman remembered, calling the house "a shack that was one of about eight or ten others located in what looked more like an alley than a street."[35]

From these humble beginnings, Dizzy would first rise to fame as a media darling. His celebrated accomplishments on the field came later. "If he is led in the right direction," wrote *Post-Dispatch* columnist J. Roy Stockton, "he should develop into the best box office attraction the Cardinals ever had." Stockton wrote those words in January of 1931 when Dizzy's resume consisted of one major league game. The Newspaper Enterprise Association (NEA) syndicated a 10-part series on Dean that summer.[36] "The Cardinals sent Dizzy Dean to Houston," wrote *New York Times* columnist John Kieran, "but they can't keep him out of the papers." In September, Kieran referred to him as "the eccentric fireman on the slab," as Dizzy was wrapping up his final minor league season, a campaign in which he won 26 games, including both ends of a doubleheader in July.[37]

In his rookie year, he won 18 games for the Cardinals and became a 20-game winner for St. Louis the following season as his achievements began catching up with media attention. (He led the league in strikeouts in both years.) When Paul joined the club in 1934, Dizzy looked out for the financial interests of his brother just as his wife always fought for him. Three years younger than Dizzy, sportswriters would sometimes refer to the younger Dean as "Daffy." He was anything but. One writer called him Harpo, for the silent Marx brother. "Dizzy does the talking for the family. Paul is his stooge. He just puts in about a word an hour to keep Dizzy going," said manager Frisch in spring training.[38] But the brothers shared an unbreakable bond, forged by their years in deep poverty and chopping cotton to survive. Paul "believed in Dizzy, and Dizzy believed in Paul," remembered teammate Jim Mooney. "They were two very close boys."

The Cardinals paid Paul $3,000 his rookie season, an amount his brother believed insufficient. That June in Pittsburgh, Dizzy went on strike, claiming he wouldn't return until the team paid Paul more money. (He also had strong opinions about his own $7,500 salary.) Dizzy's protest got the brothers nowhere. Their paychecks remained the same. Dizzy soon returned to the club. The incident became one in a long list of clashes involving the Cardinals and the volatile Dean.

Things got more serious in August. Following a Sunday doubleheader loss to Chicago (Paul lost the first game, Dizzy the second), the Cardinals departed for an exhibition game in Detroit against the Tigers. The brothers skipped the contest and remained in St. Louis. Dizzy claimed he had a sore arm. Paul said his ankle was lame.[39] The Cardinals weren't buying it. The club fined Dizzy $100 and Paul $50.[40] Dizzy tore up two uniforms in protest and was shocked to find the team had deducted the cost ($36) from his paycheck on top of the fine.[41] When the duo refused to take the field on Tuesday because of the fines, Frisch suspended them. The matter went before Commissioner Landis.

The hearing got underway at 10:00 a.m. the next Monday in a suite at the Park Plaza Hotel. Landis expected to catch the noon train back to Chicago. He had to make new arrangements as the debate stretched on for more than four hours. Breadon and Rickey brought along manager Frisch, two coaches, two players (shortstop Leo Durocher and pitcher Jesse Haines), two secretaries, and the trainer and treasurer. All but secretary Mary Murphy and treasurer Bill DeWitt Sr. (who also served as Dean's business manager) testified in the matter as vice president Rickey assumed the role of prosecuting attorney. The

Cardinals even brought the two torn uniforms. Dizzy and Paul were left to fend for themselves.

With reporters standing just outside the door and able to hear, thanks to an open-air transom above the suite, Landis watched as traveling secretary Clarence Lloyd claimed Dizzy told his teammates in the clubhouse he had no intention of going to Detroit, with Dean then launching into an imitation of Rickey "pulling his hair" at the idea of losing part of the $3,800 guarantee paid to the Cardinals for the exhibition game.

The Cardinals and Dean argued over everything from his behavior in the minor leagues at St. Joseph and Houston to Dizzy's brother, Elmer, who was offered a job as a vendor that season at Sportsman's Park. "I thought you were going to give Elmer a good job in the concession department," Dean shouted at Rickey. (Elmer was offered a job as a peanut vendor, but soon returned to the same position in Houston. "Ain't what it's cracked up to be," he told reporters after visiting Sportsman's Park.) At one point, things got heated between Dean and the man who signed his paycheck. "Don't you call me a liar, Dizzy!" yelled Breadon. "Well, then don't call me a liar," Dean responded.[42]

In the end, Landis upheld the right of the Cardinals to administer justice as the club saw fit. The fine, uniform damages, and a seven-day suspension ($50 a day) cost Dizzy $486.[43] Dean "was flabbergasted," wrote reporter Martin J. Haley. "His facial expression indicated he couldn't believe what he had just heard."[44] After the hearing, photographers tried to get him to shake Frisch's hand. He refused. He also wouldn't shake Breadon's hand. The same photographers spent ten minutes trying to get him to cheer up, "but not the slightest smile creased Dizzy's countenance." A picture in the next day's *Globe-Democrat* showed four men with sullen expressions. Three of them – Dean, Frisch, and Landis – looked straight ahead at the camera. Breadon was staring at Dizzy.

*****

There was a reason Breadon and Rickey tolerated Dean's antics. A less talented player would have been quickly dispatched, but Dean's unique abilities brought more victories to the team and attracted more fans in the stands. (A long-held view by many was that club executives viewed his outbursts as good for business.) He attracted constant media attention because he was always telling stories and making predictions. One of his most memorable calls came in spring training of 1934. "I think we'll win forty or forty-five games," Dean told reporters of what he expected from him and his brother in the upcoming season. "I'm pretty good and I believe that Paul is almost as good as I am. It will mean that the other six pitchers need to win only fifty games and that will give us the pennant."[45]

Dizzy had won 20 games the year before, but his brother hadn't pitched a single inning in the big leagues. It was an outlandish prediction that soon became an ironic one. It was likely the only time in Dizzy's career he underestimated what he and Paul could deliver. The brothers won 49 games for the Cardinals. The other pitchers on the staff won 36 as the 95-58 St. Louis team won the National League pennant. With a record of 21-5 when his suspension began, Dizzy saved his best for last.

Dean went 9-2 with two saves over the last six weeks of the season. Over 37 days, he appeared in 15 games (including seven of the last 10), completing eight of them with four shutouts. His thirtieth victory came on the final day of the regular season, a complete-game shutout of the Reds.[46] The Cardinals celebrated a pennant on a Sunday and began the World Series on Wednesday against the Detroit Tigers. It featured seven games in seven days, with not a single day off for travel. It would be the defining week of a defining season.

Wednesday, October 3. The Cardinals win the opener 8-3 with Dean getting the complete-game victory. That evening, Dizzy joins actors Joe Brown, George Raft, and Will Rogers at a Detroit radio station to address Admiral Richard Byrd, on his second expedition to Antarctica. Dean greets the explorer – "Hello, big Byrd down in Little America" – and makes another prediction. "I think if they pitched me the whole four days I would win all four of them."[47] He also wires Branch Rickey – collect. "This American League is a pushover," he boasts.

Thursday, October 4. Dizzy and Paul travel to Dearborn to have breakfast with Henry Ford.[48] Dizzy asks for, and receives, an autographed baseball from the automobile magnate and invites him to buy the Cardinals. "I won 30 games for Sam Breadon, but I'm sure I could win 50 for you."[49] The brothers return to the ballpark on time thanks to a police escort. Dressed and on the field before the game, Dizzy grabs an instrument from a band member positioned behind home plate. Thirty years before Bob Uecker pulled his famous stunt, Dean became a tuba player. "Gimme a week at this," he tells the musician from whom he had borrowed the brass sousaphone, "and I'll have your job."

Friday, October 5. After taking the train to St. Louis following an extra-innings Detroit victory, the Cardinals take a 2-1 Series lead with Paul Dean getting the victory in front of 34,000 fans at Sportsman's Park. Detroit strands 13 runners and Dizzy is warming up in the bullpen in the ninth inning, but Paul manages to complete the game. Both brothers are photographed before the contest with the governor of Arkansas. Dizzy also poses with Will Rogers, the mayor of St. Louis and the city's police chief. After the game, he walks out of

Sportsman's Park and is offered a ride in an automobile with New York plates. Breadon, fearing the men were gamblers or kidnappers, has Dizzy removed from the ride and installs twenty-four-hour police protection for both brothers. (A grand jury indicts Bruno Richard Hauptmann for the kidnapping and murder of the baby son of Charles Lindbergh three days later.)

Saturday, October 6. In the fourth inning, the Cardinals need a pinch-runner on first base. As Frisch looks around the dugout for a candidate, Dean sprints on the field.[50] The next batter hits a potential double-play groundball to second base. But when the Detroit shortstop makes the relay throw to first base, the ball hits Dizzy in the head and bounds "up into the air at least 60 feet, dropping into right field."[51] The Cardinals carry an unconscious Dean off the field.[52] ("The blow that floored Dizzy would have knocked down two elephants," wrote Grantland Rice.) Regaining his senses in the clubhouse, he initially refuses to go to St. John's Hospital for X-rays.[53] Dr. Robert Hyland, the team physician, later diagnoses him with a slight concussion, but no fractures.

Sunday, October 7. Dean is back on the mound, going eight innings and allowing three runs, two earned. Detroit pitcher Tommy Bridges is even better. The Tigers win 3-1 and take a 3-2 Series lead.

Monday, October 8. Dizzy has a limousine waiting for him when the train arrives in Detroit. He returns to the home of Henry Ford and is once again late to the Cardinals clubhouse. "I'm tryin' to get Henry to buy this ballclub," he explains to Frisch. "I'll get you a raise if he does." Dean watches from the dugout as his brother earns his second straight complete-game victory. Later that day in Memphis, Tennessee, a man wanted on charges in West Virginia walks into the sheriff's office and turns himself in. He explains to authorities he'd "rather be in jail than to hear Paul and Dizzy brag about that game today."

Tuesday, October 9. Dean shuts out the Tigers, winning 11-0, in a game best remembered for Joe Medwick's hard slide into Detroit third baseman Marv Owen, sparking a near-riot among Tigers fans and resulting in Commissioner Landis removing Medwick from the game for safety reasons. Actor and comedian Rogers is among those congratulating Dean in the Cardinals clubhouse afterward. "We done it, didn't we boy?" Dizzy tells him.

The seven days featured five starts from the Dean brothers and four victories. It also included five days of round-the-clock security coverage, two visits to Henry Ford's house, and a single tally each for tuba playing, a live address to Admiral Byrd, and a concussion-induced hospital visit. Dizzy also had a daily nationally syndicated column (ghostwritten by columnist Stockton).

At the age of 24, he had crossed the line from baseball star to cultural phenomenon.[54] Even his former employer wanted to take some credit. "The

Army trained him," read a recruiting poster at Fort Sam Houston. At the victory parade in St. Louis the next day, Dizzy wore "a white African sun helmet and carried a toy rubber tiger," noted one dispatch. He and Paul left the parade and hopped on a plane to Oklahoma City, where they began a barnstorming tour that evening. A week later, baseball writers named Dizzy the National League's Most Valuable Player. In November, the brothers appeared in a vaudeville show at the Roxy Theatre in New York and shot a movie short for Warner Brothers. Not for the last time, Dizzy would draw comparisons to Babe Ruth. "In one respect, he overshadows Ruth," wrote Dan Parker of the *New York Daily Mirror*. "He has a keen sense of humor and spouts drolleries that would do credit to Will Rogers – if, indeed, they wouldn't be an improvement on his stuff."[55]

He returned to St. Louis in late November to talk with Breadon and Rickey. Afterward, he mused out loud about buying the club someday. "Me and Paul ought to have enough money pretty soon to buy it," he told reporters. (From May 1933 to November 1934, Dean earned $66,911.83 from non-baseball activities.)[56] In December, Dean called Breadon to tell him he had signed his contract for 1935. But he soon had second thoughts. By February, he was asking to be traded. Peace and harmony didn't last long. With Dizzy and the Cardinals, they never did.

*****

After 1934, Dean's demands grew larger, his win totals became smaller, and his negotiations with the Cardinals simultaneously became more contentious and less serious. ("Breadon, Frisch Give Dizzy Horse Laugh," read one headline.) He demanded $25,000 in 1935. He signed for $17,500 plus a $1,000 bonus. He bumped his request to $40,000 the next year. The Cardinals paid him $22,185. In 1937, he announced he wanted $100,000 to play baseball before quickly reducing the number to $50,000 and claiming he would quit before playing for less. The Cardinals called his bluff. "I believe the Cardinals and Dean would benefit if Dizzy would make good his threat to retire for a year," said Breadon. After asking the Cardinals to put him on the voluntarily retired list, Dean signed for $25,500.[57]

The Cardinals had openly shopped Dean the previous fall, with cash offers coming in as high as $250,000 for his services. But each time, Rickey would up the demand, asking for players to be included, which killed the trade talks.[58] Dean won 28 games in 1935, 24 the next season, and just 13 in 1937, when he broke his toe pitching in the All-Star Game and returned too quickly. Along the way, a seemingly endless parade of drama featured a fistfight in a hotel lobby between the Cardinals and two reporters started by Dean, a suspension by National League president Ford Frick (Dean had called him and an umpire the two biggest crooks in baseball), and more shouting matches with management. Holed up in a New York City hotel one offseason, Breadon, Dean, and Frisch were discussing a contract, with Rickey listening and shaving in an adjoining room. An irate Rickey would occasionally pop his head in, waving a razor while dressing down Dean. "G'wan back in there and cut your throat," Dizzy responded.[59] To the horror of his bosses, Dean announced, on his twenty-sixth birthday, plans to buy an airplane. "There won't be any backseat drivers. All Diz will have to do is sit down. I'll handle the stick," said Pat. Rickey described Dizzy as having "inexplicable" impulses. "Dean is like an oil burner without a governor," he said.

Breadon and Rickey dealt with Dean for the last time as a player in the spring of 1938. The Cardinals traded him to Chicago for three players and $185,000 in cash. In three seasons with the Cubs, he won 16 games. After making a single appearance in 1941, he officially retired in May. At the age of 31, he took a job as the Cubs first base coach, the equivalent of a Hollywood star becoming a production assistant. But even in a dramatically less consequential role, Dean still managed to capture headlines. In early June, he was fined $50 and suspended for five days after a run-in with an umpire. Later that month, word spread that a brewery was considering hiring Dean as a broadcaster. In early July, the news became official. Dean was leaving Chicago for a broadcasting job in St. Louis. Falstaff signed him to a three-year $25,000 deal ($5,000 for the rest of 1941, and $10,000 for each of the next two seasons) to announce Browns and Cardinals games.[60]

After attending the All-Star game in Detroit, Dean arrived in St. Louis on the morning of July 9.[61] Hundreds of fans greeted him at Union Station as a band played Auld Lang Syne. KWK, his new radio station home, was there to interview him. Dizzy shared the mic that morning with Joe DiMaggio, who had also arrived on the train from Detroit. (DiMaggio would later replace Dean on Yankees broadcasts.)

After tossing baseballs to the assembled crowd, Dean hopped into an open-air car, with the band and several automobiles following him to the Park Plaza for a breakfast reception. "The Great One came home today," wrote Robert Morrison in the *Post-Dispatch*. The man who had spent years talking to the public through newspaper reporters could now speak directly into the microphone to his legion of fans. Baseball broadcasting in St. Louis would never be the same.

*****

His first broadcast came on Thursday night, July 10. Along with announcers Johnny O'Hare and Johnny Neblett, Dean described a 1-0 Yankees victory over the Browns as DiMaggio extended a hitting streak to 49 games. It would end at 56, exactly one week later in Cleveland. DiMaggio had broken the previous American League hitting streak record of 41, set by Browns first baseman George Sisler in 1922. In a pre-game ceremony, Sisler and DiMaggio shook hands at home plate. Former Cardinals great Rogers Hornsby, who owned the National League hitting streak record at the time (33 games), was among the Sportsman's Park crowd that evening. Dizzy also participated in the pre-game ceremonies, telling fans he hoped to be as good as a broadcaster as he was "on the rubber," and later telling his radio audience he had predicted in spring training that the Cardinals would win the pennant. "Except for his arm," noted one account, "Old Diz hasn't changed a bit."

Others disagreed. "Although he still is somewhat of a riot in the press box, old Diz isn't the fire-eating popoff he used to be," claimed an *Associated Press* story later that same season, citing his occasional empathy for both umpires and struggling pitchers. "Don't get discouraged, brother. I know just how you feel," Dean said on the air after Cardinals pitcher Lon Warneke gave up home runs to three straight batters.

He brought an insider's knowledge of the game to the booth combined with a fan-like intensity. At pivotal moments, he'd bite his fingernails, tear soda straws, break pencils, knock over chairs, and slap his broadcast partners on the back "until their teeth bent against the microphones," observed one reporter. At times, he'd get so caught up in the action, that he could no longer talk or even observe. "You take it, Johnny. I can't watch," he once said as the Giants loaded the bases. He slid the microphone over to his partner and proceeded to put his hands over his face until the play was over.[62]

He often preferred to stand instead of sit, crouching over the table with the microphone bent backward. Speaking in his Ozark accent, batters "swang," runners "slud," and fielders "throwed." Outfielders could "skitter" across the grass and batters occasionally looked "hitterish." His audience loved it. "He's great and for God's sake don't teach him English," wrote a businessman from East St. Louis.

Dean would regale his audience with songs ("Wabash Cannonball" was a favorite, recorded in 1954) and stories of Texas cattle, Mississippi catfish and Gashouse Gang glory days.[63] "That reminds me of ol' Pepper Martin," he said one evening with Cardinals third baseman Whitey Kurowski at the plate attempting a sacrifice. "He couldn't bunt a basketball." One year, he let the son of utility player Deb Garms broadcast portions of three different games. "Dizzy – he's my best friend," said David Garms. "I started when I was five, but I'm six now."[64] Dean didn't keep a scorecard, wouldn't recite statistics (called them "statics") and would joke about what the catcher and pitcher talked about during meetings on the mound (dinner plans). Entertaining and opinionated, there was never a doubt about which side he was rooting for. "I'm a Cardinal rooter, first, last, and always," he said in 1942, a year in which a poll claimed 82 percent of the greater St. Louis area radio audience preferred Dean's broadcast to the competition.[65] Spectators began bringing portable radios to the park to see the action while listening to Dizzy. He averaged 1,600 fan letters a month. "Diz had a method and a style all his own. Nothing like it before," said Mel Allen, who worked with Dean in 1950 and 1951 on Yankees broadcasts. "Good lord – he was an extrovert."[66]

The confidence he displayed on the field carried over to the broadcast booth. "The possibility of failure probably never entered his mind," believed Blattner. "If you run out of words to say, you just say the same ones over," Dean told a reporter. He once called former teammate Medwick, then with the Dodgers, the most unpopular athlete to visit Sportsman's Park among fans and players. Upset over umpire Bill McKinley's call in one game, he told his audience, "They shot the wrong McKinley." When wartime restrictions prevented him from discussing the weather, he found a workaround for rain delays. "I can't tell you folks why this here game is stopped, but I'll tell you what. If you just stick your head outside the nearest window, you'll know what I mean."

In Dizzy's voice, an hour became "are," and an error was spoken like "air." If he couldn't pronounce a player's name, he gave it a memorable twist. "I liked to have broken my jaw tryin' to pronounce that one," he said of Chicago Cubs pitcher Ed Hanyzewski. "But I said his name just by holdin' my nose and sneezing." A radio station owner in Dallas once tried to hire him as a disc jockey and have him introduce classical music. He turned down the offer, explaining "I can't even pronounce everybody's name in the Cleveland Indians' infield."

Couldn't do it or wouldn't do it? Those who worked closely with Dean over the years believed there was a strategic method to his madness. "That Diz was the smartest dumb man in the country," said Ray Doan, who organized Dean's postseason barnstorming tours and ran a longtime baseball school in Hot Springs, Arkansas. "He acts like he can't pronounce big words. That's all a fake. He's smart and sharp – and a grand guy."[67] Blattner recalled one inning where Dean played it straight. "He actually did a standard play-by-play and put things together pretty well. The actual structure was good, so unlike all the chaos he usually specialized in." During the commercial break, Dizzy changed his mind. "That's enough o' that poop. Now I'm going to start making some money,"

Dean proclaimed. "And he slaughtered the next inning above and beyond recall," said Blattner.[68]

In 1943, Falstaff published "The Dizzy Dictionary and What's What in Baseball," which defined certain terms he used on-air and included stories and opinions from the Great One.[69] Sample chapter headings included "Who's the Greatest Pitcher in the World? (Let's Look at the Record);" "Who's Got the Greatest Throwin' Arm in the World? (Not Countin' Days It Was Sore);" "Who's the Greatest Hitter in the World? (When He Wants to Be);" and "Who's the Greatest Runner in the World? (Not Countin' Days I Was Tired)."

Descriptions defined in the book included a "fiddle hitcher," a pitcher who has lost his stuff "so he takes to fiddle hitchin' to get them batters out." A weak hitter was termed a "buttercup," while a pitcher who could only throw slow pitches was called a "cunny thumb." Umpires were "guessers," and a "Foul Screecher" was a "ladies' day fan who screams at every pop foul." Dean also explained everything from why the Cardinals originally thought he was lefthanded (because of how he hunted squirrels with rocks. As a righthander, "I squash them squirrels up something turrible [sic]."), to taking credit for Giants manager John McGraw leaving the game. (Dean claimed he circled the bases and scored the winning run on a bunt.) While not always truthful, the book was entertaining. "He's priceless," wrote Arthur Daley in *The New York Times*.[70]

Dean did all this while still playing baseball. No longer throwing to major league hitters didn't mean that Dizzy had stopped pitching. Just days after beginning his broadcast career, he threw three innings for the Class D Sioux Falls Canaries. He frequently appeared in exhibition games and barnstorming tours (broadcasting during the week and pitching on weekends).[71] Satchel Paige was a favorite opponent. Paige and his Kansas City Monarchs faced off against the Dizzy Dean All-Stars at Wrigley Field in May of 1942, drawing nearly 30,000 fans. A week later, in Washington D.C., the two teams attracted 22,000, the largest crowd to ever watch a non-major league game at Griffith Stadium. The games caught the attention of Commissioner Landis and the U.S. government, as Dizzy's team featured former professional players now serving in the military. The War Department proceeded to block any furloughs for servicemen to participate in sporting events. While not mentioning Dean specifically, Landis issued a memo in early June blocking the use of major and minor league parks for games "allegedly played 'For Relief' but actually as commercial enterprises." Three days after the Wrigley Field contest, the Cubs and Reds played a war relief game in the same venue, attracting just under 10,000 fans, a third of what Dean and Paige drew.

Not stated by Landis was that in an era of segregated baseball, a Dizzy–Satchel matchup was destroying the myth that white fans wouldn't turn out to watch black athletes. It's another moment in Dean's life rich in irony. The son of a Southern sharecropper helped pave the way for improved race relations and cracked open the door that Jackie Robinson walked through five years later. Dean and Paige's "barnstorming tour saw ballparks that normally walled off blacks let them sit where they wanted. It brought in white reporters along with white fans. And when good ol' boy Dizzy Dean praised blackball legend Satchel Paige, followers of all hues pricked up their ears," wrote Paige biographer Larry Tye.[72] (The new rules didn't stop Dean and Paige from competing; they just shifted to smaller venues. A 1944 game in Belleville, Illinois, across the Mississippi River from St. Louis, attracted 4,000 fans.)

Not everything Dean attempted met with success. He once broadcast an NFL football game over a Dallas radio station. "The only play I called right was the kickoff," he said. Dizzy called referees "umpires" and "those guys wearing striped pajamas," and described the head linesman as "a guy with a gun who must be low on ammunition or a poor shot because I ain't seen him hit anybody." His play-by-play description ended after nine plays, with regular announcer Gordon McClendon taking over the broadcasting chores. "If I hadn't had that guy to carry the ball, it shore would have been a mess," said Dean.[73]

Just as in his playing career, Dean had encounters that strained relations with sportswriters and league officials. Columnist Stockton, Dizzy's one-time ghostwriter and author of a book on the Gashouse Gang, once ordered Dean, his wife, and a friend out of the press box. As president of the local chapter of the Baseball Writers' Association, Stockton was protecting his turf and following the rules. The press box was for working members of the media, not for friends and family. "If we police against our own wives and friends, why should we make any special dispensation for Dizzy Dean?" he said. Dean later went on air and claimed he was asked to leave because reporters were jealous that he scooped them on many stories. Thanks to the emergence of the next popular St. Louis broadcaster, the rivalry between print and radio in the city would only grow in the coming years.

Dizzy's old nemesis, Judge Landis, served as an impediment to his early broadcasting career. With both the Cardinals and Browns appearing in the Fall Classic in 1944, Dean was poised to do something he had never done – broadcast a World Series. *Variety* reported in August that Gillette, the radio sponsor of the Series, wanted Dizzy as part of the coverage. "Dean would be a terrific radio attraction among baseball fans and others not keenly interested in the game," insisted the publication. Commissioner Landis, who had the final call on broadcast assignments, said no. "Landis' specific objections to Dean have never been published, but it's thought he prefers to keep Diz silent during any air presentations of baseball classics for fear that one of his much-publicized 'colloquialisms' might backfire," *Variety* explained. *Washington Post* columnist Shirley Povich agreed. [74] Dean "doesn't know how to middle-road it," wrote Povich. "Landis likes calm detachment by the broadcasters." The All-St. Louis World Series did not feature a single local announcer. Landis went with an all-New York crew of Don Dunphy, Bill Slater, and Bill Corum. (Dunphy and Slater called Giants and Yankees games that season. Corum was a columnist for the *New York Journal-American*.)[75] The New York *Daily News* reported Dean was "burned up because he was ditched from the announcer's booth in favor of Bill Slater."[76] A "burned up" Dizzy didn't stick around to watch. He left for his Texas home before the games began.[77]

Landis may have ignored Dizzy but *The Sporting News* did not. Just weeks after the World Series, the St. Louis-based publication named Dean its "No. 1 play-by-play broadcaster of the year." Noting that Dean and partner Johnny O'Hara (who won the award in 1943) became the first announcers to broadcast the entire season of two major-league pennant winners, publisher J.G. Taylor Spink called Dean a "terrific radio favorite in the St. Louis area."

"Contrary to the belief of some, Dizzy is no clown on the air," read an editorial in the weekly paper. "True, he uses an informal colorful style, establishing his own rules of grammar. But this only adds to the interest in his broadcasts, which give listeners an accurate picture of what is transpiring on the diamond, based on Dean's own intimate knowledge of the game."[78] Thanks to a lengthy hunting trip, Dizzy didn't find out the news for weeks. He acknowledged the recognition in a wire to *The Sporting News*. "Many thanks, Brother," it read in part. "I will try always to keep faith with the honor given me." In a single decade, Dean had gone from being recognized as best on the field to best in the booth.

But when 1945 rolled around, his microphone was silent. Falstaff relinquished its option to broadcast Browns and Cardinals games. "Dizzy's chatter from the ballpark booth was very amusing to many of his listeners but there was also some severe criticism of him when he injected his political views into his sports broadcasts last fall," wrote W.J. McGoogan in the *Post-Dispatch*. (Dean was a vocal backer of President Roosevelt.) "This, however, does not seem to have had anything to do with the dropping of the program."[79] Dizzy signed a new five-year contract with the brewery over the winter and now spent his time doing promotional events for his employer.[80] The absence of the "terrific radio favorite" meant local listeners now had more time to enjoy the new man in town. It was a big break in the burgeoning career of Harry Caray.

Like Dean, Caray was young and brash. Both were opinionated and controversial, with a distinctive style that alienated a few but one that was embraced by many. However, Dizzy had the tailwinds of fame and fortune behind him when he stepped foot in the booth. Harry, who had only recently moved back to St. Louis, was starting from scratch. From the perspective of 1945, the new voice of St. Louis baseball would go on to achieve the near-impossible: Harry Caray would make Dizzy Dean a footnote in the annals of Cardinals broadcast history.

---

[1] Bryant and Dean played golf together frequently in pro-am tournaments around the South. On the day of Dean's funeral, Bryant recalled a tournament in Pensacola, Florida in 1969. "Dizzy doesn't like to be alone, but he had come to Pensacola without [wife] Pat. So, every morning about 5:45, Diz knocks on mine and [wife] Mary Harmon's door, looking for somebody to converse with." *St. Petersburg Times*, July 21, 1974.

[2] *Baseball Digest*, September 1951.

[3] *New York Times*, May 3, 1952. Herman Mankiewicz wrote the script for the movie, the same man who wrote the screenplay for *The Pride of the Yankees* about the life of New York Yankees slugger Lou Gehrig. He is best known for writing the screenplay for *Citizen Kane* with Orson Welles. Actor Dan Dailey bore "a striking resemblance to Dean." *The Sporting News*, March 19, 1952. Dean was reportedly paid between $50,000 and $100,000 for the movie rights to his life story. Payments were spread out over multiple years to reduce taxes. The film debuted in St. Louis on April 11, 1952, but was shown in St. Petersburg, Florida in March. Al Lang organized the event, featuring a cocktail party and dinner for 125 invited guests. Dean was expected to attend but did not show. *The Sporting News*, March 26, 1952.

[4] "His real estate in recent years has included a mansion in the most expensive section of Dallas' Highland Park suburb, several smaller residences, an office building at Lancaster, Texas, and a number of farms," wrote Frank X. Tolbert. Dean said his brother had also invested his baseball earnings into real estate. "Paul has done better than me, though," he conceded. "He got three times his money back from most things he bought. I usually only got twice my money." *Saturday Evening Post*, July 14, 1951.

[5] Both Dean and Pepper Martin had signed bats in 1936. Wildcatter S.A. Murphy discovered oil on the property – estimated at 300 to 500 barrels a day – in 1938. Dean and Martin received 10 acres total – five each. *St. Louis Globe-Democrat*, June 25, 1938.

[6] The Dean-Poladian Carpet Company was in Phoenix, Arizona. He purchased it in late 1963.

[7] "When Dean was hired as a member of the Yankees' broadcasting team, he declared that being on Topping's payroll was nothing new for him because he had been taking money from Dan for years," wrote Red Smith. *New York Times*, May 22, 1974.

8 Dean considered the run for Governor in 1967. Dizzy Dean Enterprises, Inc. was formed in Mississippi in 1961 and announced plans for a charcoal briquet manufacturing plant in the town of Wiggins. By 1965, "Ole Diz Charcoal Briquets" were being distributed and marketed nationwide. *The Clarke County Tribune* (Quitman, Mississippi), November 12, 1965. The company became a subsidiary of Hood Industries, Inc. in 1969. By that time, it employed 100 people. Ibid.

9 Appearing on Hope's radio program, Dean inadvertently dropped his script just as the entertainer asked him where he went to school. Without skipping a beat, Dean replied, "Well, Bob. I'll tell you. Me and (boxer) Maxie Rosenbloom was roommates up at Harvard together." Hope then tossed aside his script and the two men chatted off the cuff for ten minutes. *St. Louis Globe-Democrat*, July 14, 1942.

10 Other birthdates he would claim were February 22 and August 22. Multiple reports listed his birth year as 1911, even though the earlier date was widely known early in his career. "It was January 16, 1910, just when one of those Oklahoma thunderstorms was on, I was born," Dean wrote in one installment of a series of syndicated articles about his early life. *St. Louis Star*, August 20, 1931. "According to his own records Dizzy was born January 16, 1910 in Lucas, Ark," wrote *Houston Press* reporter Andy Anderson in 1934.

11 Ironic since Dean was a Democrat. In 1935, a York, Pennsylvania woman asked him to sign a card that included the words "13th Ward Republican Club." Dizzy told her he would sign it if he could cross out the word "Republican." She agreed and Dean signed his name. *The Scranton Times*, October 16, 1935. Years later, he got into a nightclub fight in Florida with a man arguing over the Democratic presidential nominee in 1952. Dean's choice was Harry Truman but Charles Clark of Polk County, Florida preferred Richard Russell of Georgia. Clark wound up with a black eye, was freed of an assault charge, and received a 30-day suspended sentence for drunkenness. Dean was not charged. *The Sporting News*, March 19, 1952.

12 Staten, Vince. *Ol Diz: A Biography of Dizzy Dean.* HarperCollins Publishers, Inc. 1992. The book includes a picture of the application.

13 Former Spaulding, Oklahoma mayor Johnny Mayfield claimed in 1997 that Dean attended high school there in the mid-1920s. "And someone said the only time he came to school was when they had a baseball game." *The Daily Oklahoman*, September 7, 1997. The town hosts an annual "Dizzy Dean Day." Earlier comments from Paul Dean also support the idea of additional education. "Diz left school in 1926, while he was in the Seventh Reader at Spaulding, Oklahoma." *The Sporting News*, August 1, 1951. Pat Dean claimed, and both Roy Stockton and Bob Broeg wrote, that Dean's education ended in the fourth grade.

14 One year, the family planted a crop in Brazoria, Texas but soon left. "The grasshoppers got it," explained their father, Albert Dean, "and we left in June for Lexington, Oklahoma, where we chopped cotton through the season."

[15] "I didn't see my brothers, 'cept Paul, for a long time. But it wasn't nine years like some folks say. Only four." *Baseball Digest*, September 1951. To another writer, Dean said that Elmer was stuck at the train tracks for about 20 minutes, then likely took a wrong turn. "That was in 1925 and we didn't see him again until 1930." *Saturday Evening Post*, July 14, 1951. According to Dean biographer Robert Gregory, Elmer "was 21, had no money, had never been on his own, couldn't read or write, and was retarded." Gregory, Robert. *Diz: Dizzy Dean and Baseball During the Great Depression*. Viking Penguin. 1992. In 1951, Dean said he was not with the family when they were separated from Elmer. "When Elmer was lost, I was in the Army at Fort Sam Houston, Texas." *The Sporting News*, August 1, 1951.

[16] *Baltimore Sun*, October 5, 1934. That same fall, he told a whopper of a story about a game when he claimed to be ten years old. "We were living in Oklahoma then, and I remember a semi-pro team wanted me to chunk against the Oklahoma City Teachers' Team. They wanted Paul, who was eight, to play shortstop. So I told'em if they'd send us a couple of mules to ride to the park – it was about 15 miles away – we'd play. So Paul, who was only eight then, and me rode over. I pitched and Paul played shortstop. I only gave'em four hits and Paul hit a home run, and we won easy." *St. Louis Star-Times*, October 3, 1934.

[17] Gregory, *Diz*. "Dizzy was probably the best ball player and worst soldier ever to hit Fort Sam Houston," said Sgt. John H. Podmenick. *Austin American-Statesman*, July 11, 1935.

[18] "I bought Diz out of the Army with the money I earned (picking cotton)," said Paul Dean. *Tallahassee Democrat*, July 21, 1974. Dizzy once gave his father the credit. "I'll never forget how he handed me six $20 bills." *The Sporting News,* April 2, 1952.

[19] *San Antonio Express*, October 3, 1965. "The last winter I was in uniform, my dad was pickin' cotton and finally got himself a shack on Rattlesnake Hill in San Antonio." *The Sporting News*, April 2, 1952.

[20] Ibid. With Dean asleep one evening during his shift, his co-workers affixed the electrodes from a Model T truck to Dean's hands and turned the crank. It took two turns to grab his attention. "He didn't know what had hit him," a co-worker recalled. "He jumped up and ran crazily across the street and then ran back rubbing his hands and screaming: 'it eeches, it eeches.'"

[21] Staten, *Ol' Diz*. Other reports have Dean signing for a bonus anywhere from $50 to $300. Dizzy claimed he was paid $300 a month. Curtis was a scout for the Cardinals minor league team in Houston. Staten wrote that the contract was dated May 25, 1929.

[22] Curtis died in 1937 at the age of 57 following a battle with pneumonia. *New York Times*, February 28, 1937. At the time of his death, Curtis was living in Waco, Texas where his local paper would refer to him as "Silent Don." He worked for decades for the Missouri-Texas-Kansas (MKT) Railroad. A West Virginia native, he played minor league baseball from 1901 to 1908. *Waco News-Tribune,* February 27, 1937.

[23] The eight teams were located in Rochester, New York; Houston, Texas; Danville, Illinois; St. Joseph, Missouri; Shawnee, Oklahoma; Scottdale and Waynesboro, Pennsylvania; and Greensboro, North Carolina. *St. Louis Post-Dispatch*, November 9, 1930.

[24] *New York Times*, April 29, 1943.

[25] Not everyone agreed with Rickey's contention. Author Curt Smith quoted an unidentified Rickey associate in the 1930s as saying, "Rickey was never all that fond of Dean, partially because Diz often called him Branch." Smith, Curt. *America's Dizzy Dean*. The Bethany Press. 1978. Over the years, Dean was quoted as calling him Branch, but whether he said it to his face is another matter.

[26] *St. Joseph Gazette*, May 30, 1930.

[27] *St. Louis Star*, September 29, 1930. Dean's debut came after the Cardinals had already clinched the pennant. He was not on the postseason roster. He was later asked why the Cardinals didn't win the World Series. "Dean didn't pitch," he said.

[28] Dean returned to Charleston after the 1931 season, pitching for the locals against the Cape Girardeau Capahas. Cape Girardeau native and former St. Louis Brown Elam Vangilder pitched for the Capahas. Vangilder struck 22 and allowed only two hits – both by Dean – in beating Charleston 4-0. *Sikeston Standard*, October 13, 1931.

[29] Leonard Koppett once referred to this era of Cardinals players as "a collection of uninhibited nuts." *The Man in the Dugout: Baseball's Top Managers and How They Got That Way*. Crown Publishers, Inc. 1993.

[30] "I'm through with the Cardinals and I'm going home," Dean told a newspaper reporter (likely Roy Stockton) shortly before leaving the team hotel. The source of the dispute was a request to wire Dean's wife $100. Dizzy claimed the club rejected the request, an allegation denied by Rickey. *St. Louis Post-Dispatch*, June 15, 1932.

[31] Dean claimed he was not yet 21 and his father had not signed his contract, making it invalid. The Cardinals found documents and old contracts that established his true age. "I'm 22 all right. I musta been thinkin' of my brother Paul's birthday," said Dizzy. Gregory, *Diz*.

[32] After being shipped to his third team in 1931, Paul Dean was so unsure of his ability that he refused a photographer's request to strike a pitcher's pose. He preferred to play shortstop. But on the mound, others had no doubt about his ability. "I saw this boy Dean pitch and he's nearly ready for the majors," Western Association president Dale Gear wrote to Branch Rickey. *The Paterson (NJ) Evening News*, October 20, 1934.

[33] The Cardinals returned Dizzy to Houston on May 2. Paul was sold to Columbus on May 5. Did the Cardinals purposely separate the brothers? A report at the time only noted that Columbus had a larger roster limit than Houston and that Paul may have a better chance of sticking with the Ohio club. *Fort-Worth Star-Telegram*, May 6, 1931. The Cardinals owned both teams. Dizzy had spent April with the major league club but never appeared in a game. He had clashed with manager Gabby Street in spring training, the same camp where Rickey restricted him to $1 a day.

[34] Exactly *when* they met is a source of debate among Dean biographers. Author John Heidenry wrote that they first met in 1929 and resumed dating when he returned in 1930. She had been married twice before; one of the marriages had been annulled, with the other ending in divorce. Dizzy was once asked if he had heard the rumor that Patricia had screwed half the men in town. "Sure, I heard it. I'm one of them. That's why I want to marry her." Heidenry, John. *The Gashouse Gang: How Dizzy Dean, Leo Durocher, Branch Rickey, Pepper Martin, and Their Colorful, Come-from-Behind Ball Club Won the World Series – and America's Heart – During the Great Depression.* Public Affairs. 2007.

[35] Staten, *Ol' Diz.*

[36] "He is the most colorful player that baseball ever produced," read an editor's note before one of the stories. *The Capital Times* (Madison, WI), August 20, 1931. Ralph A. Anderson of the *Houston Press* wrote the series.

[37] *New York Times*, May 20, 1931 and September 15, 1931.

[38] Ibid, March 23, 1934.

[39] Both Dizzy and his wife would later claim he didn't go to Detroit because he was upset at losing to the Cubs. Frisch later claimed the brothers attended a barbecue chicken dinner that evening outside Belleville, Illinois. Heidenry, *The Gashouse Gang.*

[40] Breadon explained the difference in fines was because Dizzy was older and was paid more money. He also explained that this was Paul's first offense and he was influenced by his brother.

[41] Dizzy had torn up one uniform and was walking out of the clubhouse when he ran into Ray Gillespie of the *Star-Times.* The reporter asked Dean if he would tear up a second one so his photographer could capture it. Dean agreed to do it.

[42] When Breadon was explaining Dean's many breaches of discipline, Dizzy would reply to each, "He lies, judge. The man lies." *Saturday Evening Post*, July 18, 1959.

[43] Paul Dean received a three-day suspension estimated at roughly $20 a day. (He had already returned to the club before the hearing.) Combined with the $50 fine, his total came to slightly more than $100.

[44] *St. Louis Globe-Democrat*, August 21, 1934.

[45] *St. Louis Star-Times*, March 12, 1934.

[46] Dean's 29th victory of the season had come just two days earlier. It also was a complete-game shutout of the Reds. He appeared in 50 games in 1934, 33 as a starter and 17 as a reliever. A July 1 game against the Reds went 18 innings. Dean pitched the first 17. In his previous start, he went 8 2/3 innings against the Giants, leaving the game tied at 7. Reliever Jim Mooney retired the only batter he faced. The Cardinals scored in the bottom of the ninth inning to win the game. The official scorer awarded the victory to Dean and the save to Mooney.

[47] "You can't win four straight games," sportswriter Grantland Rice told Dean. "I know I can't, but I can win four outta five," Dizzy replied. Staten, *Ol' Diz.*

48 Ford's company paid $100,000 to become the exclusive sponsor of 1934 World Series radio broadcasts. Graham McNamee was part of the NBC broadcast crew. France Laux was one of two play-by-play announcers for CBS.
49 Gregory, *Diz*.
50 Frisch received heavy criticism for allowing Dean to pinch-run. Sportswriter Paul Gallico called it "probably the greatest World Series boner in the history of baseball." *Los Angeles Times*, October 7, 1934.
51 *St. Louis Globe-Democrat*, October 7, 1934.
52 About thirty minutes later, the team announced to fans that Dean was "O.K." Lacking a public address system in the stadium, a man with a megaphone made the announcement multiple times to separate areas of the park.
53 The story Dean and others told that the headline in the paper the next day read – "X-RAYS OF DEAN'S HEAD SHOW NOTHING" – was just that, a story.
54 "In each era, there are shining stars such as Theodore Roosevelt, Dizzy Dean and others who excelled in their fields," said Dr. Ira Sassaman, a Williamsport, Pennsylvania pastor, in 1945.
55 *The Sporting News*, October 25, 1934. Parker also wrote the lines for the Dean brothers' show on Broadway.
56 Staten, *Ol' Diz*.
57 The 1937 contract was originally for $25,000, making Dean tied with Dazzy Vance for the highest-paid pitcher in baseball. Dean talked Breadon into an increase. "Now, look, for $500 extra, you'll make me the highest-paid pitcher in the game, and you'll have the honor of being the fellow who paid it," Dizzy told his boss. "I believe that was the only argument I ever lost in signing a ballplayer," said Breadon. *St. Louis Star-Times,* January 25, 1941.
58 The Dodgers offered $250,000 for Dean, but Rickey countered by asking for the cash and pitcher Van Mungo. After the 1936 season, Dean called his teammates "a bunch of bushers." Outfielder Terry Moore responded on a radio show. "As one busher to another, Diz, I really saw a great pitcher in Carl Hubbell. I hope to live to see the day when you can act and pitch like him." *Brooklyn Times Union*, October 15, 1936. Hubbell's Giants won the National League pennant.
59 *Washington Post*, February 4, 1935.
60 A local advertising agency, Sherman K. Ellis, suggested Dean to Falstaff. Gregory, *Diz*. One of Dizzy's reported inspirations for the broadcast booth was pitcher Bobo Newsom. While injured in the minor leagues in 1933, Newsom wandered into the broadcast booth and helped call a game at Wrigley Field in Los Angeles. Early in his major league career, "he happened to compare notes with Dizzy Dean, telling Diz how much he enjoyed the experience," wrote Jim McConnell. "Dean's playing career ended shortly thereafter, but inspired by Bobo, he took to the microphone." *The Inland Valley Daily Bulletin*, October 18, 2010.

[61] In his first official duty for his new employer, Dean hosted a reception for Falstaff at the All-Star game.
[62] *St. Louis Post-Dispatch*, August 3, 1941.
[63] The 1954 record featured Dizzy Dean and His Country Cousins singing "Wabash Cannonball" on the A-side and "You Don't Have To Be From The Country" on the B-side. Both songs can be found on YouTube. Dean once performed "Wabash Cannonball" in a duet with concert singer Jessica Dragonette.
[64] *St. Louis Globe-Democrat*, September 4, 1944.
[65] With the Cardinals and Dodgers locked in a tight pennant race, Dizzy did a Western Union "ticker game" between Brooklyn and Boston late in the 1942 season from the KWK studios at the Chase Hotel. When the Braves raced out to an early lead, Dizzy announced on the air, "If the Braves win this game here tonight, all of you come down here to the hotel tonight, and my sponsor [Falstaff] will put on a big party for you with a lot of free beer and sandwiches." To the relief of Falstaff executives, the Dodgers rallied to win the game. *The Washington Post*, January 8, 1945.
[66] Smith, *Voices of The Game*.
[67] *Quad-City Times*, (Davenport, Iowa), February 28, 1960. Columnist Jimmy Powers spoke with Dean at the 1946 World Series. "Dizzy Dean spoke to us for 15 minutes hand running and never once split an infinitive. Any resemblance to Dizzy's ghost-written Ozark dialect is strictly coincidental and corny." New York *Daily News*, October 9, 1946.
[68] Smith, *Voices of The Game*.
[69] Bill Bartelson was hired in the summer of 1941 to be Dean's public relations manager and ghostwriter. He left in 1943 to join a Chicago advertising agency. *The Sporting News*, July 24, 1941, *Chicago Tribune*, December 8, 1943.
[70] *New York Times*, September 13, 1943. Also see *Kansas City Times*, May 19, 1944. Dean would call a lefthanded pitcher a "cockeye," and a regulation nine-inning game "union hours." *Boston Globe*, September 8, 1944.
[71] Weekend broadcasts at Sportsman's Park during World War II were restricted until 1944. The Browns and Cardinals feared out-of-town customers wouldn't attend. They were correct, but for different reasons. "Gas and tire rationing virtually … eliminated the out-of-town motorist customer from the picture," wrote J. Roy Stockton. *St. Louis Post-Dispatch*, March 12, 1944.
[72] https://www.historynet.com/barnstorming-aces-satchel-paige-and-dizzy-dean.htm
[73] *Fort-Worth Star-Telegram*, November 24, 1947.
[74] *The Sporting News*, August 24, 1944 (reprinted from the August 16 issue of *Variety*). *Washington Post*, August 25, 1944.
[75] Corum was a Missouri native. He later served as president of Churchill Downs and is credited for coining the term "Run for the Roses" to describe the Kentucky Derby. The 1944 World Series was carried exclusively over the Mutual Network. In an editorial, the *St. Louis Post-Dispatch* called the New York announcers "technically good, all right. But

we'll take Dizzy Dean and Johnny O'Hara. They're good, too. As a matter of fact, they're better." *St. Louis Post-Dispatch*, October 7, 1944.

[76] New York *Daily News*, October 3, 1944.

[77] *The Sporting News*, October 12, 1944.

[78] Ibid, November 2, 1944. Johnny Neblett left the broadcast team after the 1941 season. Dean and O'Hara later left KWK to broadcast games on WEW for day games and WTMV for night games. "During the 1920s, O'Hara roamed the world as a shipboard radio operator," *The Sporting News* once noted. Before coming to St. Louis, he called games in Chicago for the Cubs and White Sox. He started at KWK in 1936. O'Hara taught code to Air Corps radio instructors during World War II at the St. Louis University Army Air Forces' Radio Instructor School. He also owned an orange ranch in Florida. O'Hara died of cancer at the age of 59 in 1963.

[79] *St. Louis Post-Dispatch*, March 1, 1945. Curt Smith wrote that after Dean voiced his political preferences, "many baseball broadcasts carried a tagline disclaiming any Dean views as his own." Smith, *America's Dizzy Dean*. Dean attended one evening of the Democratic National Convention in 1936. He didn't meet Roosevelt, but told Postmaster Jim Farley, "You tell the big boss 'Ol Diz' will be pulling for him." Gregory, *Diz*.

[80] Dean signed a five-year contract that paid him $20,000 annually. In 1945, he spoke at military hospitals, showed movies of the World Series, and appeared three times a week on a Falstaff-sponsored radio program. *St. Louis Globe-Democrat,* June 15, 1945. The radio show was syndicated throughout the Midwest and South. "Dean will appear as announcer and storyteller..." *The Sporting News*, April 12, 1945. He avoided military service during World War II because of a perforated eardrum.

Bombers, Flyers, Stretch, and Gabby

By the time Dizzy Dean was broadcasting his first baseball game, Harry Carabina had a new name, a new job, and was living in a new city. Starting his broadcast career in 1940 at radio station WCLS in Joliet, Illinois, he adopted the last name of Caray thanks to station manager Bob Holt (who previously worked at KMOX). It has a quicker sound, Holt told him. "While my first reaction was negative, I decided, why not?" Harry recalled. "I had no paternal relatives, I was starting a new job in a new town. So, I became – legally – Harry Caray. Forever."[1] He was also likely aware that Harry Carey ("ey" not "ay") was a well-known actor at the time. Around the time Carabina changed his name, Carey was nominated for an Academy Award for Best Supporting Actor in the 1939 movie *Mr. Smith Goes to Washington*.[2]

In Joliet, Caray called everything from summer softball to winter bowling leagues. The athletic schedules of two high schools and a junior college kept him busy in the spring and fall. His dayside routine included a "Man on the Street" program. In the summer of 1941, it aired six days a week at 12:45 and 6:45.[3] He also got his first taste of announcing major league baseball, recreating Cubs and White Sox games, condensing each contest into a thirty-minute broadcast.

Before the end of the year, Caray had left Joliet for Kalamazoo, Michigan. He took a job as sports director at WKZO. The radio station was owned by John Fetzer, who would go on to build a broadcasting empire of radio and television properties, wealth that would later allow him to own the Detroit Tigers. Fetzer convinced his fellow owners in the 1960s to pool their network broadcast revenue and share the money equally.

At Kalamazoo, Fetzer and station general manager Ray Hamilton assembled one of the greatest radio lineups of all time. Caray was sports director. Paul Harvey was news director. The legendary newsman shared characteristics of three great Cardinals broadcasters. Like France Laux, Harvey was an Oklahoma native. Both men grew up in law enforcement families. Laux's father was a judge. Harvey's father was a police officer killed in the line of duty when his son was just three years old. Four years after Laux left KVOO in Tulsa for St. Louis, 14-year-old Paul Aurandt (Harvey was his middle name) was escorted into the station by a high school teacher who told the manager: "This boy needs to be on the radio."[4] He started as an unpaid gofer, but it was his beginning in a medium he would never leave.

Like Dizzy Dean, Harvey had a passion for golf. "I don't know if this is true or not, but he loves golf, loves to bet, and he plays to win," remembered longtime St. Louis radio executive Tim Dorsey. "The story is that when he wins he'll only take a check as payment. Then he posts them on a wall and never cashes them."[5]

Like Caray, Harvey developed trademark phrases instantly recognized by millions ("Stand by for news"; "Now you know ... the REST of the story"). Both men worked at KXOK radio in St. Louis (Harvey before Kalamazoo, Caray afterward). Caray's first wife was from the St. Louis suburb of Webster Groves. Harvey's one and only wife grew up in nearby University City. He met her while working at KXOK. Lynne "Angel" Cooper was the youngest of five daughters of a University City judge. She went on to earn undergraduate and master's degrees from Washington University. She was hired at KXOK after answering an ad from the station. Her car, a 1938 Nash Lafayette coup, was parked outside the studios when she met her future husband on an elevator. "Is that your pretty car out front?" Harvey asked her. He needed a ride to the airport and promised to buy her dinner. "Boy, I thought these radio people are fast," Angel remembered. "But I looked at him, heard that voice, and I thought: This fellow is going places. I wonder what makes him tick."[6] They were married in June of 1940, just the beginning of Harvey's many connections to St. Louis and the greater Missouri area that would eventually include three farms and a museum in Branson that celebrates his family history.[7]

During his time in Kalamazoo, Harvey would occasionally fill in for Caray. "He [Caray] teased him all the time," remembered Carl Lee, who would later become president of Fetzer Broadcasting.[8] "Paul did a sufficient job but sports just weren't his specialty." Both men would do man-on-the-street interviews, something Caray would occasionally struggle with if the topic wasn't sports. "He used to sweat all over the equipment," said Lee, who was chief engineer at the station before he became a media executive. "One day out on the street, at the corner of Main and Burdick, I plugged his microphone into the amplifier and because his hands were all sweaty and slobbery, it sent a huge jolt up his arm and knocked him off his feet!"[9]

Caray was on firmer footing behind the microphone calling games, something he did for Western Michigan football and basketball. The station also carried Detroit Tigers baseball. Harry did pregame and postgame shows for the local affiliate. He also got the opportunity to do baseball play-by-play for the first time in his life, broadcasting games of a local semi-pro team in a tournament. For the first time, listeners heard him say, "It might be ... it could be ... it IS a home run!" Caray also believed it was the first time he used "Holy cow!" on the air. "It was forceful, exciting, and certainly couldn't offend anyone," Harry recalled. "And, of course, more important than any of the above, it was the only exclamation I could come up with that didn't involve profanity."[10]

Various profiles of Caray throughout the 1950s and 1960s include the detail that he also spent time in Grand Rapids, Michigan. "I kept writing letters," Harry once told members of the Elks in Alton, Illinois about his early days in radio. "I ... moved to Kalamazoo and then to Grand Rapids," he said in 1960.[11] But over time, any mention of living or working in Grand Rapids, just like the credit he once gave his first wife for his start in radio, simply faded away.[12]

By the summer of 1943, Caray was classified as 1-A and expected to be drafted. He quit his job in Michigan and returned to Missouri. He wanted his wife and young son (Harry Christopher "Skip" Caray Jr. was born in 1939) to be with family if he were to enter the military. Harry's poor eyesight at the induction physical led him to be reclassified as 1-AL, limited service. "I'm very myopic," Caray wrote in his autobiography. "I couldn't see the scoreboard at Sportsman's Park, let alone the eye chart across the room." Harry was spared from military duty but found himself unemployed with a family to feed. Perhaps it was just a coincidence or maybe he had help, but Caray soon took a job at KXOK. (Not only had Paul and Angel Harvey worked at the station, but so had WKZO station manager Hamilton, who held the same title in St. Louis.) [13]

He started as a staff announcer but was soon doing a sports show.[14] In January 1944, Caray was appointed sports editor of the station. He hosted "Sports From A Different Angle" every night in addition to covering all play-by-play duties for KXOK.[15] Back in his hometown and two months shy of his 30th birthday, Caray was now ready to introduce his St. Louis listeners to a style that borrowed heavily from America's most famous gossip columnist.

*****

Radio pioneers of the 1930s and 1940s profoundly impacted the (mostly) men who followed in their footsteps. As a sportscaster for NBC, Bill Stern called boxing matches and the first televised baseball game in 1939.[16] He was most famous for a fifteen-minute show called *The Colgate Sports Newsreel*. "Stern eulogized the great, the near-great, the obscure. His fantastic tales broke all rules," wrote John Dunning, the author of *On The Air: The Encyclopedia of Old-Time Radio*. "He told of horse races won by dead jockeys, of armless and legless baseball players, of the profound if tenuous effect that sports had on the lives of great national statesmen." One man who paid close attention to Stern's delivery was Caray's one-time colleague. "Newsman Paul Harvey displays unmistakable Stern influence today in his daily 'news' reports," Dunning wrote in 1998. "Harvey ... borrows heavily from Stern's personal style – the long pause, the repetition, the hyped emphasis – to lift ordinary events out of the ordinary."[17]

Like Harvey, a newsman who found inspiration in a sports broadcaster, Caray looked outside his immediate field to find his model. Harry didn't want to be France Laux or Dizzy Dean. He wanted to be Walter Winchell. "I read his columns regularly and I loved his radio broadcasts," Caray remembered. Winchell, a former Vaudeville performer, had a gossip column syndicated by more than two thousand newspapers and a Sunday night radio show that was the most popular program in the country by the late 1940s.[18] Wearing a cocked Fedora and camping out at Table 50 in New York's famed Stork Club, Winchell would trade tidbits and rumors about America's rich and powerful with his many contacts, information that could make or break careers if he decided to make it public. In a country of 75 million adults, 50 million of them either read his columns or listened to his broadcasts.[19] "Walter Winchell may have been wrong, but he was never in doubt," Caray believed. "You might not have agreed with him, but you always listened to him." Caray had Winchell in mind when he took to the air in St. Louis. "I just didn't read scores – I went wild. I editorialized. I 'Walter Winchelled' like crazy," Caray told author Curt Smith.

"Every night at ten-fifteen, I'd be on the air blasting, ripping, praising, and slashing. I would editorialize, and I would break real scoops. I'd tell the truth. I used – perhaps overused – stories from sources I described as unidentified and unimpeachable, another Winchell trademark," he recalled for his memoir.[20] "Broadcasters had never before done things like that in St. Louis. They had always left that kind of work for the newspapermen, for the columnists and beat writers from the *Globe-Democrat* and *Post-Dispatch*."

It wasn't long before the columnists and beat writers noticed. They didn't like what they heard. "He was awfully tough to deal with," said Broeg. "[In] his nightly editorials he'd say, 'Despite what you read in the papers' ... Well, after a while you get pretty sick of it." Broeg also discovered something else about Caray during his early St. Louis years. The man loved to argue. "I found that his exaggerations of the game were one thing, but he was difficult to have a drink with in those days. You'd say black was black and he'd say it was white. All of a sudden, his eyes squinting behind those thick glasses, he'd say something derogatory." More than words would be exchanged. "One time Gus Mancuso, who succeeded Gabby Street as his associate, had to pull me off of him. Another time, Dixie Walker, coaching for the Cardinals, had to pull me off of him," recalled Broeg, who served in the Marines in World War II. "I don't mean that he wouldn't have fought but I just said, 'Harry, the hell with it. You go your way and I'll go my way.' And that's what we did."[21]

Globe-Democrat columnist Bob Burnes had a similar take. "I had my share of squabbles with Harry through the years," he said in 1970. "My biggest beef came years ago when he might be on the road and would reveal something that 'you won't see in the St. Louis newspapers.' Often we had carried the thing he was talking about days earlier."[22] Like his *Post-Dispatch* counterpart, Burnes could only take so much. "I know Bob Burnes of the *Globe-Democrat* finally did the most insulting thing," Broeg remembered. "We just cut him out of the news."

Caray may have been initially oblivious to the cause, but he noticed the slight. "The strange thing was, in all my years in St. Louis, I rarely got my name in the newspapers unless something negative occurred," he observed. He was the subject of a lengthy and fawning profile in 1949. (It didn't come from the *Post* or *Globe*, but the *Star-Times,* which owned KXOK.) Under the headline, "IT MIGHT BE! IT COULD BE! IT IS!" Caray talked about receiving 1,500 letters a week and being so popular that he had to remove his name from the phone book. It was his last major profile by St. Louis print media until the late 1960s.

By the time he arrived in Chicago, Harry had absorbed the lesson. In 1971, after his first year with the White Sox, Caray invited members of the press who traveled with the team to dinner – one or two at a time. Harry picked up the tab at one of his favorite restaurants, the Pump Room, and gave each of them the same kind of tape recorder he used for his job.

The Chicago media never cut Harry Caray out of the news.[23]

*****

Within months of debuting on KXOK, Caray's new show proved so popular that station management moved its time slot to 5:45 p.m. The last year of his life without baseball play-by-play duties featured the only all-St Louis World Series. It was in this atmosphere, with local interest in sports at a peak, and a nation weary from war, "that I started to make a name for myself in St. Louis," Caray remembered.

When the baseball season ended, Harry really got busy. The Griesedieck Brothers Brewery, one of three area beermakers heavily involved in sports marketing at the time (Falstaff and Hyde Park were the other two), decided to blanket the airwaves with sponsorships. That winter, the brewery started sponsoring "everything from college basketball to the American Hockey League, from boxing to Ping-Pong to wrestling," Caray recalled. He would know. Through their advertising agency, Ruthrauff & Ryan, the brewery hired him to broadcast the events. Harry called St. Louis Flyers hockey with Leo Carbol, Shrimp McPherson, and Ralph "Bouncer" Taylor (hockey was the first play-by-play Caray ever did in St. Louis), Golden Gloves boxing with sports columnist Sid Keener, Benny Kessler and "Kid" Regan, and St. Louis University football with former high school coach Bert Fenenga. He also announced wrestling matches from the Arena and did the play-by-play for St. Louis Bombers basketball.[24]

Griesedieck Brothers had been awarded sponsorship of Cardinals and Browns baseball for 1945 over WIL. Executives planned to hire a well-established broadcaster to lead the coverage, with former Cardinals manager Gabby Street serving as color analyst. Caray would serve as the number three man in the booth. Harry, though, had other ideas.

He first pleaded his case to Oscar Zahner, the advertising agency vice president. "You need someone young and vital," Caray told him. "You need *me*." Zahner reiterated the message that the focus was on finding a big-name broadcaster. But Caray wouldn't take no for an answer. He decided one day to show up at the office of brewery president Ed Griesedieck. "You don't need Mel Allen or Bill Stern," Caray told him. Griesedieck replied that his preference was for someone similar to France Laux. "I can have a cup of coffee and read my newspaper, and even though he doesn't miss a play, I don't have my concentration interrupted," he explained.

It was all the opening Caray needed. "Can you read the newspaper while I'm announcing?" Harry asked him. The answer was obvious. Its impact resonated with Griesedieck immediately. He made up his mind that day. The brewery had found its new lead announcer.[25]

The third man in the broadcast crew came the next year. Campbell "Stretch" Miller arrived in St. Louis for an audition in November of 1946. With Caray on the West Coast covering baseball meetings, Miller worked Harry's 15-minute show on KXOK and wrestling from Kiel Auditorium on Friday night, a high school football game and a St. Louis Flyers hockey game on Saturday, and the St. Louis Bombers basketball game against the Chicago Stags on Sunday. He met with executives from Griesedieck Brothers and their advertising agency on Monday. They only had one criticism. Don't say "Stags," they told him. Instead, they preferred he said "Chicago" since Stag Beer was a local competitor. Miller would work with Caray until Griesedieck Brothers' sponsorship of the Cardinals ended in the 1950s. "Harry Caray and I did more sports during a year than any other announcers in the business," Miller wrote in his autobiography. "We sometimes worked in conflict with each other. I would be doing a basketball game on one station and Harry would be doing a hockey game on another. By actual count we did more than 350 sporting events a year for several years, all for the same sponsor."[26]

Born in St. Louis and raised in Chicago, Miller weighed 16 ½ pounds at birth, the thirteenth child and seventh son of Scottish parents who immigrated to America in the 1890s. As a teenager, he worked at the Cooper-Carlton and Sisson Hotels in Chicago, two side-by-side establishments that frequently served as the resting place for visiting major league teams. It was here that he came to despise Babe Ruth. "Perhaps he mellowed later, but those years he was a blustering, crude, loud-mouthed person who treated all of us youngsters shabbily," Miller remembered.[27] He also came to appreciate Hall of Fame pitcher Walter Johnson. "He was one of the kindest gentlemen I ever met in sports, and until I got to know Stan Musial, I never knew a professional athlete with such a common touch, who was a real 'nice' guy without being sticky about it, and who was liked and respected by everyone."

Standing 6'4" and weighing 190 pounds by his senior year in high school, Miller was a talented basketball player. A college basketball star during this period was Charles "Stretch" Murphy, who played at Purdue. Westbrook Pegler, working then at the *Chicago Tribune*, covered one of Miller's games. "If his name isn't 'Stretch,' it should be," Pegler wrote, giving Miller a nickname that would stick for the rest of his life.

By the time he was in college, he had grown an inch and played on the first conference basketball championship team in Illinois State history. He broke into radio in 1935, making $12 a week for station WJBC in Bloomington. Listeners around the country first heard his voice in 1936 when President Roosevelt made an appearance in the Illinois city as part of a whistle-stop tour. Miller covered the event and when CBS asked WJBC to feed the broadcast to the network, Stretch had the honor of introducing the President to the nation. Moments before going live, Miller began worrying about how to pronounce Roosevelt's middle name – Delano – while also spotting the President's wife in the crowd. Then it came time for the introduction. "And now, ladies and gentlemen, the President of the United States, Franklin ELEANOR Roosevelt."[28]

Stretch had better luck with baseball. He called play-by-play for the Bloomington Bloomers, a minor league team of the Cardinals in the Three-Eye-League. Burleigh Grimes, who won 17 games for the 1931 World Series champion Cardinals, was the manager. Grimes "spoke two languages very fluently," Miller recalled: "English and profanity." The ground-level broadcast booth was located just behind home plate, meaning the distance between the microphone and Grimes' frequent disagreements with umpires was short. "It was on a spot only a few feet in front of me that Grimes and the umpire would meet, stand nose to nose, exchange pleasantries and proceed to make references to each other's ancestry," remembered Miller.

Stretch later joined WCBS radio in Springfield, Illinois (call letters later sold to the Columbia Broadcasting System for their flagship New York station). He left to become an officer in the Navy during World War II, serving in the Pacific theater. "Our duties were to transport Army and Marine personnel and their equipment for various island invasions," he explained. After the war, he rejoined the Springfield station but hesitated to return to unscripted play-by-play after spending years in the military. "Four-letter words, and even some longer ones, were part of every sailor's vocabulary," Miller wrote in his memoir. "I didn't return for several weeks, not until I had control of my words so that the station wouldn't lose its license."

His play-by-play work eventually caught the attention of Zahner, the advertising executive who worked on the Griesedieck Brothers' account. (The 1946 Springfield Browns were an affiliate of the St. Louis American League franchise.)[29] Just like Caray, he broadcast everything in St. Louis involving a ball that could be kicked, thrown, or shot as well as other sports such as golf, wrestling, and boxing. Because he worked so frequently with Harry during this era, no one knew Caray's strengths and weaknesses better than Stretch.

"Football and basketball were not Harry's cup of tea," Miller claimed. Because of bad eyesight, Caray often called the wrong ball carrier. He had a creative way of correcting himself. For example, Harry would say "Smith" on a touchdown run, when it was actually "Jones" who ran the ball into the endzone. Realizing the mistake, Caray would improvise. "Smith laterals to Jones, and Jones goes in for the touchdown," he would say. "He had done this on several occasions while doing St. Louis U. games," Miller remembered.

In 1947, the announcer for the Preakness, Clem McCarthy, famously called the wrong winner of the race. A search was soon on for the next broadcaster of horse racing's triple crown. Harry approached his advertising manager about calling the races. "Sorry, Harry," he was told. "You can't lateral a horse!"

Caray struggled with distances in basketball games, saying shots occurred from 40 to 50 feet when they were taken from a much shorter range. When Kentucky's Cliff Hagan threw a full-court-length desperation shot at the end of a game against St. Louis University, Caray told his radio audience, "That would have been the longest shot in the history of basketball – 125 feet!" (A college basketball court is 94 feet long.)

Caray, Miller, and Street often appeared together at events involving their beer sponsor. One year, the trio spoke to a gathering of the company's truck drivers. With several hundred assembled for what they presumed to be an all-male event, Harry told a few dirty stories and so did Gabby. Stretch was halfway through one ribald tale when he spotted a lone female near the back. He toned down the punchline and finished with some cleaner stories. He then sought out the woman to apologize. She explained to him that she had been driving a truck for ten years, ever since her husband died. "Those stories are pretty tame," she told him. "Now I could tell you some pretty goddam good ones!"

With Caray and Street calling the contests, Miller's responsibilities with the Cardinals were the pregame and postgame shows and plenty of pitches for his sponsor.[30] The advertisements for Griesedieck Brothers were often done live, but sometimes Stretch had to spend time in a studio filming a spot. He would show up at 6:00 a.m. for shoots that could drag on for hours. If anything was off – a bottle out of place, an issue with the lighting, one wrong word – the production crew would have to start all over. One day, they were still shooting the ad at noon and Miller was so bloated from swigging beer he could hardly speak. (It was legal to drink in the ads at the time.) With the cameras rolling, he let out a loud, long burp that had his floor crew and cameraman laughing. "It's all right for you clowns to laugh," Stretch told them, "but I have to drink this damned slop." Griesedieck officials got such a kick from the outtake they made a copy to show at sales meetings and other gatherings.

*****

Miller may have been Caray's most frequent broadcast partner during the Griesedieck Brothers' years of sponsorship, but Harry's favorite and most influential co-worker of this era was the other man in the Cardinals' broadcast booth. "Harry learned baseball from Gabby," Miller believed, a view that Caray embraced and extended. Street was not just Caray's teacher; he was also like the father that Harry never had. "I listened to Gabby and learned, and not only about baseball; I learned many of the most important lessons about life," Caray wrote in 1989. "No partner I've ever had meant as much to me as he did."

Charles Evard "Gabby" Street was born in Huntsville, Alabama in September of 1882.[31] After high school, he spent time at South Kentucky College and began playing professional baseball in the Kitty League at Hopkinsville, Kentucky in 1903. His big break came in 1904 when a recently signed player for the Cincinnati Reds refused to play on Sundays. The Reds and the unflinching athlete soon parted ways. That player, Branch Rickey, was a catcher, just like the man who replaced him. Street made his major league debut on September 13, 1904. Rickey and Street's career paths would intersect for decades.

Gabby played for Cincinnati and Boston the following season before returning to the minor leagues to catch in the Pacific Coast League for the San Francisco Seals. He was asleep in the Golden Gate Hotel one April morning when he was awakened by a rumble deep in the ground. "I rubbed my eyes, looked out the window and saw buildings crumbling, and having heard whispers of quakes, started for the street. If I live to be a hundred, I shall always remember that scene. The 'Beauty and the Beast' and the 'Babes in Toyland' companies [theatrical troupes] were living in the same hotel and what the female members of those troupes wore as they hiked for the exits are nobody's business. As we hit the street, en masse, the rear of the hotel collapsed and the water tank on the roof, halved by the second shock, washed every one of us. I walked through showers of brick and mortar to the Golden Gate Park, where I spent the night."[32] The 1906 San Francisco earthquake struck at a magnitude of 7.9 on the Richter Scale, destroyed nearly 500 blocks, killed an estimated 3,000 people, and left half of the city's 40,000 residents homeless.

Street survived the earthquake's aftermath and eventually returned to the big leagues. In 1908, he joined the Washington Senators, where he became known for catching Walter Johnson and snagging a ball dropped from near the top of the Washington Monument. A local journalist, Preston Gibson, hatched the idea for the monument stunt, betting colleagues that Street could pull it off after watching him catch high pop-ups during Senators games. Gabby was up to the challenge. "Gibson at first tried rolling the balls out on a trough to give them a good start away from the monument," Street remembered. "The first few, however, hit the side and bounced off. I didn't even get close on one or two others. Then we changed sides, to get the benefit of the wind." After 12 dropped balls, Street still hadn't made a catch. "As luck would have it, I snagged the thirteenth and last ball."[33] The final baseball, dropped from one of the observation windows at a height of 550 feet, was labeled, dated, and promptly forgotten.[34] In the summer of 1931, a former neighbor of Street's was rummaging through her attic when she discovered the relic. Twenty-three years after the famous catch, Street and the baseball were reunited.

Johnson, who debuted with the Senators a year before Gabby arrived, loved throwing to Street. "He never hit much, but what a receiver he was – big fellow, a perfect target, great arm, slow afoot, but spry as a cat on his feet back of the plate, always talking, always hustling, full of pep and fight." Johnson and Street were batterymates for four seasons, a period in which the pitcher won 77 games. "In 1910 and 1911, he was the greatest receiver I ever saw," said Johnson.[35] He was also durable. Gabby once caught 16 straight games over the course of nine days and set a record for catching chances in 1909 (924) that stood for decades.

Street finished his big-league career with the New York Highlanders (Yankees) in 1912, the same team that Rickey ended his playing career with five years earlier. The two men would later manage both the Browns and Cardinals. They met in World War I as members of the Chemical Warfare Service. Serving on the battlefields of France were Major Rickey, Captains Christy Mathewson and Ty Cobb, and Sergeant Street. "It was not strange if these four sometimes talked baseball," noted one dispatch.[36] It was here that Rickey first encouraged Street to consider a career as a manager.[37]

Street had an independent streak and a mind of his own. He arrived in France as a sergeant but was briefly demoted to private ("after having a row with my company commander over how to run the war," he once explained). He was later reinstated to the rank of sergeant and frequently called "Old Sarge" for the rest of his life. Unlike the other three baseball men he served with, Street was assigned to a combat division. "I was one of the first 50,000 to get over and took part in three major engagements: Chateau-Thierry, Saint-Mihiel, and the Argonne." In the Argonne Forest in early October of 1918, a machine-gun bullet from a German plane hit Street in the right leg. Awarded the Purple Heart for his wound, Gabby's days on the front lines came to an end.

Back in America after the war, he played and managed in the minor leagues for the next decade. *The Sporting News* offered two versions of how he came to St. Louis. In 1923, while managing in Joplin, Street recommended Tommy Thevenow to Rickey. The Cardinals signed the shortstop who later became one of the stars of the 1926 World Series. Rickey remembered the favor and promised to find Street a major league job. In another version of the story, owner Sam Breadon met Street in 1928 when Gabby was managing the Knoxville Smokies. The Cardinals had stopped in Tennessee after spring training. Impressed with his ability running the minor league team, Breadon offered him a job as a coach with the Cardinals the following season.[38]

In between those two events, Gabby came to a crossroads in his life. "Six years ago, I was just one of the drifters, pretty much of a has-been," he admitted in 1931. And once again, Rickey was there to offer advice. "I always liked a drink or two, maybe more. I'm not telling you any secret when I say I liked it too much for my own good. Branch Rickey knew it; told me I could be a first-class manager if I straightened out and got down to business." Street took his words to heart. "Somehow, this hit home."

As a coach with the Cardinals in 1929, Street had one job. "I was a babysitter. That's what Sam Breadon really hired me for." Street's babysitting duties meant keeping an eye on pitcher Grover Cleveland Alexander, another man who battled the bottle. "I got with the Cardinals only because they needed somebody to wheel old Alex around and keep him dry," Street once told the

Boston Globe's Jerry Nason. "I knew a few bartenders by their first name myself!"[39]

While Street may have known a few bartenders, Alexander knew even more. He proved to be quite elusive. Street lost track of him one day just a few hours before Alexander was scheduled to pitch. In a panic, he rushed to Breadon's office to tell him the news and offered to resign. "The season of 1929 had reached the middle stages when Street came to me and told me he wanted to quit," Breadon recounted. "He said he could not keep tab on Grover and that he felt he was not earning his salary as detective and guardian for Alex. However, I refused to accept his resignation."[40]

Street coached for a Cardinals team that won 78 games and finished in fourth place in the National League. It also featured one of the more unusual managerial carousels in team history. The previous year's team had won a pennant but not a single World Series game that October against the Yankees. Embarrassed by the sweep, Breadon had major league manager Bill McKechnie and minor league manager Billy Southworth swap jobs. Promoted from the Cardinals' top farm team in Rochester, Southworth lasted just 88 games in his first stint as Cardinals manager. In July, Breadon reversed his earlier decision. "I realize that I took the World Series last fall too much to heart," explaining why he brought McKechnie back.[41] But less than a month after returning, McKechnie announced he wanted to enter politics. He ran for tax collector in his hometown of Wilkinsburg, Pennsylvania, and stated he would retire from baseball if he won the Republican nomination. He lost the primary in September and returned to the Cardinals. Breadon now had mixed feelings about his manager. He felt bad for demoting him after winning a pennant in 1928, but also thought the team would be better off with a new pilot. He hesitatingly offered him a contract for 1930. "Why don't you wait awhile, Bill," Breadon asked him, "and see if you can't find something better somewhere else?" McKechnie took the advice and soon signed on to manage the Boston Braves.[42]

Street had managed the team for a game during the transition in July and for a few games in September when McKechnie left the team to campaign.[43] Breadon, an admirer of his coach, made the obvious choice. Street became the Cardinals seventh manager in five years when he signed a contract in October. The 47-year-old former major league catcher and World War I veteran had spent 26 seasons in professional baseball for 18 different teams before joining the Cardinals, the majority of them in the minor leagues. The only pennant-winning team he had been a part of was the 1922 Joplin Miners. His luck would soon change.

In his first two years as Cardinals manager, his club won two pennants and a World Series, meeting the Philadelphia A's in the World Series in back-to-back seasons. St. Louis players and sportswriters discovered Street had two passions: talking and tobacco. During train trips, "He'd sit back, smoke a pipe I bet was 100 years old, and tell stories," said Pepper Martin. "He was a first-class lobby-sitter, smoked a pipe furiously – loading it from a tobacco pouch the general dimensions of a lady's handbag – and punctuating his tales with atomic clouds of smoke," wrote the Boston Globe's Nason. "Street, a tireless storyteller, entertained the players nightly with his tales of war and romance, baseball and balderdash," remembered columnist Roy Stockton.

He was appropriately nicknamed Gabby, but not for the reason many imagined. "Down South, if you see a black boy and want him, and you don't know his name, you yell, 'Hey Gabby,'" Street said in 1930. "It works in St. Louis, too, and if you don't believe it, try it. To me, all black boys have been Gabby and I got my nickname from the use of that word, and not, as many commonly believed, because I am a chatterbox," said the man born in Alabama seventeen years after the end of the Civil War.[44]

Like many of the team's managers before him, Street discovered Breadon had a short leash. A year after winning the World Series, the Cardinals finished in sixth place. The following season, with the club just a game over .500 in late July, Breadon made the call. The owner replaced Street with Frankie Frisch, the club's longtime second baseman. "I am leaving with the best of feelings for Mr. Breadon," said Street. "He gave me a great chance when he made me manager, and I am grateful for it."[45]

He returned to the minor leagues, this time as manager only (before joining the Cardinals, he caught 72 games for the Knoxville Smokies at the age of 45), led the Browns for a single season in 1938, and served as the pilot of the ill-fated St. Louis entry in the National Professional Indoor Baseball League in the fall of 1939. (The St. Louis Pandas were part of an eight-team league that folded after just a month of play.)[46] He broke into broadcasting in 1940, calling Cardinals and Browns games with Ray Schmidt. In 1941, he joined France Laux and Cy Casper in describing games at Sportsman's Park. He later went to Kansas City to do radio work for the minor league Blues. In the spring of 1945, he joined Caray, his final broadcast partner.

The two men were born 32 years apart. One had played, coached, and managed in the big leagues, while the other was a rookie baseball broadcaster. Despite the differences, they quickly bonded. "We connected right away, almost instantly," Caray remembered. "We understood each other. I was young, I was inexperienced, but that never bothered Gabby, who had seen it all. He found it refreshing; he said it made him feel young again."[47]

During the baseball season, Street lived at the Melbourne Hotel, located at the intersection of Lindell Boulevard and Grand Avenue. Harry would pick him up every morning before a game. The duo would stop for food and drink at the end of the day. "That's how the relationship really grew," Harry recalled. "That's where the confidences were developed. Not at the ballpark. Not at work. But away from the ballpark. Over a ham sandwich and a beer. That's when Gabby did his most important teaching. That's when I learned the most important lessons."

Competing for listeners against France Laux and Johnny O'Hara on a rival station, Caray and Street managed to generate some early publicity for themselves. Reprising his Washington Monument moment in May of 1945, Gabby caught two of three balls dropped from the Civil Courts Building in St. Louis at the age of 63. He later called that moment – and not the one in D.C. – his greatest catch. "That was almost 40 years later and any man who thinks he is as good at 63 as he is at 26 better have his head examined." The event was part of a war bond drive that netted hundreds of thousands of dollars. Caray threw the balls off the building to his broadcast partner. "They had to strap me up on the roof to throw the ball," said Harry, "and I was scared to death."

At Sportsman's Park, the duo was among the pioneers who set the template for the modern broadcast; the professional announcer doing the play-by-play joined by an ex-jock who provided the color. "We showed how to put your broadcast team together – the main guy, me, aided by the former athlete – we did it the way you should," Caray said years later. *Look* magazine counted seven ex-jocks in the broadcast booth by 1950.[48] The one that caught columnist Don Meiklejohn's eye was Street. "He's pro-Cardinal from the word 'Scat' since he managed the Red Birds in the early '30s," he wrote, a description many would also apply to Caray. "Every ball hit by a Cardinal is hit 'like a bullet,' and he can rationalize a defeat by saying, 'Every game we lose in June, we don't have to lose in September.'"[49]

Street's deep experience in the game allowed him to see things others couldn't. From the broadcast booth, he could spot when pitchers indicated what they were about to throw. "There's one fellow in this league who grimly closes his lips as he is about to throw a fastball and opens his mouth when he tosses a curve," he once told Taylor Spink of *The Sporting News*. "If you have a pair of glasses [binoculars], bring them to the park some afternoon and keep them on the pitcher. You'll see many things that will astonish you."[50] Sometimes he didn't have to look at the pitcher. He once correctly called on the air several deliveries from Cardinals pitcher Murry Dickson just by focusing on the opponent's third-base coach. In a game against New York, Street noticed that every time Giants coach Red Kress put his hand to his mouth, Dickson was about to throw a curve.[51]

Caray and Street's on-air performances even won over some of their toughest critics, the St. Louis print media. "These two announcers have done a bang-up job throughout the season," raved the *Globe-Democrat* in a 1949 editorial, arguing the two men should be considered to broadcast the World Series. "The provincial East, of course, believes it has the best, as always," the paper added.[52] "The importance of the fine broadcasts of Harry and Gabby cannot be minimized," wrote Bob Burnes a year later. "Their commentary has made fans Cardinals conscious over a wide area."[53]

During broadcasts, "Gabby combined ... knowledge with a folksy, homespun philosophical charm," believed Caray. "If you had to compare him to a contemporary sportscaster, Tim McCarver would be the closest. Gabby could explain everything perfectly, but he could also make you laugh. He was just a natural."

"Gabby was one of the great storytellers of all time," stressed his other broadcast partner. "It used to be that, when rain interrupted a game, we would switch to the studios and play music until play was resumed," explained Miller. "Not with Gabby around. He could talk, telling stories and anecdotes for the greater part of an hour and seldom repeat himself."

Street could literally talk all day. "His supply of stories was so great that, on speaking trips, he could speak at a school assembly in the morning and tell stories that kids would enjoy. That noon, he would speak at a luncheon and tell stories for adult men and women, and then at night, he would speak at some stag banquet and tell some of the dirtiest sports stories you'd ever want to hear," Miller recounted.

A broadcast natural and a self-described "chatterbox," even Street had his limits. He and Caray once reconstructed a game between the Cardinals and Dodgers at Ebbets Field that lasted nearly three-and-a-half hours. Gabby, who enjoyed his cigars as much as a pipe, went through six stogies during the broadcast. Exhausting his vocal cords and his lungs, Street "said goodnight in sign language," according to one account. The next day, he had to have his dentures recapped.[54]

The years of smoking and drinking took their toll. In 1945, and again in 1949, Street underwent operations for cancer. The 1949 surgery kept him in the hospital for a month. Street had a malignant growth in his throat. While boarding a train in Chicago in August of 1950, he collapsed. An ambulance was scheduled to meet the train when it arrived in St. Louis to take him to the hospital. But Street recovered during the journey home, blamed the heat for his collapse and refused medical attention. He was on the air that night with Caray at Sportsman's Park.

In January of that year, Street was honored by his adopted hometown of Joplin. Gabby had made his offseason home in the southwestern Missouri city ever since he managed the Joplin Miners. In 1923, he married Lucinda Chandler in Joplin, where the couple raised two children.[55] They bought a southern plantation-style home, where Gabby could be seen every spring and fall tending to the garden or working in the yard.

He gave a speech on juvenile delinquency in 1937 that resonated with local leaders. The Downtown Lions Club in Joplin launched the Gabby Street Leagues for boys ten to sixteen, giving youth the opportunity to play organized baseball. Thirteen years later, the city said thanks, staging Gabby Street Day. The local school system canceled classes for the afternoon, giving 7,000 students the opportunity to attend a parade and the dedication of a new ballpark named in Street's honor. A city street was renamed Gabby Street Boulevard. That evening, 650 people paid $5 each for a banquet that honored Street, money that went toward expanding youth baseball. By 1950, some 4,000 Joplin boys had played in the leagues. "Gabby Street is the greatest thing that has happened in Joplin in 50 years," said Chamber of Commerce president William Markwardt.[56]

Caray emceed the evening event. He was part of a Cardinals contingent that arrived in Joplin from Saint Louis on a special Pullman car. Musial and other players such as Joe Garagiola, Red Schoendienst and Enos Slaughter also made the journey along with executives from Griesedieck Brothers. "I hope I may some day be one-tenth the catcher Gabby Street was, and one-sixty-fourth the man he is," Garagiola told the audience.[57] Many of the same people made an identical trip a little more than a year later, under dramatically different circumstances.

Street had traveled to Peoria for an old-timers baseball event in January of 1951. He became gravely ill by the time he returned home to Joplin and was immediately hospitalized. In addition to cancer concerns, he was battling a heart ailment that quickly escalated into pneumonia. By the end of the month, he had been placed in an oxygen tent and hospital visits were limited to immediate family. On February 2, Caray gave a speech in Terre Haute, Indiana, where he asked the crowd to stand in a moment of silent prayer for Street.

He died on February 6 at the age of 68. Pallbearers at his funeral three days later included Caray, former Cardinals outfielder Ray Blades, team scout Runt

Marr, and advertising executive Zahner. Also making the train trip from St. Louis were Ray Schmidt, Street's first broadcast partner, Ed Griesedieck and other executives from the brewery.[58]

On the day Street died, Caray showed up early at the KXOK studios to write a monologue on his mentor and describe to his audience the impact his broadcast partner had on his life. But every time he started to type, he'd stop, crumple up the paper, and throw it on the floor. Harold Neusitz, the public relations director for Griesedieck Brothers, was with Caray and described the broadcaster as being in a state of shock. By the time Harry was scheduled to go on the air at 5:45, he had nothing prepared. He just spoke from the heart.

"Since noon I have been fiddling with the typewriter, for if there is anybody who should be able to write a beautiful eulogy from the very core of his heart, it should be me. But I couldn't – I haven't been able to write a thing," Caray told his radio listeners. "I can't think of an important thing to write about Gabby Street. All that keeps running through my mind are a million miscellaneous things that could hardly be of interest to you – that loving laugh, for example; that philosophy of life. I was associated with Gabby going on seven years, but we didn't work a single day together. We just laughed, lived, and argued," he said. "I can't forget our many talks which would branch off into so many different facets – religion, politics, intimate personal problems," Caray confessed.

"The public will miss him, but I know that I will miss him far more. For he wasn't just a friend, he was almost a father – in fact, the closest thing to one I have known, and I am so happy tonight that he knew how I felt about him."[59]

Fifteen years later, Street was posthumously inducted into the Missouri Sports Hall of Fame. Once again, Caray spoke publicly about his first broadcast partner. "Gabby could talk because he lived through so much," he told the audience at the Tiger Hotel in Columbia. "To be able to have this man as my friend is the greatest thing that could have happened to me."[60]

*****

Miller continued to work with Caray for a few more seasons after Street's death. His busy St. Louis schedule ended a year after Anheuser-Busch bought the Cardinals. He was replaced on the broadcasts by a young announcer named Jack Buck. Stretch briefly did freelance media work in St. Louis before leaving to do television and radio in Peoria and write columns for the local paper, the *Journal Star*. For many seasons, he was the voice of Bradley University basketball. He also managed to return to St. Louis every year for the annual Elks Sports Celebrity Night. Miller had emceed the event in its early years (a role later assumed by Garagiola and then Buck). When Caray left the Cardinals after the 1969 season, Miller was among those contacted by KMOX executive Bob Hyland to see if he would be interested in the position. "But I begged off," Stretch revealed. "Told him I was too old." That same year, he broke a bone in his foot. Instead of healing, it gradually weakened. Concerned medical officials sent him to the Mayo Clinic in Rochester, Minnesota for a ten-day observation. Miller was diagnosed with Lou Gehrig's disease.[61]

He was honored with a "Stretch Miller Weekend" in St. Louis in 1971. Following a Saturday night reception, the wheelchair-bound Miller did some play-by-play on the Cardinals Sunday broadcast until rain interrupted the game. During the delay, Jack Brickhouse interviewed him for nearly half an hour on the Cubs telecast. Longtime friends he reminisced with on that emotional day included sportscaster Bob Buck (Jack's brother), France Laux, columnists Broeg and Burnes, Cardinals general manager Bing Devine, and Musial, who still remembered his son's birthday. "How's that November 21st son of yours?" Stan asked him.[62] (Miller's son, Bob, was born on Musial's birthday.)

At his final Elks Sports Celebrity Night banquet, Miller's wife had wheeled him out of the room at the end of the evening only to be confronted with a set of stairs. "We waited for a while and no one offered to help until Stan Musial and Red Schoendienst came along and without hesitation each grabbed a wheel and helped me up the stairs," Stretch remembered. "It was a typical performance by two men I have long contended are the finest gentlemen in baseball."

Miller passed away in October of 1972 at the age of 62.

---

[1] Caray, *Holy Cow!*
[2] John Ford directed Carey in 25 silent westerns. He made his film debut in 1908 and appeared in more than 300 movies in his career. He died in 1947 at the age of 69. A black widow spider bite was thought to be an aggravating condition. At his funeral, Burl Ives sang a cowboy ballad, and John Wayne recited his favorite poem. He was buried wearing cowboy boots, a black suit and a shoestring tie. His son, Harry Carey Jr., was also an actor.
[3] "When you are in Joliet, be sure and visit the 'Man on the Street' at the corner of Chicago and Van Buren." WCLS advertisement in *The Star* (Tinley Park, Illinois), July 18, 1941.
[4] *New York Times*, March 2, 2009.
[5] *St. Louis Post-Dispatch*, May 10, 1998.
[6] Ibid. Angel did on-air work for KXOK. She had answered an ad for the station looking for ideas around educational programming. Her future husband was the director of special projects.

[7] "All our big family gatherings were in Missouri," Paul Harvey Jr., the Harveys' only child, told *Missouri Life* magazine in 2017. The farm in Maries County, north of Rolla, had belonged to his mother's side of the family since the early 1800s. Shortly after her marriage, Angel Harvey's father gave the couple a farm in Franklin County. "I don't have much confidence in this radio thing," he told the newlyweds. "Now, when this radio thing fails, you'll have something to keep you going." But the place they cherished the most was their land in Jefferson County. "The dearest place to my parents on earth was a farm 18 miles south of St. Louis," Harvey Jr. said. They dubbed it "Reveille" in honor of their dog. Located just north of Kimmswick, the 300-plus acre farm was once described as "a collection of well-kept white buildings in the rolling green countryside. The bluffs of the Illinois shore, across the Mississippi River, are in the distance." Like his other two homes (one in suburban Chicago, the other in Phoenix), the Missouri farm was set up to handle broadcasts of "Paul Harvey News" and "The Rest of the Story." Son Paul Jr. wrote the scripts for "The Rest of the Story" for many years, a show that was Angel's idea. She was the first producer ever inducted into the Radio Hall of Fame. Angel Harvey passed away at the age of 92 in 2008. Paul Harvey died in 2009 at the age of 90. *Missouri Life*, April 14, 2017. *The Springfield News-Leader*, November 8, 2016. *St. Louis Post-Dispatch*, May 10, 1998. The Paul Harvey Jr. Museum is located inside the World's Largest Toy Museum Complex in Branson. It opened in 2016.

[8] WKZO radio went on the air in 1930. The television station debuted twenty years later. In 1986, Fetzer sold WKZO-TV and five other stations for $480 million. "Television turned things around for us," remembered Lee. *Kalamazoo Gazette*, June 1, 1989.

[9] Butera, Paul J., *Good Day! The Paul Harvey Story*. Regnery Publishing, Inc. 2009.

[10] Caray was not the first to use "Holy Cow!" on the air. By the 1930s, Halsey Hall was using the expression on Minneapolis radio, and so was Jack Holiday in New Orleans.

[11] *Alton Evening Telegraph*, February 3, 1960.

[12] Caray does not mention living or working in Grand Rapids in his autobiography. WKZO was often listed as a Kalamazoo-Grand Rapids station (the two cities are about 50 miles apart), but comments from Caray and early profiles make a distinction between the two cities. "After two years [in Joliet], he moved on to Kalamazoo and later to Grand Rapids, Michigan." *Globe-Gazette* (Mason City, Iowa), January 11, 1957. It is possible that Caray wanted to give the impression that he had more radio experience in more markets than he actually did. He was not beyond resume inflation. *The Sporting News* once noted that Caray was "active in sports at high school [true] and the University of Missouri [false]." *The Sporting News*, January 13, 1944.

[13] Harry didn't acknowledge any help in getting hired at KXOK. "I knocked on the door of every radio station in St. Louis. I handed out resumes and auditioned for anyone who was willing to listen." Caray, *Holy Cow!*

[14] "Bob Cochran, St. Louis golfer ... will be a special guest on Harry Caray's sports program over KXOK, the Star-Times station (630 kilocycles), this evening at 10:15 p.m." *St. Louis Star-Times*, July 27, 1943.

[15] *St. Louis Star-Times*, January 3, 1944. The man Caray replaced, Jerry Burns, was drafted.
[16] Stern broadcast the Columbia-Princeton college baseball game in May. The Reds-Dodgers broadcast at Ebbets Field occurred in August.
[17] Dunning, John. *On The Air: The Encyclopedia of Old-Time Radio*. Oxford University Press. 1998.
[18] "Much of Winchell's fortune was his voice," wrote Dick Cavett. "Sharp, tangy, forceful and dramatic, it produced goosebumps over the radio, where voice was all." *New York Times*, December 4, 2009. "With his gift for 'slanguage,' as Winchell called it, he either invented or popularized such terms as 'scram,' 'G-man,' 'pushover,' 'making whoopee,' 'infanticipate,' 'Reno-vated' (for a quickie Nevada divorce), and 'Ratzis' and 'swastinkas' (for Hitler acolytes)." https://www.thedailybeast.com/walter-winchells-ghost-still-haunts-a-media-biz-that-divides-america. Winchell later became the narrator of *The Untouchables* television crime series. He was the inspiration for Burt Lancaster's character in the movie *Sweet Smell of Success*.
[19] Gabler, Neal. *Walter Winchell: Gossip, Power, and the Culture of Celebrity*. Alfred A. Knopf, Inc. 1994.
[20] Early 1944 newspaper ads for the show indicate it aired at 10:45 p.m. after airing at 10:15 p.m. the previous year.
[21] Wolfe and Castle, *I Remember Harry Caray*.
[22] *Southern Illinoisan*, May 8, 1970.
[23] "The Chicago market was better for him," said Broeg. "And, I think by that time, he was wiser. He went there, in effect, with his hat in his hand, dealing with the press and got along admirably, which he hadn't done here." Wolfe and Castle, *I Remember Harry Caray*.
[24] He also broadcast some high school football games. In December of 1949, Caray went to Charleston, Missouri to call a game between Festus and Sikeston. Before 4,500 fans, Sikeston defeated Festus 14-0 in the Polio Bowl. Sikeston *Daily Standard*, December 2, 1949.
[25] Griesedieck died in March of 1955 at the age of 59. He had been suffering from a heart condition. He became president of the brewery in 1942 after the death of his brother, Robert Griesedieck. The Griesedieck family traced its brewing history back to Stromberg, Germany in the 1700s. They started making beer in the St. Louis area in the 1850s.
[26] Miller, C.A. "Stretch:" *"One Guy Called Me Stench."* Illinois Graphics, Inc. 1972.
[27] Ibid. As a bellboy, Miller once delivered ice to Ruth's room. Instead of getting a tip, Ruth told him to contact the team's traveling secretary for free tickets. When he knocked on the door of the traveling secretary and made the request, the Yankee official called Ruth to say he was out of tickets. Ruth replied that he hadn't received any bellhop service that day, and the kid was lying. "What could I do?" wrote Miller. "It was my word against the great Ruth's. So I didn't get the ticket, but Ruth lost a fan."

[28] Ibid. According to Miller, Roosevelt began his address by saying, "My friends of BLOOMINGDALE."

[29] In his autobiography, Caray describes Zahner as "a little Napoleonic type of guy, about 5'6", with a tiny bristle of a mustache and a real brisk, all-business kind of walk. He was a great executive, and he was used to getting his way. He ran his office with an iron fist."

[30] Miller's pregame show included "baseball gossip, and 'Mystery Man' and 'Controversy of the Month' contests." *The Sporting News*, April 21, 1948.

[31] Some accounts list Street with a birth month of February or the year as 1883. Findagrave.com has a picture of his tombstone with the date of September 30, 1882. https://www.findagrave.com/memorial/13263215/charles-street

[32] *The Sporting News*, October 2, 1930.

[33] *St. Louis Post-Dispatch*, September 16, 1931. The article, part of a 12-part series on Street, was written by *Associated Press* sports editor Alan Gould. Street received a $500 prize for catching the ball on the morning of August 21, 1908. He caught Walter Johnson's 3-1 victory over the Detroit Tigers that afternoon. "Looking up was no good," he once explained regarding the monument catch. "I got a crick in my neck. Somebody suggested that I keep my head down and he [the person assisting him] would tell me when to reach out and grab the ball. We had a couple of dry runs on that and a couple of people almost got beaned, including me. Finally, we were down to the 13th ball. When it was about 50 feet from the ground, the guy who was helping me – and had a C-note bet – hollered. I looked up and the ball smacked in my mitt. It knocked me down, but I held on to it." *The Anniston Star*, February 8, 1951.

[34] A newspaper report that day estimated the ball was travelling at a rate of 135 feet a second. *The Evening Star* (Washington D.C.), August 21, 1908. According to Taylor Spink of *The Sporting News*, the ballistics department of the Army later calculated the speed of the ball at 240 feet a second or 290 miles an hour. *The Sporting News*, August 20, 1947. A speed of 240 feet per second is actually 163.636 miles an hour. "Though it was announced at first that Street's catch was the first ever made off the monument, it later developed that William (Pop) Schriver, a Chicago National catcher, had performed the same trick 14 years earlier. Billy Sullivan [White Sox catcher] and a few others matched the feat later on." *The Sporting News*, February 14, 1951.

[35] *St. Louis Post-Dispatch,* September 21, 1931. Street actually played far more games in 1908 and 1909 (131 and 137) than he did the next two seasons Johnson references (89 and 72).

[36] Street believed Cobb was the greatest all-around player he ever saw. "He could do everything, and what a terror he was on attack! He had a 90-horsepower brain that nobody in the game could keep up with," he said. "Ballplayers and fans never really understood Cobb. He was a Jekyll and Hyde personality. Some days, he was a great guy, easy to get along with. Others, you couldn't go near him." Ibid. September 24, 1931.

[37] Ibid. September 23, 1931.

38 *The Sporting News*, February 14, 1951.
39 *Boston Globe*, February 7, 1951.
40 *St. Louis Star-Times*, August 10, 1931. According to Sid Keener, Alexander was scheduled to pitch that day but never showed up. "A sprinkle of rain arrived at 2 o'clock that afternoon and the game was canceled. It was postponed because Alex was not around to pitch, and not because of the damp condition of the playing field, although the official announcement was to the effect that rain had caused the cancellation."
41 *St. Louis Post-Dispatch*, July 23, 1929.
42 *The Standard Union* (Brooklyn, NY), October 8, 1929. McKechnie was elected to the Hall of Fame in 1962. His major league managerial career included time in Pittsburgh, St. Louis, Boston, and Cincinnati. His teams won four pennants and two Word Series titles – 1925 with the Pirates and 1940 with the Reds. He remains the only manager to win National League pennants with three teams.
43 McKechnie lost to the incumbent. He received just 1,329 votes out of 4,705 votes cast.
44 *The Sporting News*, October 2, 1930.
45 Although Street had warm feelings toward Breadon, he had a different opinion of Frisch. "I hope he has plenty of trouble, the so-and-so," he said in August of 1934. "Frisch caused me plenty of gray hairs and he's got a lot of them coming. And he'll get them too, so I can get some satisfaction out of knowing that things always even up in the end." Street believed Frisch played an instrumental role in getting him ousted from the manager's job. *Los Angeles Times*, August 31, 1934. Frisch denied the charge and claimed he tried talking Breadon into keeping Street until the end of the season. "I did not think I was ready yet to become manager," Frisch told columnist Joe Falls.
46 Although called a baseball league, the teams were playing an indoor version of softball. "It is played much the same as softball," wrote reporter W.J. McGoogan. "The ball is 12 inches in circumference with outside seams, and is stamped 'Official League Softball.' The bat is a softball bat. Pitchers throw underhanded. Bases are 60 feet apart and the pitching box 42 feet from home plate." *St. Louis Post-Dispatch*, November 28, 1939. Home games were played at the St. Louis Arena. A general admission ticket was 40 cents. Wrote one critic: "If this is baseball, some evening we are going to invite some of the boys over in our basement for a game of 'regulation' football." *The Washington Missourian*, December 7, 1939. Although an eight-team league, only seven teams actually played games. The Chicago franchise never organized. The St. Louis Pandas played six contests and lost five of them. The league dissolved on December 22, 1939. Hall of Fame baseball player Tris Speaker was league president.
47 Caray, *Holy Cow!*
48 Other former jock announcers were Dizzy Dean, Harry Heilmann, Waite Hoyt, Bump Hadley, Mickey Heath, and Jack Graney. Graney was the first. "From 1932 until advancing age and the demanding schedule of major league baseball forced his exit

from radio, Jack Graney was THE voice of the Cleveland Indians," wrote Ted Patterson. http://research.sabr.org/journals/jack-graney

[49] *The Pomona Progress Bulletin*, July 5, 1950.

[50] *The Sporting News*, August 20, 1947. "Being a catcher, I suppose I have made a special study of that [pitch-tipping]," Street said with a smile. "A catcher can always tell – if he is a smart catcher – what the pitcher is throwing, even if he does not have a sign."

[51] Ibid, May 21, 1947.

[52] *St. Louis Globe-Democrat*, September 14, 1949.

[53] Ibid, June 13, 1950.

[54] *The Sporting News*, May 26, 1948. Decades later, Caray would work with Steve Stone, another former player who would smoke cigars in the booth.

[55] Street's son, Charles E. Street Jr., received the Distinguished Flying Cross in 1953. A Marine jet fighter pilot, he flew 93 missions during the Korean War.

[56] *The Sporting News*, February 14, 1951.

[57] *Joplin Globe,* January 20, 1950.

[58] Just two months after attending Street's funeral, Schmidt passed away at the age of 44. Suffering from a liver ailment, he died on May 23 in a St. Louis hospital. Street's will, revealed in probate court just a few days after his funeral, left the vast bulk of his estate to his wife. It had been signed in 1931 and witnessed by Jim Bottomley and Chick Hafey.

[59] *The Daily Standard* (Sikeston, Mo.), March 2, 1951.

[60] *The Sporting News*, November 5, 1966.

[61] *Alton Evening Telegraph*, March 6, 1970. "I told him [Hyland] I was too old," the 59-year-old Miller told columnist Jim Bell. "And then what happens? They hire Jim Woods, who must be in his mid to late fifties."

[62] Bob Buck was Jack's younger brother. Before joining KMOX-TV (now KMOV) in 1971, he worked as the sports director of a television station in Peoria.

The Rookies of '45, The Battles of '46

The year 1945 marked the beginning of Caray's baseball broadcasting career, the end of a war, and the changing of the guard in baseball's ruling regime. Peace and the death of Commissioner Landis the prior year greatly accelerated changes to the sport. "Baseball, not unlike American society, would never be the same," wrote William Marshall, author of *The Pivotal Years 1945-1951*. "The winds of change were already carrying the seeds that would alter baseball's physical, economic, and social makeup. Landis's death was the beginning of a new era."

Both players and owners embraced the opportunities in this new era. Things unimaginable before the war quickly became a reality. Players tried and failed to unionize but banded together long enough to extract concessions from owners in 1946, receiving a minimum salary of $5,000 and a pension plan that paid $50 a month (for five years of service) or $100 a month (for ten years of service) for retired players. (Cardinals shortstop Marty Marion was instrumental in getting the plan started.) That same year, Mexican owners tempted American players to join them south of the border. Dozens of them did, including a few Cardinals.[1] A year later, a handful of black players in the United States joined their white counterparts on the same major league fields.

Branch Rickey led the charge in breaking baseball's color barrier when he signed Jackie Robinson. His one-time protégé, and now Yankees president Larry MacPhail, had a decidedly different view on the subject. "There are few, if any, Negro players who could qualify for play in the major leagues at this time," MacPhail concluded just weeks before Robinson signed with Brooklyn. Writing about baseball owners of this era, columnist Dan Parker saw two distinctive camps, the "Young Turks and their Old Guard predecessors."[2]

Those dividing lines between the two weren't always clear. While MacPhail and Rickey disagreed on black players in the major leagues, both men went to court to prevent players from fleeing to Mexico. Alone among owners, Sam Breadon took the time to meet with the men who controlled Mexican baseball, drawing a $5,000 fine and the ire of baseball's new commissioner, Happy Chandler. (The fine was later rescinded.)

Baseball's Old Guard looked to the game's past for guidance. Since the Black Sox scandal from a quarter-century earlier, officials remained haunted by the specter of gambling. Cardinals prospect Hooper Triplett received a lifetime ban in August of 1946 for betting on games. "Gamblers damned near ruined the game once and if they bore in again, they will finish it," MacPhail told Chandler.

The game was changing in ways large and small. When it came time to travel, teams now had choices. After the fifth game of the 1946 World Series, the Cardinals took a train back to St. Louis. Red Sox players left Boston on an airplane. That season, the Yankees became the first club to charter flights for all away games. Broadcasters began traveling as well. Mel Allen became the first announcer to provide live descriptions of all road contests.[3] Re-creations, like train trips, were slowly fading away.[4]

Day games were also disappearing from the calendar, nowhere more than in St. Louis.[5] The Browns and Cardinals led the charge for more night baseball in the 1940s. The 1945 Cardinals scheduled 46 of their 77 home games under the lights, including every single weekday game. The Browns' schedule featured 43 night games.[6] (By contrast, Rickey's Dodgers planned seven games under the lights. Across all of baseball, 236 night games were scheduled, with games in St Louis representing 38 percent of the total.)

Night or day, trains or planes, segregated or integrated, the pace of change to American life in the immediate aftermath of the war was confusing and challenging to many, including the most powerful man on the planet. "I find Sherman was wrong," President Truman said in December of 1945. "Peace is hell."

*****

"The United States emerged from the Second World War a giant among midgets. A country with 7 percent of the world's population produced 42 percent of its manufactured goods, 43 percent of its electricity, 57 percent of its steel, 62 percent of its oil, and 80 percent of its cars," wrote authors Alan Greenspan and Adrian Wooldridge. "For twenty-five years after the war, the economy boomed." Greenspan and Woolridge called this era the "Golden Age of Growth."[7] Baseball owners in St. Louis didn't get the memo, approaching this new period as if a return to the Great Depression was imminent.

Cardinals owner Breadon was busy selling players. Brothers Mort and Walker Cooper threatened to hold out for more money after each signed to play the 1945 season for $12,000. Breadon responded by selling both. He sold staff ace Mort first, dispatching him to the Boston Braves in May for pitcher Red Barrett and $60,000. After the deal, *The Sporting News* noted that player sales over the previous two decades had netted the Cardinals $850,000.[8]

Over the years, so many St. Louis players made their way to the National League squad in Boston, the team became known as the "Cape Cod Cardinals."[9]

But many of the player sales had taken place when Rickey was running the farm system, stockpiling talent, and building for the future. Breadon had cut back on minor league investments and was now eating his seed corn. Like a magician with a favorite trick, Breadon looked to pull cash out of a hat seemingly every season. The next year, catcher Walker Cooper was sold to the New York Giants for $175,000.[10]

Less than a year after winning their first and only American League pennant in St. Louis, the man who ran the Browns was busy selling out. In a surprise move (columnist Sid Keener called it a "startling transaction"), team president Don Barnes sold all his stock in August of 1945 to Richard Muckerman, who had steadily been acquiring an interest in the team over the past several seasons.[11] With the additional shares, Muckerman now controlled 56 percent of the stock in the franchise and became team president.[12] Barnes was now out of baseball. He would be remembered as the man who almost moved the Browns to Los Angeles.[13] Over the next decade, the Browns would be sold three more times and leave St. Louis.

It was these two franchises, one whose reign of dominance was about to end, and the other whose time in St. Louis would soon expire, that Caray described every day from April to September from his perch in the Sportsman's Park broadcast booth. The rookie baseball broadcaster, who owed his start in St. Louis partly to vision issues, would make his debut alongside two rookie players; one who nearly lost an eye and the other who lost an arm.

*****

The Browns 1945 season is best remembered for a single player and his missing right arm. Pete Gray benefitted from his talent – hit .333 as the Southern League MVP in 1944 – and war-depleted rosters across baseball. An *Associated Press* survey found 79 percent of the 1941 opening day lineups were now either in the armed services or employed as essential workers.

Gray lost his right arm in an accident when he was six years old. He fell off a truck and got his arm stuck in the wheel. After being rushed to the hospital, Gray's right arm was amputated above the elbow. The right-handed Gray then taught himself how to throw and bat lefthanded. "His left arm was overbuilt – almost as big as my thigh," a former batboy once recalled.[14] By the age of 16, Gray was earning $100 a week playing semi-pro ball for teams near his hometown of Nanticoke, Pennsylvania. His first audition for professional baseball came for the other St. Louis team. "The first pro team I ever tried out for was the St. Louis Cardinals," Gray recalled years later. "They held a camp in Minersville. I still remember they gave me No. 48."[15] Gray's performance didn't earn him a contract with the Cardinals. Undeterred, he hopped on a bus to Hot

Springs, Arkansas and Ray Doan's baseball camp. A skeptical Doan became a true believer after Gray caught every ball hit to him. Doan tried to get Gray a job with a Class D minor league team, but the conversations would always end abruptly. "He'd say, 'I got this one-armed outfielder named Gray,' but they'd scream back, 'Are you nuts?' and hang up real quick," Pete once told a sportswriter.[16]

He returned to semi-pro baseball, where in New York his performance for the Bay Parkways caught the attention of *Newsweek* magazine. The publication stressed that Gray played "not because of his box office value as a curiosity but because he really is an asset." (Gray was hitting .449 at the time.)[17] He broke into professional baseball in 1942, and after his banner year in the Southern League two years later, the Browns paid $20,000 for him to play in St. Louis.

Gray's first big league game was Caray's first major league broadcast. The defending American League champions opened their season at Sportsman's Park. (The Cardinals played that day at Wrigley Field.) On the same day Griesedieck Brothers bought ads in the local papers touting "Play-By-Play Nite and Day with Harry Caray and Gabby Street" on their seven-station network, Gray started in left field and batted second against Detroit. The Browns beat the Tigers 7-1 on a cool spring day, with Gray getting his first big-league hit and scoring a run.

Adding Gray to a team coming off a World Series appearance, the Browns saw dollar signs. "Because the Browns have won a pennant and because they have in Pete Gray, the one-armed outfielder, one of the best box-office attractions in the business, they are being besieged with requests for exhibition games," columnist Roy Stockton noted shortly before the season began.[18]

"Pete Gray Browns' Greatest Drawing Card Since Sisler" read a headline in the *Washington Post* the following month.[19] While the story largely praised the Browns outfielder, it also noted that "on ground balls he does appear at a slight disadvantage. The fraction of a second he needs to shed his glove and grasp the ball for the return to the infield might provide a break for a fast base runner."

Years later, some of his teammates would seize on Gray's shortcomings and blame him for the team's third-place finish. "We would have won the pennant again if it hadn't been for Pete Gray," believed former Browns infielder Ellis Clary.[20] "Pete did great with what he had. But he cost us the pennant in 1945," said teammate Mark Christman.[21] Statistics don't support those contentions. While Gray clearly struggled against big-league pitching – .218 batting average with no home runs and 13 RBI – he only played in 77 of the team's 151 games and just 64 contests in the outfield. (The other 13 were as a pinch-hitter or pinch-runner.) In the 54 games he started, the Browns' record was 33-21 (winning percentage of .611). The team's tally when he was not in the starting lineup was 48-49.

While Browns officials would stress they would never exploit Gray – "Luke" [Sewell] would never play Gray merely for the sake of his possible value as a gate attraction," general manager Bill DeWitt said before the season – skeptics in the press and on his own team, Sewell included, thought otherwise. "When I got him, I knew he couldn't make it," the manager recalled. "He didn't belong in the major leagues, and he knew he was being exploited. Just a quiet fellow, and he had an inferiority complex. They were trying to get a gate attraction in St. Louis."[22]

"The pitchers didn't want Gray out there," said Clary. "Nobody did. He was strictly for show, to draw some fans." Gray's addition to the roster sparked resentment among some of his teammates who called him a "bush bastard" and picked on him mercilessly. "Them guys would think up shit to pull all the time," Clary remembered. "And they tortured him, teased him all the damn time."

Gray's fear of being exploited extended to the offseason. A Hollywood executive offered him $15,000 for a movie about his life story, but he turned it down because of a specific request. They wanted Gray – who was bald – to wear a hairpiece. "Gray said, 'I won't do it. No dice,'" recalled DeWitt. He did play in a postseason barnstorming tour in California arranged by Browns traveling secretary Charley DeWitt. "We played eight games against the [Pacific] Coast League All-Stars and I got $1,000 a game plus all my expenses," said Gray. "I made more in two weeks than all year for the Browns, but I got homesick and went home."

Regardless of how his teammates received him, Gray's impact resonated far beyond the Browns. "Gray was seen as an inspiration for thousands of veterans maimed in the war, and he visited Walter Reed Army Hospital in Washington to meet with amputees," wrote Richard Goldstein in *The New York Times*. "He was also a role model for handicapped youngsters."[23]

One of those handicapped youngsters was Nelson Gary Jr. The California native was just two years old when he lost his right arm in an accident. Two years later, he was in St. Louis to watch Gray perform for the Browns. "I'm gonna be a ballplayer just like Pete," Gary Jr. told a reporter. "I got a bat and a ball and a uniform and I'm a right fielder." During his St. Louis visit, Gary sat on Gray's lap while being interviewed on a local radio station. The next day's *Star-Times* pictured Gary, Gray, and a beaming KXOK host. Caray's arm was draped around the shoulder of the four-year-old boy.[24]

"Pete Gray has done something for Gary that doctors could not do," said the boy's father. "He has taught him to attain balance – by kicking a football" (with his right foot), adding that the exercise "did wonders." Gray had also told the child to carry things across his shoulders to help his balance and build strength. A later x-ray of the boy's spine surprised his doctor. "He had expected to find a curvature," said Gary Sr. "It was so perfectly straight he was amazed."

The younger Gary, who wanted to be called "Pete," went on to play high school and college baseball as an outfielder, just like his hero. Playing for Occidental College in 1962, his successful squeeze bunt drove in the winning run in the deciding game that gave the Tigers a conference championship.

"We get a lot of mail from servicemen who have lost an arm or leg and from their parents, too," Gary's father said in 1945. "They all mention Pete Gray."

*****

Absence defined the 1945 Cardinals roster, with the team's stars scattered around the globe. Stan Musial spent the year in the Navy, playing baseball in Hawaii. Enos Slaughter was on the Pacific island of Tinian when the *Enola Gay* took off on its fateful mission to Hiroshima. Terry Moore was stationed in Panama and Harry Walker was racing across Europe with General George Patton's Third Army. "Sometimes we'd be 30 or 40 miles back of the German lines just like the scouts in the Old West," Walker remembered.[25]

That spring, heavy rains and a rising Ohio River flooded Cotter Field in Cairo, the Cardinals' wartime spring training home. Batting practice stopped. Fishing in the infield began. Owner Breadon moved the team back to St. Louis to finish preparations for the season. It marked the first time since 1919 that the Cardinals conducted spring training in their hometown.

Despite a challenging spring and numerous losses to the military, the Cardinals got good news when a promising prospect was discharged from the Army. A *Post-Dispatch* profile in March called him Al (short for Albert), but Cardinals fans would know him as Red. Before joining the Army, Red Schoendienst led the International League in hitting with a .337 average at Rochester. He returned to the minor league team in 1944, but played in just 25 games before Uncle Sam came calling. But the Germantown, Illinois native, who had been hit in the eye with a nail while building fences as a teenager, had his military duty cut short when his eye ailment resurfaced.

When he was discharged from the Army, the vision in Red's left eye was estimated at 20/100. The Cardinals had him work with Dr. Alvin Mueller (brother of former Cardinals outfielder Heinie Mueller). The eye doctor used heat applications and vision exercises to bring Schoendienst's vision to 20/40. "What possibilities that boy would have if he had complete vision," said manager Southworth. "There is no telling how far he could go. Even so, he seems destined for a great career."[26] Appearing primarily as an outfielder, Schoendienst hit .278 and stole a league-high 26 bases for a Cardinals team that won 95 games.

Unlike Gray, who never appeared in the big leagues again after 1945, Schoendienst enjoyed a nearly two-decade career. He also battled eye problems for years. "He had to go twice a day in the winter to the eye doctor," his wife, Mary, recalled years later.[27] He experimented with eyeglasses in 1955 but announced after the season he was abandoning them, opting for additional eye exercises. He also contended with a chronically sore shoulder. Team physician Dr. Robert Hyland had diagnosed him with a shallow shoulder socket early in his career.

The Cardinals traded him to the New York Giants in 1956, who sent him to Milwaukee a year later. Schoendienst would enjoy two pennants and one World Series title with the Braves. He hit .300 in the 1958 Series against the Yankees despite being sick. Weeks later, he was diagnosed with tuberculosis. "Under the circumstances, there is grave doubt that the Redhead will ever play again," Bob Wolf wrote in *The Sporting News*.[28]

Schoendienst proved the skeptics wrong. He spent five months in the hospital, but returned for a handful of games in 1959. He later returned to the Cardinals as a player and coach, making his last appearance on the field in 1963. Caray was there for his first at-bat at Sportsman's Park and his last game as a big leaguer. By the time Harry left St. Louis, Red had added two more pennants and a World Series title to his resume, this time as a manager. Both men briefly worked for Charlie Finley's Oakland A's in the 1970s (Schoendienst was a coach in 1977 and 1978) and were honored in Cooperstown on the same day in 1989.[29] "Harry, we're still going strong," Schoendienst said at his Hall of Fame induction ceremony speech.

The 1980s also saw a rejuvenation of appreciation for Gray and his relationship with the boy who also lost his right arm in an accident. Gary's visit to St. Louis in 1945 was his second time seeing Gray. The year before, at the age of three, Gary and his family traveled to Tennessee to watch him play for the Memphis Chicks. The visits became a summertime ritual.[30] A picture of the pair hung at the Hall of Fame. ABC turned the relationship into a movie in 1986. *A Winner Never Quits* explored their inspiring story and the longtime connection between the duo. Keith Carradine portrayed Gray and Huckleberry Fox Jr. played Gary in the television movie a critic described as "filled with warmth and heart." The producer of the film grew up with Gary. James Keach's older brother had played high school baseball with him in California. To convince the publicity-shy Gray to get on board with the project, Keach showed up unannounced at the Nanticoke, Pennsylvania tavern Gray was known to haunt. The visit sparked a five-hour conversation between the television producer and the former player. "My argument to him was this," Keach said. "Don't you want people to appreciate your triumph in your own lifetime?"[31]

Gray's lifetime extended another sixteen years.[32] He died in 2002 at the age of 87. After the Browns, he spent four seasons in the minor leagues before returning to his hometown, where he lived a quiet, unassuming life and received occasional questions from kids as to how a man with one arm could play in the major leagues. "I'd just look at them and say, 'You know, son, there's a lot of guys with two good arms that don't make it.'"

*****

During this era of transition, some things remained constant. The National and American Leagues, born 25 years apart, had separate histories and unique identities. Just as in seasons before and decades to come, the rivals preferred competition over cooperation. When the Yankees sold pitcher Hank Borowy to the Chicago Cubs for $100,000 in 1945, MacPhail was criticized by fellow owner Clark Griffith for diluting the talent of the American League. "We ought to keep our own stars in our own league," said Griffith.[33] MacPhail's decision impacted the pennant race in the rival circuit, a battle that came down to the Cardinals and Cubs. Borowy beat the Cardinals three times in September. Chicago finished three games ahead of St. Louis.

There was another factor. As the two-team race for the pennant developed late in the season, Breadon spoke confidently about his team's chances. "We're gaining speed and it looks like the Cubs are faltering," Breadon told a reporter. "Anyhow, I've made [World Series] reservations for the Cardinals in both Detroit and Washington." That same week, rainouts in a series against Brooklyn led Breadon to schedule a doubleheader on a Friday, with the Dodgers due in Chicago for a series against the Cubs the following day. An angry Dodgers team swept the doubleheader. Critics circled in on the owner's decision that backfired. "That may well have been the clincher," wrote Arthur Daley in *The New York Times*, "and the money-conscious Breadon may have muscled himself out of some World Series swag."[34]

Despite no postseason play, the business of baseball marked a banner year in St. Louis. The 1945 season represented the first since 1928 in which the local teams' combined attendance exceeded one million. The Cardinals drew 595,220 and the Browns attracted 482,986 to Sportsman's Park. The numbers were even better on the road, with 870,452 coming out to ballparks to see the Cardinals and 737,370 turning out to watch the Browns. The road figure for the

Browns was just 7,644 fewer than the pennant-winning team of the previous year. "Pete Gray did his bit in holding up the 1945 figures to last year's levels," wrote Fred Lieb in *The Sporting News*.

For the Cardinals, Breadon declared a $3 a share dividend for the third straight year, money that largely went into his pockets. (He owned approximately 77 percent of the team.) With the sale of the Browns and both teams coming off a profitable season, baseball officials saw stability in St. Louis. "There is no longer serious talk of moving either of the St. Louis clubs," Yankees president MacPhail said in September.[35]

Breadon was at the peak of his power and popularity in the mid-1940s. He served on the Committee of Ten, the owners charged with writing a new major league agreement, and on baseball's four-man nominating committee, tasked with finding the new commissioner.[36]

Considered more press-shy and reserved than his one-time lieutenant Rickey, Breadon felt increasingly comfortable giving his opinion on various topics. When manager Southworth left the Cardinals after the 1945 season to manage the Boston Braves, Breadon touted his replacement, Eddie Dyer. "I consider him the best judge of young ballplayers in the country, which makes him priceless at times like this," Breadon said, referring to Dyer's experience managing in the minor leagues and the blitz of players coming home for the 1946 season. "When Rickey was younger, I believed he was the best judge of young ballplayers in the country, but today I think that distinction goes to Dyer," Breadon believed. "When Rickey left the club in 1942, a lot of persons thought it would probably be the end of the Cardinals as a factor and the end of Breadon's luck."[37]

The end of the Cardinals as a factor and the end of Breadon's luck happened sooner than anyone expected. Caray's good fortunes were just beginning. At the end of the season, Griesedieck Brothers again took out an ad in the local papers. "Thank You Fans ... for your fine reception of our baseball broadcasts this year," the ad began. "You have shown you appreciate the interesting, enthusiastic style in which Harry Caray brings the game to you," stated the sponsor.

But not everyone was sold on Caray's style. "When Harry first started, he kind of talked a little fast," remembered Bea Higgins. "And the people at the brewery, I remember them calling my boss [Oscar Zahner] and saying, 'I don't think he's going to work. He talks a little bit fast.' My boss said, 'No. He's good. He's got something. Just hang in there.' And, of course, he turned out to be right." Higgins worked as Caray's personal secretary for twenty-five years, doing double duty at first when she was an employee of the advertising agency that handled Griesedieck Brothers. She eventually quit that job and worked for Caray full-time. Early in his career, Caray told her there were always two things he wanted to buy if he had money – a suit of clothes from an exclusive men's shop and a convertible. "And he got them both," she recalled. A big part of her job was handling the considerable volume of mail Caray received. She would read the letters. So would Harry. Every single missive. "He was a fan's person and I know with the mail, he read every letter and signed every letter. And he'd get upset if a fan didn't like him because he wanted to be liked."

Evidence of Caray's popularity with the fans could be seen in how the radio competition responded after the 1945 season. The Hyde Park Brewing Company ended its broadcast sponsorship. Falstaff reemerged as a promoter and swapped out France Laux for another familiar and popular voice. St. Louis baseball fans now had a new choice to make when it came time to listen to baseball games on the radio: Harry Caray or Dizzy Dean?[38]

*****

When the Cardinals celebrated "Dizzy Dean Day" at Sportsman's Park in September of 1933, the pitcher received a new Buick Coupe, purchased by a group of grateful fans.[39] After the contest, thousands loitered outside Sportsman's Park, hoping to give their hero another round of applause. But Dean wanted no part of it. Dizzy jumped 15 feet from a clubhouse window to the street below in order to escape the adoration.[40]

Confident and boisterous in public, Dean was always more reserved (and grammatical) in private. While he craved the spotlight, he also had moments like the day in St. Louis, where he preferred privacy to praise. "Dizzy had two personalities," believed Eldon Auker, who opposed Dean and the Cardinals in the World Series as a member of the Detroit Tigers and pitched for the Browns when Dizzy began his broadcasting career. "The rest of the world saw the more colorful Dizzy Dean, the one the media preserved for eternity. In reality, he was as refined a gentleman as I ever looked at from across the table," Auker wrote in his autobiography.[41]

Like Caray in later years, who would line up beer bottles on the ledge of the broadcast booth in view of the fans, Dean wanted to present the appearance of enjoying his sponsor's products when the reality was quite different. "I never did see Dizzy drink a beer, certainly not at his house anyway, but he was happy to say he drank Falstaff regularly," Auker said. "He wasn't only a great pitcher, but a great pitchman."

Buddy Blattner shared Auker's view. "Diz liked to feed the impression that he liked to drink," stated Dean's broadcast partner in the 1950s. "Well, I never saw Diz take a drop prior to or during a game in all my years with him." On a

Friday night before a weekend broadcast, Dean preferred the privacy of his hotel room. "On the 'Game of the Week,' we'd get in a town on Friday, and Diz would get a suite and he wouldn't leave," Blattner remembered. "We'd even have dinner up there. So there were conflicts. And America still thought of him, nonetheless, as a wild man, a harmless, lovable wild man, drinking and eating up a storm."[42]

Dean also shared Caray's sense of theatrics and always knew when he was on the stage. Put a camera, recorder, or notebook in front of him, and the shy, reserved Dizzy would disappear. Dean and a reporter proved a perfect match – one had plenty of lines and the other had plenty of quotes for the next day's edition. Dizzy's favorite topic was always Dizzy, but he also found time on occasion to mention his brother, stories of games long since passed, and salary battles with Breadon and Rickey.

With his brother Paul pitching at the Cardinals farm team in Houston, Dean called on Breadon to bring him up during the late stages of the 1942 pennant race. "With me up here broadcasting and Paul down there throwin'em in, how could we lose?" he asked. A year later, when the Army rejected him for military service because of an impaired eardrum, he told reporters the military had made a big mistake. "If they had only tooken [sic] me in, this here war would be over in less time than I ever spent listening to a speech by Branch Rickey."

Even when he wasn't talking about himself, others were. "Let me tell you something," Frankie Frisch said in 1944. "Diz should be in the big leagues right now." Dean's former manager believed he could still play as a first baseman. "The guy really was a natural."[43] (Frisch would repeat the claim in 1959. "He could hit, was a good runner, and a great fielder.")[44]

Grantland Rice once asked Joe DiMaggio about the best-pitched game he had ever seen. "That's easy," the outfielder replied. "It was the game Dizzy Dean pitched against the Yankees in the 1938 World Series." Dean's style with the Cubs had changed dramatically since his arm injury the year before with the Cardinals. "He was a crippled duck now. He had no arm," remembered the Yankee Clipper. "So what happens? Here comes these dinky-dinks floating up to the plate. No speed at all. Not much of a curve. Just a shot put. But they would come at tough spots. Low and inside – around your shoulders – just balls you don't like. Balls that are hard to hit solidly," DiMaggio told Rice. "This game convinced me that Dizzy Dean was one of the greatest of all time. Think what he must have been when he had his arm. I'm glad I was in the other league when he was right."[45]

While his arm was no longer healthy, Dean still had plenty of verbal fastballs to offer reporters. In the spring of 1946, Dean regaled a Boston reporter with a story of the time he met Red Sox owner Tom Yawkey. "It was at a victory celebration [after the 1934 World Series] and nobody was feeling any pain," Dean recalled. "You're just the kind of ballplayer I'd like to have," Dean said Yawkey told him. "I'd pay a half-million bucks if I could get you. I think Tom was serious and not talking through his beer. And I sure wish he could have bought me because I'd still be pitching and be in my prime dragging down about $40,000 a year and not working for peanuts like I used to with the Cardinals. That Yawkey is a great guy."[46]

In a single interview, Dean managed to recapture the glories of the past, imagine a greatness still to come, and take a swipe at the stinginess of the Cardinals. It was the perfect Dizzy story.

Unlike his counterpart, media mentions of Caray in 1946 were rare. No reporters asked for his opinion, any criticisms he offered were not covered, and any controversial comments were still to come. Press coverage of the broadcaster focused on his job. He spent time with the Browns in Anaheim, California and the Cardinals in St. Petersburg, Florida, as the spring training travel ban was rescinded.

The big story in March was the return of players from the war. Nearly 400 major league players were serving in the military in 1945. That number dropped to 22 a year later. Ballplayers treated this period as a homecoming celebration. "Oh man, we were fearless," remembered Joe Garagiola, then a 20-year-old rookie Cardinals catcher. "Anything you did, you felt you were ahead of the game. Not that you'd been in the trenches necessarily. No matter *what* you'd done, you were so glad to be back."[47] Breadon dealt with the glut of talent by doing more sales. In addition to Walker Cooper, second baseman Jimmy Brown ($30,000), outfielder/first baseman Johnny Hopp ($40,000), and first baseman Ray Sanders ($25,000) were sold before the season began.

A postwar economy featured an inchoate television industry that was slowly gaining steam. Just 16,500 TV sets were sold in 1945. That amount would be sold every day by the early 1950s. There were worries over inflation (Bob Broeg reported from spring training in Miami, where a New York Giants player was shocked to find a seven-dollar tab for a ham sandwich and Coke), while attendance boomed at big league parks. The numbers around the game totaled seven million higher than the year before with ten of the 16 teams – including the Cardinals – drawing more than a million. (The Cardinals drew 1,061,807, while the Browns attracted 526,435.)

A country gaining exposure to new technology was also one facing new challenges – Winston Churchill gave his "Iron Curtain" speech in Fulton, Missouri in March – and one battling age-old problems. An America of 1946 was still one where a sitting U.S. Senator felt comfortable admitting he was a member of the Ku Klux Klan and did not believe African-Americans had a right to vote. "The best time to keep a nigger away from a white primary in Mississippi was to see him the night before," Senator Theodore Bilbo told *Meet the Press* (a radio program at the time). "It is good diplomacy and good strategy to keep them from voting," said the Mississippi Democrat.[48] But an increasingly vocal portion of the population had a decidedly different take on race relations. "When people are let alone, they get along together," read a letter to the editor of the *Post-Dispatch* in February. "There is proof abundant – the admission of Negroes to Sportsman's Park grandstand, their admission to St. Louis University, mixed prize fights, democratic seating at Symphony concerts – all occur without incident."[49]

Breadon, who moved to desegregate the grandstand at Sportsman's Park two years earlier, would make a choice after the 1946 season that would have a huge impact on the careers of both Dean and Caray. Other owners instrumental to Harry's life in St. Louis and Chicago would also have career-altering moments. Bill Veeck bought his first major league team in 1946, leading a syndicate that purchased the Cleveland Indians. He later sold the franchise, with profits from that venture invested into the St. Louis Browns. Gussie Busch wasn't involved in the sport in 1946. He wasn't even a baseball fan. But he did become president of Anheuser-Busch in August when his brother passed away.

By August, a controversy that originated in St. Louis had now generated nationwide headlines for a month. It involved Dean and an unlikely foe. Or perhaps English teachers were the perfect foil. Tired of what they viewed as Dizzy's abuse of the language on the air, the English Teachers Association of Missouri filed a complaint with government officials.

Or did they?

*****

It began with a single paragraph in a newspaper column. On the morning of Thursday, July 11, readers of the *Globe-Democrat* opened the second section of the paper featuring "Women's News" and a "Feature Forum" to see a Leonard Lyons column that included this entry in the third-to-last paragraph.

"The English Teachers Association of Missouri has complained to the FCC [Federal Communications Commission] about the sports broadcasts of Dizzy Dean, protesting that his assault against syntax may affect the language of their pupils. It was Dean who reported: 'He slud into third base.'"[50]

Lyons wasn't a local journalist. He wrote from New York, where his column was syndicated. He focused primarily on the arts, entertainment, and politics, not sports. His column's name – "The Lyons Den" – was reportedly devised by

Walter Winchell. Despite no sources and no quotes in the 41-word story, it didn't take long for other media, fans, and Dean to react.

In a column for *United Press*, Dean claimed he was three years old when his mother died and he and Paul had to pick cotton to make ends meet. "I guess we didn't get much education," Dean wrote. "But I ain't dumb. I know most of the folks listening are from my part of the country – mostly from the Ozarks. They like it."

He found plenty of support for his view. "He started with nothing. He came up the hard way," wrote syndicated columnist Henry McLemore. "No, you mustn't take Diz off the air, St. Louis. You're lucky to have him in fact."

Local media agreed. "It doubtless jars the English perfectionists to hear Dizzy remark that "Musial (which he invariably pronounces Muzel) is standing confidentially at the plate," and that the "players have returned to their respectable positions," and that Kramer "throwed one high on the outside," but the idiom has its attractions," wrote the editors of the *Globe-Democrat*. "We don't expect such from the always correct Mr. O'Hara [Dean's partner] or Mr. Caray, and we never heard it during the many years France Laux relayed the play-by-play, but such lapses represent the eccentric Arkansan in the natural pose of a man who makes no claim to erudition but speaks by ear, pretty much as does Gabby Street, who entertains so acceptably on another station," read an editorial that appeared the day after the Lyons column. "Dizzy ain't no teacher," one fan wrote to the paper. "Don't emulate him. Enjoy him!"

Near the end of August, seven weeks after the original story appeared, Jimmy Powers wrote in the New York *Daily News* that "school teachers are still hounding Dizzy Dean in a desperate effort to improve the diction of Missouri's youngsters."

Dean kept the story alive with another column in early October. "I come close to getting in a jam this summer," he wrote for *The American Weekly*. "But what looked like would be disastrous turned out to be goodastrous," Dean said, repeating a line he used on the air. Dizzy echoed many of the claims from his July column – noting his upbringing and the support from fans – and managed to weave in some familiar grievances that had nothing to do with English teachers. "Me and Paul" [were] "about the lowest-paid pitchers on the staff," in 1934, Dean complained. Still bitter about a $500 bonus at the end of a season from twelve years before, Dean wrote, "That just shows you how a man is or ain't appreciated."[51]

Whether or not he was appreciated or underpaid, Dean had once again demonstrated his power as a media magnet in a season remembered for one of the all-time great Cardinals' teams. St. Louis and Brooklyn ended the season with identical records. In a best two-of-three format in baseball's first-ever playoff, the Cardinals clinched the pennant with two straight wins. "You ain't awolfin', boy!" Dean could be heard exclaiming from the victorious locker room as he interviewed players.[52] Declaring he had predicted the Cardinals victory (Dean was always making predictions), Dizzy took credit the next day. "Well, I looked purty good, as usual," he wrote for his syndicated column.

But not good enough for baseball's biggest stage. The commissioner again shot down Dean's bid to broadcast World Series games. Dean was "in line to do the radio job," according to columnist John Lardner (son of Ring Lardner), but "Chandler made a political appointment of one of the radio announcers for the Series."[53] Showing newfound maturity, Dean didn't immediately retreat to his Texas ranch as he did in 1944 when passed over. Appearing on the field before a game in Boston, photographers captured him tossing a baseball while wearing a suit and sporting a ten-gallon hat.[54] His byline appeared on a column every day during the Fall Classic, where he expressed frustration at the length of the Series that featured a shift against Ted Williams and Slaughter's scoring of the winning run in the seventh game on what many recall as a single by Harry Walker. (It was officially recorded as a double.)[55] "For Heaven's sake, if we don' git this thing over with pretty soon well [sic] be late for spring training," he wrote after Game 5. When the Series concluded, he again took credit for predicting the outcome and reminded his readers of his busy schedule. "I had 179 straight days of broadcastin' the games," he claimed.

In a year that marked his return to the airwaves, Dean also managed to keep alive for months a story that should have ended shortly after it began. "There is evidence that the English Teachers Association has been wrongly accused of criticizing Dizzy's speech. The secretary reports that no such complaint has been made officially through her office," *The Sporting News* noted at the end of July. "It ain't right," one teacher complained to the St. Louis-based publication. "We've been given a bum rap."[56]

Writing for the *Missouri Historical Review* in April 2002, authors Patrick Huber and David Anderson noted: "A thorough search of the FCC's published records for the period July-August 1946 revealed no such grievance lodged by the English Teachers Association of Missouri, any group of teachers, or any individual teacher. It appears the 'School Marms' Uprising' was nothing more than a publicity stunt designed to generate even higher ratings for Dean's already popular broadcasts on WIL or to sell more copies of the *Globe-Democrat*."[57]

Who would engage in such a stunt and why? "The authors of the apparent hoax (perhaps Lyon himself?) will probably never be known for certain," Huber and Anderson concluded. "Nor will the exact motives behind it."

While we will never know if Dean was a party to the hoax, the controversy gave him a forum to discuss his broadcasting style while generating publicity and sympathy from fans and media alike, even drawing attention from the *Saturday Review of Literature*. Editor Norman Cousins believed Dean possessed "the strongest, best lubricated, and most frequently used voice apparatus the national pastime has ever known."[58] Dean had a long history of manufacturing publicity for himself (e.g., tearing up a uniform for a photographer) and loved practical jokes (e.g., pretending to be a carpenter in team hotels). It's also worth noting that Street and Caray had engaged in a (more transparent) publicity-generating stunt the previous season when they simulated Gabby's famous catch of a baseball dropped from the top of the Washington Monument. Did Dean, or his sponsor, feel compelled to answer in the year of his return?

The late 1940s were a time of growth for the beer industry – 1947 set a record for consumption – but also an era of increased concentration.[59] More than a dozen breweries dotted the St. Louis-area landscape at the war's end.[60] A few years later, the number had shrunk to eight, with four considered large multi-million-dollar breweries. Both Falstaff and Griesedieck Brothers had scale, but the former was considerably larger than the latter. (Falstaff was the fifth-largest brewer in the United States by 1949, Griesedieck ranked 35th among 430 nationwide breweries.)[61] The smaller Griesedieck, however, blanketed the airwaves of St. Louis during this era, sponsoring various sports. On the Griesedieck-backed baseball network, Caray's partner also enjoyed reliving the glories of the past. But unlike Dean, Street could do so without drifting into self-pity and resentment.

Whatever they did or did not do, the publicity proved to be more pyrrhic than purposeful. Dizzy didn't know it yet, but his days as a broadcaster for the Cardinals were over.

*****

Despite the Cardinals appearing in their fourth World Series in five seasons, no St. Louis broadcaster worked the 1946 World Series. Gillette, the sponsor of the radio broadcasts, and Commissioner Chandler chose Arch McDonald (Washington Senators) and Jim Britt (Boston Braves and Red Sox) to call the play-by-play, a move that provoked serious agitation in St. Louis.[62] Carried over KWK in the city, the station reported receiving 866 complaints after the third game. McDonald was the focus of the backlash, with many fans finding his announcing "dull and lifeless."[63] To make the situation even more awkward for Chandler, the former Democratic Senator from Kentucky who resigned to become commissioner, McDonald was running for Congress as a Democrat in Maryland. Chandler denied politics played any part in the selection of announcers.[64] Acting St. Louis Mayor Albert Schweitzer filed a protest with Gillette the next day, stating that area fans were "highly displeased" with the broadcast and requested that Caray, Dean, O'Hara, or Street be paired with a Boston announcer to finish the Series. The request was ignored. But the controversy wasn't forgotten.

"The World Series is over, but as far as radio, the sour taste lingers on," *Variety* reported at the end of October. "Thousands of squawks by wire, postcard, letter and phone calls thundered into network headquarters and individual stations complaining about the subpar work of the announcers."

The next month, *The Sporting News* reminded its readers of what could have been had Gillette and Chandler gone in a different direction, naming Caray its top National League announcer. "His versatility, frankness, enthusiasm, and thorough familiarity with the game have built up a wide following for Caray on his play-by-play broadcasts," wrote Taylor Spink. It's easy for a Cardinals fan to close her eyes and picture a scene with Harry behind the mic for Game 7. What excitement he would have generated in his audience describing Slaughter's "Mad Dash" to the plate. But since Caray didn't make the call, perhaps it's only appropriate that no audio from that play survives.

Beyond the award from the St. Louis weekly, more permanent appreciation for Caray's work soon arrived. In January of 1947, Breadon called a news conference on Saturday, the eleventh, alerting local newspapers and radio stations by sending a telegram. Speculation immediately focused on the possibility he was either selling the team or stepping down from day-to-day management. Instead, he surprised the press by announcing an exclusive radio arrangement with the Griesedieck Brothers Brewery. No longer would multiple radio networks carry Cardinals baseball. Instead, local outlets WEW and WTMV would serve as flagship stations for a small two-state network, with Caray and Street broadcasting all games, home and away. In 1947, plans called for the duo to broadcast road games directly from ballparks in Chicago and Cincinnati, but rely on wire reports to re-create games from other locations.[65] Buried in the coverage was a note that the Cardinals, for the first time, would broadcast a limited number of games over television station KSD.[66]

What reporters really wanted to know was why Caray and not Dean. Breadon gave his clearest response to that question the next day in a telephone interview with *Post-Dispatch* columnist John Wray. "We didn't choose Harry

Caray and Gabby Street over Dean and O'Hara because we thought they had better mike personalities," Breadon said. "Nor did we give the exclusive rights to Griesedieck company because they outbid rivals." Instead, Breadon focused on the two local radio stations that carried the games. "The Griesedieck company, with its inter-city hookup, reaches a wider field," he stressed. (WEW, broadcasting on AM and FM in St. Louis, would carry only day games, while WTMV, located in East St. Louis, would air all contests.) "Our choice was purely because of that angle."[67]

Dean's biographers saw different motives. It was a need for a "conventional" and "dignified" broadcast, wrote Robert Gregory. Calling Breadon "greedy and wise," Curt Smith believed that the Cardinals owner distrusted "Dean's proclivity for the unknown." Vince Staten quoted an explanation from Paul Enright, who worked at WTMV radio. Enright believed advertising manager Oscar Zahner made the call. "What bothered Zahner was that we [WTMV] had to make money any way we could and on Sunday we had about eight colored quartets on right before the game." Griesedieck Brothers "didn't want its baseball games immediately after black music programs," Staten wrote. If the brewery didn't like this arrangement, it waited years to make a change. The Cardinals continued to broadcast their games locally over WTMV and WEW through the 1948 season. It wasn't until 1949, with the club under new ownership, that Griesedieck-sponsored broadcasts returned to WIL (where they originated in Caray's first season).

A variety of factors aligned after the 1946 season to expand media coverage. The Yankees had already set the precedent for home and road broadcasts.[68] With the Cardinals celebrating their sixth World Series title under Breadon, their third in just the past six seasons, the timing was right. The Cardinals had leverage, a popular product, and a poor competitor in the city. The Browns finished 1946 in seventh place in the American League. Manager Luke Sewell resigned at the end of August.

The Cardinals made more money from the new arrangement (an estimated $50,000 or more from Griesedieck Brothers versus $30,000 total from the two breweries), but does doubling the number of broadcasts available to fans make Breadon "greedy?" While he controlled the majority of stock in the team, he also had a responsibility to maximize the value of the franchise to his limited partners.

With the value of the Cardinals in mind, the owner was positioning his property for an exit. Breadon's health was not good after serious injuries following a horseback riding incident. "The thiamin chloride he'd taken after a fall from a horse in 1939 no longer was a magic elixir," recalled Broeg. In his history of the Cardinals, the longtime St. Louis sportswriter also wondered if "the cancer that would take his life in May 1949 had made its early inroads."⁶⁹

As for the choice of Caray, the St. Louis native was no longer a novice in the broadcast booth. He had two seasons of Cardinals baseball under his belt and his offseason calendar was populated with seemingly every sporting event in the city. He had quickly become THE voice of St. Louis sports. *The Sporting News* honor was validation of his talent.

Caray had another factor in his favor, one long remembered by him and also cited by Broeg. The Cardinals held a team dinner at Ruggeri's restaurant on Sunday night following the last regular-season game. Both St. Louis and Brooklyn lost that Sunday, setting up their playoff series. What was supposed to be a celebration of another pennant-winning team would have to wait, a pause that set the tone for a more somber gathering. Serving as master of ceremonies for the event, columnist Stockton told the crowd to stand for ten seconds of silence in tribute to "the man who made the close race possible." Citing multiple player sales and the players who jumped to the Mexican Leagues for more money, it was obvious to all Stockton was referring to the Cardinals owner. "I hope Sam hasn't cut the baloney too fine," he told the assembled. (In his autobiography, Caray described Stockton as "a bitter and eternally angry enemy of the Cardinals owner," and that he "ripped into Breadon with a vicious relentlessness.")

"Everybody was furious at Roy," recalled Broeg. "Harry Caray was one of them. But that didn't bother Stockton. He could have knocked Caray on his ass," said the Stockton colleague and Caray critic.⁷⁰

An indignant Caray followed Stockton to the microphone. "I just gave them a little speech from the heart," he remembered. He spoke of the many postseason appearances of the Cardinals and the World Series checks that came with it. He talked about Breadon's generosity, citing his support of Grover Cleveland Alexander and other players who had fallen on hard times after their careers were over. When he finished, Breadon sought him out. "Young man, that was awfully nice of you. I will never forget it."⁷¹

So while Breadon had reasons to select Caray, he also had reasons to shy away from Dean. The two men had famously and publicly battled over compensation during Dizzy's playing days, a sticking point that Dean never failed to mention in his conversations with reporters years later. Dizzy's "proclivity for the unknown" extended to his behavior outside the broadcast booth.

Dean loved to gamble. The same month that Breadon made his decision, Grantland Rice told the story of playing golf with Dean and Babe Ruth. "These two had at least a dozen bets," Rice wrote.[72] While broadcasting for CBS in the 1950s, "The only time he'd really get upset during a game is when he'd told a person how to bet on a game and then his advice turned sour," remembered Blattner.[73] As a player, he'd been spotted more than once at racetracks and made at least one wager during a game, betting that he could strike out Vince DiMaggio four times. He did, but only after telling his catcher to drop a foul ball pop-up during DiMaggio's fourth appearance at the plate. By the 1940s, he was consistently betting on game outcomes. "You're sending bets by the clubhouse boy to the saloon on the corner. You're broadcasting the game and you're betting on the game," Commissioner Chandler told him in a closed-door meeting. "Make your choice," Chandler recalled telling Dean for his autobiography. "Quit betting or I'm taking you off the air."[74]

Breadon had delivered a similar ultimatum to Rogers Hornsby after the 1926 season, becoming so uncomfortable with his player/manager's ways he demanded that he swear off the habit in exchange for signing a new contract. When Hornsby refused, Breadon traded him to the New York Giants. Chandler and Dean's closed-door meeting didn't occur until 1948, but his earlier exploits had been well documented. It was just one more data point that Breadon potentially weighed when making his choice.[75]

Despite Dean's baggage, it's worth remembering just how popular he was on St. Louis radio and the risk Breadon took by going with Caray. Bill Bartleson helped hire Dean in 1941 when he worked for Falstaff. (He also worked as his ghostwriter for several years.) "A rival brewery was also sponsoring the Cardinals games on another station, and they were beating us in ratings 2-1," he recalled in 1960. "I signed him to a contract in midseason and by October, our baseball broadcast had a 4-1 edge in listeners. The people just ate it up."[76] Five years after his debut, even with Caray and Street as competition, Dizzy still dominated the airwaves. "Radio surveys for 1946 showed that Dean had the largest baseball following in St. Louis," said Browns general manager DeWitt.

On the night of Breadon's announcement of the new radio arrangement, reporters tracked down Dizzy in Dallas for comment. "They can't do that to me," he insisted.

But they did.

---

[1] Infielder Lou Klein and pitchers Max Lanier and Fred Martin left the team for Mexico in May. Lanier was 6-0 with a 1.93 ERA at the time of his defection. He rejoined the Cardinals in 1949.

[2] *Saturday Evening Post*, October 6, 1945.

Holy Cow St. Louis!

³ Yankees president MacPhail had first offered the job to Red Barber. The two men had a long relationship that dated back to their days together in Cincinnati. But Dodgers president Rickey matched MacPhail's offer – three years and $100,000 and Barber decided to stay with the Dodgers. Allen called Yankees games in 1946 with Russ Hodges.

⁴ The Washington Senators were the last club to have broadcasters travel with the team in 1955. See https://sabr.org/bioproj/person/arch-mcdonald/

⁵ "Like the horse, day baseball practically became extinct in St. Louis as the town was educated to night baseball and Sunday doubleheaders," wrote Dan Parker. *Saturday Evening Post*, October 6, 1945.

⁶ *St. Louis Post-Dispatch*, March 21, 1945. Other than Sundays, the only day games the Cardinals scheduled were four games on Saturdays and two holiday twin bills. The Cardinals had 12 Sunday dates on their schedule. Eleven of them were doubleheaders.

⁷ Greenspan, Alan and Wooldridge, Adrian. *Capitalism in America. A History.* Penguin Press. 2018.

⁸ *The Sporting News,* May 31, 1945.

⁹ The Braves were the National League's version of the St. Louis Browns, a struggling franchise in a two-team town. Over a thirty-year span, from 1917 to 1946, the Braves never finished higher than fourth in the standings. The franchise relocated to Milwaukee in 1953, a year before the Browns departed St. Louis. By 1946, the Braves roster included former Cardinals Mort Cooper, Johnny Hopp, Danny Litwhiler, Ken O'Dea, Ray Sanders, and Ernie White. Pitcher Johnny Beazley joined the Braves in 1947. "Cape Cod Cardinals Gone," read a *Boston Globe* headline in 1950. *Boston Globe*, January 22, 1950. "The name 'Cape Cod Cardinals,' because of its geographical inaccuracy, was not used much hereabouts," noted the paper. "But you heard it a lot in the Midwest." Billy Southworth managed the Braves from 1946 to 1951.

¹⁰ Breadon did have his limits when it came to cash deals. In June of 1945, Philadelphia Phillies general manager Herb Pennock offered Breadon $250,000 for shortstop Marty Marion and third baseman Whitey Kurowski. Breadon turned it down. "I might as well sell the franchise as let Marion and Kurowski go," he told Pennock. *New York Times*, June 5, 1945.

¹¹ Barnes was known as an aggressive marketer during his time as an owner. "Baseball virtually became a sideline at Sportsman's Park under the Barnes regime as loud-speaker plugs for the park-owned fried-fish concession and a brand of cigarettes filled in the quiet moments between cracks of the bat," Parker wrote. *Saturday Evening Post*, October 6, 1945.

¹² Muckerman was previously a vice president of the team. "Rumors circulated in local baseball circles for the past several months that Muckerman and Barnes were not hitting it off as big-shot directors," wrote Keener. Both men denied the charge. However, "Barnes seemed extremely nervous, apparently indicating he was withdrawing from major league baseball under deep regrets." Muckerman was

reportedly upset that Barnes would not declare a dividend after the 1944 season and preferred to reinvest the money back into the team. *St. Louis Post-Dispatch*, July 22, 1962. When he purchased a controlling interest in the Browns, Muckerman served as vice president of the City Ice & Fuel Co. His grandfather had arrived in St. Louis in the 1840s from Germany and started the Polar Wave Ice & Fuel Co. The company sold to City Ice & Fuel in 1925. Muckerman was also a director at Tower Grove Bank in St. Louis and owned a hotel in Guaymas, Mexico. *St. Louis Star-Times,* August 10, 1945, and *The Sporting News*, August 16, 1945.

[13] Was the Browns planned move to Los Angeles legitimate? *The Sporting News* was skeptical. "Of course, this was chimerical. Barnes had a motive, too. He was fighting for more night games, and got them through the development of war conditions. The Browns in Los Angeles, without another American League club in San Francisco, would have been marooned as if on a desert isle." *The Sporting News*, December 13, 1945. Barnes later spoke publicly about the possible move, telling Vincent X. Flaherty he was encouraged to move by Breadon. "He was going to pay me a quarter million dollars to leave town." *Pittsburgh Sun-Telegraph,* January 8, 1946. While stating the arrangements weren't complete, Breadon told Fred Lieb the Cardinals were prepared to take over the cost of lights and pay the Browns' rental fee for the use of Sportsman's Park. *The Sporting News,* January 17, 1946. (The Browns later bought Sportsman's Park from the Dodier Realty Co.)

[14] Oklahoma City *Journal Record*, July 15, 2002.

[15] "They [the Cardinals] had a tryout in Minersville [in Schuylkill County] back in the mid-thirties," Gray told *Pennsylvania Heritage* magazine. "There were over six hundred others there and each of us had a number on our back. After they called my number, they watched me for a few minutes and said I'd never make it in organized ball. What was I going to say? So I just turned around and headed back home." *Pennsylvania Heritage*, Spring 2003.

[16] *Baltimore Sun,* March 14, 1982.

[17] Golenbock, *The Spirit of St. Louis.*

[18] *St. Louis Post-Dispatch,* April 1, 1945.

[19] *Washington Post*, May 23, 1945.

[20] Golenbock, *The Spirit of St. Louis.*

[21] Mead, *Even the Browns.*

[22] Ibid.

[23] *New York Times*, July 2, 2002.

[24] *St. Louis Star-Times,* June 26, 1945.

[25] Powell, Larry. *Bottom of the Ninth: An Oral History on the Life of Harry "The Hat" Walker.* Writer's Showcase Press. 2000.

[26] *The Sporting News*, September 6, 1945.

[27] *St. Louis Post-Dispatch*, July 23, 1989.

[28] *The Sporting News*, November 26, 1958.

[29] After the 1978 season, Schoendienst returned to St. Louis and coached for every Cardinals manager from Ken Boyer to Tony La Russa.
[30] Gary saw Gray every summer until he was ten years old.
[31] New York *Daily News,* April 11, 1986.
[32] "Gray had been a hard drinker at one time but gave up booze in 1976," wrote Peter Goldstein. "He has no visible source of income since leaving baseball. Townsfolk will tell you, however, that he always has good luck at filling a straight, and found easy marks who challenged him in pool and in golf, a game he plays in the low 80s and drives a ball more than 200 yards." Gray was 67 at the time. *Baltimore Sun,* March 14, 1982.
[33] *Washington Post,* July 31, 1945.
[34] *New York Times,* September 19, 1945.
[35] Rickey disagreed with MacPhail's assessment. "It is not exactly a secret that St. Louis cannot support two major league clubs," he said in August. "The situation in St. Louis is complicated. There is a vast Negro population there and it has not yet got into the habit of supporting major league baseball." *The Sporting News,* August 23, 1945.
[36] Browns president Barnes also served on both committees.
[37] *The Sporting News,* November 15, 1945.
[38] With a cartoon showing Dean and partner Johnnie O'Hara riding a microphone like a horse, Falstaff took out ads in St. Louis newspapers in April 1946 announcing Dizzy's return. "Baseball ala Dizzy Dean is not just another play-by-play," the ad read in part. "It's a riotous roundup of ribbing, and rare, original Deanisms."
[39] Dean was honored on Sunday, September 17. Four days earlier, he had won his twentieth game of the year.
[40] *The Sporting News,* May 24, 1945.
[41] Auker, Eldon with Tom Keegan. *Sleeper Cars and Flannel Uniforms: A Lifetime of Memories from Striking Out the Babe to Teeing It Up with the President*. Triumph Books. 2001.
[42] Dean's weight ballooned after his playing days were over. Appearing at the Old-Timers' Day game at Yankee Stadium, "Dizzy admitted to 255 pounds." He claimed to weigh 185 when pitching in the 1934 World Series. *New York Times,* August 9, 1959.
[43] "I know that you've heard Dizzy say that he was the world's greatest pitcher, the best baserunner, the heaviest hitter, and the best fielder. Just between you and me – I wouldn't want Diz to get more swell-headed – he was all of that," Frisch told Arthur Daley. *New York Times,* July 16, 1944.
[44] *The News* (Paterson, New Jersey), August 26, 1959.
[45] *Pittsburgh Post-Gazette,* January 3, 1946.
[46] *Boston Globe,* May 19, 1946.
[47] Smith, *Voices of the Game.*
[48] Bilbo was the author of a book called *Take Your Choice: Separation or Mongrelization*. Republican Senator Robert Taft of Ohio called Bilbo "a disgrace to the Senate."
[49] *St. Louis Post-Dispatch,* February 4, 1946.

[50] *St. Louis Globe-Democrat*, July 11, 1946.
[51] *San Francisco Examiner*, October 6, 1946.
[52] *St. Louis Globe-Democrat,* October 4, 1946.
[53] *Boston Globe*, October 11, 1946.
[54] "Up till today there was considerable argument about the 10-gallon hat which Mr. Dean has been wearing since the Series came to Boston," wrote Lardner. "As every baseball student knows, Diz only has a 5-gallon head."
[55] Many that day, including Bob Broeg, believed it should have been scored a single, with Walker advancing to second on the throw to the plate. "Slaughter actually scored easily, really on a single," he wrote. Broeg, Bob. *Bob Broeg's REDBIRDS: A Century of Cardinals' Baseball.* River City Publishers, Limited. 1987 (Revised Edition).
[56] *The Sporting News*, July 31, 1946.
[57] Huber, Patrick and Anderson, David. "Butcherin' Up the English Language a Little Bit": Dizzy Dean, Baseball Broadcasting, and the 'School Marms' Uprising of 1946." *Missouri Historical Review*. April 2002. Dean and O'Hara broadcast over WIL in 1946. Caray and Street had carried games on the station in 1945, but switched to WEW and WTMV the following season.
[58] Ibid.
[59] There were an estimated 40 million beer drinkers in the country. The average beer drinker in 1947 consumed 857 10-ounce glasses, or 80 more than in 1946. *The Bergen Evening Record,* July 7, 1948.
[60] In early 1946, the *Post-Dispatch* counted 13 breweries in the St. Louis area: Anheuser-Busch, Falstaff, Gast, Griesedieck Brothers, Columbia, and Hyde Park, all in the city. Fischbach was in St. Charles. Illinois breweries were Griesedieck-Western and Star-Peerless in Belleville, Ems in East St. Louis, Bluff City in Alton, Schott in Highland, and Mound City in New Athens. *St. Louis Post-Dispatch,* February 10, 1946.
[61] *St. Louis Post-Dispatch,* December 25, 1949. Anheuser-Busch was the largest and oldest of the St. Louis breweries, but not the largest beer seller in the country at the time. "Anheuser-Busch sales for the past few years have been exceeded by Schlitz and Pabst of Milwaukee and Ballantine of New Jersey."
[62] Gillette considered televising the 1946 World Series, but ultimately rejected the idea. *The Sporting News*, August 21, 1946. The first televised World Series came the following year.
[63] "It is one thing to be impartial in broadcasting a game. It is something else to broadcast a game with the same lack of animation with which the treasurer of the Mortician's Association might read his annual report." *The Sporting News*, October 16, 1946. The St. Louis-based publication quoted from a story in the *East Side Journal* (East St. Louis, IL).
[64] *St. Louis Star-Times*, October 10, 1946.
[65] *The Sporting News*, January 22, 1947.

⁶⁶ Newspaper columnists Roy Stockton and Ellis Veech served as broadcasters for the early television games. (Caray and Street did a pregame show.) Veech was the sports editor of the *East St. Louis Evening Journal* from 1936 until he died in 1960. He served as the official scorer and statistician for the National League at Sportsman's Park/Busch Stadium for many years. Veech was at the center of a 1952 controversy that saw an umpire suspended. In a game between the Browns and Tigers, umpire Bill McGowan ejected a player in the Tigers' dugout and refused to give his name to the media. "Tell them I'll write them a letter," said McGowan. "We didn't know you could write," was the reply he received from the press box. "If you guys could write, you'd be in New York," McGowan fired back. According to Veech, McGowan also made obscene gestures toward the press box. Tom Duffy, Veech's boss and managing editor of the paper, was so outraged by the incident that he sent a letter to Browns ownership saying his paper would boycott coverage of American League games until McGowan apologized. *Globe-Democrat* sports editor Bob Burnes wired a letter of protest regarding McGowan's actions to American League president Will Harridge, who responded by suspending the umpire. Working from 1925 to 1954, McGowan "was the best umpire in the American League," according to ballplayers. He founded an umpire school in 1938. It remains active to this day as the Wendlestedt Umpire School and is the only independent umpire school recognized by minor and major league baseball. In poor health, he retired in 1954, with the American League voting to give him a lifetime pension. He died a few days later. McGowan was inducted into the Hall of Fame by the Veterans Committee in 1992. *The Sporting News*, August 13, 1952; *New York Times*, December 10, 1954.

⁶⁷ *St. Louis Post-Dispatch*, January 13, 1947.

⁶⁸ "Several other cities, including Brooklyn, New York, and Chicago, have broadcast both road and home games in the past, Breadon pointed out." *St. Louis Globe-Democrat*, January 12, 1947.

⁶⁹ Broeg, *Bob Broeg's REDBIRDS*.

⁷⁰ Golenbock, *The Spirit of St. Louis*.

⁷¹ "Harry Caray was a company man," said Broeg. "He always knew when a Breadon or Busch was in charge. But Caray could be very tough on anybody who didn't sign his checks." Ibid. The two men didn't always have an acrimonious relationship. Broeg "suggested he [Caray] would take the town by storm," after appearing on Harry's radio show in 1944. "As a Marine covering the famous St. Louis Streetcar World Series between the Browns and Cardinals, I was impressed after Caray's 30-minute radio show and said so." *St. Louis Post-Dispatch,* February 22, 1998.

⁷² *St. Louis Globe-Democrat*, January 14, 1947. In 1936, Dean won $190 from Ruth during a Florida golf tournament. That same year, he won an $80 bet with George Jacobus, a Sarasota, Florida golf pro. When Jacobus refused to pay, citing a technicality, Dizzy's wife, Pat, walked into the pro shop, took a $50 golf bag and $30 worth of balls, and walked out without paying. "That guy, Jacobus, thinks we're a couple of saps, does

he, well, ask the son of a bitch how he likes this mess of turnips." Gregory, *Diz*. Dean bought a racehorse that same year, naming it "Kizzy D," Pat's pet name for her husband. Described as a Texas-bred, dark chestnut filly, "She can run as well as I can pitch," said Dean. *Miami Daily News*, December 27, 1936.

[73] Smith, *Voices of the Game*.

[74] Chandler, Albert B. with Vance Trimble. *Heroes, Plain Folks, and Skunks. The Life and Times of Happy Chandler*. Bonus Books. 1989. A grand jury named Dizzy as a co-conspirator in a 1970 gambling scandal. (He had placed bets for a friend and made payoffs for him.) Dean testified as a witness for the government and wasn't charged with a crime. https://retrosimba.com/2020/02/24/how-dizzy-dean-got-ensnared-in-federal-gambling-probe/

[75] The Cardinals owner had other points to consider. Three months before Breadon announced his decision, Dean denied a report that he was leaving St. Louis for Pittsburgh to broadcast Pirates games. *The Sporting News*, October 23, 1946.

[76] *The Minneapolis Star*, August 25, 1960.

Biggie's Boys and The Man

The final seasons of Caray broadcasting for Griesedieck Brothers were among the most tumultuous years in St. Louis baseball history. The years 1947-1953 saw deaths, debuts, divorce, team sales, ballpark stunts, threats, feuds, court battles, and a prison sentence for an owner. The flurry of activity reflected a change in the pace of American life.

"Open dates even during the winter months are a thing of the past now at ballpark offices. 'Twas different years ago. Business was slack, and you could drop in, sit around and gab about this and that, maybe pick up a feature story or a little news, or perhaps fill out an inside straight," wrote *Globe-Democrat* sports reporter Martin Haley in January of 1947. "That's gone now. If you drop into a ballpark office today, everybody's busy, so busy you excuse yourself for breathing part of their air."[1]

"American life was speeding up significantly," wrote David Halberstam, author of *The Fifties*. "The nature of the American family was changing and so was the family dinner." After getting a $5,000 loan, the McDonald brothers opened a small drive-in restaurant in San Bernadino, California. They eventually cut their menu from 27 to nine items and turned hamburger making into an assembly line process. "BUY'M BY THE BAG" read their sign out front. The cost was 15 cents each. Future San Diego Padres owner Ray Kroc got his first look at the company that made his family billionaires in 1954.[2]

In St. Louis, Breadon's decision to expand the Cardinals radio network to include road games came at the perfect time. In the previous two decades, his team had gained popularity by winning ballgames and scheduling Sunday doubleheaders. "By nine a.m., when the gates opened on Sunday, the whole section instantly filled up with brown-bagging out-of-towners," remembered Broeg.[3] New rules after the 1946 season made those Sunday doubleheaders harder to schedule. One of the concessions players had extracted from owners was eliminating twin bills following night games. In 1947, the Cardinals played twelve Sundays at Sportsman's Park, but only one featured a doubleheader.[4]

Compared to the modern game, mid-20th century baseball featured smaller gloves, shorter games (average time less than two-and-a-half hours), and a sport living in the shadow of Babe Ruth; a base-to-base affair punctuated by the periodic longball. Ralph Kiner led the National League in home runs in 1950 with 47. Dom DiMaggio led the American League in stolen bases with 15. A player weighing more than 200 pounds was a rarity. Weightlifting was discouraged. "We were told that loose muscles were better, and that's what we believed," said Schoendienst.[5] In an era where cars were large, gas was cheap, and Milton Berle became television's first superstar, the Cardinals second baseman was among a group of players setting a standard for what was possible in the post-war years.

Before the war, it was common for ballplayers to return home in the offseason to work as day laborers: on construction crews, in factories or on farms. By 1950, the average baseball salary was $11,000. The players weren't rich, but they weren't poor, either. ($11,000 translates to roughly $137,000 in 2023 dollars.) Increasingly, those who drew a paycheck from the game wanted to be their own boss and go into business for themselves. Nowhere was this entrepreneurial ethic more prominent than in St. Louis. Enos Slaughter owned a jewelry store in Belleville, Illinois. Manager Eddie Dyer had an insurance business and oil interests in Texas. After his playing days ended, Marty Marion owned a minor league team in Houston and tried to buy the Minneapolis Lakers.[6] But the locus of this dynamism centered around a group of five men who either called St. Louis home or grew up in the city. Their mutual admiration society featured longtime friendships and plenty of business deals. Three of them played for the Cardinals. Four of them played major league baseball. They all prospered in what Harvard economist John Kenneth Galbraith would soon term *The Affluent Society*.[7]

*****

The snowball that started this avalanche of connections was the oldest of the five, and the only one not to play the game. Julius "Biggie" Garagnani grew up on the Hill, the Italian section of St. Louis, just like his friends Yogi Berra and Joe Garagiola. Born in 1913, Garagnani was twelve years old before either of the two future major league catchers was born. By the time he was twenty-six, Biggie was a married man and operating his first restaurant, the Brass Key.[8] Gregarious and outgoing, the restaurateur was instrumental in both Berra and Garagiola receiving early honors at Sportsman's Park. (This was old hat for Garagnani. In 1939, Jack "Red" Juelich, another product of the Hill, made his debut for the Pittsburgh Pirates. When the Pirates played in St. Louis in August, Biggie organized a parade and a presentation of gifts.) Garagiola's night of honor came first, during his rookie season. Before a game against the Cubs in September, more than 25,000 fans, including more than 1,000 from the Hill, saw Garagiola receive a new Nash automobile, two suits, and six white shirts.[9]

The next year, 1947, Berra was scheduled for recognition in August when the Yankees came to town for a series against the Browns. But there was a problem. The game was set for the afternoon. Garagnani went to the Browns to see if the affair could be switched to the evening because, as one columnist put it, "the people on the Hill work when the afternoon sun is shining." The Browns told him no. Biggie went to Yankees manager Bucky Harris, who also turned down his plea. (The Browns needed the Yankees' consent to change the game time.) Garagnani decided to write a letter to Yankees president MacPhail. Biggie's persistence paid off. MacPhail agreed to move the contest to a night game. "What we gave Joe Garagiola, we'll give Yogi," Garagnani explained. "No less, no more. They're both our boys."[10]

The following spring, with both the Cardinals and Yankees training in St. Petersburg, Berra and Garagiola, neighbors and friends since childhood, made the trip together. Garagnani drove them. Down in Florida, Cardinals owner Breadon liked to suit up in the mornings and play baseball with a group of cronies. One year, Biggie was Breadon's partner in a game of pepper.[11]

By this time, Garagnani had moved on to his second establishment, Biggie's Steak House, located on Chippewa. With his many baseball connections, Biggie's restaurant became a favorite hangout of players. (Carmen Berra worked as a waitress there before she was married. It's where she and Yogi met.) One of the players who enjoyed dining at Biggie's was Musial. In 1948, Stan made a decision that benefitted his bottom line, and one other players would soon adopt. Instead of spending his winters in his native Pennsylvania, he decided to make St. Louis his year-round home. "I think it's wise for a baseball player to make his home where he's made his reputation," he later reflected.

"I decided to go into some kind of business in St. Louis. I didn't know what," Musial recalled. "I almost decided on the insurance business. At the same time I was doing a little duck-hunting with Biggie and eating in here. He had good steaks and salads. He knew I was looking around and one day he said, 'How'd you like to go in with me?' Just that casual. I said I thought I'd like it. I looked over his books and we became partners."[12] Musial was 28 years old.

The business partnership was officially born in January 1949. The restaurant was renamed Stan Musial and Biggie's Steak House. It would be Musial's first outside business investment ($25,000 for his half-interest in the establishment, to be paid to Garagnani out of profits), but far from his last. Over the years, the two men would partner in everything from banks to bowling alleys.

While they shared Midwestern roots and the same religious faith, Schoendienst, the final member of this quintet, was largely outside Garagnani's considerable orbit. But just as Biggie influenced Stan, Musial's business acumen impacted Schoendienst. By the 1960s, Red's business resume looked remarkably similar to his longtime teammate: a board of directors seat at a local bank, real estate holdings, and an interest in two bowling alleys.[13]

In fact, all five men would eventually own bowling alleys, reflecting a boom in the sport in the postwar years and the social ties of their Catholic faith. (A picture in the *Globe-Democrat* once featured the wives of Garagiola, Garagnani, and Schoendienst making plans for the Annual Tea of St. Raphael, the Archangel Parish.) Schoendienst partnered with his brother Julius, Berra bought a bowling alley with teammate Phil Rizzuto in New Jersey, and Garagiola, Garagnani and Musial went together to purchase Redbird Lanes in St. Louis.[14] "Bowling was a huge part of the Catholic Church in medieval times," Travis Boley, curator of the International Bowling Museum and Hall of Fame in St. Louis, once explained to *The New York Times*. "It was a religious game. Martin Luther was an avid bowler."[15]

By 1951, all five were married men. All but Garagnani were 30 years old or younger.[16] Everyone but Schoendienst, whose father was an Illinois coal miner, was the child of immigrants. "They differed from their parents not just in how much they made and what they owned but in their belief that the future had already arrived," wrote Halberstam about the men and women who came of age after World War II. "Above all, they were confident in themselves and their futures in a way that [older people] growing up in harder times and poorer neighborhoods, found striking."[17]

From hunting in the winter to baseball in the summer, the bonds and business ties between these men would only grow in the coming years. No one did more to spread the legend of Berra's malaprops – "Yogisms" – than Garagiola. Garagnani would remain Musial's business partner until he died of a heart attack in 1967. Schoendienst became Stan's roommate on the road. "Red and I just seem to like the same things and the same leisurely pace in which to do them, hunting, fishing, and golfing in the offseason, sleeping late on the road, taking our time cooling off after a game before slowly eating the best dinner in town," said Musial. "We like to read to improve ourselves – Red didn't get a college education, either – and occasionally we'll take in a movie or a live show on Broadway."[18]

The lights of Broadway – or any other street – shone brightest for the two biggest stars of the group, both on and off the field. Berra, the St. Louis native, and Musial, the lifelong Cardinal, each won three MVP awards in their respective leagues. "Berra is the best player in baseball, except for maybe Musial," Casey Stengel said in 1955, the year Yogi earned $50,000, making him the highest-paid catcher in major-league history. His salaries for the next two seasons – $58,000 and $65,000 – made him the highest-paid player in the American League.[19] In 1958, Musial earned a $100,000 salary, becoming the first in National League history to hit six figures. Late in the 1959 season, Taylor Spink wrote in *The Sporting News* that a Musial for Berra deal would be the first trade of the offseason. It didn't happen. Musial retired with the Cardinals in 1963, the same year Berra played his last game for the Yankees.[20]

At the peak of their careers, both men saw heavy demand for their appearances in the offseason. Writer Tom Meany dined at Musial's restaurant one evening and later complimented him on the steak. "I'm glad to hear the food is still good," Musial told him. "I have so many speaking dates in the winter that I hardly ever get the chance to eat here."[21] Berra was the most requested Yankees player in the winter months. (Like Musial, he sought permanent residence close to where he played, settling in suburban New Jersey in the early 1950s.)[22] "Yogi only says two things to me before a speech – 'Write it out,' and 'Rehearse me,'" said Jackie Farrell, who worked in the Yankees front office. "All he wants is a four-line introduction and then he invites the kids to ask him questions." Signing autographs after speaking one night in Trenton, New Jersey with a blizzard approaching, Farrell and a state trooper had to take the fountain pen out of Berra's hand. "Yogi was hurt," Farrell recalled. "He said, 'You could have made enemies for me of those last three guys.'"[23]

Playing in New York helped Berra earn plenty of endorsement deals. He pitched everything from bicycles to cigarettes and became a vice president of the company behind Yoo-Hoo, the chocolate-flavored drink.[24] Instead of taking a salary, he took stock in the business. At the bowling alley he opened with Rizzuto in Clifton, the cocktail lounge was shaped like Yankee Stadium. The grand opening featured appearances from manager Stengel and all his Yankee teammates.[25] By this time, "Yogi Berra is quickly becoming one of the richest men in baseball," noted biographer Jon Pessah.

The same could be said of Musial in St. Louis. By the mid-1950s, Musial and Garagnani owned multiple restaurants and were the second-largest shareholders in Brentwood Bank in suburban St. Louis.[26] His original steakhouse with Biggie moved to Oakland Avenue in 1960. By 1965, Garagnani estimated its value at $4 million. As for his partner, "He's happy. He takes out his $200,000 a year," said Biggie.[27] Musial's plowed the money into new investments, including a radio and television station in Lake Charles, Louisiana, purchased with partners for $2.2 million, and three hotels – two in Florida and the Airport Hilton in St. Louis.[28] As a player, he endorsed Chesterfield cigarettes, Lifebuoy soap, and Winthrop shoes.[29]

"A man lives pretty high when he is a player," Cleveland Indians third baseman Al Rosen told the *Wall Street Journal* in 1955. "He travels first class, stays in the best hotels, eats fine food and hobnobs with important people. When his career is over, he usually isn't satisfied to go back to a small town and operate a gas station."[30]

Part of the reason Musial and Berra thrived in business was people found them both likable and trustworthy. In 1973, long after both men had retired, a research company surveyed 2,500 men to ask their opinion of athletes across various categories. Musial ranked No. 1 in "Like Person as an Individual" and "Trust Person's Endorsement." Berra also scored highest in the same two categories, ranking fourth in likeability and third in trust.[31]

Because Musial was more than five years older than Berra, everything seemed to happen just a little earlier for Stan. Musial made it to the big leagues at the end of the 1941 season. Berra debuted at the end of the 1946 campaign. Cooperstown came calling for Stan in 1969. Yogi was inducted into the Hall of Fame in 1972. Musial received the Presidential Medal of Freedom from President Obama in 2010. Berra received the identical honor from the same President in 2015.

Musial loved to play the harmonica. ("Take Me Out To The Ballgame" was an annual favorite at the Hall of Fame.)[32] Berra was involved in a famous harmonica incident. While managing the Yankees in 1964, Berra heard infielder Phil Linz playing one on a team bus following a loss. The manager told the player to knock it off. Linz didn't hear the request. "He said to play it louder," a mischievous Mickey Mantle told him. When he did, Berra knocked the harmonica out of his hands. The Yankees proceeded to go 30-11 the rest of the season to win the pennant and play the Cardinals in the World Series.

At a time of a growing civil rights movement, Musial supported Democratic Party politics, but was no social crusader.[33] "He was like Gil Hodges," Jackie Robinson told author Roger Kahn. "A nice guy, but when it came to what I had to do, neither one hurt me and neither one helped." Testifying before a House antitrust subcommittee in 1957, Musial told members of Congress, "I think everybody likes baseball the way it is," when asked if antitrust statutes should cover the game. He added that he supported the reserve clause, the language that bound a player to his team in perpetuity.[34] "He not only accepted baseball mythology but propounded it," wrote his one-time teammate Curt Flood. "There was no conscious harm in him. He was just unfathomably naïve."[35]

Naïve and simple were how the press frequently caricatured Berra. But a second image of the player ran counter to the one in the public imagination. "Berra can be cold and aloof to visitors and he can be distrustful of writers, and yet utterly ingenuous with friends away from the game who want a favor of him," Irv Goodman wrote in *Sport* magazine in 1958. His wife described him as "temperamental. Not like [opera singer] Maria Callas, but pretty moody."[36]

Both men had their vices. As a middle-aged man, Musial started smoking (years after he had endorsed Chesterfield cigarettes).[37] "I didn't start smoking until I was 35, 36. A year ago, I quit. Yesterday, I took it up again and you see what I'm doing, smoking with both hands," he confessed to a reporter in November of 1960. "Well, when I go to spring training that will stop. I'm one of those guys who can quit."[38] Berra liked to drink straight vodka on the rocks. But according to teammate Mantle, three or four would be his limit. "Me, I'd just be starting," said Mickey.[39] Rooming with Rizzuto on the road, Berra didn't like being alone and hated going to sleep. When he would finally grow tired, he always had a request for his teammate. "He insisted on hearing a bedtime story. In self-defense, just so he could get some sleep, the Scooter would calm the savage beast in Yogi by telling him the story of 'The Three Little Pigs,' 'Snow White,' or 'Little Red Riding Hood,'" wrote Rizzuto biographer Gene Schoor.[40]

The biggest chink in this multi-million-dollar armor occurred with a breakup of the relationship between Garagiola and Musial after Garagnani passed away. Garagiola filed suit against Musial, his wife, Garagnani's widow and son over the operations of Redbird Lanes, their bowling alley partnership.[41] The suit was settled and the bowling alley sold in 1987, years after their playing days ended and long after all the men had become wealthy, famous, or both. By the late 1980s, outside of Stan the Man Inc., Musial had largely wound down his outside business affairs. The lawsuit, Jack Buck later wrote, "was a dagger in Stan's heart."[42]

Before their split, Garagiola – who filled reporters' notebooks with endless tales of growing up with Berra – offered enthusiastic and frequent praise of Musial. With Stan closing in on 2,500 career hits in the summer of 1955, Garagiola estimated that if every Musial hit were laid end to end, it would stretch from St. Louis to Columbia, a distance of 120 miles. That same year, he entertained reporters with the story of his immigrant father, who buried his savings in cans in his backyard for decades. But with Musial now on the board of directors of a regional bank, Papa Garagiola felt comfortable digging it up and placing it in the hands of the local lender.

The postseason is where Musial and Berra parted ways. Stan never played in another World Series after 1946. From 1947 to 1963, from the time Yogi became a regular in the Yankees lineup until the last game he wore the pinstripes, the Cardinals finished second five times, just twice after 1949. During that same 17-year timeframe, Berra went to 14 World Series, winning ten rings. ("He'd fall in a sewer and come up with a gold watch," Stengel once said of his star catcher.) Every World Series Musial played in came before the television age. All 14 of Berra's Fall Classics came with live broadcasts. Some of Yogi's World Series moments – jumping into the arms of pitcher Don Larsen following his perfect game in 1956 comes to mind – are burned into the collective consciousness of baseball fans. "Berra bounced up, raced out to the mound, and leaped into the big pitcher's arms, like an oversized kid greeting papa," wrote Broeg, who was in Yankee Stadium that day.

Musial's biggest moments on the national stage during this period came at the All-Star game. At the 1955 matchup in Milwaukee, Musial led off the bottom of the 12th inning with the game tied. Berra, the starting catcher for the American League, was still playing. Chatting at home plate, both men admitted they were tired. Musial proceeded to hit the first pitch for a game-winning home run. Stan still holds the career record for most All-Star game home runs with six. But one or even two All-Star games in the summertime (the leagues met twice from 1959 to 1962) are no match for the magic of October baseball.

The unkindest cut for St. Louis fans is that the two could have been teammates. "When I was 16, Rickey told me I couldn't run and would never make the majors," Berra said in the winter of 1947, a story he would repeat over the years and one that never failed to make Cardinals fans cringe.[43] So Yogi signed with the Yankees instead and proceeded to get years of postseason attention, accolades, and money. (He collected $82,979 from those 14 World Series.) Musial's glories were largely appreciated by a Cardinals fanbase, still growing despite some challenging years, thanks to an ever-expanding radio network and the man behind the microphone who loved to watch Musial play.

Stan the Man was Caray's favorite player.

*****

"When I am asked to name the best player I've ever seen, I don't have to think about it," Caray wrote in his autobiography. "It's not even a debatable question as far as I'm concerned. The answer is simple. Stan Musial." From 1947 to 1963, with Caray calling all games home and away, Stan sparked the memories. Harry provided the soundtrack.

In 1948, Musial won his third and final MVP award. In a season in which Caray broadcast over a 43-station network, Musial led the National League in runs (135), hits (230), doubles (46), triples (18), batting average (.376), RBI (131), on-base percentage (.450), slugging percentage (.702), and total bases (429). He missed a triple crown by a single home run. Stan hit 39. Ralph Kiner hit 40.[44] A five-hit game in May at Ebbets Field (one of four five-hit games he had that season) cemented his reputation among Dodgers fans, forever making Stan "the Man" among the Brooklyn faithful.[45]

"I remember Sunday, May 2, 1954, which might have been his best day of all," Caray stated. "The Cardinals were playing the New York Giants in a doubleheader and I called every inning." In the first game, Musial went 4-4 with three home runs and six RBI in a 10-6 St. Louis victory. In the nightcap, a 9-7 win for the Giants, Stan hit two more home runs. "No one had ever hit five home runs in one day," said Caray. "And as I recall, Musial hit three more balls right on the nose, each time sending Willie Mays toward the flagpole in center field."[46] Caray described each at-bat over a Cardinals radio network that had more than doubled in size to 92 stations.[47]

In 1956, *The Sporting News* named Musial its Player of the Decade.[48] A season later, the year he turned 37, Musial hit .351. Cardinals public relations director Jim Toomey calculated that Stan came to the plate that season with 171 runners in scoring position. He drove in 102.[49]

Career hit number 3,000 came at Wrigley Field in May of 1958. It wasn't supposed to happen that way. When the Cardinals left St. Louis for a series in Chicago, Musial was two hits shy of the milestone. After he got a hit in the first game, manager Fred Hutchinson announced Musial would take a seat the next day. Stan was sunning himself in the bullpen when he got the call to pinch-hit in the sixth inning with the Cardinals down 3-1. Before a crowd of just 5,692, he came to the plate with a runner on second base and one out, when he connected for a hit off pitcher Moe Drabowsky. "There it is! Into left field! Hit number 3,000!" Caray screamed into his microphone. "A run has scored! Musial around first, on his way to second with a double! Holy cow, he came through!"

After a brief celebration in which photographers stormed the field and the ball was presented to Musial, Stan's day in uniform was through.[50] After the game, one of the photographers asked him if he knew who the blonde woman was who kissed him on his way back to the dugout. "I'd better," Stan replied. "She's my wife." The ride back to St. Louis featured cake, champagne, and gifts. Caray presented Musial with a pair of diamond cuff links. The Illinois Central train made multiple stops, as adoring fans turned out to pay their respects. "It was like a triumphant parade," Caray remembered (later calling it his "greatest day" in baseball). Hundreds roared their approval when the Cardinals pulled into Union Station that night. "I know now how Lindbergh must have felt when he returned to St. Louis," Musial told the crowd.[51] The trip is also recalled for another reason. "This would be the Redbirds' last team trip by train – memorable!" wrote Broeg.

In St. Louis the next night in front of 20,000 fans, Musial connected for hit number 3,001 in his first at-bat, a home run that landed on the right field roof.

In May of 1962, Musial surpassed Honus Wagner as the all-time hits leader in the National League. "I got it! I got it!" Stan screamed after hit number 3,431. At the All-Star game that year in Washington D.C., Musial chatted with President John F. Kennedy. It was the second time the two men had met. On the 1960 campaign trail in Wisconsin, JFK told Stan, "They tell me you're too old to play ball and I'm too young to be President, but maybe we'll fool them." Two years later, Musial was again an All-Star and Kennedy was in the White House. "I guess we fooled them, all right, Mr. President," Stan told him. Musial's last day in a Cardinals uniform came 54 days before the President was gunned down in Dallas.

When he decided to retire in 1963, Musial made the announcement on an August night at Grant's Farm in St. Louis. "Baseball has been my life," he said as he wiped away tears. "There's nothing like playing and hitting." That evening, he heard praise from teammates, front-office executives, columnists Broeg and Burnes, and the man who described so much of his career on the radio. "Stan, if it hadn't been for you and your feats, I couldn't have lasted on this job as long as I have," Caray told him. "You made my job easier."[52]

As his career wound down, praise poured in from all over baseball. "He's my kind of player," said Ty Cobb. "He has the power of Nap Lajoie, the stamina of Eddie Collins, and is steady as old Honus Wagner." Cobb believed Musial was "a better player than Joe DiMaggio in his prime."[53] Cubs outfielder Billy Williams called Musial his favorite player. Hall of Fame third baseman Pie Traynor remembered the minor league injury that turned Stan from pitcher to outfielder. "Musial, if he hadn't hurt his throwing arm, would have been a perfect player. I never saw anyone better at turning first base at full speed in an almost square turn without losing a stride."[54]

His batting stance, once described by a former player as "a kid looking around the corner to see if the cops were coming," always drew interest and scrutiny. "Musial's stance is unorthodox," wrote *Associated Press* reporter Joe Reichler. "Before squaring off on the left side of the plate, he limbers up with a hula-like motion, bat held above his head, hips and shoulders waggling. It never fails to draw a laugh from the crowd, especially on ladies' day. Before the pitch, he goes into a crouch in the far outside corner of the batter's box, stands motionless as a statue, his feet close together, knees bent, body slanted forward." Leo Ward, the longtime traveling secretary of the Cardinals, first saw the stance when Stan debuted in 1941. "All I could think of then, was how the heck was he ever going to hit the ball?" Caray credited Rickey, running the

Cardinals at the time, for being "smart enough not to tamper with Stan's unorthodox swing."[55]

What Harry remembered and appreciated most about Musial didn't occur on the baseball field. It's what happened after the games were over and the crowds had largely dispersed. There would always be some young fans looking for a Musial autograph when he left the ballpark on a late Sunday afternoon. "At the end of one of those marathon dog-day doubleheaders, other ballplayers might duck the crowd. And who could blame them, really?" Caray asked. "But when Musial came out, it was different," he remembered. "Forty-five minutes, an hour. It didn't matter. Stan would not flinch. He would not complain. He would always have a smile or a kind word. He even carried pictures of himself to give away. He figured it was just as much a part of his job as hitting home runs or making great catches. And he was right, of course. I think it's a real shame that more athletes haven't developed Musial's sense of and flair for public relations."

Stan's final game occurred on Sunday, September 29. He began the day driving from his home to the stadium with actor Horace McMahon, star of the television show *Naked City*. McMahon flew in from Connecticut for the special occasion. Musial was Godfather to the actor's son.[56] On the way to the clubhouse, he ran into Joe Medwick, outfielder for the Gashouse Gang. "Fellows," Stan announced to the press, "this is the guy I replaced as the regular left fielder 22 years ago." A short time later, Musial's trip down memory lane continued as general manager Bing Devine stopped by. "Bing and I broke in together in the Cardinals organization in 1938," Stan recalled. Someone asked him how many hits he'd like on his last day. "How many [career hits] do I have now?" he asked. Told the number was 3,628, he said, "I'd like 3,630 ... I like the nice, round figures."

In a pregame ceremony on the field, Caray had a request. "Please hit one more out on Grand Avenue today." Stan didn't hit a home run, but he did get two hits on his final day, both past the rookie Cincinnati second baseman Pete Rose, who would later break Musial's record for career hits in the National League. The pair of singles balanced the ledger for Stan – 1,815 at home to match his 1,815 hits on the road. "Take a good look, fans. Take a good look," Caray told his audience during Musial's final at-bat in the sixth inning. "Remember the stance. And the swing. You're not likely to see his likes again."

Musial went into the Hall of Fame in July of 1969 following an incredible weekend of news. On Saturday, Massachusetts Senator Ted Kennedy gave a nationally televised address, explaining his role in a car accident that led to the drowning death of Mary Jo Kopechne. On Sunday, the Apollo 11 astronauts who landed on the moon returned to American soil. On Monday, Cooperstown honored Stan. Caray made the trip from St. Louis after calling an 8-2 Cardinals victory on Sunday over a 101-station radio network, 26 stations more than any other team in the National League.[57] Before his own day of honor two decades later, it was the only trip he ever made to the Hall of Fame. "Stan broke down, and I cried, too," he remembered.

In 1971, Harry upped the ante. This time, he linked himself to Musial in a prideful statement, but one tinged with anger and bitterness. In January, Chicago baseball writers held their annual dinner. Commissioner Bowie Kuhn attended, as did St. Louis native Earl Weaver, fresh off a World Series championship as manager of the Baltimore Orioles. But the big draw that night was Caray, on the verge of his first season with the White Sox. "Still larger than life," wrote Bob Logan in the next day's *Chicago Tribune*. "Virtually all of the dozens of baseball figures, writers, radio-TV men and sports scene hangers-on there last night joined the pilgrimage to Caray's table to exchange greetings," he noted. When it came time for Caray to speak, he delivered a message he knew would get a reaction back in his hometown.

"There were just two names in St. Louis," Harry told the crowd. "Stan Musial and me."[58]

---

[1] *St. Louis Globe-Democrat*, January 17, 1947.

[2] Kroc, the man who turned McDonald's into a global franchise operation, died in 1984 with an estimated net worth of $600 million. His widow, Joan Kroc, died in 2003. Among the many gifts in her estate were $60 million to Ronald McDonald charities, $200 million to National Public Radio, and $1.5 billion to the Salvation Army. In 1988, she gave the Salvation Army $92 million to build a community center in San Diego.

[3] Smith, *Voices of the Game*.

[4] Baseball owners moved to eliminate doubleheaders following a night game in December of 1946. "Those grand people from the country, baseball fans who journeyed long distances to attend Sunday doubleheaders in St. Louis, apparently don't have the same standing that they once enjoyed," wrote Roy Stockton. *St. Louis Post-Dispatch*, December 8, 1946. Breadon announced plans for the Cardinals to broadcast home and road games a month later.

[5] *Sports Illustrated*, April 16, 1990. Average home runs per game in 1950 were 1.79 compared to 1.40 in 1989. Average stolen bases per game were 0.60 in 1950 versus 1.57 in 1989. By 2019, the numbers were 2.78 for home runs and 0.94 for stolen bases. Teamrankings.com

[6] During his playing career, Marion worked at a printing company in the offseason owned by St. Louis businessman Milton Fischman. In 1957, the two men joined forces in an attempt to buy the Minneapolis Lakers and move the team to Kansas City. The pair offered $150,000 but a group of Minneapolis businessmen raised $200,000 to keep the

team in Minnesota. It was a short-lived success. The Lakers moved to Los Angeles in 1960.
[7] Galbraith published the book in 1958.
[8] Garagnani married Theresa Lydon in 1937. Like her husband, she was active in the family restaurants for decades. In June of 1943, police raided the Brass Key, located at 5453 Magnolia Avenue. The raid took place on a Sunday night. Once inside, police found 12 persons in the bar, "several of them drinking highballs." Garagnani was arrested and booked for violation of the Sunday closing law. *St. Louis-Globe-Democrat*, June 7, 1943.
[9] One newspaper report put the crowd from the Hill at approximately 1,800. Joe's mother received a bouquet of roses and his father was presented with a wristwatch. Garagiola contributed a two-run double in the game won by the Cardinals 10-1. Garagnani was a member of the organizing committee that featured a priest, a judge, and Louis G. "Midge" Berra, Yogi's second cousin and unofficial "King of the Hill." *St. Louis Globe-Democrat,* September 6, 1946, April 21, 1962.
[10] *St. Louis Post-Dispatch*, August 10, 1947. Musial biographer James Giglio described Garagnani as "notoriously cheap toward those who frequented his restaurant regularly … Yet, he could show considerable generosity toward friends, employees, and others in need." Giglio quotes Garagiola, who described Biggie as "tactful as a sledgehammer." Giglio, James N. *Musial: From Stash to Stan.* University of Missouri Press. 2001.
[11] Ibid, March 27, 1949. "Most observers say freely that the Cardinals will regret it if they ever give up this Sunshine City as a training base," wrote Roy Stockton about the setup in St. Petersburg. "The facilities are excellent, the weather is the best to be found anywhere and the fan interest is consistent year to year." The Musials and Garagnanis shared a beach cottage in the spring of 1949.
[12] Ibid, November 27, 1960. Garagnani credited Bob Hannegan, who briefly owned the Cardinals with Fred Saigh, for instigating the partnership. "Hannegan said, 'Can't you see he wants to be your partner?' Suddenly, I woke up," Biggie told columnist Joe Hendrickson. *Pasadena Independent*, June 7, 1965.
[13] "Red is a director of an East St. Louis bank, owns two bowling alleys and a productive 160-acre farm in Illinois, and operates a rest home in St. Louis which accommodates 65 guests." *Los Angeles Times*, August 27, 1967.
[14] When Cardinals outfielder Terry Moore retired after the 1948 season, he bought a bowling alley, partnering with his brother Frank and Sid Salomon Jr. They purchased the Regina Lanes at 6000 Natural Bridge Avenue. The price tag was estimated at $200,000. The name was changed to Terry Moore Bowling Lanes. Broadcaster France Laux was the bowling manager. *St. Louis Post-Dispatch,* December 21, 1948.
[15] *New York Times,* December 10, 2000.
[16] All but Garagnani also lived until their nineties. Schoendienst died at the age of 95, Musial 92, and Berra and Garagiola at 90.
[17] Halberstam, David. *The Fifties.* The Random House Publishing Group. 1993.

[18] *St. Louis Globe-Democrat*, August 22, 1954. Musial would later write the forward to Schoendienst's autobiography. "Red and I are as close as brothers," he stated. After the 1946 World Series, Schoendienst and his five brothers (all but one played professional baseball) went on a barnstorming tour throughout Missouri and Illinois. The opposing team featured Berra, Garagiola, and Dodgers outfielder Pete Reiser. *The Sporting News*, January 23, 1965.

[19] The Society for American Baseball Research (SABR) lists Berra's salaries of $58,000 in 1956 and $65,000 in 1957 as the highest in all of baseball. *https://sabr.org/research/article/mlbs-annual-salary-leaders-since-1874/*. *The Sporting News* reported Musial's salary in those years at $80,000.

[20] Spink, the longtime publisher of *The Sporting News*, was a big Musial fan. Hearing whispers that the Cardinals were about to trade Musial to the Philadelphia Phillies in 1956, he phoned Stan to give him a heads-up. Musial then reportedly told Cardinals management he would retire before being traded. Trade plans were quietly dropped. *Wall Street Journal*, May 29, 1975. (Broeg disagreed. "Truth is, Stan would have gone, if traded.") Spink dined one evening with a Chrysler executive. Later, his daughter-in-law asked about his reaction. "Boy, he was dull," Spink replied. "He didn't even know who Stan Musial was." *Los Angeles Times*, April 7, 1986. Broeg served as Spink's ghostwriter. "If he wanted a story written about a person or situation with which I was in disagreement, I would write using his name, not mine. Happily, that didn't happen often." Broeg, *Memories of a Hall of Fame Sportswriter*.

[21] Musial and his restaurant were featured in a 1971 episode of the ABC television show *That Girl*, starring Marlo Thomas. While speaking engagements and travel kept him occupied in the winter, Musial was actively involved in the management of the business. "Musial has that long-established fondness for accounting," noted a story in the *Post-Dispatch*. He also had strong opinions about the restaurant's design and layout. "We always keep a baseball atmosphere, some of my trophies in front, but we change in the main room [every three years or so.] I didn't like the job we had just before this one. It was a little too effete for a steakhouse." *St. Louis Post-Dispatch*, November 27, 1960.

[22] "I am paying in on annuities. I am also buying Savings Bonds," Berra said in 1951. "Another thing, if I spend my winters in New York, I can get into some business. I believe I can make better connections than in St. Louis." *The Sporting News*, March 14, 1951.

[23] Ibid, January 23, 1957.

[24] Berra's long list of endorsements included Camel cigarettes, Shelby bicycles, Savoy clothing, and Doodle Oil [fishing] bait. By the mid-1950s, he was earning $15,000 or more from his endorsement deals. Pessah, Jon. *Yogi: A Life Behind The Mask*. Little, Brown and Company. 2020.

[25] Dan Daniel wrote that Berra and Rizzuto each invested $75,000 in the 40-lane bowling alley. After it was sold in 1962, Berra invested in a saloon with his brother. *The*

Sporting News, December 24, 1958, January 12, 1963. Mantle invested in a 32-lane bowling alley in Dallas that cost $200,000. According to Daniel, Mickey put up 90 percent of the money. Mantle also had a half-interest in a $300,000 motel in Joplin, Missouri.

[26] Garagnani told a St. Louis paper that he and Musial were the second largest shareholders in Brentwood Bank. *St. Louis-Globe Democrat,* April 3, 1956. "Our first place was Biggie's Restaurant and two years ago we bought Garavelli's Cafeteria. The two places did more than $1 million of business last year," Musial told the *Wall Street Journal*. The paper noted that Musial owned an interest in a third restaurant, two real estate companies and was elected a director of Southwest Bank of St. Louis. *Wall Street Journal*, October 4, 1955.

[27] *Pasadena Independent*, June 7, 1965. "I never had a feeling that Stan flaunted his money," said former teammate Jim Brosnan. "He and Schoendienst together were a couple of good guys who deserved all they got. They didn't lord over anyone." Golenbock, *The Spirit of St. Louis*. Fred Corcoran was Musial's business manager. When asked about Musial's salary and wealth, he replied, "I never talk about my friends' financial affairs. Let's just say Stan gets a very large salary and is a very wealthy man." *The Napa Register*, August 8, 1962.

[28] *Lake Charles American-Press*, July 2, 1964. The group paid $2 million for television station KPLC and $200,000 for KPLC radio. A 1975 Copley News Service article names the three hotels: the Ivanhoe in Miami Beach, the Hilton in Clearwater, and the Airport Hilton in St. Louis. The St. Louis hotel, purchased in 1973, underwent a $22 million renovation in 1984 and was sold in 1985. The buyers, Delphinance Development Corp., defaulted on their loan in 1987 and lost control of the property. *St. Louis Post-Dispatch*, October 3, 1987. Following Biggie's death, Musial's partnership continued with Jack Garagnani, Biggie's son. Their company also managed hotels. Eight months into a 10-year contract to manage the Majestic Hotel in St. Louis, the hotel owners ousted Stan Musial & Biggies Inc. as manager. At the time, the company's principals were Jack Garagnani and Stan's son, Dick Musial. Eight months after being removed by the Majestic owners, Stan Musial & Biggies Inc. was awarded $600,000 for being "wrongfully removed" as managers. *St. Louis Post-Dispatch,* January 17, 1988, September 1, 1988.

[29] The Winthrop ad featured both Stan and his son Dick. The Lifebuoy ad featured Musial and wife Lillian. "I never dreamed Stan's soap had such luxurious lather," she quipped. *The Sporting News,* September 10, 1947, July 14, 1948.

[30] *Wall Street Journal,* October 4, 1955.

[31] The Poll was conducted by Alan R. Nelson Research. Twenty national advertisers each paid $6,000 for the results. "Not bad for an old, retired ballplayer," Musial said to Joseph Durso when told of the survey results. *New York Times*, December 19, 1973.

[32] "I close my eyes when I play the harmonica," Musial said. "I'm glad I didn't hit that way." *St. Louis Post-Dispatch*, August 4, 1987. Over the years, Musial played the

harmonica with country musician Roy Clark (at an Iowa bar one night following a golf tournament) and trumpeter Al Hirt (both at Musial's restaurant in St. Louis and Hirt's club in New Orleans). *Los Angeles Times*, March 15, 1984.

[33] Musial and his wife once gave a reporter of the *Los Angeles Times* a tour of their home in Ladue. In a room adjoining the dining room, nearly every inch of wall space was covered in pictures. "This wall over here is some of the Presidents we have known. You'll notice a lot of Democrats, but we do have one Republican," she explained with a laugh. "Reagan entertained all of us Hall of Famers the Friday before he was shot," said Stan. "We were all at the White House." Ibid.

[34] *New York Daily News*, June 26, 1957.

[35] Flood, Curt with Richard Carter. *The Way It is*. Trident Press. 1971.

[36] *Sport*, May 1958.

[37] Musial is pictured in a Chesterfield cigarette ad that appeared in *The Sporting News* during the 1946 World Series. Before him, every Chesterfield ad in the St. Louis weekly that year featured a female endorser. He was one month shy of his 26th birthday. *The Sporting News*, October 16, 1946.

[38] Ibid, November 27, 1960. Musial put cream and sugar in his coffee until he and Schoendienst had breakfast with Ty Cobb one morning. "You should cut out one of them," Cobb told him. Musial stopped putting cream in his coffee. Cobb also told Musial, 35 at the time, to start drinking wine with dinner.

[39] Devito, Carlo. *Yogi: The Life & Times of an American Original.* Triumph Books. 2008.

[40] Schoor, Gene. *The Scooter: The Phil Rizzuto Story.* Charles Scribner's Sons. 2002.

[41] At issue was a $750 monthly management fee Dick Musial and Jack Garagnani each received over a period of three years. The total amount contested was $54,000. Garagiola claimed the arrangement was made without consulting him and that the two men didn't perform the services. The bowling alley had also loaned Stan Musial and Biggie's Inc. $130,000, which was repaid.

[42] Buck, Jack with Bob Broeg and Rob Rains. *Jack Buck: "That's a Winner!"* Sagamore Publishing. 1997.

[43] *St. Louis Star-Times*, January 21, 1947.

[44] Broeg wrote that Musial lost a home run that season due to a rainout, but the evidence is lacking. "Several researchers have come up empty in trying to locate this missing round-tripper," wrote Glen Sparks at Dazzy Vance Chronicles. https://dazzyvancechronicles.wordpress.com/2017/11/30/did-rain-wash-away-a-musial-home-run-and-triple-crown-in-48/

[45] While often credited to Brooklyn fans, it's unclear exactly when and where Musial first acquired the moniker. A UPI account at the end of Musial's career traced it to a series at Ebbets Field in 1948. Broeg thought it came from a series in 1946. In September of 1946, St. Louis sportswriter W. Vernon Tietjen referred to Musial as "the hitter even Brooklyn's hostile fandom refers to as 'The Man.'" *St. Louis Star-Times*,

September 25, 1946. A database search at newspapers.com shows references to "Stan the Man" increased sharply in 1948, particularly in the latter part of the season.

[46] Jack Buck largely corroborates Harry's account, saying, "Caray was on the air for all five homers." But while Harry recalled three hard-hit outs to Willie Mays, Jack remembered just one. Musial "might have had another [home run] with the longest ball he hit all day but it was to straightaway center and was caught by Willie Mays." Buck, *Jack Buck*.

[47] Walker, James R. *Crack of the Bat: A History of Baseball on the Radio*. University of Nebraska Press. 2015. The author lists the number of team radio stations for 1936-2001 in an appendix. 1936-1958, *The Sporting News*. 1959 and 1961, *Sponsor*. 1960 and 1962-2001 are from *Broadcasting* and *Broadcasting & Cable*.

[48] The announcement came in July of 1956, in the middle of a season in the middle of a decade. Did an ulterior motive by publisher Taylor Spink explain the odd timing? See endnote 20 of this chapter.

[49] Broeg, *Memories of a Hall of Fame Sportswriter*.

[50] "I should have left him in," Hutchinson admitted later.

[51] *St. Louis Post-Dispatch*, May 14, 1958.

[52] Ibid, August 13, 1963.

[53] "I don't want to argue with Ty Cobb," said Musial when informed of his comments, "but I can't say I was ever as good as Joe DiMaggio." New York *Daily News*, April 18, 1962.

[54] *The Sporting News*, August 2, 1969.

[55] Rickey appeared in a television show on KMOX-TV (now KMOV) in St. Louis the night before Musial's last game. Back with the Cardinals as a consultant, Rickey spoke of Musial's "true" batting stance once the ball left the pitcher's hand. "He is no longer in a crouch and his bat is full back and so steady a coin wouldn't fall off the end of it," he said. "There is no hitch. He is ideal in form." *The Sporting News*, October 12, 1963.

[56] McMahon played Lt. Mike Parker in the ABC police series and received an Emmy nomination for his role. "I once ran into Stan and Red in a little restaurant in New York, their favorite place," remembered Jim Brosnan. "Stan and Red were eating with a Hollywood actor – he became the star of a detective show on television – I had just come in, and they introduced him to me. They left, and he came over and sat down, and we talked. I thought, 'That was a real nice thing that Stan and Red did.' The two of them had passed along this TV star to me. It was the kind of thing you did if you were a Cardinal. You were introduced to the friends of players as if you were likely to be a friend of theirs, because you were a Cardinal." Golenbock, *The Spirit of St. Louis*.

[57] With 75 stations, the Cincinnati Reds had the second-most in the National League. Over in the American League, the Minnesota Twins also had 101 stations in their network. Walker, *Crack of the Bat*.

[58] *Chicago Tribune*, January 11, 1971.

Ticker Talk, a Death Threat, and a Sale

In the summer of 1947, visitors to St. Louis could board a Public Service Co. bus for a four-hour tour of the city. The company had a fleet of 10 buses, half of them in use every day of the week, with tours offered twice a day. Morning or afternoon, the cost was the same – $2.88. The curious sightseers got a first-hand look at Forest Park and the St. Louis Zoo, heard historical trivia – the cornerstone of the DeSoto Hotel was "laid by none other than President Harding" – and from the cobblestone streets of the Landing, peered across the Mississippi River to East St. Louis, Illinois. "A city of 100,000 with the largest horse and mule market in the world," their driver would explain.

From a script that made the Chamber of Commerce beam, the tour guide pointed with pride to the houses in the Central West End. "We're pretty much a home-minded city," bus driver Chris Reiterman told his audience one July day. "Thirty percent own their own homes." South Broadway, not far from the site of the current Busch Stadium, was once known as "Frenchytown, the city's bargaining, bickering, haggling center, so crowded on Friday and Saturday nights, you can't get by," the driver related. Further south was an area dominated by the descendants of Germans who settled there in the 1800s. "We sometimes call them the 'scrub Dutch,'" said Reiterman.

In between Frenchytown and Dutchtown, then and now, is the Soulard Market. Just south of there, in an area Reiterman described as "Little Bohemia," he called attention to the homes in the neighborhood. "Notice the scrubbed steps, the washed windows, the clean appearance of all these houses, old though they are. Good, God-fearing, hard-working people live in them, and most of them work for Anheuser-Busch." With those words, the tour made its longest stop of the day. Fully one hour of the four-hour expedition was consumed by a visit to the brewery that typically ended with two glasses of beer for the guests. ("Of course, when we had the Baptists in town the other week, I skipped this stop," Reiterman admitted. "You have to use your discretion.")[1]

In 1947, the Anheuser-Busch campus occupied 70 square blocks and employed 6,000 people. The company claimed it paid $96,000 daily in federal taxes. The largest brewery in the city was the fourth largest in the country, a great disappointment to new company president Gussie Busch. Despite a salary of $132,222, the largest in the city that year, he was not a happy man.[2] Busch didn't like being fourth largest at anything. Third or even second was no better. "Being second isn't worth shit," he once told a reporter. "These years were the low point for Gussie," wrote Peter Hernon and Terry Ganey, authors of *Under the Influence*, a history of the Busch dynasty. Under Gussie's leadership, the company would greatly expand its operations in the decades to come. When Anheuser-Busch broke ground for its brewery in Newark in 1950, the company's first outside St. Louis, Gussie turned the first spadeful of earth. By 1968, the company operated breweries in six American cities, with two more under construction.[3] Over that time, Busch's competitors would come to realize his ambitious and ruthless ways, something his family had already experienced.

Busch's father had willed the Shooting Grounds, a large farm in neighboring St. Charles County with a hunting lodge, to Gussie and his brother, Adolphus III. When Adolphus died in 1946, his will called for his property to be distributed to his wife and daughters. Gussie, who used the grounds to hunt ducks and geese, rope calves, and entertain friends and politicians, somehow bought his brother's family interests from the estate. "To this day," Hernon and Ganey wrote decades later, an Adolphus heir "doesn't know what happened."[4]

Around the time he took control of the Shooting Grounds, he was also pouring his efforts into restoring Grant's Farm.[5] Prohibition and the Great Depression combined to make the era Anheuser-Busch's greatest challenge. Before he committed suicide in 1934, Gussie's father, August A. Busch Sr. had to sell off many of the animals that roamed the 200-plus acres of the family estate. (Tessie, an elephant, was sold to Ringling Brothers Circus.)[6] Gussie, an enthusiastic outdoorsman and animal lover since his youth, focused on making the family home his private zoo. By the time it opened to the public in 1954, Grant's Farm boasted more than 1,000 creatures and 100 different species from six of the seven continents.

Just as with brewery tours, visitors to Grant's Farm could sample some fresh Anheuser-Busch libations. But those marketing efforts would pale in comparison to when A-B took control of a local sports team, and a baseball game was somehow squeezed in between endless pitches for a frosty cold Budweiser. The duo of beer and baseball would soon make Anheuser-Busch the dominant brewer in the country. But even then, Busch expressed frustration with the locals. As late as 1957, "St. Louis beer drinkers preferred Falstaff or Griesedieck Brothers."[7]

A decade earlier, on those summer days when Reiterman was touting the city's virtues to out-of-towners, visitors and locals alike were reminded of Busch's competitors every time they turned on their radios. On WIL, Dizzy Dean described Browns baseball and invited his listeners to enjoy a "Premium Quality Falstaff." Over WEW AM/FM and WTMV, Harry Caray called the action for the Cardinals and reminded fans that Griesedieck Brothers beer was "brewed with imported Bavarian hops."[8]

*****

Dean's season began just as his offseason ended; with plenty of complaints about Breadon's decision that made him a former Cardinals broadcaster and a full-time announcer for the Browns. While the three St. Louis daily newspapers largely offered only perfunctory coverage of the move – "Newspaper versus radio rivalry for the advertising dollar was intense," remembered Broeg – other media outlets had no such constraints. "Baseball next summer is not going to be like it used to was, as far as the Cardinals are concerned. We might as well face it," read an editorial in the weekly *Webster News-Times*. "The game is going to be a drab and dreary affair. At least for Cardinal radio sitters. Dizzy Dean is not going to be on the air for them," pronounced the publication from Caray's hometown of Webster Groves.[9]

The decision received even greater scrutiny and criticism outside the St. Louis area. While conceding he had never heard Dean describe a baseball game, *Richmond Times-Dispatch* columnist Chauncey Durden nevertheless felt compelled to write an entire 800-word piece on the topic. "From what we've heard and read, Dean's broadcasts were a far cry from the usual baseball broadcast," Durden informed his Virginia readers.[10] In Chicago, one writer viewed the situation through a constitutional lens. "All who cherish the inalienable right of free speech and abhor censorship as well as students of Elizabethan English, view with dismay Sam Breadon's decision to deny Dizzy Dean the privilege of broadcasting the Cardinals' home games next season," wrote Jack Clark in the *Chicago Sun*.

The Browns' decision to have Dean broadcast all their games came just two weeks after Breadon's announcement. So while Dizzy still had a microphone to say whatever crossed his mind, being passed over for Cardinals broadcasts stung him deeply. The raw emotions were on display at a testimonial dinner in April for new Browns manager Muddy Ruel. On the eve of baseball's opening day, the man who broadcast games for the St. Louis American League team focused his speech on the man who controlled the city's National League franchise. "Now let me tell you something about this guy Breadon and his penny-pinching business. I got a raw deal from Sam all the time I pitched for them there Cardinals," he told the audience at the Knights of the Cauliflower Ear banquet. Recounting his salary history as a player with the Cardinals, Dean revisited issues with Breadon in 1930, 1931, and 1934, the amount of money the Cardinals received when the team traded him to the Cubs in 1937, and even mentioned salaries paid to current major league players Bob Feller, Hank Greenburg, and the star of the Cardinals. "What does Breadon pay Stan Musial?" he asked. "He ought to get $60,000. Shouldn't he?" He fired a few more shots at Breadon before winding up his speech and returning to his seat. "Minus applause," noted Fred Lieb.[11]

"I guess we can't treat our players so badly, as this is the first world championship club we've ever had on which we didn't have a holdout," said Breadon, to roaring approval when it came his time to address the audience.

His world-champion Cardinals opened their season the next day in Cincinnati. Caray and Street traveled to Crosley Field to describe the action, but other than visits to there and Chicago, the broadcasters still relied on re-creations for road contests. Breadon's choice to call Cardinals games had one big advantage over Dean. Caray enjoyed recreating games from brief Western Union ticker descriptions.[12] Dizzy did not. "There shouldn't be broadcasts of this kind," a frustrated Dean said on the air one night while reading the wire. "[Browns infielder Sam] Dente up. Ball one. Strike one. Ball two. Folks, there's no use fooling you: the inning's over, but we just have to read you this stuff to make it sound like a ball game."[13]

Caray embraced the theater. At the beginning of the broadcast, he and Street would announce it was a re-creation and they would be working from information provided by Western Union. "But once we were into it, the fantasy was never interrupted," Caray said. "The key to working the wire was imagination, employing a little poetic license. To be able to do this was absolutely essential." The ticker provided only minimal information (e.g., B1 for ball one, S2 for strike two), leaving plenty of time for broadcasters to improvise and ad-lib. Caray and Street kept a picture of the park where the game originated in front of them, complete with the size, dimensions, and locations of the grandstand and bleachers. Their performance was so engrossing, "the station and newspapers have been compelled to answer many queries as to whether it is a ticker game, or the original, and wagers have been placed on the outcome," noted *The Sporting News*.[14]

Additional challenges came from lengthy delays in receiving updates, which occurred frequently. "When that happened, I would provoke an argument down on the field or maybe a disturbance in the stands that slowed play, or I would have a sandstorm kick up and have the players request time out to wipe their faces," Caray remembered. "We tried to keep the flow of the game intact, as if we were really there, and we developed a real sense of timing, of broadcasting give-and-take."

Flow of the game was never a consideration for Dean. He filled the gaps with whatever was on his mind at the moment, be it a song, favorite foods, or remembrances of seasons past (and occasionally falling asleep). Near the end of the 1947 season, Dean and partner Johnny O'Hara launched into a debate over who would win the upcoming World Series. A Browns baserunner stood at first base for 15 minutes until Dean, suddenly remembering the ballgame, announced he had scored on a base hit.

"The contrast between Dean and Caray is violent," wrote *New York Herald Tribune* columnist John Crosby. "Caray is an [sic] hysterical, rabidly pro-Cardinal announcer who shouts himself into exhaustion over any play larger than a foul tip. His broadcasts of telegraph games are little horrors of fakery. He uses recordings of crowd noises and the crack of a bat, invents endless phony details ('Kurowski is taking a long lead off first. Throw to first. Back in time.') that obviously are not carried on the wire, and almost goes out of his mind when any Cardinal gets as far as first base."[15]

Crosby's criticisms came as a rare moment of national scrutiny for Caray. In the early part of his career, Harry had support from the hometown *Sporting News* (winning broadcasting honors from the publication in 1946, 1948, 1950 and 1951), but otherwise, the men who controlled and critiqued the media largely ignored him. "Baseball has become a diversion of housewives," nationally syndicated columnist Red Smith wrote in 1949. "The gentle doves who formerly wept through the long afternoons over the misadventures of soap opera heroines have become so bemused by the accents of Red Barber or Jimmy Britt or Byron Saum or France Laux that they have crowded the men out of the grandstand."[16] A year earlier, when the All-Star Game came to St. Louis, it was Laux, and not Caray or Dean, who was tapped to be a member of the broadcast crew.[17]

*****

The Cardinals and Dodgers were the National League's greatest rivalry of the 1940s. From 1941 to 1949, St. Louis or Brooklyn won every NL pennant but two. Of the seven seasons Brooklyn or St. Louis won the title, the other team finished second five times. St. Louis native Mickey Owen played for both teams. Pete Reiser was born in St. Louis, played minor league ball for the Cardinals and played the majority of his career with the Dodgers. Joe Medwick won a triple crown with St. Louis in 1937 and was traded to Brooklyn in 1940. The man in charge of the Cardinals when all three of them were signed to professional contracts famously switched sides after the 1942 season.[18] Rickey, the architect of the modern farm system in St. Louis, engineered the breaking of baseball's color barrier in Brooklyn. In the summer of '47, the combination of old rivals and new entrants brought a boiling rivalry nearly to a breaking point.

Jackie Robinson made his major-league debut on April 15. His first game against the Cardinals came less than a month later, in early May at Ebbets Field. The day after the series concluded, *New York Herald Tribune* editor Stanley Woodward dropped the bombshell claim that the Cardinals were coordinating a league-wide strike against Robinson when the Dodgers came to St. Louis later in the month. The strike was averted when Breadon alerted Ford Frick to the possibility. The National League president responded by saying any striking player would be suspended, a message passed along to the players.

The ending of any strike talk did little to abate the intensity of the rivalry on the field. "I don't think we had any personal love for anybody on the whole club, and I'm sure they didn't for us," shortstop Marion said of the battles with the Dodgers. At Ebbet's Field in August, Robinson was playing first base when Enos Slaughter hit a groundball on the infield. Slaughter spiked Robinson as he crossed the bag. "All I know is I had my foot on the inside of the bag. I gave Slaughter plenty of room," said Robinson. "I never spiked anyone intentionally in my life. Anybody who does, doesn't belong in baseball," maintained Slaughter. [19]

Caray makes no mention of the incident in his autobiography (as a re-created road game, he likely didn't know the details until he read the paper the next day), nor did he mention another spiking of Robinson the following month.[20] This time, he witnessed the event at Sportsman's Park. In the bottom of the second inning in a game on September 11, Garagiola grounded into a double play, making contact with Robinson as he crossed first base. "He cut my shoe all to pieces," Robinson said after the game, adding that he didn't think the Cardinals catcher did it intentionally. But when it came time for Robinson to hit in the top of the third, the two men had to be separated by the umpire. "Umpire Reardon stepped between them, shoving Garagiola away," noted reporter Martin Haley.

Caray, who would tussle and trade barbs with players and managers alike throughout his career, idolized Walter Winchell and loved to stir the pot with on-air commentary, suddenly became Switzerland when calling baseball games with Robinson. He was neutral.

"While all this was going on, I was neither a crusader nor a social commentator, I was a baseball announcer," Caray recalled. "I talked about how he played the game. Just the same way I talked about how Stan Musial and Ralph Kiner and Pee Wee Reese and Andy Pafko and the other great stars of the National League played the game." Caray admired Robinson, calling him, with the possible exception of Willie Mays, the most exciting player he had ever seen and "the greatest base runner who ever lived." Whatever he said about Robinson drew plenty of attention and criticism.

"Our radio station was picked up in all the southern states when I was in St. Louis. And I used to get letters from people all the time calling me racist names because I loved Jackie Robinson," Steve Stone remembered Caray telling him. "They called me a 'you-know-what-lover' because I thought he was a great player. Can you believe that crap? What makes people so damn sick?"[21]

*****

In the summer of 1949, the Cardinals received an unsigned letter from someone threatening to blow up the park and kill Caray. The *St. Louis Globe-Democrat* broke the story on the morning of July 29, the same day the Cardinals began a three-game series at Sportsman's Park against the Dodgers. Under the banner headline, "HARRY CARAY GETS DEATH THREAT," the story explained how Caray received protection from police the day before, with authorities guarding the booth and detectives roaming the park "looking for suspicious characters." The handwritten letter had a St. Louis postmark and was sent to the team, not the broadcaster. Cardinals management turned it over to the FBI. While Caray acknowledged FBI agents had questioned him about its content, he told reporters, "I have received no threatening letter and I have asked for no protection from the police." He downplayed the threat at the time, saying, "I don't think there is anything for anyone to worry about. Out of about 35,000 letters a year, we're bound to get a few unpleasant ones."[22] With a squad of 50 patrolmen and detectives in and around the park for the weekend, the series against the Dodgers came and went without incident. (All three games drew more than 30,000 fans.)[23]

Years later, Caray would captivate reporters with the death threat tale, while conflating its timeline with another memorable milestone. Instead of tying the threat to the beginning of a series against Robinson and the Dodgers in 1949, Caray remembered it as validation in his battles with Dean to become the voice of the Cardinals in 1947. "The Cardinals had to decide on Diz and me. Now Diz did a good job for Diz, but my partner, Gabby Street, and I did a better job of selling the ball club," he remembered. "Now [advertising executive] Oscar Zahner was the man who had to make the decision on who would get the job, and I finally win. I get the job, but now I want the money that Diz is getting. Zahner says, 'Harry, Diz gets the publicity. He gets his name in the papers and you don't.' Zahner and I go to the theater that night. We're still haggling over the money."

He recalled to more than one reporter how the story broke that evening. "I'm at the theater as all this is going on. Now the morning papers came out at 9 at night. So Zahner and I are walking out of the theatre and this newsboy is yelling, 'Read all about it. Harry Caray receives death threat. Read all about it.' I can't believe my ears. I'm dreaming, I think. There's this big crowd and I push my way through and buy a paper. Hell, there's this big headline like war had been declared. So I hand the paper to Zahner and say, 'You sonuvabitch, Dizzy Dean never got publicity like this.' I got my money. I was a cocky kid in those days."[24]

*****

The September 1947 series where Garagiola and Robinson had a heated exchange ended with the Dodgers leaving town up by 5.5 games over the second-place Cardinals. The final standings told a similar story. Brooklyn won 94 games to claim the National League pennant. St. Louis won 89 games to finish second. Manager Dyer blamed the finish on Musial's appendicitis, Howie Pollet's arm troubles (the lefthander won 21 games in 1946, but just nine in 1947), and injuries to Slaughter. A horrible start to the season (in last place with a 9-19 record in mid-May) and bad luck conspired against them. For the season, the Cardinals scored six more runs than the Dodgers and allowed 33 fewer, but won five less games than their rival.[25] "St. Louis lost this year because it tried to stand pat with a world championship outfit that had played a little over its head and was a little past its peak," concluded columnist Hy Turkin in the New York *Daily News*.

Two-and-a-half weeks later, the same paper published a report that Larry MacPhail, who had just sold his interest in the Yankees, was planning to meet with Breadon about possibly buying the Cardinals.[26] Both men quickly denied the report.[27] While the newspaper had the wrong buyer, rumor became reality a month later.

A Browns season that began with Dean in the broadcasting booth ended with him on the mound. The team signed Dizzy to a contract in mid-September, much to the disappointment of their manager. Upset about not being told about the decision, Ruel responded with a terse "No comment" when asked by reporters if Dean would be used in a game. Dizzy wanted the chance to pitch again (he hadn't appeared in a big-league game since 1941) and was so eager to get back in uniform that he signed a contract for a $1. "This is the first baseball contract I signed without first turning it back for more money."[28] Ownership needed the crowd they knew it would attract. Both got their wish in the final game of the year.

In the third inning against the White Sox at Sportsman's Park, Dean came to the plate with a striped bat he called his "zebra model" and was told by the umpire it was illegal. (One account described it as a miniature bat.) He returned to the bat rack and grabbed a red-striped one, "this one was even more grotesquely decorated," noted the *Post-Dispatch*. He promptly lined a single to left field. When the next batter hit an infield ground ball, Dean was out at second base, but not before he made a hard slide into the bag. He came up limping, but managed to pitch the next inning before departing to cheers. In four innings, Dean allowed three hits and issued one walk, but gave up no runs. The Browns lost the game, 5-2, their 95th loss of a last-place season. The crowd of 15,916 was the team's third largest of the season.

Still upset about the publicity stunt, Ruel didn't manage the final game, turning the duties over to coach Fred Hofmann. While the manager was still in the park (he spoke to reporters from the clubhouse afterward), Browns management missed the affair entirely. Owner Muckerman, general manager DeWitt, and two other officials, all accompanied by their wives, left at noon for New York to attend the World Series. Writing of Dean's final appearance in a big-league game, *New York Times* columnist Arthur Daley noted, "there was something disgraceful about it from the long-range point of view. Dean is not to blame. The Browns are to blame. It's a sad state of affairs when baseball has to stoop to the hippodrome and the circus in order to draw customers."[29]

From May 7 to the last day of the season, the Browns spent all but two days in last place. The team drew just 320,474 fans for the year, a drop of more than 200,000 from the previous season. A home game on July 14 attracted just 478 fans. In November, the club announced that the final tally on improvements to Sportsman's Park came to $700,000. (DeWitt later revised the figure to $775,000.)[30] The original estimate was $180,000. Muckerman's Browns had purchased the ballpark from the Dodier Realty Company in the fall of 1946, paying a half-million dollars for the privilege.[31] With ownership of both antiquated real estate and a flailing franchise, Browns management now had two bottomless pits. Over the next few months, the club would sell players that returned nearly $500,000, embarking on a vicious cycle of poor performance and the selling of talent, which only guaranteed more bad teams.[32] The World Series of 1944 already seemed like a distant memory.

While the Browns were busy selling players, Breadon was selling out. On November 25, he announced the sale of the team to Postmaster General Robert Hannegan and real estate investor Fred Saigh.[33] The price tag was $4,060,000. Breadon's share came to a little more than $3 million. He would spend the last years of his life on his other business passion, real estate development. Suffering from cancer, Breadon died in May of 1949 at the age of 72. He would be remembered as a tightfisted owner to some, recalled as generous to former players by others, and celebrated for the most successful ownership reign in Cardinals history.[34]

While championship baseball would be his ultimate legacy, the selection of Caray would be his enduring final gift to Cardinals fans. Breadon's exit from baseball closed the first chapter of Harry's baseball broadcasting career. Caray had described a successful and stable franchise when he began calling Cardinals games in 1945. In Harry's first three years, the Cardinals won one World Series title and were the defending World Series champions for the other two. New owners brought new challenges and a new landscape. Comparisons between Caray and Dean would fade. One of Dizzy's biographers wrote that "he frequently lashed out at Breadon on Browns broadcasts."[35] With the ex-owner out of the picture, Dizzy's complaints would largely focus on the inept team he described daily. The 1948 Browns lost 94 games, one less than the previous season. The American League franchise, increasingly desperate for money, would look to the Cardinals to help solve their financial woes.

At Breadon's retirement dinner, Muckerman joked that he didn't field an offer for his team the entire night. The attendance at the event by the Browns president reflected an era of mutual cooperation between two franchises that shared a park, and whose players and managers had often worn the uniform of both teams in their careers. This amiable sibling rivalry would soon take a darker turn and more closely resemble a nasty domestic dispute. The battle between the St. Louis teams escalated almost from the moment Hannegan and Saigh took control of the Cardinals. It would eventually wind up in court where the source of the troubles would be revealed.

It all began with the Cardinals radio deal and the broadcasting of road games.

---

[1] *St. Louis Star-Times*, July 28, 1947.
[2] Ibid, June 13, 1949.
[3] A 1968 newspaper ad lists the six brewery locations as St. Louis, Newark, Los Angeles, Tampa, Houston, and Columbus. Plants were under construction in Merrimack, New Hampshire and Jacksonville, Florida.
[4] Hernon, Peter and Ganey, Terry. *Under the Influence: The Unauthorized Story of the Anheuser-Busch Dynasty*. Simon & Schuster. 1991.
[5] Busch paid $800 for four buffaloes in 1947. "At Grant's Farm, they will join herds of many kinds of deer, Sicilian donkeys, an English stag and long-horned Texas steers, which roam the extensive grounds." *St. Louis Star-Times*, October 1, 1947.

[6] "His [August Sr.'s] extensive menagerie had become a costly drain as the Depression worsened," wrote Hernon and Ganey. The size of Grant's Farm has been reported over the years at 215, 273, and 281 acres. The "Big House," where many Busch family members lived, and 22 acres, remained private, even after large parts of Grant's Farm opened to the public. *St. Louis Post-Dispatch*, May 1, 2021.

[7] Hernon and Ganey, *Under the Influence*. Stag was another beer hugely popular with the locals. Another branch of the Griesedieck family controlled it – the Griesedieck Western Brewing Co. In 2019, 90 percent of Stag's business was in St. Louis or southern Illinois. *Belleville News-Democrat*, June 17, 2019.

[8] Quotes describing Falstaff and Griesedieck come from 1947 newspaper ads.

[9] *Webster News-Times* (Webster Groves, Missouri), February 6, 1947.

[10] *Richmond Times-Dispatch*, January 16, 1947.

[11] *The Sporting News*, April 23, 1947. With the world champion Cardinals opening on the road in Cincinnati and Jackie Robinson making his major-league debut at Ebbets Field, Commissioner Chandler made the curious decision to spend opening day 1947 in St. Louis watching the Browns and Tigers. (National League president Ford Frick was in Brooklyn.) "We are going through a crisis in the sports world," Chandler told columnist Sid Keener. "I have sent direct bulletins and instructions about gambling to the owners. I will expect them to watch and curb that evil. For myself, I have arranged to patrol every park when the season opens. My representatives and agents will watch for evidence of gambling, if any, and, if they find open betting, they will forward the reports to my office." Keener finished the story by noting that while the commissioner didn't name names, he was "hot on the trail of two certain big league officials." *St. Louis Star-Times*, April 15, 1947. The interview came five days after Chandler had suspended Dodgers manager Leo Durocher for the season. When the Cardinals unveiled six new advertising signs on the outfield walls in the spring of 1950 (three in left field, three in right), two new huge "No Gambling" signs were placed between them. *St. Louis Star-Times,* March 28, 1950.

[12] Western Union charged $27.50 a game to provide the ticker service from any major league park. In the early 1950s, the Liberty Broadcasting System provided a daily re-created game to its network of affiliates around the country. Liberty recorded various sounds and noises from major league ballparks as well as the local rendition of the Star-Spangled Banner to use in the broadcasts. Because of its own large network, the Cardinals refused to cooperate with Liberty. *Tampa Bay Times*, June 1, 1975.

[13] *The Sporting News*, August 28, 1948.

[14] Ibid, July 30, 1947.

[15] Reprinted in the *Washington Post*, September 28, 1947. He was more complimentary toward Dizzy. "Maturity and fame have quieted Dean considerably," Crosby wrote. "The fact that Dean, a former Cardinal and a National League player, should be calling the games of the team that occupies the cellar position in the American League is a triumph of commerce over art."

[16] *Miami Daily News*, June 7, 1949.

[17] Mel Allen and Jim Britt broadcast the 1948 All-Star Game over the Mutual Broadcasting System. "France Laux, veteran St. Louis ballcaster, turned in a capable recapping job," noted *The Sporting News*. Laux and Dean broadcast Browns games in 1948.

[18] After the final out of the 1942 World Series, "Rickey let out a terrific cheer," an unnamed informant told *Dayton Daily News* sports editor Si Burrick. "Then he said, 'We've won this World Series, and I've done my work. Now I can leave that blankety-blank-blank-blank of a Breadon happy!'" *Dayton Daily News*, November 26, 1947.

[19] Fifty years later, Enos was telling the same story. "I played the game like it was supposed to be played," he told a Robinson conference audience at Long Island University. He sounded more contrite responding to a fan a year earlier. Slaughter's typewritten, four-paragraph letter ended with this sentence. "I am sorry this incident has caused so much controversy." Slaughter was responding to Seth Swirsky, who wrote to more than 650 baseball players. He published their replies in a book. *Baseball Letters: A Fan's Correspondence With His Heroes.* Kodansha International. 1996. Slaughter's reply: "It was a low throw and Jackie pulled his foot off the bag. When he placed it back, his foot was in the middle of the base. I had no recourse but to unintentionally step on his ankle. Ken Burns [the documentary filmmaker] made the remark that I 'sliced his thigh open,' but there was no blood whatsoever. I do not know where he finds his sources, but I wish he would share them with me! Burns continually hangs up on me when I have called him to question him about these falsehoods. I am sorry this incident has caused so much controversy." Swirsky told *Post-Dispatch* columnist John McGuire that Slaughter "probably feels sorry about it." He also wrote to Marty Marion, on deck when Slaughter scored the winning run of the 1946 World Series. What was on Marion's mind watching Slaughter run? "To tell the truth – I don't know what I was thinking," Marty replied. Sharing a birthday with pitcher Nelson Briles, Swirsky wrote the former Cardinal about the final game of the 1968 World Series and his reaction to Jim Northrup's triple on a ball where Curt Flood slipped in the outfield. "My heart sank as I realized we were not going to repeat as World Champions," wrote Briles. "Life goes on! Have a glass of wine on me!"

[20] While not specifically mentioning the Slaughter or Garagiola incidents, Caray did write that by playing first base, Robinson "was really vulnerable to the bigots – and there were an awful lot of them." Caray, *Holy Cow!*

[21] Stone, Steve with Barry Rozner. *Where's Harry?: Steve Stone Remembers His Years with Harry Caray.* Taylor Publishing. 1999.

[22] *St. Louis Globe-Democrat, St. Louis Star-Times*, July 29, 1949. The letter writer had reportedly threatened to throw a tear gas bomb at Caray and ended with the statement: "Get someone else to broadcast your games." Fred Saigh denied reports that the letter contained a threat to blow up the ballpark. *St. Louis Post-Dispatch*, July 29, 1949. Caray said the only unpleasant letter he had personally received was from a

fan in Peoria, Illinois upset about his coverage of a recent series against the Dodgers in Brooklyn.

[23] Ibid, July 31, 1949. The *Globe-Democrat* called the weekend matchup the "Little World Series." The Saturday night crowd included Missouri governor Forrest Smith and the Archbishop of St. Louis, Joseph E. Ritter, credited with desegregating Catholic schools and hospitals in the St. Louis area. He conducted the world's first Mass in English at Kiel Auditorium in 1964. Caray wrote that the FBI's attention "cooled off" after a few days. "They were convinced that no one was going to kill me, so they went back to crime-busting. Much to my relief, I was able to go back to having fun." Caray, *Holy Cow!*

[24] *Sarasota Herald-Tribune*, March 7, 1975, *Florida Today*, March 30, 1975. Caray also told a version of the story in his autobiography, claiming it occurred in 1948. The *Florida Today* story incorrectly calls Zahner "Oscar Zonith." The year of the incident, 1949, Dean wasn't broadcasting any baseball. Tom Dailey and Johnny O'Hara called the Browns games. Dean hosted *Grandstand Managers*, a television show on KSD. By claiming Zahner was making the choice, Caray also appears to be confusing this episode with his initial hiring as a baseball broadcaster in 1945. Zahner's advertising agency represented Griesedieck. Dean had a contract with Falstaff. Finally, since Caray received protection from police that very day and had spoken to reporters about it, it defies credulity that he would be shocked the story would be in the newspaper.

[25] Based on run differential, the Cardinals projected to win 91 games, the Dodgers 87 games.

[26] New York *Daily News*, October 5 and 23, 1947.

[27] *Brooklyn Daily Eagle*, October 23, 1947. "This is the first I've heard of any meeting," said Breadon. "Any rumors that I am going to buy into any ball clubs, skating rinks, hot dog stands, or anything else for the next year are absolutely false," said MacPhail.

[28] *The Sporting News*, October 1, 1947. After the season, *Long Beach Press-Telegram* columnist Frank T. Blair wrote that Vern Stephens told him, "Dizzy undoubtedly received a percentage of the Sunday gate for his part in luring the fans through the turnstiles." *Long Beach Press-Telegram*, October 5, 1947.

[29] *New York Times*, October 16, 1947.

[30] "Sportsman's Park was bought in the fall of 1946 for $500,000 and extensive improvements that were made prior to the opening of the 1947 season cost us another $775,000," said DeWitt. *The Sporting News*, March 28, 1951.

[31] The Browns paid $50,000 in cash and borrowed $450,000. There were two 10-year notes – one at $350,000 at four percent interest payable in 120 monthly installments and the other for $100,000 on identical terms. Dodier Realty & Investment Co. became a wholly-owned subsidiary of the Browns. Total annual income for the real estate operation was $77,500; $30,000 in rent from the Browns, $35,000 from the Cardinals, $5,000 for park advertising, and $7,500 rent for retail stores under the stands. Taxes were estimated at nearly $30,000. Annual payments on the notes totaled $46,200,

leaving little margin for error. Ibid, November 26, 1947. James Paulson Ball, the son of former Browns owner Phil Ball, was asked why Sportsman's Park was sold for $500,000 when construction of the stands cost $650,000. "What else could you use it for?" Ibid, October 23, 1946.

[32] The biggest deal occurred on November 17, 1947, when the Browns shipped pitcher Jack Kramer and shortstop Vern Stephens to the Boston Red Sox for six players and $310,000 in cash. "The deals stemmed the financial tide momentarily, but they set the ball club back so far that it never recovered," wrote W.J. McGoogan. *St. Louis Post-Dispatch,* July 22, 1962.

[33] Breadon and Hannegan "had been neighbors for years and shared a mutual admiration for baseball," noted an *Associated Press* story the day after the sale was announced.

[34] "Breadon was looked upon in one extreme or another. People either liked him or they didn't. He was called a tight old skinflint by some, and he was actually called kind and generous by others," wrote Si Burrick. "Rickey always implied ... that the reason he paid the Cardinals such miserly salaries in his St. Louis days was that he always had Breadon's restraining hand over him." *Dayton Daily News*, November 26, 1947. "Sports page readers frequently got a distorted notion of the Cardinals owner, colored by ignorance and provincialism," wrote Red Smith.

[35] Staten, *Ol' Diz.*

Mavericks and Exiles

When Bob Hannegan ascended to the title of Cardinals president, he became the first native St. Louisan to ever run the franchise. 1948 turned out to be quite a year for the one-time St. Louis University athlete and Democratic Party power broker.[1] The man Hannegan helped become a U.S. Senator and Vice President became the first Missourian elected to the White House in the fall when Harry Truman defeated Thomas Dewey. (The iconic photo of Truman holding up a newspaper with the headline "Dewey Defeats Truman" was snapped at Union Station in St. Louis.) That same year, Hannegan's Cardinals drew more than one million fans and again finished second in the National League. The 1949 Cardinals did even better, winning 96 games and setting a franchise attendance record of more than 1.4 million, a mark that wouldn't be eclipsed until the team moved into a new ballpark seventeen years later.

Hannegan's partner was once the subject of a fawning profile by columnist Roy Stockton, who saw in Fred Saigh the combined attributes of Breadon and Rickey. "Both men plus a little more. All of the idea production that made Rickey so valuable. All the business astuteness of Breadon."[2]

Meanwhile, the team's broadcaster proved so popular with fans that local radio stations began playing the "Harry Caray Polka."[3] The song featured composer Glenn Young's band and a vocal group called "The Base Hits." Caray could be heard on the recording with his staple phrases ("Holy Cow!" ... "It Might Be..."). "As polkas go, this is as good as most," wrote a reviewer in the *Post-Dispatch*.[4] Harry became so associated with "Holy Cow!" he wrote a syndicated column under the title and applied for a trademark.[5]

He expected to invoke the phrase often. No, these were no longer Breadon and Rickey's Cardinals, but the team still appeared formidable. The Cardinals finished first or second every year for nine straight seasons, the club had the best player in the league in Stan Musial, and one of the owners had ties that reached all the way to 1600 Pennsylvania Avenue. What could go wrong? As it turned out, quite a bit.

Hannegan, in poor health, sold out his interests in the Cardinals to Saigh in January of 1949. "My physician has advised me that the tension and pressure of the work as president of the Cardinals is not conducive to the completion of the health program he has outlined for me," read a statement he issued to the press. Saigh paid between $866,000 and $1 million for Hannegan's share of the team ($700,000 in cash and securities valued between $166,000 and $300,000).[6] While press reports at the time indicated both men had owned roughly the same amount of the franchise, Broeg always insisted Saigh was the larger shareholder of the two from the beginning (70/30 split).[7] Regardless, Saigh now controlled an estimated 90 percent of the stock and became the club's third president in fourteen months.[8] Hannegan died of a heart attack in October at the age of 46, just five months after the team's previous president, Breadon, had passed away.

The new man in charge of the team, the 43-year-old Saigh, had worked as a relatively obscure criminal lawyer in town until a series of large-scale commercial real estate transactions in the late 1940s. Combined with the purchase of the Cardinals, Saigh had engineered deals conservatively estimated at $15 million in about three years. "Everywhere St. Louisans are asking the same question: Where does this latter-day Golden Boy get the dough?" a reporter for the *Star-Times* inquired in August of 1949.[9] Among those who wanted an answer to that question was Commissioner Chandler, who went so far as to hire a former FBI agent to investigate Saigh's finances. The commissioner and the owner would repeatedly clash over the next few years and both men would suffer for it. Chandler lost his job. Saigh would later go to prison.

As for the man behind the microphone, Caray's professional life boomed while his relationship with his wife deteriorated. After he told her he no longer loved her, Harry set up residence at the Sheraton Hotel in August. Three months after the couple separated, their divorce became final.

The same year Hannegan died and Caray divorced proved to be a season of frustration for Saigh's Cardinals. After 149 games, St. Louis had a 1.5-game lead over Brooklyn. The Cardinals then dropped four of their last five contests. The Dodgers won three of their last four to edge their rivals for the pennant by a single game. "I wonder when we're going to get this close again," Broeg said to manager Dyer on the train ride home following the last game of the season.

Saigh also had other worries. In April, the Browns filed a lawsuit against the Cardinals, seeking to evict them from Sportsman's Park. Later, under oath, the Cardinals president would concede no other parks in St. Louis were suitable for his team, and acquiring a new property would take two to three years. He also angered his American League counterparts when he claimed the Browns needed refinancing and suggested the club move to Baltimore. "Mr. Saigh does not know anything about our club, and it is none of his business what we do about the club or its finances," said Browns president Bill DeWitt.

The final intervening years between Breadon and Busch were grim for both St. Louis teams. After the 1940s, the Cardinals were headed in one direction. Down. After the 1940s, the Browns were going one way. Out. But the man who began his baseball broadcasting career calling games for both teams would not only survive but thrive during this interregnum. Caray would emerge from this transition with a new wife and new broadcast partners, and would soon be touting the virtues of a new beer.

*****

"Caray has gone completely overboard. Did you hear a remark he made before the start of the Cardinals-Cubs game last Wednesday night?" asked a columnist in the summer of 1949. "There seem to be some Cub fans here," Harry had said. "They've got a lot of guts to boo the Cards with the Cubs in eighth place."[10]

Assertive and secure in his role by the late 1940s, Caray was no longer a rookie baseball broadcaster. "Holy Cow, how he eats, breathes, and lives each game he broadcasts!" one fan exclaimed in a letter to the *Post-Dispatch*. In July, a picture of a shirtless Caray broadcasting from his booth at Sportsman's Park appeared in *The Sporting News*. "He obligingly put on his trousers for the photographer," noted the publication.

The relentless pace he had maintained since his return to St. Louis was on full display in 1949. In addition to live or re-created broadcasts of every Cardinals game, he still had his nightly show on KXOK radio. His offseason play-by-play broadcasts included St. Louis University basketball. In February, Caray had launched a campaign to have Billiken boosters show up for a game against the Oklahoma A&M Aggies (now Oklahoma State) with cowbells in hand. The effort had its roots in the same matchup from a year earlier when a handful of Aggies' fans had descended on Kiel Auditorium with the noisemakers and nearly rivaled the audio output of 10,000 Billiken faithful.[11] With Caray sounding the drumbeat, area fans responded.

"A radio announcer's gag turned Kiel Auditorium into a first-class bedlam for the Oklahoma Aggie-St. Louis basketball game here Saturday night," the *Daily Oklahoman* recognized the next day. "Harry Caray, local sportscaster, suggested that fans all bring cowbells – traditional noisemakers of the Stillwater Cowboys – to the game, and at least 10,999 of the 11,000 fans must have responded. The decibel rating probably was ten times any noise ever generated for the Aggies on their home court."[12]

The basketball game was not the only event at the venue that evening. "The Cowbell sonata provided an unusual background for a cowboy concerto being given by Gene Autry, in another section of Kiel Auditorium, separated from the basketball arena only by a stage curtain."[13] While the effort was not a total success – the Aggies won the game 40-37 against the Billikens, the defending N.I.T. champions – there was no doubt that Caray's pitch had considerable influence. "St. Louis University officials estimated they could have sold 50,000 tickets for the contest, had seats been available. Ducats were selling for as much as $35 a pair on the street five hours before the game."[14]

When the Billikens best player, All-American Ed Macauley, was honored by St. Louis University High School in April, Caray served as master of ceremonies. In constant demand as MC or an after-dinner speaker, Harry traveled the region, spreading the gospel of Cardinals baseball, touting the virtues of Griesedieck Brothers beer, and broadcasting local sports. In November, he trekked about 150 miles south to Charleston, Missouri (where Dizzy Dean spent an offseason nearly two decades earlier) to broadcast a high school football game. In 1951, Caray's third straight year broadcasting the "Polio Bowl," the event drew a crowd of more than 5,000 and was carried over an eight-station radio network.

Small towns would virtually shut down for the day when Caray arrived. Appearing in Mattoon, Illinois in February of 1950, an afternoon parade honoring Harry attracted more than 1,000 people. That evening, Caray, joined by Musial, spoke at a dinner for 200, then answered questions from an estimated 1,800 people at the local high school auditorium.[15] One year during the baseball season, Caray traveled more than 170 miles to Paducah, Kentucky to broadcast three innings of a minor league game over the public address system. The Kitty League game between Paducah and Owensboro drew 2,600 fans.[16]

Appearances like the ones in Charleston, Mattoon and Paducah helped Caray maintain his connection and popularity with listeners who heard Cardinals games on the radio but rarely saw them. But the man who charmed rural audiences still had his issues with St. Louis sportswriters. "'The Canary,' as many called Caray, didn't have many friends in print media," said Broeg, who missed a fistfight one year between Caray and a sportswriter with the *Star-Times* because he didn't make the road trip. On a different trip, Broeg, Caray and Street were all traveling with the team for a series in Pittsburgh. In the first inning of the final contest, Musial lined into a triple play. The Cardinals lost the game 6-2. On the train after the game, Caray insisted Musial should have bunted and Street agreed with him. Cardinals captain Terry Moore disagreed and told them exactly what he thought about the proposed strategy. "I've never heard Tee Moore as angry, but that was Caray for you," Broeg remembered. "He has an ability to draw out emotion, whether positive or negative."[17]

His biggest fight of 1949 ended not with a bang, but a whimper. His busy schedule meant he rarely spent time with his family. The neglect took its toll on his wife. In November, she testified that Harry was "cold and indifferent," claimed he ignored her in the presence of family and friends and preferred reading the newspaper to engaging in conversation with her. In the divorce settlement between Harry and Dorothy Caray, a judge ruled that he pay $200 a month in alimony and $375 a month in child support for the couple's three children: Harry Jr. (Skip), Patricia, and Chris. The entire matter took 20 minutes before a judge in Clayton. Harry, who urged reporters "to bury" the story when the news first broke, didn't appear in court.[18]

*****

When team president Saigh announced media plans for 1949, the Cardinals radio network was already considered the largest in baseball. Coverage that spread across 54 stations in seven states by the end of the previous season expanded by 15 stations and two additional states for the new year.[19] From 1948 to 1959, the Cardinals averaged 73 stations in their network, nearly double their closest rivals.[20] AM radio exploded after World War II, with the number of stations in the country more than doubling from 1946 to 1950. "The end of the Second World War is often seen as the beginning of the end of radio's golden age and the beginning of television's ascendancy," wrote *Crack of the Bat* author James Walker. "However, for baseball on the radio, both nationally and locally, it was the true golden age."

An expanding media market meant increasing values for media rights. Those values had jumped considerably since Breadon told his fellow owners in 1936 that the Cardinals received $16,000 from two stations for the right to broadcast games. The agreement with WTMV and WEW that expired after 1948 was believed to be worth about $50,000 annually. The 1949 deal, with a new radio station (WIL AM and FM), was estimated at between $75,000 to $100,000 a year.[21]

The middle of the twentieth century straddled two distinctly different eras of communication. In January of 1949, Cardinals pitcher Murry Dickson discovered he had been traded to the Pittsburgh Pirates by a neighbor in Leavenworth, Kansas, who had heard it on the radio. Dickson later heard the news on the radio and read it in the newspaper the next day. A letter from Saigh and the Cardinals informing him of the move arrived four to five days later. By 1952, CBS television would use UNIVAC computers to process election totals and relay the results to viewers nationwide.

Baseball magnates were as challenged as anyone by the communication crosswinds. Owners jealously guarded their territorial rights. In 1942, Breadon discovered WGN radio in Chicago was re-creating a Cardinals-Cubs game in Sportsman Park. He had it halted mid-broadcast. "We are sorry, ladies and gentlemen, but we are forced to terminate this telegraphic report of the Cubs-Cardinals game from St. Louis," Jack Brickhouse informed his listeners.[22]

While major league teams relaxed their rules after the war, owners still had issues when it came to their farm teams. Minor leagues had an agreement with the Majors to restrict broadcasts to within 50 miles of a minor league park. After a Joplin radio station carried St. Louis games on back-to-back nights with the local minor league club playing at home in the spring of 1951, the Cardinals told KFSB management that continuing to do this would result in cancellation of the service. (As an affiliate station, KFSB was free to carry Cardinals games, just not when the Joplin club played a home game at the same time.) The station responded by filing a lawsuit, naming the Cardinals, the Joplin club, Griesedieck Brothers, and their advertising agency, Ruthrauff and Ryan, as defendants.[23] Disputes over media rights and territories would continue until 1961 when Congress passed the Sports Broadcasting Act, "which codified the right of professional sports leagues to sell their rights collectively."[24]

Until then, sports media offerings were still in their Wild West phase. Upstart and rapidly growing industries always attract iconoclasts and outsiders. The market for baseball on the radio was no different. Thanks in large part to baseball broadcasts, one media concern had a spectacular rise and an equally stunning flameout. Its ascent and downfall were aided on both ends of the slope by a man who started his broadcasting career in St. Louis and the St. Louis beer company that signed his paycheck.

*****

When Dizzy Dean broadcast his one and only football game in November of 1947, Gordon McLendon was his partner. The first play Dean called was a 70-yard touchdown by Cleveland Browns running back Marion Motley. "There goes big Motley around end," McLendon recalled Dean saying. "He's at the 35, the 40, the 45, 50, 55, 60." Hoping to steer his partner in the right direction without correcting him on the air, McLendon kicked Dean underneath the table. Dizzy got the hint. Sort of. "Motley's back at the 50 ... and here the big fellow comes again ... the 45, the 40, the 35 ..."[25] After the game, McLendon was still optimistic about Dean's future in the industry, telling reporters the station would try to make Dean a regular football announcer. Dizzy had different ideas. "I'll stick to baseball announcin' and farmin', football's too rough."

Dean and McLendon had broadcast the re-created game from the basement of the Oak Cliff Hotel in suburban Dallas, where station KLIF had made its debut earlier in the month. While Dizzy indicated he was done with football, McLendon was just getting started in sports broadcasting. The two men made quite a pair. If anyone could match Dean's audaciousness and verbosity, it was the man who would be called the "Maverick of Radio."

McLendon, who graduated from Yale with a degree in Oriental studies, served in the Pacific during World War II as a Japanese language officer. On an island in the Western Carolinas, he noticed how servicemen stopped what they were doing to listen to baseball games. After the war ended, he attended Harvard Law School, but couldn't shake his fascination with sports radio. He and his father first bought a station in Palestine, Texas, and soon secured the paperwork to launch KLIF. McLendon grew a radio network from that outpost that eventually encompassed 458 stations across the country. At its peak, the Liberty Broadcasting System offered 16 hours of daily programs, including six newscasts, variety shows and a crossword-puzzle-based quiz show.[26] But the heart of its programming was re-created baseball games, with McLendon the network's biggest star.

He called himself "The Old Scotchman" and presented himself to his radio audience as a grizzled broadcast veteran. In fact, when he started his radio career, McLendon was just 26 years old and had only *seen* one major league game years ago as a child. Like Caray, he loved the theater of re-creation. He had his engineers tape crowd noise from the local Dallas minor league team and weaved the sounds into his broadcasts. He later refined the ambient noise experience, recording sounds from major league parks. "When you heard a Liberty broadcast of a game at Fenway Park," wrote columnist Scott Ostler, "the hecklers and peanut vendors had Boston accents."[27] His hotel basement studio featured a Louisville Slugger bat suspended from the ceiling. He would tap it with a smaller souvenir bat or a lead pencil to recreate the sound of the bat hitting the ball.[28] The office bathroom also played a role in the recreation, as a young Lindsey Nelson would soon discover. "My first day on the job, I was looking for the men's room," remembered Nelson, who would go on to broadcast games for the New York Mets and San Francisco Giants. "But the door was locked because they were using it for the public address announcer effect, to create an echo chamber."[29]

Nelson was among a group of announcers who got their baseball broadcasting careers started with Liberty, a clan that also included longtime

Dodgers broadcaster Jerry Doggett and Don Wells, the original voice of the Angels. McLendon's fans included author Willie Morris, who tuned in from Yazoo City, Mississippi. "Under his handling, a baseball game took on a life of its own," he wrote. "He made pristine facts more actual than actuality." Nearly 500 miles north of Yazoo City, a St. Louis beer company also took notice of McLendon's growing network. Falstaff signed on as a sponsor.

Information about contests came from a variety of sources. Liberty would eventually negotiate an agreement with Western Union to secure the ticker feed of major league games, but until then, McLendon took whatever information he could get, however he could get it. He frequently hired rooftop observers equipped with binoculars near major league parks. With the Dodgers, Giants, and Yankees all in New York, he came up with a different approach. "I figured out I could get six teams at once by placing a guy in a hotel room in Brooklyn," McLendon remembered. "He could listen to broadcasts of all three New York teams and give us the play-by-play over the phone."[30]

Any breakdowns in communication didn't faze McLendon. He welcomed them. "If the teletype broke down for 45 minutes, he wouldn't panic. He'd rejoice," remembered *San Francisco Examiner* columnist Dwight Chapin. "That would give him a chance to talk about non-existent fistfights in the stands, rabid dogs running loose on the field or record numbers of foul balls ricocheting all over the park." As a 19-year-old aspiring broadcaster, Wes Wise joined Liberty in 1949. "Gordon would come up with wild stuff out of his mind to get us through those delays," he remembered. "He'd have a fan jump out of the stand and run into center field to Joe DiMaggio to shake his hand."[31]

Before the 1951 season, Liberty and Falstaff announced plans for a national network of games and a second, smaller network of stations for the St. Louis Browns. The Liberty – Falstaff partnership was a lifeline to the Browns, who had started the previous season without a radio sponsor and no coverage outside the city. The new Browns radio lineup featured 25 stations in four states, with Buddy Blattner and Howie Williams describing the action.[32]

Successful and gaining increasing momentum, McLendon's syndicate began to create headaches for the baseball establishment. The game already had a longtime broadcast partner in the Mutual Broadcasting System, which had an exclusive contract for the All-Star Game and World Series. Mutual launched its own Game of the Day in 1950 with live, not re-created broadcasts. While Liberty offered its affiliates a choice of a day or evening game, Mutual featured only day games, and (initially) only broadcast Monday through Saturday, leaving nights and Sundays untouched, the times when people were more likely to attend in person.[33]

As baseball attendance at the major league, and especially minor-league level, began to wane in the early 1950s, officials fingered Liberty as a source of the problem.[34] The vast majority of teams stopped cooperating with McLendon's network, which by 1951 had begun incorporating more live ballpark broadcasts. Baseball had dramatically increased its rights fees (from $1,000 per season in 1949 to more than $225,000 by 1951), and Western Union (with baseball's backing) refused to sell its services to McLendon.[35] Falstaff decided to jump ship, abandoning its sponsorship of Liberty for the Mutual chain, and announced Dizzy Dean would be behind the microphone for the network in 1952. He would do both national broadcasts and also return to St. Louis to cover the Browns. (He had spent the previous two seasons working for the Yankees.) For the first time in team history, the St. Louis American League franchise would broadcast all home and road games from the scene of the action. Dean would be paired with Blattner, the beginning of a broadcast partnership that would last for years.[36]

Baseball was the core offering of McLendon's syndicate. Meeting a wall of resistance from the sport's establishment, confronted with soaring costs, no cooperation from Western Union, and no sponsor, the Liberty Network discontinued its broadcasts. McLendon filed a $12 million anti-trust lawsuit against baseball owners. It was later settled out of court for a fraction of the contested amount. (McLendon claimed he received $250,000.)

Even without baseball, McLendon would be remembered for a fabulous career. He is credited as one of the pioneers of Top-40 and all-news radio formats, owned a group of large-market radio stations, was a longtime movie producer (John Wayne was a friend), became one of the largest shareholders of Columbia Pictures, and operated a chain of movie theaters. But none of that captured the thrills he got from baseball. "I never had the fun and I never will have the fun again that I did broadcasting games," McLendon said decades later. Years after his exile, he was still bitter about the experience. "The 16 S.O.B.s" is how he described the baseball owners to an *Oakland Tribune* columnist in 1981, calling one of them a "magna cum laude graduate of Alcoholism University."

"The owners claimed Liberty was ruining minor league baseball as well as the majors," said Wise, McLendon's one-time broadcast partner. "But others felt just the opposite – that it was creating additional fans. Those points could be argued forever."

*****

In his own way, Cardinals president and owner Saigh was just as much the maverick and outsider as McLendon. Both men started their sports-related careers in the same month. Both men would become fantastically wealthy after getting rebuked by baseball. Both would come to resent the men who controlled the game.

Saigh's partner, Hannegan, was a prominent political and business insider. The St. Louis native, who once worked in his youth as a peanut vendor at Robison Field and claimed membership in the original Knothole Gang, resigned from two positions, Postmaster General and his board position with the Browns, to become president of the Cardinals.[37] Breadon, Hannegan's friend and neighbor, had operated his automobile dealership in the city for nearly two decades before getting involved with the Cardinals. Muckerman, the majority owner of the St. Louis American League team, was an ice and fuel company heir. He purchased the team from Barnes, president of the American Investment Company and Public Loan Corporation.[38] Barnes got involved with the Browns at the same time as DeWitt, whose spouse was a close friend of Barnes' daughter. (The two women were avid horse riders and had met on the bridle paths.) DeWitt's long involvement in the game started with Rickey, who had leveraged his relationship with real estate developer Bill Zeckendorf to get his preferred price when selling out his ownership interests in the Dodgers. The same year Rickey left Brooklyn, Zeckendorf and Sidney Salomon Jr. purchased Hampton Village, a St. Louis real estate development owned by Breadon and partners.[39] Salomon was an assistant to Hannegan when he was Postmaster General and later partnered with him in an insurance company. DeWitt and his brother, Charley, purchased Muckerman's interests in the Browns in 1949.

These men – Barnes, Breadon, DeWitt, Hannegan, Muckerman, Rickey, and Salomon – largely controlled St. Louis baseball for decades. (Salomon would later become the first president of the St. Louis Blues.) DeWitt and Rickey spent their entire professional lives in baseball. Breadon, Barnes, Hannegan, Muckerman, and Salomon all had longtime business interests in St. Louis, with many of them active in Democratic Party politics. Breadon was a longtime backer of the party, Hannegan had served as chairman of the Democratic National Committee before he became Postmaster General, and Salomon would later become DNC treasurer and chairman of John Kennedy's 1960 Presidential campaign. At various times, he owned stock in and had board positions with both the Browns and Cardinals. (Saigh's successor, Gussie Busch, also fits this profile; active fundraiser for the Democratic Party with longtime business concerns in the city.)

In the clubby world of St. Louis sports ownership, Saigh stood out from his peers. The Illinois native had come to town in the mid-1920s after attending college at Bradley and Northwestern. The early days of his career would later raise questions – and eyebrows. He had connections to a law firm that represented mob interests, testified for the defense in a sensational blackmail and kidnapping case, had a reputation for piling up parking tickets, and was recognized as the brains behind a vending machine company that went bankrupt.[40]

Two decades later, he had transformed into a successful tax and corporate attorney who attended luncheons at the Noonday Club, described as "an exclusive midday eating place," where businessmen talked shop and arranged deals. But his low profile meant few people outside his immediate orbit were even aware of him. "Nobody would have included him in the first fifty or even the first 100 outstanding citizens of St. Louis, whereas ... Sam Breadon ... would have been high on anybody's first 10," wrote Stockton.[41]

That began to change when Saigh successfully led investor groups in the purchase of the Syndicate Trust Building (housing the Scruggs-Vandervoort-Barney department store) and the Railway Exchange Building. (Famous-Barr was a tenant.) "I owned the two largest buildings in the city," Saigh claimed. Owning trophy real estate gave him cache and ensured his phone calls got returned. Knowing Breadon owned some undeveloped property in town, Saigh reached out to him when a tenant needed warehouse space. The real estate deal didn't materialize (this was the land where Breadon had intended to build a new ballpark), but it did spark conversations that ultimately led Saigh and Hannegan to purchase the Cardinals.

Saigh's legal background came in handy during his tenure with the Cardinals, an era characterized by disputes, feuds, lawsuits, and legal maneuverings. Several of the issues he had to navigate involved marketing and media rights.

Shortly after taking control of the team, Saigh and Hannegan met with Browns management in Florida. The Browns made it clear they did not like their rival's radio deal. "The trouble arose over radio broadcasting," said Saigh. "They wanted us to discontinue broadcasting our on-the-road games." The protest fell on deaf ears. If Breadon gets the credit for starting the Cardinals radio network, it was Saigh who aggressively expanded it. By the early 1950s, the list of affiliates included more than 90 stations stretching across ten states.

During this era, the Cardinals would host an annual "Radio Appreciation Day," which featured the crowning of a "Queen of Beauty" among a field of young female contestants from the team's listening audience. Festivities would take place before a Sunday home game, always drawing a big crowd. Caray and Street would serve as masters of ceremonies and on the panel of judges. While the event was always fraught with potential for Caray to make an inappropriate comment ("I'll bet you, Gabby, there weren't any beauties like these back in

1900," he said one year), the event generated plenty of publicity and goodwill throughout the region.[42]

"I'm fascinated by Saigh's success," said Browns president DeWitt in 1949. "Saigh's promotion ideas have been terrific," he said while also paying tribute to the Cardinals radio broadcasters, noting a large crowd for a weekday afternoon game in August. "I believe the tremendous radio play announcers Harry Caray and Gabby Street have been giving the club was greatly responsible for this turnout."[43] The Cardinals had continuity on the radio while Browns broadcasts featured a revolving door. From the time the Cardinals began their home-and-road radio network until the Browns left town, the American League team changed its broadcast pairings every year.

The Cardinals also ambitiously experimented with television during its early days. In 1948, the franchise broadcasted 55 games on the new commercial medium at a time when St. Louis had more major league teams (2) than TV stations (1). In 1950, two years before the Browns, the Cardinals ended wire report re-creations and announced Caray and Street would travel with the team for all games. The duo was now doing all television broadcasts as well. Caray became both a voice and face of the franchise at a time when he had battles with both the owner and manager.

"I fired [Caray] about three times," Saigh said years later. "Harry was a great second-guesser, and our manager, Eddie Dyer, would come to me and threaten, 'Either Caray or me!' So I'd fire Caray for a day or two, and they'd kiss and make up, and we'd hire him back."[44] Caray irked Dyer with constant sniping and criticism on the air and in print. "It could be," Caray wrote in his *Holy Cow!* column in March of 1950, "that this is Eddie Dyer's final year as manager of the St. Louis Cardinals, unless they win the pennant!"

Saigh claimed to have limited control over Caray – "Griesedieck Beer had hired him, not me, and they paid me for his broadcasting, and even though I would fire him, it was up to them, really," – he did have the final say on Dyer. When the 1950 Cardinals finished fifth in the National League, Saigh made a change. At a Sportsman's Park news conference from the president's office after the season, Dyer announced he wouldn't return as manager. Caray was in the building at the time, but not in the same room, at the request of team management, who feared an "incident" between the broadcaster and former skipper.[45] (Broeg wrote that Dyer had frequently called Caray's criticisms "vicious." Dyer also had issues with Saigh, claiming that Breadon had offered him and his Houston oil partners the first option to purchase the team. He was also upset over the sale of Dickson to the Pirates. "They said they didn't need the money," he said before the beginning of the 1949 season, "but I need a 15-game winner to replace Dickson.")[46]

Saigh did get some good news in 1950. The lawsuit the Browns filed against the Cardinals was settled in favor of the National League club. The team's lease on the park – which the Browns contended was non-assignable following the sale – was still in good standing. But when the Browns decided to invest new money in the park, the Cardinals president was unhappy with the results. "Without even consulting us, the Browns went ahead and painted the iron bars around the [grandstand] boxes as well as the railings right down to the street, in their own colors, orange and brown. They forgot the Cardinals colors completely," he said. Browns president DeWitt described the colors as orange and maroon, to which his Cardinals counterpart replied, "it's not maroon – it's their dirty brown."[47]

Saigh's biggest challenge – and what ultimately led to his downfall – had to do with his relationship with Chandler, the commissioner with a long history in politics. The president of the Cardinals and the commissioner feuded over a scheduled Sunday night game in St. Louis. Saigh backed down after Chandler told him it couldn't be done.[48] Saigh criticized Chandler after the commissioner negotiated a six-year, $6 million television contract with Gillette as the sponsor. "Television is in its infancy," said Saigh. "Television rights worth $1 million [annually] today may be worth several million two or three years from now."[49] (He would later call it "the biggest financial error in baseball history.")[50] His media ideas included opinions that angered his fellow owners. Saigh believed visiting teams should share in the revenue generated by home-team television agreements, an idea Dodgers owner Walter O'Malley called "socialistic." (Two months after Chandler announced baseball's new TV deal, O'Malley's Dodgers signed a media rights contract with the Schaefer Brewing Company that paid the club $3 million over five years.)[51]

Saigh's Cardinals also managed to ruffle a few media feathers in St. Louis in the middle of a long homestand. "WOMEN INVADE THE PRESS BOX AT SPORTSMAN'S PARK," read the headline of the *Post-Dispatch* in June of 1949. "The presence of the newcomers has put a damper on the uninhibited flavor of press box conversations," observed the paper.[52]

But Saigh reserved his sharpest elbows and strongest opinions for Chandler, a commissioner who demanded loyalty and was sensitive to criticism. (He would write letters to reporters when he disagreed with their stories.) Saigh, on the other hand, was "quite unabashed, and quite loud," wrote columnist Shirley Povich. One of his loudest criticisms involved Chandler's ownership of a Kentucky radio station that carried baseball games over the Mutual network. "Is it a healthy situation for baseball's commissioner to be tied up with Mutual through his own station in Versailles, Kentucky, and through other connections to the extent that NBC or CBS or others do not have a chance to bid on television or radio?" he asked.

By this time, Chandler had made it known that he had what he exaggeratingly termed an "FBI file" on Saigh.[53] The commissioner hired a former FBI agent to dig into Saigh's past and compile a dossier that revealed embarrassing information about the man who owned the Cardinals (e.g., received 31 parking tickets as a hurried attorney rushing to court) but no smoking gun regarding the source of his money.[54]

Much of the information in the dossier surfaced in a series of articles by *Los Angeles Examiner* columnist Vincent X. Flaherty. Saigh responded by accusing Flaherty of being "a Chandler stooge" and admitted that he had scrutinized the commissioner's past dealings. "I have a thick file on Chandler and I'll match it against the file he has on me," he told Povich. "Two can play at that game."[55]

The nasty battle soon got even uglier. In March of 1951, a Boston columnist cited both the Flaherty columns and an anti-Semitic "letter-writing campaign out of Kentucky" that attacked Saigh "in unspeakable language."[56] (Saigh, whose father had emigrated from Syria, was not Jewish). That same month, with Saigh leading the charge, baseball owners voted 9-7 against offering Chandler another term as commissioner.[57] Chandler left office in July but didn't forget about his nemesis. (A *Saturday Evening Post* profile a few years later described him as "a man who never forgets to pay off his grudges.") Saigh was indicted on income tax evasion charges just nine months after Chandler left baseball. Saigh always suspected the former U.S. Senator from Kentucky was behind his legal troubles.

Saigh was learning the hard way how difficult it was to play politics with a well-connected politician. In between the commissioner's ouster and the owner's indictment, a new man arrived on the scene. Saigh would soon be absorbing more lessons, this time from baseball's ultimate maverick.

Bill Veeck purchased the Browns in the summer of 1951. Decades before he became a Caray booster in Chicago, Veeck was a Caray and Saigh foe in St. Louis.

"The battle of St. Louis was on again," wrote author William Marshall, "this time in earnest and to the death."

---

[1] Hannegan played both baseball and football at St. Louis University in the 1920s. *St. Louis Globe-Democrat*, January 28, 1949.

[2] *St. Louis Post-Dispatch*, October 2, 1949.
[3] "I listened to Caray religiously when I was a lad in Missouri, never missed him," wrote sports columnist Corky Simpson. "I won't do it here, but I could recite most of the words to the 'Harry Caray Polka.'" *Tucson (AZ) Citizen*, June 11, 1984.
[4] *St. Louis Post Dispatch*, September 6, 1950.
[5] The columns had three sections, "It Might Be," "It Could Be," and "It Is," and would close with the line, "You don't have to take part in a sport to be a good one." He applied for the trademark in 1951, the same year Red Barber applied to copyright the phrase "The Catbird Seat." *The Sporting News*, March 28, 1951. Grant DePorter, the president of Harry Caray's Restaurant Group, told the *Chicago Tribune* that Caray's "Holy Cow!" was patented in January of 1999. *Chicago Tribune,* July 19, 2005.
[6] The transaction included 250 shares in the Locust-Ninth Realty, Co., a concern that held the Century and Syndicate Trust Buildings in St. Louis. The *Globe-Democrat* reported that the shares were worth an estimated $166,000. *St. Louis Globe-Democrat*, December 21, 1949. Saigh later estimated "it could be liquidated for $100,000 to $300,000." *St. Louis Post-Dispatch*, January 10, 1950. Saigh would later claim he paid $1.2 million for Hannegan's shares to match an offer Hannegan received from Joe Kennedy.
[7] Selling fifty percent of a team for roughly $1 million seems baffling when the two men paid more than $4 million for the franchise just 14 months before. (On the day the sale was announced, the *Star-Times* speculated that Saigh may have paid Hannegan as much as $2 million.) This would seem to jibe with Broeg's belief that Hannegan's stake was only 30 percent. However, in 1950, Saigh testified that Hannegan held 1,731.7 shares in the franchise, slightly more than 50 percent of the stock. Saigh said the Cardinals purchased 1,731 shares. He personally purchased the fractional share. *St. Louis Post-Dispatch,* January 10, 1950. Ray Gillespie reported Hannegan's total shares at 1,731.96. *The Sporting News,* January 28, 1950.
[8] By early 1950, Saigh held all the stock in the Cardinals except for seven shares, whose owners "insisted on holding for sentimental reasons," wrote Roy Stockton. *Saturday Evening Post*, May 27, 1950. But in 1952, a congressional subcommittee looking into baseball's antitrust exemption found the Cardinals had four shareholders, with 1,837 total shares outstanding. Saigh held 1,667. *The Sporting News*, June 4, 1952.
[9] The day before the 1947 sale was announced, columnist Bill Corum reported that Breadon was selling the Cardinals to "Hannegan, a member of President Truman's cabinet, of course, and the man most responsible for his being President, the Skouras brothers of motion picture fame, Sidney Salomon Jr. of St. Louis, and one or two other St. Louisans." Saigh's name was not mentioned. Spyros Skouras was president of Twentieth Century Fox, his brother Charlie headed the chain of Skouras Theaters on the West Coast, while another sibling, George, ran the theaters on the East Coast. Corum wrote that not only were Breadon and Hannegan next-door neighbors, they "always have been intimate friends." Corum, who wrote for *International News Service*, later

expressed skepticism that health was the only reason behind Hannegan's sale in 1949. "I can't somehow escape the feeling that there must be something, in addition to considerations of health, behind the sudden switch." *St. Louis Star-Times*, January 28, 1949.

[10] *Southern Illinoisan*, July 7, 1949.

[11] As the play-by-play voice of Oklahoma A&M basketball, Curt Gowdy first met Caray at an Italian restaurant in St. Louis in 1948. Gowdy and A&M coach Hank Iba were having lunch when Caray walked in. Gowdy was in awe. "I had my mouth open about a foot." *Boston Globe,* February 20, 1998.

[12] *The Daily Oklahoman*, February 27, 1949. The *Post-Dispatch* called it "a new record crowd of 11,624 persons who rang cow bells loud and long in Kiel Auditorium." Vendors sold cowbells outside the venue, small ones for fifty cents, large ones for a dollar. *St. Louis Post-Dispatch*, February 27, 1949.

[13] Autry, who would later own the California (Los Angeles) Angels, died in October of 1998, eight months after Caray.

[14] *The Daily Oklahoman*, February 27, 1949.

[15] *Daily Journal-Gazette* (Mattoon, Illinois), February 21, 1950.

[16] *The Sporting News*, August 15, 1951. Caray made the trip with Gus Mancuso, Gabby Street's replacement in the broadcast booth.

[17] Broeg, *Memories of a Hall of Fame Sportswriter*.

[18] Dorothy Caray's suit against her husband made the front page of the *Globe-Democrat*. "Holy Cow! Harry Caray's Wife Sues To Tune Him Out," read the headline. *St. Louis Globe-Democrat*, October 29, 1949. Settlement came two weeks later. Ibid, November 11, 1949.

[19] Ibid, February 1, 1949. Figures for network affiliates varied during a single year. It was common to add stations during the season. A Griesedieck Brothers Beer ad at the end of the 1949 season claimed the Cardinals radio network "embraced 69 stations in 9 states." *The Sporting News*, October 5, 1949.

[20] The closest to the Cardinals during this era were the Boston Red Sox and Milwaukee Braves (1953-1959), who averaged 38 stations a season. Walker, *Crack of the Bat*.

[21] *St Louis Globe-Democrat* and *St. Louis Post-Dispatch*, February 1, 1949. The *Post-Dispatch* put the value of the previous deal at $50,000, while the *Globe-Democrat* placed it at $55,000. WIL was in the process of boosting its signal from 250 to 5,000 watts and was moving to 1430 on the AM dial. (The FM signal could be heard at 97.3.) The station also announced that "arrangements have been made to provide a service for listeners with push-button radios, this service of changing the push button to the new frequency to be made free of charge if the set owner desires and phones WIL." Total radio and television dollars for the club in 1950 totaled $189,365. *The Sporting News*, June 4, 1952.

[22] Ibid, October 1, 1942.

[23] *St. Louis Post-Dispatch*, May 6, 1951.

[24] Walker, *Crack of the Bat*.
[25] *Oakland Tribune*, May 10, 1981.
[26] Walker, *Crack of the Bat*.
[27] *Philadelphia Inquirer*, June 15, 1979.
[28] "We hung a regulation bat from the ceiling and used one of those souvenir bats against it to make the sound of the hit," said Wes Wise, one of McLendon's broadcast partners. "Some have written we made the noise by hitting a grapefruit. I never quite understood that." *The Times* (Shreveport, Louisiana), May 19, 1979. "To simulate the sound of ball against bat, the Old Scotchman would plunk a lead pencil against a Louisville Slugger suspended from the ceiling," wrote columnist Dwight Chapin. *San Francisco Examiner*, April 17, 1981. McLendon once described it as a "nickel bat."
[29] *The Times* (Shreveport, Louisiana), May 19, 1979.
[30] *Oakland Tribune*, May 10, 1981.
[31] Wise was drafted into the military during the Korean War. Lindsey Nelson was his replacement. Wise later served three terms as mayor of Dallas.
[32] *The Sporting News,* April 18, 1951. Williams had previously worked with Arch McDonald broadcasting games of the Washington Senators. In addition to the Browns, Falstaff had a second smaller network of stations that featured Chicago Cubs baseball broadcasts by Bert Wilson. Ibid, April 15, 1953. Bill Veeck once described Wilson as suffering "from a curious astigmatism. He was never able to see a bad play by anybody wearing a white uniform."
[33] Walker, *Crack of the Bat*. With Liberty out of the picture, Mutual adopted a different strategy. "Game of the Day broadcasts again will be carried *seven* days a week by Mutual stations under the sponsorship of Falstaff Brewing Corporation of St. Louis..." *The Sporting News*, January 21, 1953.
[34] "Major league game broadcasts are making big league fans – not fans of your hometown clubs," Browns vice president Charley DeWitt told a group of minor league officials meeting in Dallas. *Alton Evening Telegraph*, October 20, 1950. Headline: "Radio Will Kill Minor Leagues Says DeWitt."
[35] Walker, *Crack of the Bat*.
[36] "All Brownie games next summer – at home and away – will be broadcast over station KXOK by Bud Blattner direct from the scene of action. Dean will be in the booth with Blattner 'from time to time,' the sponsor Falstaff Brewery announced." *St. Louis Post-Dispatch*, December 2, 1951.
[37] "I used to sell peanuts when the games were at the old Robison Field, which is now beside Beaumont High School," Hannegan told reporters on the day he became president of the Cardinals. "There were two years in my youth that I entered the Tuberculosis Day marathon (a 10-mile race which ended in the ballpark) just to get in free to see a ballgame. I was a member of the original Knothole Gang, too." *St. Louis Post-Dispatch*, November 25, 1947.

[38] The American Investment Company was a consumer loan operation. Profits of $235,632 in 1935 grew to more than $1.4 million in both 1940 and 1941. By 1943, its subsidiaries operated 102 loan offices in 13 states. *St. Louis Star-Times*, February 26, 1943.

[39] Breadon had passed away by the time of the transaction. His interest was held in his estate. Hampton Village had about 100 stockholders but was largely owned by Breadon, Harry Vollmer, and Harry Brinkop. The property sold for $2.5 million. *St. Louis Star-Times*, January 6, 1950.

[40] Saigh shared office space with attorney Sigmund Bass. Both men's names were mentioned in one of the most sensational kidnapping cases of the 1930s. Saigh had done legal work for both Dr. Ludwig Muench and his wife, Nellie Tipton Muench. She was one of the suspected ringleaders of the plot. The case involved the kidnapping of Dr. Isaac Kelley in April of 1931. Nellie Muench was believed to have convinced the kidnappers to target Kelley, claiming she moved in the same social circles. After he was taken from his home on the night of April 20, Kelley was moved to multiple locations over the next week.

Assigned to cover the story, *Post-Dispatch* reporter John T. Rogers received a call from a man with instructions to meet at a location. Rogers picked up the man in his vehicle at that spot, and the two men eventually made their way to a gas station near East St. Louis, Illinois. After the man abruptly left the vehicle, Rogers discovered Kelley standing by the side of the road with his eyes taped shut. Rogers interviewed Kelley for two-and-a-half hours before reuniting him with his family. Angelo Rosegrant was convicted of kidnapping Kelley on October 4, 1934, and sentenced to 20 years in prison.

For her suspected role in the case, Nellie Muench was acquitted the next year. Attempting to gain sympathy from jurors during her trial, Muench claimed to have a baby. In fact, she had bought a baby for $50 from a St. Louis couple. The infant died before she was acquitted. She then bought a second baby from a 19-year-old Pennsylvania woman and blackmailed a doctor colleague of her husband's with whom she was having an affair, asking him for money to avoid revealing the baby's "true" identity. After her acquittal, the second child's mother demanded her baby back and brought suit against Muench. Along with her husband, her attorney, and a friend, Muench was found guilty and sent to prison.

During the kidnapping trial, Muench's maid testified that Saigh was seen at the Muench home in April of 1931, just before Kelley was abducted. Asked by the prosecution about the men visiting the Muench home in the days before the kidnapping, Ida Wilzer named "Rosegrant and a lawyer named Saigh." Called as a witness for the defense, Saigh told the jury he "first met Dr. and Mrs. Muench about 1929," calling them "wonderful people." But he also claimed he never went to the Muench home with Rosegrant. "I did not know Rosegrant then, and I do not know him now," he said in October 1935. One of the kidnapper's ransom notes directed those seeking Kelley's release to get in touch with "Sig Bass." The kidnappers initially asked for $250,000 and later reduced their demands to $100,000. *St. Louis Post-Dispatch*, October 3, 1935, Marshall, *Baseball's Pivotal Era 1946-1951*, and https://becker.wustl.edu/news/kelley-kidnapping/

August A. Busch Sr. (Gussie's father) was rumored to have a fascination with Nellie Muench. Hernon and Ganey, *Under The Influence*. Saigh's vending machine operation was covered in the author's previous work. See *Mr. Rickey's Redbirds: Baseball, Beer, Scandals & Celebrations in St. Louis*.

[41] *Saturday Evening Post*, May 27, 1950.

[42] "Sportsman's Park is usually jammed" [for Radio Appreciation Day], noted a Florida columnist. *St. Petersburg Times*, March 10, 1953. Caray's comment to Street about beauties back in the day comes from a letter to the editor under the heading: "A Boner by Harry Caray?" *St. Louis Post-Dispatch*, July 10, 1950. The 1951 winner, Miss Janice Brown of Joplin, Missouri, represented KFSB, the station that had filed a lawsuit against the Cardinals just three months before the event. Two pictures of her with Caray (one with him kissing her on the cheek and the other with her holding a KFSB sign) were published in the August 15, 1951 issue of *The Sporting News*.

[43] *The Sporting News*, August 17, 1949.

[44] Golenbock, *The Spirit of St. Louis*.

[45] *St. Louis Post-Dispatch*, October 17, 1950.

[46] "I don't like to say anything derogatory about Mr. Breadon while he's sick," Dyer told NEA sports editor Harry Grayson in April of 1949, "but it is true that he gave me his word that I would have first crack at the club's purchase." Grayson wrote that he first heard of the promise from Commissioner Chandler. In 1950, a New York paper reported that Dyer had the option to purchase the team if Saigh decided to sell, a claim Dyer denied. "I have no agreement with Mr. Saigh about that." *The Sporting News*, August 2, 1950.

[47] "They forgot the Cardinal colors completely – even though most of the people who come to Sportsman's Park during the summer are there to see the Cardinals and not the Browns," said Saigh. *The Sporting News*, April 18, 1951. Red-colored seats in the upper deck were repainted green. Ibid, March 28, 1951.

[48] Even though several other sporting events had been played on Sunday nights in St. Louis (e.g., hockey and basketball games), Chandler claimed it would conflict with church services and not be in the best interests of baseball. National League president Ford Frick ruled that the game would violate league regulations. Saigh claimed his decision was based "entirely" on Frick's ruling. *New York Times*, June 13, 1950.

[49] *St. Louis Globe-Democrat*, December 27, 1950.

[50] New York *Daily News*, December 13, 1953.

[51] *New York Times*, February 28, 1951. The deal covered both television and radio.

[52] *St. Louis Post-Dispatch*, June 30, 1949. The women were Western Union teleprinter operators. "Western Union said the women operators were needed because of a growing shortage of men telegraphers who use the old Morse code system."
[53] *St. Louis Post-Dispatch*, August 6, 1950.
[54] Chandler acknowledged in February of 1951 that he had conducted investigations into Saigh and Yankees co-owner Del Webb. "These are the only two major league owners we have investigated, but our probe turned up nothing detrimental to baseball." *Washington Post*, February 4, 1951. "People forget that I had acquired some important assets in those two department-store deals," Saigh told Stockton. *Saturday Evening Post*, May 27, 1950. Saigh's attorney would later say that in the early 1940s, when Saigh's law business "wasn't too good, he got into the manufacturers' agent business and acted as a broker representative for a number of out-of-town concerns, selling various products, in addition to practicing law." *St. Louis Globe-Democrat*, January 29, 1953.
[55] *Washington Post*, February 12, 1951.
[56] Marshall, *Baseball's Pivotal Era, 1945-1951*.
[57] Browns president DeWitt also opposed Chandler. The commissioner had upset the club on two occasions. He unsuccessfully attempted to intervene and block Dean's appearance in uniform in 1947. The next year, Chandler succeeded in blocking the Browns' plans for attaching a ticket to the All-Star Game to a season-ticket purchase.

The wedding of Harry's parents, May 1913. Harry was born a little more than nine months later.
(Family photos courtesy of Nick and Malon Argint)

Harry's father, Christopher Carabina. He disappeared from his son's life when Harry was a young boy.

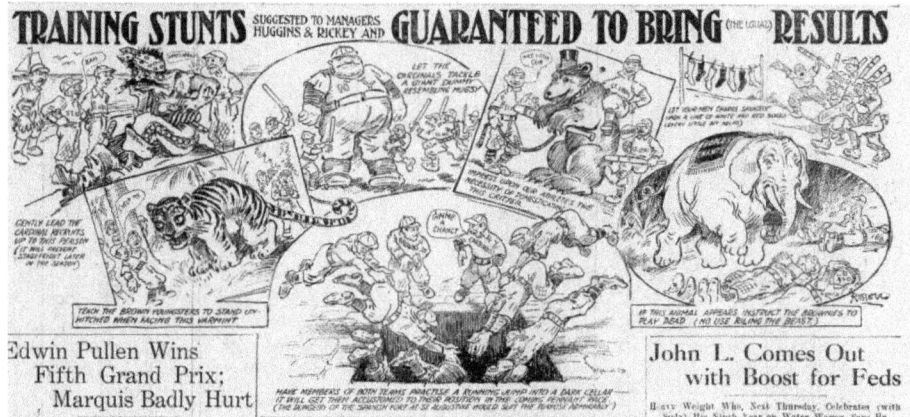

On the day Harry was born, March 1, 1914, the *St. Louis Globe-Democrat* featured this cartoon of baseball players jumping into a cellar. "It will get them [the Browns and Cardinals] accustomed to their position in the upcoming pennant race." (Newspapers.com)

Harry grew up on Lasalle Street in St. Louis.

Before he lived with his uncle John and aunt Doxie, Harry attended their wedding with his parents. Harry (seated in front) has his left arm perched on his mother's leg. Harry's father is standing on the right.

Harry's mother, Daisy (also known as Tasica), with her second husband, Sam Capuran.

At Webster Groves High School, Harry played baseball and basketball and sang in the Glee Club.
(front row – fourth from right)

When Sam Breadon (seated) sold the Cardinals to Robert Hannegan (center) and Fred Saigh (not pictured) in November 1947, Harry (left) was there to cover the event.
(Mo. Historical Society, St. Louis. Sam Breadon Collection)

From 1945 to 1950, Harry called Cardinals baseball with broadcast partner Gabby Street.
(St. Louis Media History Foundation)

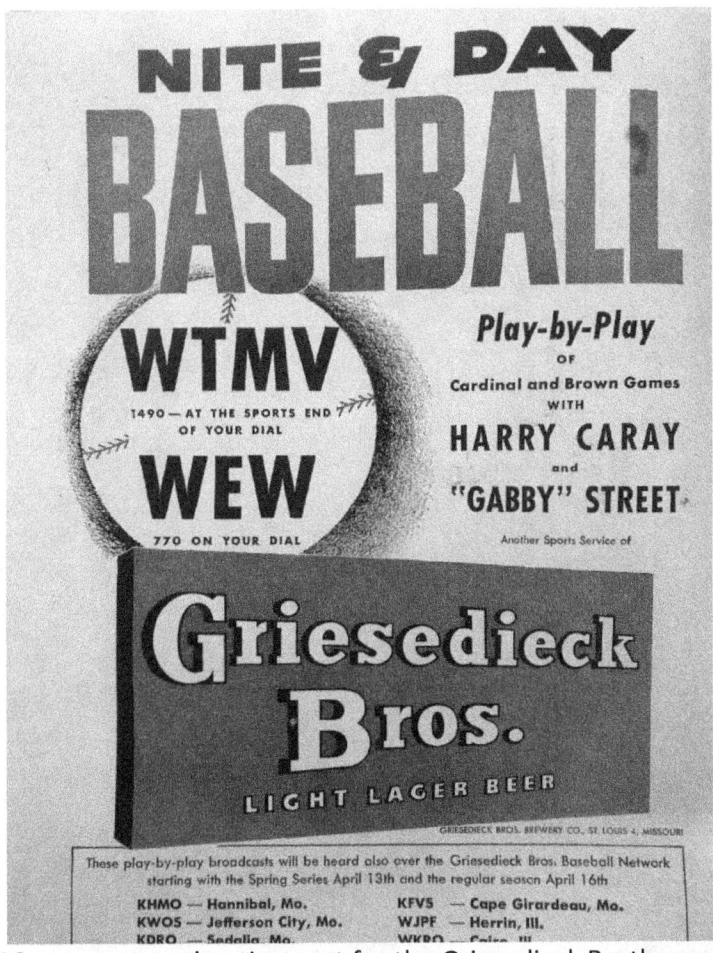

A 1946 newspaper advertisement for the Griesedieck Brothers radio network that featured games of the Browns and Cardinals.

Harry and Gabby's other partner on the Griesedieck Brothers radio network – Stretch Miller.
(St. Louis Media History Foundation)

Harry works the phone from his office at KMOX in 1955. "I'm a helluva reporter," Caray once said.
(Mo. Historical Society, St. Louis)

For many years, Harry spent his winters broadcasting St. Louis University basketball. He's pictured here courtside with broadcast partner and SLU AD Bob Stewart.
(Mo. Historical Society, St. Louis)

Harry on the beach with second wife Marian and the couple's two daughters, Michele and Elizabeth. (DignityMemorial.com)

A One-Team Town

On a Sunday afternoon in June of 1951, more than a dozen surviving members of the 1926 world championship Cardinals donned uniforms and walked onto the field at Sportsman's Park. Hearing their names called by Caray, who was on the field in a coat and tie that day, the former Cardinals took their place along the baseline to the cheers of more than twenty-thousand fans. The day before, they had gathered for a luncheon at Stan Musial and Biggie's restaurant where Saigh presented each of them with a tie clasp with the Cardinals insignia. The club president introduced the 1926 attendees, while new manager Marty Marion introduced the team's current roster. While old-timers mixed with newcomers, swapped stories, and bathed in the glow of warm memories, *Post-Dispatch* columnist John Wray pondered the future of Cardinals baseball.

"Will the Cardinals of the future have another 25 years like the past quarter-century?" he asked. Noting that "the advantage of the unique farm system is now lost," and that "more and more large gate receipts will be necessary for operating costs," he also speculated on the cost and site of a new stadium. "At the moment, the 25 years to follow promise plenty of major headaches."

What Wray outlined represented challenges to the Cardinals (the inventors of the modern farm system), issues peculiar to St. Louis (two teams sharing an aging stadium), and a general malaise and lack of confidence in the future growth of the game (sparked by higher costs and declining attendance across baseball).[1]

"Money is not free," Commissioner Chandler said months before leaving office. "American people bought $60 billion worth of stuff on time last year. They haven't the dollars for entertainment. They're staying home." Seeking to boost attendance in 1951, Saigh scheduled night contests for 53 of the team's 77 home games. "Think of it," said Chandler. "There's never been anything like it in the majors."[2]

After a banner 1949 campaign in which the team reported net profits of $1.1 million (after subtracting for taxes and using $700,000 to retire Hannegan's stock), Saigh made the 1950 club the highest-paid team in the National League. But after winning 18 fewer games and watching attendance drop by more than

300,000, he announced planned salary cuts for several players in 1951. "In baseball, as in all businesses, salaries are based on performance and the records speak for themselves," he said. (The move met with approval from the local media. "High salaries are not always an unmixed blessing. Players are too content," believed Bob Burnes. "No one on the Cardinals is going to go broke this summer.")³

Saigh's hardline stance only generated modest results. The 1951 edition, while jumping two spots in the standings to third place, won only three more games. The team president again changed managers, swapping out Marion for Eddie Stanky. For the first time since the 1920s, the Cardinals had three separate managers at the beginning of three straight seasons. While Breadon's impatience produced pennants, Saigh's restlessness only generated more of the same. Stanky's first two seasons produced back-to-back third-place finishes, the same outcome that got Marion fired. Attendance fell for four straight years. By 1953, the Cardinals and Browns *combined* numbers at the gate didn't equal what the Cardinals attracted in 1949.

The issues resonated far outside the walls of Sportsman's Park. A congressional subcommittee investigating baseball's anti-trust exemption opened the books, poured through the numbers, and asked plenty of tough questions about the state of the game. Why, lawmakers asked, does St. Louis have two teams and Los Angeles and San Francisco – cities with larger populations – have none? New York Congressman Emanuel Celler called the situation "intolerable" and insisted to reporters that St. Louis was a "one-team town."

Into this maelstrom of anxiety and discontent stepped a man with a wooden leg and a clear vision of how baseball could bring fans back to the ballpark. If St. Louis was indeed destined to have only one baseball team, Bill Veeck was determined it would be the Browns, and not the Cardinals, who would survive.

*****

As a young man, broadcaster and Caray partner Stretch Miller worked at a country club in Hinsdale, Illinois, where he and other caddies would play softball behind the clubhouse. Frequently, a 12-year-old boy would show up and watch. "I always had the feeling he wanted to join us but couldn't," Miller believed. "He was a rich man's son," Stretch recalled in his autobiography, "dressed up like Little Lord Fauntleroy, with knickers, collar and tie and a jacket." The boy was the son of the president of the Chicago Cubs. And while Bill Veeck Jr. would soon shed the coat and tie permanently for a more comfortable look, he'd stay involved in sports for much of his life.

From his father, the younger Veeck learned the importance of marketing. Ladies' Day promotions on the North Side of Chicago became a huge attraction. "I'll never forget it," said Veeck Jr. of one such promotional event in 1930. "The biggest mob of women I ever saw in one place in my life." One time after a game, his father showed him the day's receipts. The son absorbed the lesson that whatever the race or religion of the fan, the money doesn't change. "You can look at that money and it all looks the same, doesn't it? You can't tell who put it into your box office. It's all exactly the same color, the same size and the same shape. You remember that."[4]

At Wrigley Field, Veeck Jr. watched mobsters become fans (Al Capone was a frequent visitor) and planted ivy on the walls, elements of which remain to this day. "By the time I was 12," he recalled, "I decided I was going to own a baseball team." He purchased his first team, the minor league Milwaukee Brewers, in June of 1941.[5] Veeck was 27 years old.

Veeck and Miller's paths crossed again in World War II, with both men serving in the military in the South Pacific. "While visiting a fellow officer in a tented hospital, I saw Veeck," Stretch remembered. Veeck, who had enlisted in the Marine Corps, had his foot crushed by the recoil of an anti-aircraft gun. He underwent the first of more than 30 operations, which resulted in his foot and part of his leg being amputated.

Back in the States after the war, Veeck bought the Cleveland Indians in 1946. After the team drew more than 2.6 million fans and won the World Series in 1948, he sold the club the following year, needing money for a divorce settlement. He remarried in 1950 and while he had interests in a couple of minor league teams,[6] he seemed content to follow major league baseball from a distance. When a desk clerk at a San Francisco hotel asked his occupation when checking in, Veeck replied, "unemployed." He was reportedly working on a novel whose hero was a Cleveland first baseman who lost a foot in the war.[7] He also dabbled as an actor, portraying Sherman Whiteside in the play, "The Man Who Came to Dinner." Appearing at the Hanna Theater in Cleveland, Veeck and fellow cast members attracted less than $7,000 at the box office for a week's worth of shows. "It was like a day game in St. Louis," Veeck told reporters, "strictly for park employees and friends."[8]

It was at a game in St. Louis where Veeck's life took an unexpected turn. Real estate developer Roy Drachman and Yankees co-owner Del Webb came to town (Webb, also in construction, was building a VA Hospital in the city) and attended a game with Saigh.[9] The Cardinals president told the men the DeWitt brothers would likely be selling the Browns soon. The information was passed along to Veeck, who sensed an opportunity. He quickly went to work raising money to make a bid, securing backing from a variety of sources, both inside (Sidney Salomon Jr.) and outside St. Louis (Chicago's Lester Armour, grandson of a meatpacking magnate).[10]

On June 21, 1951, Veeck appeared at the Hotel Jefferson to announce a deal had been struck to buy the Browns. There was one important caveat. Bill and Charley DeWitt held 57 percent of the team's stock.[11] Veeck's group wanted at least 75 percent of the equity to consummate the deal.[12] A deadline was set for July 5 for odd-lot shareholders (some 1,400 of them) to tender their stock. The offer was $7 a share. Veeck, who emphasized he had no intention of moving the Browns out of town, began a two-week campaign to secure additional equity. Saigh and the Cardinals launched a counter-offensive. Caray was front and center in the campaign to deny Veeck.

"It was at this point that Harry Caray, on his own nightly sports program, began to implore the stockholders not to sell their stock to this well-known capital-gains hustler, this con man," Veeck recalled, believing Saigh was behind the effort. "In case there is any doubt in anybody's mind as to who hires, pays, and fires the guy who broadcasts the games for a big-league team, let me clear that up. Indirectly or directly, it is the owner of the team."[13]

Even before they worked together in Chicago, Veeck respected Caray's work. "I should say in all fairness that Caray is an excellent announcer. He does as good a job at selling as anybody on the air," he wrote in 1962. He had a dramatically different opinion of Saigh, calling him a "patsy," and writing that the Cardinals president "didn't have the foggiest notion of what he was doing." Veeck viewed the Cardinals under Saigh on a downhill slide. Because of that, "I had come into St. Louis to try to run the Cardinals out of town," he boldly proclaimed.

To do that, he needed cooperation from Browns shareholders. Just days before the deadline, Veeck was still seeking converts. "Practically all the stock we received today was from small shareholders," said Al Fleishman, a name that would feature prominently in Caray's later years with the Cardinals. In the summer of 1951, Fleishman was part of a committee working on the Browns deal. "There are a couple of stockholders controlling about 7,000 shares apiece," he told the *Globe-Democrat*. "They could put the deal over the top." At noon on July 3, a large Browns stockholder, Herbert Waltke, who initially refused to sell, changed his mind and decided to tender his 8,572 shares. The 75-percent threshold was crossed. Bill Veeck was now president of the team. Even before the ink was dry on the deal (the final paperwork wasn't signed until July 5 because of the Independence Day Holiday), Veeck plunged headlong into the most ambitious marketing campaign of his career. "My first full year in St.

Louis, I will maintain to the end of my life, was the best job of promoting I have ever done," he believed.

Veeck tracked down Browns outfielder and holdout Frank Saucier in Washington, Missouri, some 40 miles from St. Louis.[14] He and his wife rented a car, arriving at 2:30 in the morning. By 4:30 a.m., Saucier agreed to sign. Veeck immediately put up a new sign in front of Sportsman's Park. OPEN FOR BUSINESS UNDER NEW OWNERSHIP. His first weekend on the job, he treated Browns fans to a thunderous fireworks display and announced during a game that a round of drinks was on the house.

He dusted off his Cleveland playbook, hiring his old switchboard operator (Ada Ireland) to answer calls, Max Patkin, "the clown prince of baseball," to coach first base and provide laughs, and Satchel Paige to pitch. He also took a page from Caray and the Cardinals, covering a 250-mile eight-state area, giving as many as seven speeches in a single day. Veeck would charm and disarm his audiences, beginning his speeches by saying, "You're going to have to forgive me if I seem nervous. I'm not used to seeing so many people."

When he wasn't busy soliciting new business in the area, Veeck made it a point to entertain old friends and colleagues at Sportsman's Park. He moved the second floor Browns business offices to street level and converted the old offices to a ten-room apartment, where he, wife Mary Frances, and son Mike set up residence. The new digs became a frequent gathering place for players, managers, and sportswriters. Casey Stengel always liked an early dinner while others arrived for a cocktail hour.[15] More dinners would be arranged for late arrivals, and drinks would be served at all hours of the night. "On a good night the party would continue until 5 a.m. before we broke up," Veeck remembered.

Beyond his most famous marketing promotions and stunts – the at-bat for 3'7" Eddie Gaedel, Grandstand Managers' Day, appearances by the Harlem Globetrotters, and a miniature circus – Veeck just had a different perspective and approach to the game than his fellow owners. "We're still selling the game on the won-lost column. That automatically means seven of eight teams in the league are offering a second-rate product, because only one can win the pennant," he once said. "But the worst mistake is the failure to promote baseball as a delightful way to spend an inexpensive afternoon or evening."[16]

Veeck had the idea for broadcaster Blattner, who had a brief major league career, to suit up for one game, put a walkie-talkie on his back, and broadcast from the field and at the plate. The idea was shot down after the Phillies wanted $10,000 for Blattner's unconditional release. (Blattner had played his last game in 1949 for Philadelphia. In the days of the reserve clause, the team still controlled his contract.)

When a New York advertising executive wrote to Veeck, telling him he may want to consider a retractable roof for Sportsman's Park, the Browns president wrote him back. "I obtained figures for a similar plan while I was in Chicago back in 1940. The cost was in excess of $1,800,000 and by now would be more than double that."[17]

After the Browns swept a doubleheader against the Yankees at Sportsman's Park in September of 1951, temporarily knocking New York out of first place, Veeck announced free sweaters for all his players.[18] The Browns owner was a master at this type of promotion, calling attention to his own team while taking a jab at an opponent. Nowhere did Veeck do this more skillfully than in St. Louis, constantly delivering small digs and pinpricks to the club that paid him rent. It enraged Saigh and emboldened Caray to aim some of his strongest criticisms at the hometown rival.

Veeck had the walls of Sportsman's Park painted on the side of the field where the Browns conducted business but left the Cardinals' side of the park untouched "to give Saigh that grim persecuted feeling as quickly as possible," he explained. He also barred the Cardinals president from a special press room and the owner's private box. (Saigh owned the Cardinals but Veeck and the Browns owned the park.)

The psychological warfare spilled into the open a few weeks into Veeck's ownership when he wrote a letter to the chairman of the Community Chest challenging the Cardinals to a postseason series with profits going to the nonprofit group. "Since it appears neither St. Louis team is going to be engaged in the World Series this fall," Veeck explained in the letter published in the next day's *Post-Dispatch*, "it would seem that here is an opportunity for us to take part in this most important drive."[19]

On the day Veeck penned his missive, the Browns were buried in last place in the American League, but the Cardinals were in third place in the senior circuit (but ten games back of Brooklyn). Veeck had cast his line. An outraged Saigh quickly took the bait. "Poor Saigh walked, ran, or dove into every trap we set," Veeck declared. The Cardinals owner refused the postseason challenge, quickly donated $10,000 to the Community Chest (matched by Veeck), took out a series of ads aimed at female fans ("Dear Miss Lonelyhearts," one began, "I'm jealous of the Cardinals"), and wrote his own letter that made its way to the media. "Let's not forget," he wrote in late July, "that on August 10, 1942, the Cardinals were ten games behind; on September 4, 1934, six games behind; on July 2, 1946, seven and one-half games behind and went on to win World Series championships."

Saigh's appeal to history and tradition fell flat. (The 1951 Cardinals finished the season 15.5 games behind Brooklyn.)[20] It was also ironic since the team that took the greatest advantage of Redbird nostalgia during this era debuted brand new brown and white uniforms the following season.[21] Veeck's 1952 Browns began the season with Rogers Hornsby as manager, Marty Marion as a coach, and Dizzy Dean in the broadcast booth, three former Cardinals players linked to nearly every championship team from the 1920s to the 1940s.

With the story of Dean's life, *The Pride of St. Louis*, scheduled to debut in April, Twentieth Century Fox made plans for a parade, movie premier and other festivities timed to the opening of the City Series between the Browns and Cardinals. Because of Dean's affiliation with the American League team, Saigh wanted no part of it. "We do not want to take part in any promotion or any program or parade in which the Browns have a single person," he declared in a letter to a studio representative.[22] The festivities went on without participation by the Cardinals as St. Louis Mayor Joseph Darst declared "Dizzy Dean Week" in the city.[23] In May, the Browns again celebrated the Cardinals legend with Dizzy Dean Day at Sportsman's Park between games of a doubleheader with the Indians.[24] (The 23,536 in attendance represented the Browns' second-largest home crowd of the year.)

The spat over Dean came after the two teams fought over Hornsby. Veeck insisted he stole Hornsby from Saigh, who was eyeing the former slugger to replace Marion. "I couldn't allow that to happen," he claimed. [25] Veeck signed Hornsby to a three-year contract right after the 1951 season concluded. When Saigh fired Marion in November, Veeck quickly hired him as a coach for the Browns. The Hornsby hiring proved disastrous (Veeck fired him halfway through his first season, replacing him with Marion). But the all-out blitz by Veeck left Saigh on his heels. His muted response included newspaper ads and a new slogan: THE CARDINALS, A DIGNIFIED ST. LOUIS INSTITUTION read the bottom of the scorecards printed for the team at Sportsman's Park.[26] (A veteran journalist had Saigh's ear at the time. His friendship with a *Post-Dispatch* executive got the attention of local writers and national media alike. "I became uncomfortable with *Post-Dispatch* managing editor Ben Reese, because he had become pals with Fred Saigh, often sitting in the owner's box," noted Bob Broeg. "The two [Saigh and Reese] have shared a box almost every time the team has played at home," wrote columnist Red Smith. Saigh went so far as to recommend Reese as Chandler's replacement for commissioner. "Ben is a great baseball fan," Saigh told friends. "If we could get a little publicity for him, we might put him across.")[27]

While Saigh took measured steps in his battles with Veeck and the Browns, there was nothing subtle about Caray's criticisms of the hometown rival. After the Browns fired Hornsby, Caray invited him on his radio show to tell his side of the story. "I have never been associated with a fellow who likes to get his name in the paper more than Bill Veeck does," the ex-manager told the broadcaster. Hornsby found a sympathetic interviewer in Caray, who took time to defend the Hall-of-Famer. "Rog, I noticed the way you summed it up after you were dismissed. You wished Marion and the Browns good luck. That's an entirely different tenor from the stuff that is being directed at you."[28] (The "stuff" directed at Hornsby included a trophy presented to Veeck in the locker room the day Hornsby was fired.)

After a flurry of trades by the Browns following the 1952 season, Caray went on the air to express bewilderment at Veeck's moves. "Frankly, I'm confused," he began. "I had just started to believe all the wonderful things written by the Browns' publicity office about that sensational new rookie outfielder, Jake Crawford, when I read yesterday that he had been traded to the Tigers for 'Here-He-Is-Back-Again' Cliff Mapes and utility infielder Neil Berry," said Caray, who also mocked a trade that sent pitcher Tommy Byrne to the White Sox for "Third-Time's-The-Charm" Willie Miranda and pinch-hitter Hank Edwards."

"The next time somebody asks me: 'Don't you believe what you read in the newspapers?' I'm going to ask: 'Do you mean before they are traded or after they are traded?' For somehow, there sure seems to be a great difference."[29]

To the irritation of both Saigh and Caray, Veeck's playbook featured constant claiming of any Cardinal placed on waivers. When the Browns claimed pitcher Harry Brecheen, Saigh filed a protest with the commissioner. "Mr. Saigh just got tired of such maneuvers and filed his protest," said Caray. Brecheen had been a hero of the 1946 World Series for the Cardinals, winning three games, but now that he had switched sides, Caray blasted him and his new team. "How do they expect to play winning ball if they can use a 38-year-old pitcher like Harry Brecheen?"[30]

Appearing at an offseason banquet in Christopher, Illinois, Caray told the crowd the 1953 Cardinals were the team to beat in the National League and didn't miss the chance to disparage the other team in the city. "The Browns haven't proved they can play winning baseball yet," he said. "They gave the fans in St. Louis and in this area a lot of ballyhoo last winter, but they finished seventh. They sold a lot of tickets on the strength of Hornsby, Veeck, Marion, etc., but their attendance fell off badly the last half of the season after Hornsby was gone and the team didn't win."[31]

Caray had touched on the one area where Veeck could point to dramatic progress. Despite a team that won just 64 games, the Browns' attendance increased from under 300,000 to nearly 520,000, a jump of 77 percent in 1952. While Saigh's Cardinals drew more than 900,000, the figure represented 100,000 fewer fans than the prior year. "I had judged my man right, I felt, and we had him on the run," remarked an increasingly confident Veeck about his Cardinals counterpart. "We had a deal brewing with [an area television station] to carry our games, an unheard-of thing," he recalled. "It was still a local station, of course, but it was powerful enough to reach a far greater area than we had ever reached before."[32]

While the owner recognized the promise of the new medium ("Veeck believes television will eventually help baseball and he's surveying Sportsman's Park with the idea of providing better points of vantage for television cameras," wrote Roy Stockton shortly after Veeck bought the Browns),[33] he took a hardline with his fellow owners when it came to broadcasts, a stance he shared with Saigh. For all their differences, the two St. Louis owners found common ground on the issue of baseball on television. Both men believed teams should share their advertising revenue with the visiting club when televising games. Veeck went so far as to ban the Yankees from televising games against the Browns, but when New York responded by scheduling all games with St. Louis during the day (reducing the crowd and the gate split), the Browns owner backed off.[34] Saigh was just as determined and more successful with his National League colleagues, announcing television revenue splits with the Cubs and Reds for the 1953 season.[35]

This media clash was shaping up as a battle between St. Louis owners on one side, with the majority of the baseball establishment on the other. The dispute didn't last long. The one thing not in Veeck's plan to run the Cardinals out of town was Fred Saigh going to prison.

*****

When Saigh was indicted for tax evasion in the spring of 1952, he was confident he would receive a fine, but nothing more. "A top politician in high places told me over the phone that if I pleaded nolo contendere [no contest], I would be fined $15,000 and receive no jail time. (Saigh led his interviewer to believe the "top politician" was President Truman.)[36] But when the case moved to trial in January of 1953, Judge Roy Harper, a former business manager for a Cardinals minor league team, showed Saigh no mercy.[37] He sentenced the Cardinals owner to 15 months in prison, in addition to the fine. "Someone had a dagger out for me. I don't know who," said Saigh, who speculated the source of his problems may have originated inside the Internal Revenue Service. His former partner, Hannegan, had once run the agency, "and he may have made some enemies there," said Saigh. He also believed that his old nemesis, Chandler, had used his political connections to influence powerful people in Washington.[38]

The case against Saigh largely centered around the financing behind the purchase of the Cardinals, a transaction that fueled suspicion from the beginning, as his attorney acknowledged at trial. "It is hard for a man in the streets, not knowing the facts, to understand how this lawyer and Bob Hannegan, another lawyer, who had been in politics, could get the money together to buy the Cardinals, to do these big deals," said Robert H. McRoberts Sr. "There was this suspicion, there must be something wrong with it, there must be some shenanigans some place, there must be some improper influence, something that shouldn't be in the picture. That suspicion was widely expressed."[39]

Saigh had suspicions of his own, wondering why the government was so lenient with Hannegan's family and took such a hardline stance regarding his affairs. "The estate of the man who was associated with me for so long settled all government claims quietly for $5,000," Saigh explained in a handwritten statement the day he went to prison. "Claims were essentially based on the same alleged deficiencies." (Like Saigh, Hannegan's business matters had also raised questions with some in the press. A New York *Daily News* columnist once referred to him as "a struggling small-time political lawyer in St. Louis [until 1942] ... [who] died a millionaire seven years later, despite the fact that he spent six of those intervening years on Uncle Sam's payroll at government pay.")[40]

Between the verdict and his prison sentence, Saigh hastily made arrangements to sell the Cardinals. He had offers from other cities, most notably groups in Houston and Milwaukee, but decided to sell the team to local interests (at a reduced price) when Anheuser-Busch stepped forward with a bid to keep the team in St. Louis for $3.75 million. Gussie Busch, who "didn't know a foul ball from a mallard," according to Broeg, was now team president.

Typical was the reaction of *Kansas City Star* sports editor Ernest Mehl who wrote that Saigh "had been held in poor repute by his baseball associates." Mehl also quoted an unnamed St. Louis sportswriter, who told him that when A-B bought the team, "It was the greatest thing that could have happened to St. Louis."[41]

It was also a banner day for the baseball ruling class. The man now running the Cardinals quickly signaled that the days of his team raising uncomfortable questions about the game's finances were now over. Less than a month into his stewardship of the club, Busch announced the Cardinals would end their demand for a piece of television revenue from other clubs.[42] (The television revenue-sharing model would later become a staple of the NFL.)

*****

Like Saigh, Veeck had made plenty of enemies among baseball's establishment. And with Anheuser-Busch now writing the checks for the Cardinals, he believed he had no choice but to try to move the Browns. "I wasn't going to run Gussie Busch out of town. And I certainly wasn't going to run Anheuser-Busch Inc. out of town," said Veeck. "The brewery could run the club as part of its advertising budget, lose an unlimited amount of money and just write it off the company profits."[43]

He first looked to Milwaukee, but Boston Braves owner Lou Perini owned the territorial rights in Wisconsin and wasn't interested in selling them to Veeck. He then turned his focus to Baltimore. The Browns struck a deal to move to Maryland, but it needed approval from the other American League clubs. But as long as Veeck owned the team, the baseball magnates weren't interested. (The vote was 5-2 against. National League owners unanimously approved the Braves' move to Milwaukee that same week.) Veeck spent the season searching for a home. "All I do is answer: When are you moving and where?" he told a *Globe-Democrat* reporter in early September.[44] After a second attempt to move to Baltimore was again blocked, the hardball message from his fellow owners was clear.[45] The only way Veeck could get the Browns out of St. Louis was to sell the franchise. Resolution came at the end of September when Veeck announced a deal to sell the team to a Baltimore group that paid $2,475,000 for the 80 percent interest controlled by Veeck's syndicate. The move received unanimous approval from American League owners. The Browns had played their last game in St. Louis.

With Saigh in prison and Veeck now out of the game, baseball had rid itself of two of its biggest headaches in less than a year. Although he attempted to return (offered $4.5 million to buy back the Cardinals in 1964, and considered buying the Washington Senators in 1971), Saigh's withdrawal from the game was permanent. Instead, he assumed a Veeck-like role in the city as a corporate gadfly and brewery tormentor. After selling the Cardinals, he bought 28,000 shares of Anheuser-Busch stock, becoming the largest shareholder outside the Busch family. He also became one of the brewery's strongest critics, once suing Gussie Busch over his compensation and calling a company reorganization plan "a blank check to run roughshod over smaller stockholders."[46] He never attended a baseball game in St. Louis the entire time the brewery owned the franchise.

Holy Cow St. Louis!

Like his St. Louis counterpart, Veeck employed creative financing and had his battles with the IRS (he argued the value of players should be depreciated[47]), but staying away from the game he grew up with was never an option. After selling the Browns, Veeck worked as a scout, a minor-league executive, and a television color man. He considered buying Ringling Brothers and Barnum & Bailey Circus. He returned to the major leagues in 1959 when he purchased the Chicago White Sox. His third ownership reign, like his first two, was brief. Experiencing violent coughing fits and chronic concussions (Veeck thought he had a brain tumor), he sold the team in 1961. He bought them back after the 1975 season, this time with Caray on the payroll.

When Veeck turned on a public address microphone during a seventh-inning stretch that allowed the fans to hear Harry sing "Take Me Out to the Ballgame," he started a tradition at Comiskey Park that later became an institution at Wrigley Field. After he sold the White Sox for the second time, Veeck returned to the park where he got his start. The man who dressed like Little Lord Fauntleroy in his youth spent the later years of his life shirtless in the Wrigley bleachers, beer in one hand, cigarette in the other, singing along with Harry. "Another gag that worked," Veeck told a reporter one afternoon on Chicago's North Side.[48]

In poor health for years with permanent walking pneumonia (he had to have his lungs drained periodically) and lung cancer, Veeck passed away in January of 1986 at the age of 71. He was celebrated as a baseball iconoclast, a civil rights activist (in addition to signing Larry Doby, the American League's first black player,[49] he participated in the civil rights march in Selma, Alabama in 1965), and "a champion of the little guy" (the inscription on his Hall of Fame plaque). Aaron Copeland's "Fanfare For The Common Man" was played at his funeral.

After President Kennedy was assassinated, Veeck and his son went to Washington, D.C. to view the casket in the rotunda of the Capital. Security invited Veeck to a VIP area to avoid the crowds. He refused. With his one good leg, Veeck stood in line for seven hours to pay his respects to the slain President. Following his last team sale, Veeck received a lifetime pass to any park in the big leagues. He didn't use it, preferring to pay his own way. "I pay for my tickets so I can complain," he explained. "If he got in a cab, he never sat in back, he'd sit up front with the driver. If he walked in a bar, the first thing he'd do was buy everyone a drink," Caray recalled.

"Throughout his life, even as an old man, Veeck was a renegade, a hedonist, a buffoon. He loved outlaws, sought the night life, and consumed four packs of cigarettes a day. With his peg leg, bottomless appetite, and radiantly homely face, he might have been some inexplicable pirate-saint," wrote Tom Boswell in the *Washington Post*.

"He hated the New York Yankees, stuffed shirts, and anyone who went home before the ninth inning or the bars closed. In that order," said *Los Angeles Times* columnist Jim Murray.

Browns broadcaster Blattner recalled returning home with Veeck after a speaking engagement in southern Illinois. The team owner was lamenting his club's struggling offense. "Wouldn't it be great if we could get our leadoff man on base just one time?" said Veeck. "That's when he thought of Eddie Gaedel," Blattner told the *Post-Dispatch*. "He was the most intriguing man I ever met," said the broadcaster. "I don't know if he was ever tested for IQ, but he exploded with ideas."[50]

In addition to being the brains behind a defining part of Caray's legacy, Veeck was remembered for bringing a World Series title to Cleveland (still the last time the Indians have won a World Series) and a pennant to the White Sox in 1959. His second purchase of the team likely saved the Sox for the city (the club was threatening to move to Seattle) and Caray's job. The previous owner, John Allyn, fired Caray during an interview with a local television station after the 1975 season.[51] Veeck stepped up to preserve the team and re-hired the broadcaster. "I may not agree with Harry all the time. Just the same, he should be allowed to express his opinions," Veeck told reporters. (According to Jerome Holtzman, the television and radio stations that carried the broadcasts "made it clear they didn't want any part of the White Sox unless Caray was rehired.")[52]

"He and Branch Rickey have to stand out as the two greatest individual forces the game will ever have," said Caray. "Veeck was the one owner who never forgot the most important person involved in baseball was the fan."

The summer after Veeck passed away, *The New York Times* took note of the changes at major league parks. "The game today is a happening," wrote Michael Martinez. "Fans are treated to some form of entertainment from the moment they pass through the turnstiles until they trundle out the exits." Caray credited Veeck for helping make it happen. "That's what he wanted," Harry said, "to make every day at the ballpark seem like New Year's Eve."[53]

With the White Sox, Caray worked for Veeck for five seasons. Both men called Chicago home for years. (In 1978, the *Chicago Tribune* published an article entitled "101 Good Things About Chicago." Veeck was number 51. Caray was number 53.) Yet despite their similarities; two men who loved day baseball, the nightlife, pretty women, and a good argument, Caray admitted the two men were never close. "Last winter we got to talking over a bottle of beer," Harry recalled shortly after Veeck's death. "I said, 'You know, for two kindred souls, for two guys who were very much the same and had many of the same interests, we were never very good friends.' And he said, 'If we were together all the time, we'd only cover half the territory. By letting you go your way, and me going my way, we were able to cover both sides of the street.' Who but Bill Veeck would say something like that?"

---

[1] According to Gerald P. Nugent, president of the Interstate League, and reported by Stan Baumgartner, "Minor league ball is doomed in all leagues whose towns are not at least a sleeper jump away from any major league city, and the dwindling interest brought about by the major leagues' policy of killing the minors may not only consume them, but, in the end, all of Organized Ball." *The Sporting News*, February 18, 1953. The gloom extended beyond baseball. Higher costs and smaller crowds had columnist John Wray speculating on the future of high school football in St. Louis. "The pessimistic wonder how football can be continued without an improvement in the dollar situation." *St. Louis Post-Dispatch,* November 29, 1951.

[2] *The Sporting News*, April 18, 1951.

[3] *St. Louis Globe-Democrat*, March 4, 1951. The pay cut idea didn't go as well as Saigh thought it would. Schoendienst, when offered a contract with a salary reduction, refused to sign and became a holdout. He later signed for a pay raise, reported at the time as a $2,000 increase. (*Baseball Reference* lists his 1951 salary at $23,500, a $3,500 jump from 1950.)The longest holdout, pitcher Howie Pollet, didn't sign until April 10, reportedly at the same salary for which he played the previous season. The Cardinals traded him to the Pittsburgh Pirates in June.

[4] Dickson, Paul. *Bill Veeck: Baseball's Greatest Maverick.* Walker Publishing Company, Inc. 2012.

[5] Veeck and Charley Grimm, former manager of the Cubs and St. Louis native, led a syndicate that purchased the Brewers for $100,000. *St. Louis Globe-Democrat*, June 24, 1941. Before joining Veeck in Milwaukee, Grimm had been working as the Cubs first-base coach. His replacement was Dizzy Dean.

[6] Veeck had a one-third interest in the Oklahoma City Indians and, with a partner, a controlling interest in the Dayton Indians. When Veeck bought the Browns, he sold his Oklahoma City stock. The Browns owned a minor league team in San Antonio, a Texas League competitor. The Dayton club had a working arrangement with the Browns.

[7] *The Sporting News*, March 28, 1951.

[8] Ibid, January 10, 1951.

[9] Drachman, a member of one of Arizona's pioneer families, made a fortune developing Tucson. He once had lunch with Wyatt Earp. He also had a long relationship with Veeck, convincing the one-time Cleveland Indians owner to relocate the club's spring training home to Tucson. Drachman died in 2002 at the age of 95.

[10] Salomon stated that he hoped to continue as a Cardinals stockholder and "in some capacity with the Browns as one of Bill Veeck's associates." He added that Veeck "is an

outstanding figure in baseball and a real showmen and he should make St. Louis a baseball mecca of the nation." Mark Steinberg, a one-time director of the Cardinals, held a $700,000 note on the Browns. He sold it to Veeck for $500,000. *The Sporting News*, June 27, 1951.

[11] The DeWitt brothers' ownership interest in the Browns was variously reported at between 56 and 58 percent.

[12] Veeck claimed he wanted at least 75 percent for tax purposes, but also practical reasons. "If you're running a club with 51 percent control, you're working just as hard as if you had 100 percent but you're only getting half the profits." Veeck, Bill with Ed Lynn. *Veeck As In Wreck*. University of Chicago Press. 1962. Veeck claimed his group wound up with 79.9 percent of the team. Salomon later claimed he had a 20 percent interest in the Browns.

[13] Ibid.

[14] Saucier was working for an oil company in Oklahoma. He was at his parents' house in Washington, Mo. for the Fourth of July.

[15] Stengel managed Veeck's minor league team in Milwaukee in 1944.

[16] *Saturday Evening Post*, June 6, 1959.

[17] Eskenazi, Gerald. *Bill Veeck. A Baseball Legend*. McGraw-Hill. 1988.

[18] The players had previously received hats for a victory over Cleveland. *St. Louis Post-Dispatch*, September 12, 1951.

[19] Ibid, July 22, 1951.

[20] "Saigh is in for a fast sprint to the booby hatch if he tries to match Veeck's stunts," wrote *Miami News* columnist Morris McLemore. *Miami News*, July 27, 1951.

[21] The 1952 Browns uniforms, manufactured by Rawlings, eliminated the color orange. "The new uniform is simple, has class and is cut along the same lines as the Yankee uniform," said Veeck. *St. Louis Post-Dispatch*, February 17, 1952.

[22] "The Cardinals are not going to take part in any circus," said Saigh. "We're in St. Louis to play good, straight baseball." *St. Louis Globe-Democrat,* April 9, 1952.

[23] The movie premiered on Friday night, April 11, 1952, at the Missouri Theater. On stage with the actor who portrayed him, Dan Dailey, Dean called the Browns a great team and introduced five of the team's players to the audience. Ibid, April 12, 1952.

[24] Dean received a couple of prize Herefords, a goat, chickens, and other presents at the May ceremony. Ushers had to round up the chickens after they escaped from their crate. Sigma Delta Chi, the professional journalism fraternity, presented Dean with a "Doctor of Slanguage" degree. *The Sporting News*, June 4, 1952.

[25] Veeck wrote, "Saigh had sent an emissary to sound out Rogers Hornsby about replacing Marty Marion as the Cardinals manager. His emissary was thoughtful enough to pass the information on to me." Veeck, *Veeck As In Wreck*.

[26] Saigh did attempt to give away a new automobile at Sportsman's Park, but the idea was shot down by a judge, who termed it an illegal lottery. *St. Louis Post-Dispatch,* May 24, 1981.

27 Red Smith endorsed Roy Stockton for the role of commissioner. "Baseball has in the past and may in the future do immeasurably worse than employ Roy Stockton. He is a man of many gifts and fierce integrity, whose years as one of the country's finest baseball writers have given him a rich background of experience and knowledge." *Washington Post,* September 1, 1951. Ford Frick replaced Chandler.
28 *The Sporting News,* June 21, 1952.
29 Ibid, November 5, 1952.
30 A 37-year-old Brecheen went 7-5 with a 3.32 ERA and a 1.096 WHIP for the 1952 Cardinals. For the Browns in 1953, he went 5-13, but his ERA was 3.07. The Cardinals claimed Brecheen had agreed to become a coach for the team on the day waivers were asked and that the Browns had tampered by talking to him before the waivers had concluded.
31 *Southern Illinoisan,* November 7, 1952. At the event, Caray singled out *Southern Illinoisan* columnist Merle Jones. "He asked me how I could be so biased, so prejudiced, so inconsiderate of the only baseball club which had ever brought any world championships to St. Louis for 25 years," Jones wrote. The columnist then joined Caray on stage. "So we had a running debate for 10 minutes or so and I don't have any idea who won. No judges had been appointed. We both got in our licks." A picture in the next day's paper shows the two men squaring off just inches apart, face-to-face, each pointing a finger in the other man's direction.
32 Veeck, *Veeck As In Wreck.* The Browns and Falstaff announced plans in April of 1953 to televise 30 to 50 games over WTVI, a new UHF station (channel 54/part of the Dumont Network) preparing to go on air in Belleville, Illinois. *St. Louis Globe-Democrat,* April 14, 1953. In its early days, it also served as the home of CBS and ABC broadcasts. When Dumont stopped broadcasting and another outlet became the CBS affiliate, WTVI relocated to St. Louis, became KTVI and started broadcasting on channel 36. KTVI later moved to channel 2 on the VHF dial, where it resides today.
33 *St. Louis Post-Dispatch,* August 5, 1951.
34 The Indians and Red Sox also announced plans to eliminate night games against the Browns when Veeck demanded a share of their television revenue. But the Browns owner was especially critical of the Yankees, charging the club abrogated both written and oral agreements. "When the Yankees get $500,000 to televise their home games, they're not only more than compensating financially for their loss in attendance, but they're depriving us of our ordinary share of road receipts." *St. Louis Post-Dispatch,* February 1, 1953. The issue was scheduled to go to a special American League meeting when Veeck capitulated. "We figured to lose out, anyway, like we've lost out on everything else," he said. Ibid, March 23, 1953.
35 At the 1952 winter meetings, Veeck made two proposals: 1) Telecasting of all American League games be discontinued. 2) All revenue from a club's television contracts be divided into two equal parts. The team would retain one half with the other half divided among all clubs in the league. Both proposals were defeated by a

vote of 6-2. The Chicago White Sox were the only team to vote with Veeck. The National League decided that any decision to telecast must be worked out between the two teams.

[36] Golenbock, *The Spirit of St. Louis*.

[37] Harper was once secretary and business manager for the Caruthersville (Mo.) Pilots. The team played in the Northeast Arkansas League from 1936 to 1940.

[38] In a wide-ranging interview with author William Marshall, Saigh claimed Chandler got Illinois Senator Everett Dirksen to put pressure on the IRS. He also claimed that both Breadon and Hannegan had been paying some players "under the table," and when the government started its investigation, "I really couldn't defend myself." Louis B. Nunn Center for Oral History: University of Kentucky Libraries. Saigh remained bitter toward Chandler for years. After Chandler penned an article spread over two consecutive issues of *Sports Illustrated* in 1971 ("How I Jumped from Clean Politics into Dirty Baseball"), Saigh responded with a letter to the editor. "Sirs: Just read the articles by the Bluegrass Jackass. In the words of the immortal General George Patton, - - !" *Sports Illustrated*, May 17, 1971.

[39] *St. Louis Globe-Democrat*, January 29, 1953. For details behind Hannegan and Saigh's purchase of the Cardinals, see the author's previous work. *Mr. Rickey's Redbirds: Baseball, Beer, Scandals & Celebrations in St. Louis*.

[40] New York *Daily News*, August 25, 1950.

[41] *Kansas City Star*, March 15, 1953.

[42] Busch announced that the club was scrapping Saigh's media demands after a spring training dinner that included Commissioner Ford Frick, National League president Warren Giles, and representatives from the Braves, Reds, and Phillies. *St. Louis Post-Dispatch*, March 15, 1953. "The television angle is one of the more important factors in the new situation on the St. Louis club," wrote Dan Daniels. *The Sporting News*, March 4, 1953.

[43] Not everyone agreed with Veeck's assessment. "He lost his interest in St. Louis. I don't think he bought the team with the idea of moving it, but eventually he lost interest," Sidney Salomon Jr. said years later. "Oh, you'd have to know Bill Veeck. He lost interest because he wasn't getting too much praise," said Salomon, who opposed the Browns moving. "I fought against it, and didn't want it to happen. There was no alternative because Veeck had control." Eskenazi, *Bill Veeck*.

[44] Once Veeck's attempts to relocate the team became public, support in St. Louis for the Browns owner quickly collapsed. 'Return of the Villain' read a caption above a picture of Veeck when he returned to the city following the vote in March. *St Louis Post-Dispatch*, March 18, 1953. Veeck was hung in effigy at Sportsman's Park in September. A sign on the dummy read "Bill Wreck" in front and "Traitor" in the back. *St. Louis Globe-Democrat*, September 26, 1953. "Veeck has been quoted about St. Louis and baseball in various parts of the country this year. He has rapped the city and the Brownies fans. He has said that the players were happy to get away from their home

city, that they felt better on the road. He has attributed the plight of the Browns to shortcomings of St. Louis, but we have never heard him quoted as saying that perhaps he has been pretty much of a flop as a ball club builder in his St. Louis adventure," wrote Roy Stockton. *St. Louis Post-Dispatch*, August 2, 1953. "In retrospect ... I sometimes wonder if that deal was as wise as I once thought it was," Veeck said decades later. "The Browns were a total disaster." *New York Times,* June 21, 1982.

[45] Veeck's second attempt at moving to Baltimore failed in a September vote, with four owners voting against it. Cleveland, which had supported Veeck in the spring, joined Boston, New York and Philadelphia in blocking the move. *St. Louis Globe-Democrat,* September 28, 1953. "Veeck Ends Season With Strikeout," read a caption in the *Post-Dispatch*.

[46] *St. Louis Post-Dispatch*, April 18, 1979. In 1963, Saigh charged Busch with using his position as president to obtain excessive salary, bonus and stock options from the corporation. The suit was dismissed by the St. Louis Circuit Court.

[47] *Washington Post,* May 20, 1976.

[48] *New York Times,* June 21, 1982. Caray's singing at Wrigley Field wasn't immediately embraced by Cubs fans. "It's not working out," Harry told Bob Verdi. "And if we don't do it right, we might as well not do it at all. Either way, it's OK with me." *Chicago Tribune*, April 16, 1982.

[49] Tom Boswell wrote that when Veeck signed Doby, he "answered all 20,000 hate letters by hand." *Washington Post*, January 3, 1986.

[50] *St. Louis Post-Dispatch,* January 3, 1986.

[51] "If I own the club next year, Harry won't be with us," Allyn told Johnny Morris on WBBM-TV. *Chicago Tribune*, October 2, 1975.

[52] *The Sporting News*, January 31, 1976.

[53] *New York Times*, June 1, 1986.

Good Night, Skip

The early 1950s marked a time of dramatic change in Caray's life. Following the death of Gabby Street, Harry got a new broadcast partner in 1951 (Gus Mancuso), a new wife in 1952 (the former Marian Binkin), and a new boss when Anheuser-Busch purchased the Cardinals in 1953.[1] His time with Mancuso lasted three seasons, his second marriage lasted two decades, but his connection with A-B would be an enduring part of Caray's legacy. Like more than one relationship in his life, Caray and the brewery enjoyed a long partnership followed by a nasty split. But the two sides would later overcome their differences, ensuring that long after he left St. Louis, Caray remained a "Bud man."

The newly married Caray sounded and acted a lot like the old Harry. He continued his nonstop pace of travel and appearances. Ten days before his wedding, Caray was in Dallas, calling the Cotton Bowl game between Kentucky and TCU. Five days after the ceremony in Florida, he was in Keokuk, Iowa, speaking at a dinner for a new minor league team.[2]

Before and after his second wedding, his on-air antics antagonized a vocal minority of fans who kept newspaper editors busy with complaints. "That 'holy cow' expression has been worked to death, and it didn't sound smart even when it was new!" grumbled "Ex-Ball-Game-Fan" to the *Post-Dispatch* in the summer of 1950. (Harry would continue to use the phrase for forty-seven more seasons.)

"By what right can Harry Caray and the Old Scotchman [Gordon McLendon] make derogatory and caustic remarks about individual players? Aren't they paid to bring us the story of the game free and uncluttered by their own personal opinions?" asked an Iowa letter writer to *The Sporting News* in 1951.

"I am continually astounded at the broad scope of Caray's activities. Quite aside from second-guessing managers, players, umpires, club officials, sports writers, official scorers, and grounds keepers, I suspect he'll be advising mayonnaise instead of mustard for the Sportsman's Park hot dogs in the near future," railed a letter writer to the *Alton (Il.) Evening Telegraph* in 1952. It was signed by "A Cardinal fan who would rather go thirsty than buy a bottle of GB [Griesedieck Brothers] and help pay Mr. Caray's salary."

Holy Cow St. Louis!

The silent majority of fans who enjoyed Caray's descriptions increasingly saw their cause taken up in faraway places. For the first time in any numbers, Eastern sportswriters began noticing Harry's unique style. "The first of the play-by-play chroniclers to sully the tradition of strict impartiality, Caray has fathered almost an entirely new kind of sports broadcasting," claimed Pete Brown in the *St. Petersburg Times* in 1953. "It is a combination of split-hair informativeness and bleacher-seat zeal." Writing for *The Journal* in Meridian, Connecticut, columnist Frank Corkin Jr. first met Caray at a Sarasota, Florida hotel. "Out West they think he's the best," Corkin began one column. "When they mention baseball announcers Westerners say 'Harry Caray' and they're done talking."[3] Others saw a formula behind Caray's success. "One reason the Cards airings go over so well is that Caray goes heavy on 'color' and background of the teams on the field," wrote Dick Meyer, sports editor of the *Ft. Lauderdale News*. "Listeners get to feel that they know the players."[4]

Florida writers were among the first to embrace Caray because of the time he spent there every year.[5] In a more innocent age, columnists in the Sunshine State would announce the arrival date and lodging plans of prominent spring training visitors. The Cardinals broadcaster achieved Grapefruit League All-Star status in the winter of 1952. "Harry Caray, popular announcer of the Cardinals network out of St. Louis, has a Mar. 1 reservation at Bahama Shores," announced *St. Petersburg Times* sports editor Bill Beck. (Harry didn't check in until March 3. Interestingly, and perhaps not coincidentally, Caray celebrated his 38th birthday on the First.) The newlywed's second Florida visit of the year officially lasted four weeks. The tab came to $372.[6] The broadcaster's second marriage, a union that produced two children, officially lasted 22 years. The tab was significantly higher.

Both the spring training stay and the marriage ended up in court. When Caray disputed a portion of the hotel bill, Bahama Shores sued him in civil court over $116.43. Higher costs and longer legal battles lay ahead. Claiming Caray "associated with other women in a manner inconsistent with his marital vows," Marian Binkin Caray filed for divorce from her husband in 1972. When the couple made it official 17 months later, Caray and his wife divided assets estimated at $500,000.[7]

The judge awarded Marian custody of the couple's two daughters. One of them, Elizabeth, sued her father over her personal diary in 1977. "I have the diary and will not return it to my daughter," Caray told reporters in Chicago. "It was taken from her while she was in my custody and I'm sure her mother would not want it to be made public property."[8] When their other daughter, Michele, married in 1979, "the bride was given in marriage by Mr. John Del Valle of

Beverly Hills, California," according to a wedding announcement. Harry's name was not mentioned.[9]

When asked about his children in a 1985 television interview, Caray didn't mention any of his daughters – Elizabeth, Michele, or Patricia (from his first marriage) – by name. "I have three daughters, two of whom are married and have children," he told *Chicago Tonight*. "Another one who's about 24 years old now."[10] He did name his two sons from his first marriage; Chris, working for Maritz Travel at the time, and his firstborn. The one who shared his name became the only one to follow him into his profession. In a rare moment of public humility, Harry once told a St. Louis audience he wasn't even the best broadcaster in the family. That honor, he believed, belonged to Harry Christopher Caray Jr.

Radio and television audiences would know him as "Skip."

*****

Skip Caray was ten years old when his parents divorced. "I'll never forget it," he said, recalling the 1949 divorce that generated newspaper headlines in St. Louis. "Longest walk of my life. People staring at me like I had two heads."

Skip, Patricia, and Chris grew up with their mother (Caray's first wife Dorothy), once described by a writer as a "shy woman with a dry humor." Visits from their father were sporadic. "Those were difficult times – I couldn't really describe it," remembered Patricia. "It could be tough, but the love was still there. Sometimes you had to remind yourself of that."[11]

Seeing his son infrequently but knowing he was always listening to Cardinals games, Harry devised a way to communicate regularly with his oldest child. "When I was a little guy, he used to say at the 8:30 station break on the Cardinals broadcasts, 'Good night, Skip. This is the Cardinal baseball network,'" the son remembered. "And that has haunted me for years, all the way through high school. I was a pretty good football player. And I'd line up and the guy across the line would say [tauntingly], 'Good night, Skip.' And I'd start laughing. I'm not doing that to my kids. But he meant it in the right way."[12]

Skip got his first radio job at the age of sixteen, doing a weekend high school sports show for KMOX.[13] "I was a soprano in those days and I was pretty bad," he recalled.[14] After graduating from Webster Groves High School in 1957, Skip was off to the University of Missouri, where he majored in journalism and hosted a sports show on a local radio station.[15] He worked at KMOX during the summer throughout college and became a full-time station employee in 1961 following his graduation and a brief time with the Army Reserve.[16] He first paired with his father that fall, broadcasting Mizzou football, always calling his broadcast partner "Dad" on the air. "I know a guy who hasn't heard us together before must be thinking I'm talking 'bop' talk," he said in 1966. "But I've never called Dad anything but 'Dad.'"

As his personal life bled over to his professional career, the son of Harry Caray battled an identity crisis. "I tried to copy Dad's style when I was starting but it just didn't sound right," he admitted. He even used his father's signature line. "I used to say, 'Holy Cow' but got away from it because it is his trademark." When embracing his father's style didn't work, he retreated in the opposite direction. "I once thought of changing my name, but I dropped the idea."

More than once, he heard the whispers of nepotism. "I had a lot of that, and I was sick of it. If I did well, people said it was because of genes. And if I did bad, they said I only got the job because of whose kid I was." A frustrated Skip saw a double standard. It was acceptable to follow in your father's footsteps, but only for certain career choices. "It has always fascinated me that if a doctor or lawyer follows his father into practice, everybody says, 'Isn't that nice.' But if your Dad is a radio person or I guess is just someone in the public eye, they say, 'He got the job because of his Old Man.'"

Over the years, confusion and frustration melted away as Skip blazed his own trail with his own style. Gratitude and appreciation emerged. "Now I look back and see what a compliment it was to be Harry's kid," he said in 1979.

Skip's first opportunity to do baseball play-by-play came in 1963 for the Cardinals minor league team in Tulsa as part of a three-man broadcast crew.[17] He only spent half a season in Oklahoma before changing jobs. "Eddie Stanky was then the farm director and he noticed that the Tulsa radio booth was slightly overcrowded," Skip explained. "He told me the Cardinals Triple-A team in Atlanta had only one announcer. I sent the Crackers a tape, they liked it, and so I packed up at midseason and Hank Morgan, a very funny man, and I split the Atlanta games the rest of the year. I would drive to Atlanta for the summer and drive back to St. Louis for the winter for three years."[18]

His first chance to call a major league game came in Houston in 1965 when a death in the family prevented Mel Allen from broadcasting a Milwaukee Braves game. Skip's description of a Braves-Astros game came one day after Harry called a Cardinals-Astros game from the Astrodome. "Skip's appearance on the airwaves was believed to have been the first time that the son of a major league broadcaster had aired a big league game," noted *The Sporting News*.[19]

Skip's job with the Crackers ended that same season because the Braves relocated to Atlanta the following year. He applied to be the number two man in the Braves broadcast booth, but lost out to Larry Munson, who went on to have a long career as the voice of University of Georgia football.[20] Back in St. Louis full-time, Skip called St. Louis University basketball with Jack Buck and later became the radio voice of St. Louis Hawks basketball.[21] When the Hawks relocated to Atlanta, he turned down more money to announce Blues hockey, and headed back to Georgia, this time permanently.[22] "This was my chance to get out from under the Harry Caray mystique and see if I was any good," said Skip. "I had gotten to the point where I really didn't know."[23]

While Skip successfully navigated the transition from radio to TV ("When the Hawks televised their first game in Atlanta, I had to lie to [owner] Tom Cousins that I had done television before,"), his personal life was a mess. He divorced his first wife (the former Lila Osterkamp) in 1970.[24] She and their two young children – son Harry Christopher III, better known as "Chip," and daughter Cindy – moved back to St. Louis. As Skip's weight fluctuated between 230 and 290 pounds, he became addicted to amphetamines ("Without a fix, I could barely move," he once confessed),[25] and started spending his nights drinking and hooking up with women at a nightclub called the Brave Falcon Lounge. "It was Dewar's and water and let's see what happens," Skip remembered. "God, I loved that place." In his early thirties, Caray was suddenly a single man in the city. "I got divorced just when birth control came into being and before AIDS became a problem – every night was New Year's Eve."[26]

His father married Dr. Val Kunz's daughter in November of 1937, five-and-a-half years after graduating high school in Webster Groves. Skip had married the daughter of Dr. Roy Osterkamp in November of 1963, six-and-a-half years after graduating high school in Webster Groves. Now divorced with a namesake son primarily raised by his mother, Skip Caray was living his father's life. "Stories of Caray's escapades on the road are legendary," Atlanta reporter Ken Picking wrote. Thinking he was home, Skip once woke up and walked into the hallway of a Montreal hotel naked. The door to his room slammed shut behind him before he realized where he was. He huddled in a corner until a friend bailed him out. His hard-partying ways continued for much of the early 1970s. "A lot of the happiness was superficial," he admitted. "A little booze and a young lady and you sorta forget about missing your kids."

His life began to change when he met Paula Prather, who owned a hairstyling salon next to his favorite nightclub. They married in 1976 (the same year he started broadcasting Braves baseball). Suddenly, out-every-night Skip became more focused on home life. "That's where there's a difference with my grandfather," Chip Caray told a reporter years later. "My dad had a greater appreciation for the importance of family at a younger age. While he loves his job, he doesn't live his job like my grandfather did."[27] ("It's a game," Skip said more than once. "It's the toy department.")

A difference in lifestyle off the field mirrored the differences in style behind the microphone. In the 1980s and '90s, viewers could watch an over-the-top Harry broadcast a Cubs game over one cable superstation during the day, and catch low-key Skip describing a Braves game that night on a competing outlet. "He's glib, smooth, entertaining, informative, and honest," is how *Los Angeles Times* columnist Larry Stewart described the younger Caray in 1988. "If you want enthusiasm, watch Harry Caray on WGN. If you like dry wit, watch Skip Caray on TBS."[28]

Perhaps that dry wit came from his mother. But at least a part of it undoubtedly came from the man Skip partnered with on St. Louis University basketball games in the 1960s. "I think he sounds more like Jack Buck than he sounds like me," Harry once said of his son's voice.[29]

Buck was among a trio of announcers who called their first major league games for St. Louis teams and whose careers took flight in the middle years of the twentieth century. Although often skirted or overshadowed by Skip's dad, these men would go on to carve out their own prominent broadcasting niches: Buck as the voice of the Cardinals, Milo Hamilton for multiple teams around baseball, Joe Garagiola with a nationwide audience for NBC Sports. But before taking the lead chair, all three learned to play second fiddle in Harry's Caray's St. Louis.

---

[1] Ruthrauff & Ryan, Griesedieck's advertising agent, took out an ad in *The Sporting News* when searching for Street's replacement. "We are now scheduling 'Guest announcers' to appear with Caray for trial appointments as the Cardinals visit the major league cities on their schedule," it read in part. *The Sporting News*, April 11, 1951. Mancuso was officially hired in July. A former catcher whose big-league career spanned 17 seasons, Mancuso broke in with the Cardinals in 1928. He played for Street in 1930 and 1931. Caray's second marriage took place on January 11, 1952, in Miami. The new Mrs. Caray was identified as a saleswoman at the Famous-Barr store in the St. Louis suburb of Clayton. *St. Louis Post-Dispatch*, January 12, 1952. On the marriage application, Caray's age was listed as 34 (he was actually less than two months shy of turning 38) and his occupation as "salesman." His wife's age was listed as 26. *Miami Herald*, January 9, 1952. Her brother, Air Force Lt. Martin Binkin, was awarded the Distinguished Flying Cross for heroism in 1953. Binkin flew 50 combat missions as a navigator-bombardier during the Korean War. *St. Louis Post-Dispatch*, July 23, 1953. Another brother, Syl, was a one-time announcer and news broadcaster for radio station WEW in St. Louis.

[2] The Keokuk Kernels debuted in the Three-I League in 1952.

³ "Mancuso is Caray's stabilizer," wrote Corkin. "Listening to the two of them on the air is an education in baseball." *The Journal*, March 26, 1953. "The eastern style is factual, not like the Harry Caray 'we' for the home team," former player turned broadcaster Bill White said years later. "That's called western style." *St. Louis Post-Dispatch*, July 15, 1984.

⁴ *Fort Lauderdale News*, May 16, 1953.

⁵ With the Cardinals training in St. Petersburg, the team's exhibition games were broadcast locally on WTSP AM 1380. "PLAY-BY-PLAY WITH HARRY CARAY," read part of an ad in the *St. Petersburg Times* in March of 1952. The station featured home broadcasts of the Cardinals or Yankees daily at Al Lang Field.

⁶ "A complaint … claims Caray ran up a $372 bill from March 3 to April 1, 1952, while a guest at the hotel." *St. Petersburg Times*, March 18, 1953.

⁷ In addition to being granted custody of the couple's two daughters, Mrs. Caray was awarded the family home at 4 Sheraton Drive in Ladue, land valued at more than $100,000 and a cash settlement of $52,000. She also received $375 a month in support for each child. Harry paid all legal fees. *St. Louis Post-Dispatch*, April 4, 1974.

⁸ Ibid, July 16, 1977; *Chicago Tribune*, July 17, 1977. Fifteen-year-old Elizabeth Caray was vacationing with her father in Florida in the spring of 1977. The $40,000 lawsuit charged that the diary was taken by Gloria "Tuni" Griffith, one of Dutchie Caray's daughters from a previous marriage. The suit alleged that Harry threatened to publish copies of the diary and turn it over to Elizabeth's school. "It was full of a lot of interesting things," said Griffith, who took the diary to Harry after discovering a small quantity of marijuana in the hotel room shared by Elizabeth and another girl. "I took the diary to Harry. He read one page and told Elizabeth she was going home. He called her mother and she was put on a plane and sent home."

⁹ *St. Louis Post-Dispatch*, April 22, 1979. Michele Caray married Norman Stuart Cohen of Creve Coeur on April 1, 1979. After getting a nursing degree in college, Michele was employed by St. John's Mercy Medical Center as a psychiatric nurse. When Marian Caray passed away in 2010, she was identified as the mother to "Michele (Greg) McFadden and Elizabeth Caray of Phoenix, Arizona." Ibid, April 18, 2010.

¹⁰ "Good father? How would you grade yourself?" the interviewer asks Caray. "Well, no," Harry replied. "You can't be divorced and be as good a father as you would have liked to have been." https://www.youtube.com/watch?v=OrPw2tu_WDY

¹¹ *Atlanta Journal-Constitution*, May 21, 2000. The story identifies Patricia as "recently retired from Coca-Cola."

¹² *Chicago Tribune,* June 27, 1989.

¹³ The "Skip Caray Show" debuted on KMOX on June 30, 1956. The 15-minute program aired on Saturdays. *The News-Times* (Webster Groves), August 22, 1956.

¹⁴ *The Sporting News*, June 12, 1965.

[15] "I went to Missouri on a football scholarship, but a knee injury stopped what was sure to be a brilliant career," Skip laughingly recalled for a reporter. *The Columbus (GA) Ledger*, August 10, 1977.

[16] Skip taught typing and English for the U.S. Army Reserve.

[17] Doing a re-creation of a game while in Tulsa, Skip was reading the ticker when the word FOG appeared. "Hold on, folks," he told his radio audience. "Believe it not, fog is starting to roll in here. There is going to be a delay in the game, apparently. Wow, look at that stuff. It's as thick as pea soup." The game wasn't delayed. FOG meant "foul over grandstand." Skip had to quickly correct himself. "Folks, the fog has lifted just as suddenly as it came in."

[18] *Atlanta Journal-Constitution*, December 22, 1979. While the Crackers remained in Atlanta through the 1965 season, the team lost its affiliation with the Cardinals after 1963. The Crackers were the Triple-A team of the Minnesota Twins in 1964 and the Milwaukee Braves in 1965. For the Cardinals in 1963, Caray saw future St. Louis players Phil Gagliano, Dick Hughes, Johnny Lewis, Dave Ricketts, and Mike Shannon. Jim Frey, who later managed the 1984 Chicago Cubs, was also on the team.

[19] *The Sporting News*, June 12, 1965.

[20] Munson was not his only partner. "Hamilton, Larry Munson, ex-pitchers Ernie Johnson and Dizzy Dean are heard and seen over a large section of the Southeast." *The Sporting News*, June 4, 1966.

[21] Jerry Gross was fired as Hawks broadcaster after the 1966-1967 season. Gross was reportedly let go because of "editorializing in his broadcasts." *St. Louis Post-Dispatch*, May 3, 1967.

[22] Skip claimed he turned down $10,000 more a year in salary from the Blues to move to Atlanta with the Hawks. *Tallahassee Democrat*, May 22, 1983.

[23] *Atlanta Journal-Constitution*, December 22, 1979. Skip had the chance to join his father with the Chicago White Sox in 1976 but turned it down. "I'd have been stepping back into the shadow again," Skip said. "Dad was disappointed, but he understood, and I think he admired me for it."

[24] Lila Osterkamp "now lives in St. Clair (Mo.)," wrote columnist Benjamin Hochman. "When [Chip Caray] was growing up, she used to cut hair – even snipped Red Schoendienst's red locks." *St. Louis Post-Dispatch*, January 31, 2023.

[25] *Atlanta Journal Constitution*, January 10, 1982.

[26] Ibid, May 21, 2000.

[27] Ibid.

[28] *Los Angeles Times*, July 29, 1988.

[29] *Chicago Tribune*, June 27, 1989. "I learned by working with dad and Jack Buck and Joe Garagiola," said Skip Caray in 1991. "One guy's with CBS, the other used to do NBC and now is on the 'Today' show and my father is perhaps the biggest cult idol in the history of baseball. I was very lucky."

Hello Jack, Milo and Joe

Born in Holyoke, Massachusetts in 1924, Jack Buck would later credit his distinctive broadcasting voice to hawking newspapers in his youth, his time as a drill instructor in the Army, and four decades of smoking Camel cigarettes. The third of seven children, Buck's father was a railroad accountant. When Earle Buck Sr. relocated to Cleveland, his family followed him to Ohio. Jack and Earle Jr. were sitting in the bleachers at Municipal Stadium when Joe DiMaggio's 56-game hitting streak ended.

After graduating high school in 1942, Buck was drafted the following June and on the frontlines of World War II in Europe by early 1945. As a member of the 9th Infantry Division, Jack was among the first wave of American troops to cross the Rhine in Remagen, Germany. Wounded in March, Buck was in Paris when the Nazis officially surrendered. He later spent time in Berchtesgaden, Hitler's mountain fortress in southeastern Germany.

Back in the United States and out of the military by the spring of 1946, he enrolled at Ohio State University that fall. After graduating, he returned to campus to take a football class conducted by Woody Hayes. His first play-by-play broadcast came in 1949, a basketball game between Ohio State and DePaul. But baseball was his first love. "I'd fall asleep on the floor listening to baseball," Buck recalled. "And I always knew what I wanted to do." The Columbus Redbirds, the Cardinals minor league team in the Ohio capital, needed a broadcaster in 1950. "I auditioned for the job and the Columbus [president] Al Bannister knew that half my games would be re-creations.[1] He put me in his office chair, turned on the intercom system and went into an adjacent office. Bannister gave me the play-by-play report from the previous World Series and made me do an entire game, making up everything as I went. Whatever, it got me the job."[2]

After two seasons, Buck lost the position when the station switched formats. He left for a Columbus television station, where comedian Jonathan Winters was one of his co-workers. Jack returned to radio in 1953 after Ed Edwards, calling games for the Cardinals minor league team in Rochester, lost his job. "I understand he told a dirty story at a banquet of the Clockpunchers. Bing Devine, the general manager, fired him and was put in contact with me," Buck recalled. "That's how I got back into baseball." Just as in Columbus, he also worked for a local television station. "I did a weather show called Meteorological Mirth. I don't even think I can spell it."[3] What Buck remembered most about his time in Rochester didn't happen in a studio or at the ballpark. "Danny Whalen was our trainer. One time his wife pulled my daughter Christine out of Lake Ontario, when she was drowning."[4]

With Anheuser-Busch's purchase of the Cardinals, the organization began searching for new broadcasters. The club sent Buck to New York to work a televised broadcast between the Cardinals and Giants. His TV audition got him the job. "When I got to St. Louis," Buck remembered, "I found a tape [of radio broadcasts] I sent them from Rochester. It had never been opened. They hired me off that one telecast."[5]

When the Dodgers and Giants later left New York for California, Anheuser-Busch backed telecasts of the two clubs for an East Coast audience. Whenever Los Angeles or San Francisco played in St. Louis or Pittsburgh in 1958, Buck did the Budweiser-sponsored broadcast on a New York television station. The local media took notice. "He won favorable notice because of his ability to avoid descriptions of events that were obvious to the viewer and to provide, instead, perceptive background information about the game and the players," wrote John P. Shanley in *The New York Times*, while also noting Buck's busy schedule.[6] In a single week, Buck was in St. Louis Monday for a radio broadcast, Tuesday through Friday was spent in Pittsburgh, back to St. Louis on Saturday, before returning to Pittsburgh on Sunday. "When he is at home he also conducts disc jockey shows from Monday through Fridays from 3:30 to 5 p.m.," Shanley stated. Buck also did a 15-minute sports show five nights a week.

Buck's first year in St. Louis was Caray's tenth season calling Cardinals games. Harry dominated the broadcasts, with Jack's time on the air typically limited to a few innings. Even that time wasn't guaranteed. "When my dad started, Harry Caray was the main man, and he kind of let my dad know in no uncertain terms that he was the main man," said Joe Buck. "If there was something big going on in a Cardinals game, he'd tap my dad on the shoulder, and Harry would sit down and [call] it."[7] If a game went extra innings, "I might as well have gone home, because Caray was going to do all the play-by-play," Jack later wrote. "It upset him if he was not on the air when something exciting happened. I liked the opportunity to make some exciting calls, but when I saw how much it bothered him, it took some of the enjoyment out of it for me."[8]

According to Buck, his relationship with Caray got off to a rocky start because Harry had wanted a different broadcaster for the position. "He wanted the Cardinals to hire Chick Hearn, who, at the time, was a broadcaster in Peoria,

Illinois," Jack recalled.[9] Hearn didn't want the job and later went on to a legendary play-by-play career with the Los Angeles Lakers.[10]

Buck, meanwhile, seemed content to do a few innings of baseball because so many other opportunities came his way. He launched the "Jack Buck Sports Show" on KTVI-TV in 1955, got the opportunity to do the New York telecasts three years later, and in 1959, became sports director at KMOX radio. His timing with KMOX was fortuitous for two reasons. In 1960, the station ditched music and launched "At Your Service," becoming the first major radio station in the country to adopt a news-talk format.[11] The same year Buck honed his interviewing skills, his voice was absent from Cardinals baseball.[12] "I got word that I was fired just before Christmas of 1959," Jack remembered. The brewery had recently hired Buddy Blattner. The former player-turned-broadcaster had spent years on television with Dizzy Dean, but left the "Game of the Week" telecasts after the two feuded over a relationship with a new sponsor.[13] When Blattner was hired, Buck became the odd man out.

While Buck's departure from Cardinals baseball was brief (Blattner left to take a job with the expansion Los Angeles Angels), the break opened new opportunities.[14] ABC hired him in 1960 to broadcast weekend baseball games, joining a crowded field of telecasts that included Lindsey Nelson on NBC and Dean (with new partner Pee Wee Reese) on CBS.[15] While the ABC broadcasts lasted only one season, Buck stayed two more years at the network, calling everything from American Football League games to professional bowling.[16] He even went to Tokyo one year to call the Japanese All-Star baseball game. In 1963, he jumped to CBS, becoming the television voice of Chicago Bears football for three seasons before becoming the lead broadcaster on Dallas Cowboys games.[17] (Unlike today, where networks rotate broadcast crews weekly, announcers stayed with a single team for the entire season.) Buck called the 1967 NFL Championship Game, the legendary "Ice Bowl" between the Cowboys and Packers in Green Bay. ("Give me a bite of your coffee," partner Frank Gifford said to Buck during the telecast.) He also broadcast Super Bowl IV on television and seventeen more on radio. The duo of Buck and Hank Stram on Monday Night Football proved so popular people turned down their television sets to listen to the talented broadcaster and former coach. But years before Buck competed against Howard Cosell and his considerable ego, he learned to navigate the waters of Caray's prideful ways.[18]

"Caray treated me better than he did the first time we worked together," Buck acknowledged regarding his return to the booth in 1961. Even before he met Harry, Jack knew he couldn't be Harry. And he didn't try to pretend otherwise. Before leaving Rochester, a Cardinals executive sent him a tape of a

Caray broadcast with a note. "This is the way we want you to broadcast." It wasn't Buck's style. "I wasn't going to try to broadcast a game like Caray," Buck declared. "If the people in St. Louis didn't like my style, I'd have to go elsewhere." He once told a columnist in Florida, "I could never broadcast a game like Harry," before adding, "Harry couldn't broadcast a game like me, either."[19]

The two men had a few things in common: Both were color-blind; at different times, both were reportedly offered, and turned down, the chance to become the Cardinals general manager; and both enjoyed a night out on the town.[20] While Harry's late-night prowess got more attention, the pair combined for a few memorable escapades over the years. "We closed some places that have never been closed before," Buck once told an interviewer. "We closed an all-night bowling alley, an all-night bar once. We closed it. Permanently." While he often deferred to the elder Caray, Buck put his foot down, literally and figuratively, when it came time to get in an automobile. "I always drove," Jack remembered. "I wouldn't ride with him. He used to start fires with those glasses he wore."

Confident and comfortable in his own skin, Buck had a way of checking his ego as Caray's junior partner while still letting his personality shine. "Frequently irreverent but seldom irrelevant" is how one writer described him in the 1960s.[21] He often used humor to make his point. No one, not even Caray, was spared his razor-sharp wit. At the annual dinner of the St. Louis Elks in 1962, Buck introduced manager Johnny Keane while reading a series of make-believe telegrams. "Dear John," began the one from Caray. "Try to listen more closely next year."[22] When Caray was honored at a dinner in the spring of 1969 following a near-fatal accident attempting to cross Kingshighway in St. Louis (more on that later), Buck served as master of ceremonies. "What nice things can I say about Harry," Jack asked at the Knights of the Cauliflower Ear banquet, "that you haven't heard from the man himself?" Buck ended the evening by pleading with the crowd to "please drive carefully. Harry's walking again."[23]

That season marked Buck's sixteenth year as a broadcaster in St. Louis. But Jack's identity with the local baseball team – so fondly remembered today by Cardinals fans – had yet to emerge. "It was fun to be a part of it," Buck wrote of the clubs of that era, "but those were really Harry's teams." When Caray was on the field interviewing Musial in Chicago following his 3000th hit, Buck was back in the studio in St. Louis. When Harry screamed, "The Cardinals win the pennant!" on the final day of the 1964 baseball season, Buck was 2,000 miles away in San Francisco, calling the Bears-49ers football game.[24]

Nevertheless, Jack's talent could not be denied, as he racked up opportunities both locally and nationally. He broadcast from the top of the Gateway Arch when it opened in 1967 and called the first St. Louis Blues hockey game that same year. Viewers around the county watched him describe the 1965 All-Star Game for NBC and heard him on a World Series broadcast for the first time in 1968. The Cardinals-Tigers Series featured Caray on television and Buck on radio.[25] The combination almost didn't happen. Buck claimed that when Caray found out his partner got the radio gig, he initially refused to do the TV broadcasts. "I won't do it," Harry said, before changing his mind.

The combination of Caray's pettiness and domineering style had the potential to wreck any on-air chemistry. Despite the differences in approach and personality, or perhaps because of them, the two men somehow managed to click when the microphones were turned on. "I offset Harry," Buck once boasted to a writer. "Maybe people weren't ready for his type of commentary, but together we were the best radio team in the business – in all sports, for that matter."[26] Skip Caray agreed, calling the pair "the greatest announcing duo in sports history." Harry's son noted the two men played to different audiences. "Dad was the voice of the guy sitting in the bleachers with his shirt off and Jack was the emcee for the guy dressed in a dinner jacket. They worked so well together and played off each other so smoothly."[27]

"In my opinion," said Bob Costas, "and I spent a lot of time sitting in my dad's car in the driveway on Long Island fiddling with the radio dial – Buck and Caray were the best pair." [28]

Even after Caray stopped broadcasting for the Cardinals, the two men stayed in touch and occasionally crossed paths. After he left the Cardinals and KMOX, Caray continued to broadcast University of Missouri football through the 1972 season on a competing station. (Harry broadcast his first Mizzou football game in 1954. Other than the Cardinals, he broadcast more years of Tigers football than any other team.)[29] His KMOX play-by-play replacement on Mizzou football, just as with Cardinals baseball, was Buck. "Caray and longtime sidekick Jack Buck can be seen together in the MU [press box] before Tiger games," observed the Jefferson City *Post-Tribune* in 1971. "Shortly before game time, each man steps into a different broadcasting booth."[30]

When Caray returned to the National League as a broadcaster for the Cubs, he made his first trip back to Busch Stadium in thirteen seasons. "Well, I've been here two days, and I haven't been served a subpoena," he said on the air one May evening in 1982. During that same trip, *Post-Dispatch* media critic Eric Mink noted the differences in how Harry and Jack worked with their color men. "[Buck] manages to set up situations and discussions that help extract [Mike]

Shannon's expertise," he wrote.[31] As for Caray, "He does let go of the mike occasionally, but it almost hurts him to do it."

"In style, Buck is as sophisticated as Caray is earthy," Mink maintained. "Humor is another telling point of difference. Caray is like Milton Berle, broad, obvious, a knee-slapper. Buck is a mischievous imp – wry, witty, subtle, Mort Sahl-ish."[32]

In 1986, the Milton Berle and Mort Sahl of baseball began working together again. Harry and Jack taped a weekly conversation that aired Sunday mornings on KMOX. "We're like two old housewives getting together for a chat," said Caray. A year later, it was Buck, not Caray, honored in Cooperstown, a moment that raised eyebrows among some in the media. "How can the protégé get in the Hall of Fame before the professor?" asked columnist Dave Kindred.[33] (Buck downplayed the honor to a reporter. "I'm kind of sorry they opened the Hall [for broadcasters and sportswriters]. I think it kind of diminishes it.")[34]

Caray suffered a stroke in February of 1987 and missed the first six weeks of the baseball season. Jack was one of the announcers who filled in for Harry (calling an Andre Dawson grand slam off Todd Worrell). The next year in Las Vegas, Buck was one of many who roasted Caray at a tribute dinner. "We could have held this in Peoria, and it would have been cheaper for all of us," Jack told the mostly Midwestern crowd at the sellout event.[35] When the Hall of Fame finally recognized his colleague in 1989, Buck was among those extending congratulations. "Harry's not a very emotional or sentimental guy," Jack said. "But this has got to be very meaningful, one of the most important in his life. I know it meant an awful lot to me. And I'm thrilled to death, not only publicly but privately for Harry."

Two memorable multi-generational Buck/Caray moments took place near the end of Jack's career. In June of 2001, Jack briefly donned oversized Harry-style glasses and put on a Cubs cap to sing "Take Me Out to the Ballgame" during the seventh-inning stretch of a St. Louis-Chicago game. "Let's sing this song for the greatest rivalry in the history of sports," Buck told the Wrigley Field crowd, which roared its approval. When it came time in the song to declare his rooting interest, Jack disposed of the Cubs lid and put on a Cardinals cap. Chip Caray, Harry's grandson and the man who introduced Buck to the crowd that day, called it a "remarkable" moment. "I think I'm in the background looking at Joe Buck, who was doing the game on the Cardinals radio side, and he's looking at me kind of funny. I mouthed to him, 'That is awesome.' It really was."

Chip Caray became the Cubs broadcaster in 1998, the year Harry passed away.[36] Born in 1965, he grew up in suburban St. Louis listening to Buck.[37] His first year calling the Cubs was the summer Mark McGwire and Sammy Sosa staged an epic assault on Roger Maris's single-season home run record. On a Tuesday night in September, McGwire broke the record, depositing home run number 62 over the left-field wall at Busch Stadium. Joe Buck described the moment to a national television audience. Chip was broadcasting the game on WGN. His television booth was next to the Cardinals' radio booth. "When McGwire hit the home run, we watched Jack Buck stand up and applaud in his booth, with tears rolling down his face. We asked if he would be kind enough to come over and do an interview with us in the next half-inning. He very graciously appeared. Jack, who was suffering from Parkinson's at the time, came in, put on the headphones, sat down, looked at Steve [Stone], looked at me, and then said, 'So guys, what's shaking besides me?' We were sitting there stunned. Did he really just say that? All of a sudden, he starts laughing at our reaction, but that was Jack. He was just a great, great man."[38]

*****

"I can say without any fear of contradiction, that Jack and I were great friends," said the second man who joined the Cardinals broadcasting booth in 1954. "He always referred to me as an 'old friend.' That was special between Jack Buck and me," the broadcaster recalled. Milo Hamilton, though, would never say those words about Caray.

Like Caray, Hamilton had Midwestern roots, an enthusiastic broadcasting style, and a signature call ("Holy Toledo!"). Milo started his major-league broadcasting career calling Browns and Cardinals games, and later went to Chicago, working for both the Cubs and White Sox, just like Harry. Their paths crossed in both cities. But unlike Caray's relationship with Veeck, which got better with time and geography, Harry and Milo's relationship started on the wrong foot and never healed.

Hamilton arrived in St. Louis in the summer of 1953 from his home state of Iowa, hired as the first sportscaster for television station WTVI in Belleville, Illinois. (The station later moved to St. Louis and changed its call letters to KTVI.)[39] The station also carried Browns baseball games, something Hamilton got involved in because Dean and Blattner spent Saturdays and Sundays on the road for "Game of the Week." (The broadcast debuted on ABC that year. The telecast moved to CBS in 1955.)[40]

When the Browns left town after the season, Hamilton caught a break. Over the winter, he called St. Louis University basketball, games sponsored by a brewery that had just purchased a baseball team and wanted some new blood in the broadcast booth. "With my Anheuser-Busch background, I was the logical guy. So I stuck around St. Louis and joined the Cardinals broadcast team."

With the Cardinals, Hamilton quickly struck up friendships with sportswriter Broeg, Cardinals manager Stanky, and traveling secretary Leo Ward. The quartet bonded over afternoon movies, baseball, and their dislike of the man they disdainfully called "the Canary."

"I could see why [he was disliked]," said Hamilton, "as Caray had a way of getting under your skin."[41]

On road trips, Broeg, Hamilton and Stanky would even ride to the ballpark together. Once there, Broeg would go to the press box and Hamilton would drop off his briefcase in the broadcast booth.[42] The duo would then head down to the Cardinals dugout, where the manager would already be in uniform. "Stanky would act like he didn't know either one of us – after we'd been with him all day. To him, when he put the uniform on, he was in another world."

While Hamilton enjoyed Stanky's company away from the diamond, his relationship with Caray only got progressively worse. The two had first met that winter at Kiel Auditorium for a college basketball game. Hamilton was doing the television broadcast, with Caray calling the game on radio. "Nobody's going to be watching you tonight," Hamilton recalled Caray telling him. "They're all going to be listening to me on the radio."

The bravado continued when they met again for the baseball season. "Kid, don't worry about your mike being on because *I* am the announcer here," Harry told him. "Caray couldn't bring himself to treat someone in a nice way," Hamilton wrote in his autobiography. "He was just a paranoid person who didn't want anything good happening to anybody but himself. From the start, our pairing was hardly a match made in heaven."[43]

The pairing didn't last long. Hamilton traveled with Caray during the first half of the season. Buck got the assignment for the second half. With Buck and Caray on the road, Hamilton did pregame and postgame shows. When the season ended, Caray lobbied for a broadcast partner similar to Street and Mancuso, a former player who would serve as a color analyst.[44] He got his wish when the club hired Joe Garagiola. For the first time, but far from the last, Hamilton left a job, in part, because of his relationship with Caray.

He spent the next decade in Chicago, sandwiching a four-year gig as a rock 'n' roll disc jockey in between stints for the Cubs and White Sox. ("This may come as a shock to those who know me only as a baseball broadcaster, but there are some guys who will tell you to this day that I should be in the Rock n' Roll Hall of Fame," Hamilton boasted.)

With the White Sox in 1965, the team stopped in Atlanta for an exhibition game at the end of spring training. An Atlanta station, WGST, carried White Sox games, so local fans were accustomed to hearing Hamilton's voice. With the

Braves moving from Milwaukee to Atlanta the next season, the club hired Jim Fazhold to set up the club's radio network in the Southeast. Fazhold and Hamilton had worked together in television in St. Louis. A job offer soon emerged. Milo left Chicago for Atlanta and became the lead broadcaster for the Braves starting in 1966.[45]

Milo described the first ten years of major league baseball in Atlanta, with Hank Aaron's 715th home run – breaking Babe Ruth's record – becoming his signature moment. "There's a new home run champion of all time! And it's Henry Aaron!" he bellowed into the microphone on a Monday night in April of 1974.[46]

Clashing with ownership, Milo lost his job in Atlanta after the 1975 season.[47] The Braves got a new owner (Ted Turner) and a new announcer (Skip Caray) for the new year. Hamilton had a deal in place to return to St. Louis. With Buck leaving for a weekend sports show on NBC called *Grandstand*, Anheuser-Busch offered Hamilton a job as the Cardinals lead announcer. "They offered me a two-year contract and I was ready to sign it," Milo remembered. All it needed was final approval from Mike Roarty, a brewery executive. With the contract delayed, Hamilton reached out to a St. Louis friend who knew Roarty and arranged a meeting. "What if *Grandstand* fails?" Roarty asked Hamilton's contact over dinner. To Milo, the message was clear. "It meant that the team had promised Buck he could come back if need be," he later wrote. Hamilton was no longer interested. (*Grandstand* didn't work out for Buck. He soon returned to St. Louis full-time. In the interim, Bob Starr became the team's lead broadcaster.)[48]

With a return to St. Louis out of the picture, Hamilton took a job in Pittsburgh, where he replaced legendary Pirates broadcaster Bob Prince. They were big shoes to fill. Like Caray, Prince had an outsized personality, was hugely popular with local fans and loved to prowl the bars and saloons of big-league cities late at night.[49] "It was impossible to replace Bob Prince as Voice of the Pirates," Hamilton stated.[50] Nevertheless, Milo spent four years in Pittsburgh, capped off by a 1979 team that won a World Series. "There's nothing like a World Series-winning clubhouse. Whew! I got soaked with champagne," Hamilton fondly recalled. "But the championship celebration was somewhat bittersweet, as by the time the World Series ended, I already knew that I was going to work in Chicago the following year."

Back with the Cubs, Hamilton was set to eventually become Jack Brickhouse's successor. The longtime Chicago broadcaster had planned the 1980 season to be his last but changed his mind and worked one more year.

Holy Cow St. Louis!

Heading into the 1982 season, Hamilton finally had the role he wanted: Lead broadcaster for the Cubs on WGN-TV. His old nemesis wrecked his plans.

The new owners of the White Sox (Jerry Reinsdorf and Eddie Einhorn bought the club from Veeck) had a vision for broadcasting baseball that featured fewer games on free television and more contests to be carried on a pay-per-view basis. Caray, who always catered to the masses, wanted no part of it. He tipped his hand shortly after the 1981 season. "You know I don't want to leave Chicago," Caray told a reporter, "and I've enjoyed my association with the White Sox. But the Sox' new pay-TV (SportsVision) probably will not have more than 50,000 subscribers at the outset. I'm accustomed to working for hundreds of thousands of viewers and listeners – my fans – and so I certainly would consider a chance to join the WGN team."[51]

He got his chance a month later. When the owners of the Cubs and WGN, the Tribune Company, announced a news conference at the Ambassador East Hotel, the media knew exactly what to expect. (Harry lived there during the season.)[52] The one person caught off guard by the development was Hamilton. He received a call that morning from a WGN executive who told him to go to the hotel for an important announcement. When Milo pressed for details, he was only told, "We really need you there." He soon arrived and located the room of the news conference. "Moments later, to my complete surprise, it was announced that Harry Caray was going to be the lead TV announcer for the Cubs. My heart lept into my throat."[53]

Soon thereafter, a Tribune executive invited Caray and Hamilton to dinner at the Drake Hotel. Once again, according to Hamilton, Caray poured salt on the wound. "Well, kid, if I were you, I'd leave town," Harry told him. But Hamilton had a new contract, something Harry didn't know. "Caray wasn't ready for that news and looked rather upset," Milo recalled. The duo was paired together for the 1982 season with predictable results. "Harry's handling of people was poor to say the least," Hamilton believed. "It didn't matter if he was dealing with the starting pitcher, traveling secretary, the public relations person or an usher. If a player made an error on a Tuesday and it cost the Cubs the game, he rode that error for a week. He rode managers. He rode players. It didn't matter. He treated everyone the same way. In short, he was a miserable human being."[54]

For the 1983 season, Hamilton became the lead radio broadcaster (with Steve Stone joining Caray in the TV booth). Harry and Milo would do most of their broadcasts on their dominant medium, switching places for the fourth through sixth innings.[55] Passing each other on the catwalk between the television and radio booths, the two men wouldn't acknowledge each other. When it came time for Harry to sing during the seventh-inning stretch, Milo refused to participate, walking out the back of the radio booth onto the catwalk in silent protest.[56] After the 1984 season, the Cubs didn't renew Hamilton's contract. Milo blamed Harry. "This marked the third time in my life that Caray had caused me to lose my job. He did so first in St. Louis in 1954, second when [the Tribune Company] brought him in to take over the lead job for the Cubs in 1982, and third at the end of the 1984 season."[57]

Caray denied any responsibility for Hamilton's departure. "If there were any differences, Milo created them. I don't know what to say. This is the first I've heard about it. People who know the situation know I leaned over backwards to try to be nice. When we changed places and people reacted to me, hey, I can't control that. Milo's a fine announcer and I'm sorry to see him go," said Harry. "Personally, I think his ego destroyed him. He couldn't accept the fact that he's not the No. 1 guy."[58]

Hamilton soon became the No. 1 guy for the Astros, leaving Chicago for Houston, where he would remain for the rest of his career. (Astros broadcaster DeWayne Staats replaced Hamilton in Chicago. Staats, who was born in Advance, Missouri and grew up in Wood River, Illinois outside St. Louis, spent his youth listening to Buck and Caray.) In his first year in Houston, Hamilton gave an interview to *Inside Sports* magazine that kept the controversy between the two men alive with words that reverberated for years. "I don't have any respect for him or the way he goes about this business," Hamilton told columnist Bob Rubin. "He's a self-promoter. His line is how much he loves the game and the fans, but the bottom line is that he's promoting Harry Caray."

Similar remarks by Hamilton surfaced again in 1998 just days after Caray's death. "Harry felt he was bigger than the game, I don't think there's any doubt about it," Hamilton said in comments pulled from an Internet site and published by *USA Today*. (Milo would later claim the reporter was trying to bait him into saying something negative about Harry after his death, which he refused to do. Instead, Hamilton pointed him to comments from the magazine article, which the interviewer recycled to appear as new quotes.) "What kind of man says that about a colleague two days after he died? A very sick man," Skip Caray told the *Atlanta Journal-Constitution*. "This says more about the kind of person Milo Hamilton is than the kind of person Harry Caray was."[59]

For years after he left Chicago, anytime Hamilton was interviewed, the subject inevitably turned to his time with Caray. When asked to describe the relationship in 2006, Milo replied, "You'll have to get my new book that's coming out because I bury him in it."[60] The book, which soon debuted, featured multiple Caray stories and even a chapter titled "Caged by the Canary." Dutchie Caray, Harry's widow, reluctantly broke her silence in an interview with a

Chicago Tribune columnist. "I don't think Milo has shown any class at all. It is probably just to sell books. I hope nobody buys the book," she told Fred Mitchell. "I was really, really disappointed in Milo. After 25 years to bring up these things ... and Harry has been dead eight years."[61]

The week before being honored by the Hall of Fame with the Ford Frick Award in 1992, Hamilton told a reporter that during his last stint with the Cubs, he received letters from fans telling him they were turning down their TVs and listening to his radio broadcasts. "That was something Caray couldn't live with," he said.[62] Pointing out he was the fourth WGN broadcaster to be honored by Cooperstown (along with Elson, Brickhouse, and Caray), Hamilton expressed disappointment that this fact wasn't mentioned by the station. "To have four announcers who worked for the same station in the Hall of Fame would have been something to brag about."

Left unsaid by Hamilton was this foursome was not the only quartet he was a part of honored by the Hall of Fame. Milo was the last of four broadcasters with ties to the Cardinals celebrated in Cooperstown between 1987 and 1992. The third spot was claimed by a man given an early career boost by Caray. But their relationship would later fracture, and this time, it would be Harry doing most of the complaining.

*****

By the mid-1950s, Joe Garagiola had been a legend on the Hill in St. Louis for years and a major league player for nearly a decade. But his time in the spotlight was only beginning. An injury on the diamond got Garagiola to start considering life after baseball. He underwent surgery for a dislocated left shoulder in June of 1950. Hitting .347 at the time, he missed the next three months of the season. The career .257 hitter never again approached such lofty success at the plate.

In the hospital following surgery, "I made up my mind that the first chance I got, I would start planning on a new career," Garagiola recalled. "For the first time I realized I wouldn't play forever." Seeing Caray later at a St. Louis Ad Club meeting, Garagiola teased him, "I'd like to have a soft job like yours."[63] Always a talented talker and a magnet for media looking for a quote, Joe began to seriously consider leaving baseball for broadcasting following Gabby Street's death. Traded to the Pirates in the summer of 1951 and to the Cubs in 1953, Garagiola reached out to Harry Renfro, a representative of the D'Arcy advertising agency, before the start of the 1954 season.[64] Renfro lined up a potential radio job for Joe that would have paid him $12,000 a year.[65] But when the Cubs offered him $16,000 for the new season, he decided to play ball.

Garagiola's broadcasting offer got the attention of a Washington lawmaker. Colorado Senator Edwin Johnson served on a sub-committee investigating monopoly power. He was no fan of corporations such as Anheuser-Busch owning major league teams.[66] D'Arcy represented the brewery.[67] With a ballplayer of one team potentially getting courted by the owner of another team through its advertising agent, Johnson sniffed something was wrong. And that's how Garagiola found himself in the nation's capital one spring day in 1954, getting grilled by lawmakers.

Because of the Anheuser-Busch/D'Arcy connection, Johnson suspected tampering. "Suppose Renfro went to Brooklyn's Roy Campanella with an attractive broadcasting offer if he quit baseball," Johnson posited. "What would that do to the pennant race?"

"You can't compare me with Campanella," a chuckling Garagiola replied. "You're looking at a .250 hitter."[68] It was a line that launched a thousand headlines.

Traded by the Cubs to the Giants near the end of the 1954 campaign, Garagiola was ineligible for the World Series. (Nevertheless, his teammates still voted him a quarter-share of their Series earnings, roughly $3,000.) After the season, he made it official, sending Commissioner Ford Frick a letter asking to be placed on the voluntary retired list. The 28-year-old Garagiola planned to start doing media work in St. Louis.

He started working with Caray that fall, joining him on Mizzou football broadcasts. (Both men later developed a close friendship with Mizzou coach Dan Devine.)[69] Joe joined Harry in the Cardinals booth the following spring. "We had an eye on Joe for some time. He's a natural for radio," said Caray. "I poured my heart into making him an announcer."[70] During spring training in St. Petersburg, the duo did a daily live six-minute sports broadcast and then taped a 15-minute program called "Spring Training with the Cardinals," which aired each night at 8:00 p.m. When the season began, Caray enthusiastically welcomed the newcomer's contributions. "Any comment Joe wants to make, we want to hear," he told reporters.[71]

But Caray had his limits, as Garagiola would soon discover. When the All-Star Game came to St. Louis in the summer of 1957, Mel Allen and Al Helfer described the game on television. Caray and Bob Neal had the call on radio. Garagiola convinced Gillette, the sponsor, to give him airtime on both mediums. "Signs – The Secret Language of Baseball" would be the topic, as Joe planned to describe for both audiences all the non-verbal communication that takes place on the field, focusing on the catcher and the third-base coach. His broadcast partners had other ideas. "Joe knew all about signs and baseball. But Joe did not know anything about baseball announcers," said Lindsey Nelson.[72]

Garagiola struggled to get in a word on the television broadcast with Allen and Helfer. "Veteran announcers are not all that considerate. They are survivors," Nelson wrote in his autobiography. The radio broadcast was even worse. "Harry Caray and Bob Neal were the nearest thing to a never-ending sentence that had yet been invented," Nelson recalled. "Joe had gone from booth to booth and he had been turned away in the manner of a volunteer from the Salvation Army who had come up with an empty tambourine. And suddenly the broadcast was over, and Joe was almost in tears."

Nelson believed that day in St. Louis proved to be a pivotal point in Garagiola's career. "I thought there on that afternoon Joe Garagiola decided that that would never happen to him again, anywhere or anytime. And as far as I know, it never did," he said. The longtime broadcaster would later work with Garagiola on NBC's baseball coverage.[73] "I do not mean for this to be in any manner unkind when I say that Joe is an opportunist. He knows where and when to make his moves."[74]

Garagiola started making his moves long before he became a broadcaster. France Laux took Garagiola to his first public speaking engagement in 1946. "Joe was shy and timid but he was a funny guy who was a natural in front of a crowd," Laux recalled.[75] By 1961, Garagiola was logging in excess of 100,000 airline miles annually and had made speeches to groups in all but seven states. He became so associated with public speaking engagements and media appearances that people had difficulty believing he ever played baseball. "When I tell stories of the terrible days in Pittsburgh or when I played with the Cardinal champions of 1946, they think it's a gag, that I'm making it up," Joe claimed.[76]

Garagiola published his first book, *Baseball Is a Funny Game,* in 1960. "Jocular Joe is a delightful storyteller and even his throw-away lines provide snickers," wrote *New York Times* columnist Arthur Daley.[77] By September, the book had been on the *Times* bestseller list for eight weeks and Garagiola had made numerous television appearances promoting it. He appeared on Jack Paar's program for the fifth time in July.[78] In November, NBC hired Garagiola for its baseball coverage (partnering with Nelson). Joe's later duties at the network included hosting the *Today* show and filling in for Paar's replacement on *The Tonight Show*, Johnny Carson, occasionally doing both programs on the same day. ("I used to open and close the 'candy store' many nights," Garagiola remembered.)[79] He stopped doing Cardinals games after 1962, and his transition to New York was complete when he was hired to replace Mel Allen in the Yankees broadcast booth after the 1964 season.

In a decade, Garagiola had gone from practicing radio calls with a tape recorder in the basement of his St. Louis home to juggling multiple roles in the nation's largest media market.[80] Marveling at Joe's meteoric rise, *New York Times* columnist Leonard Koppett believed it could be traced back to a singular event. "The appearance before Congress [in 1954] made it all possible," Koppett stated. "Up to that time, Garagiola's quick wit and breezy manner were known only to baseball insiders. For the rest of the season, wherever Garagiola appeared, more questions were asked about his experiences as a witness, more interviews with him were printed, and more fans became aware of Garagiola's personality. It was this exposure, stemming directly from the antimonopoly hearings that made Garagiola attractive to the broadcasting industry."[81]

His stunning ascent didn't come cost-free. His relationship with Caray was perhaps the biggest casualty. There were signs in 1961 that a rift between Harry and Joe was emerging. When Garagiola missed some Cardinals broadcasts early in the season, KMOX and the local papers were flooded with inquiries. "Where's Joe?" callers wanted to know. "There have indeed been some rumors flying about out there in radioland during the past week or so. Rumors that were generated by Joe's recent weeklong absence from his customary perch alongside Harry Caray in the Cardinals-KMOX radio booth," wrote Peter Rahn in the *Globe-Democrat*.[82] The weeklong absence had an innocent explanation. With the Cardinals on the West Coast, Garagiola stayed in St. Louis to record some commercials for Anheuser-Busch. That weekend, he broadcast games for NBC (contests that were blacked out in St. Louis).[83] But Caray never bothered to explain the reason for Garagiola's absence to his radio audience. "My absence could have been explained but it wasn't," Garagiola told Rahn, "and the first thing I know there's all sorts of rumors flying around."[84]

Whatever tension that was bubbling below the surface fully emerged after Garagiola left the Cardinals broadcast booth. Before the first game of the 1964 World Series, Caray [working the games with Curt Gowdy] spotted Garagiola [broadcasting the contests with Phil Rizzuto] around the batting cage. "I walked toward him to say hello – my old buddy. He starts walking toward me – I figure for the same reason – and he walks right on by me and says, 'Hi, how are you, nice to see you.' I called him every name in the book," a flabbergasted Caray recalled.[85] "But that's Joe – as long as you can help him, you're his friend, but if you can't help him anymore he doesn't have time for you."[86]

Caray, who often commented that he had treated Garagiola better than his oldest son, never got over the slight.[87] "Garagiola bit me, stabbed me in the back," Harry said in 1987.[88] For his part, Garagiola never hid his dislike of his one-time partner.[89] "Harry says he taught me everything I know about broadcasting when we were in St. Louis. He taught me nothing. Harry doesn't like me because I'm nationally recognized and he isn't," Garagiola said at the 1977 All-Star Game. "He's a local announcer and always will be."[90] ("You can cut the animosity with a knife anytime the two cross paths," columnist Gary Deeb once wrote in the *Chicago Tribune*.)

Like his rift with Musial, Garagiola's split from Caray was permanent. Returning to St. Louis for an engagement in 1989, Joe described the relationship with his one-time mentor this way. "Harry Caray, well, he wouldn't go to my fan club meeting, and I wouldn't go to his."[91]

Around this time, these two old lions of broadcasting (Garagiola was in his sixties, Caray in his seventies) must have gotten tired of roaring at one another. "Joe is one of the best color men in the business," Harry wrote in his autobiography. Two years later, addressing the Hall of Fame crowd in Cooperstown, Joe returned the favor, acknowledging Caray (along with public relations mogul Al Fleishman and KMOX executive Robert Hyland) as instrumental to his early broadcasting career in St. Louis.

In most people's minds, that's where the story of Caray and Garagiola ended: Two St. Louis natives, once friends and partners, who went their separate ways to reach the top of their profession. But just as with the Bucks, the Caray family's relationship with the Garagiolas now spans multiple generations. Three decades later, Harry and Joe's grandsons rekindled memories of happier days.

On a spring night in 2021, the Pensacola Blue Wahoos hosted the Rocket City (Madison, Alabama) Trash Pandas in a minor league baseball game in Florida. Up in the press box, sitting ten feet apart in separate booths, were Chris Garagiola, in his fourth season with the Blue Wahoos and Josh Caray, Chip's half-brother, Skip's son and Harry's grandson, describing the game for the Trash Pandas. "To have Chris and Josh up in the booth, that's pretty special," said Trash Pandas general manager and former major league player Jay Bell. "This is a once-in-a-lifetime moment as far as I'm concerned."

Josh Caray described his style as more like his father's than his grandfather's. "I'm not as critical [as Harry]," he said. "But my mannerisms, my thinking, my tone, are a lot more like my father." Garagiola's grandson Chris admitted the goal for both was the big leagues. "To maybe look at this as a stop along the journey and during this time I happened to be just a door down from the grandson of Harry Caray, that is a very cool thing to say."[92]

Chris Garagiola's connections to major league baseball include his father, Joe Garagiola Jr., who spent years as general manager of the Arizona Diamondbacks, and his grandmother Audrie, a one-time organist at Cardinals games. Audrie's husband, Joe Sr., broadcast his last game for NBC in 1988, wrote two more baseball books, and worked as a color analyst on Diamondbacks broadcasts.

When Garagiola died in 2016 at the age of ninety, *The New York Times* called him a "Catcher Who Called a Better Game on TV." Garagiola's broadcasting philosophy, as described in his second book – *It's Anybody's Ballgame* – sounded like something Caray would have embraced. "I want the broadcast to sound like two guys sitting at the ballpark, talking about the game, with the viewer eavesdropping. It's not High Mass, and it's not a seminar – it's a ballgame."

Buck's career, especially his connections to the Cardinals, blossomed after Caray left St. Louis. Many of Buck's most memorable calls came long after Caray departed the city: Lou Brock's 3000th hit, the final out of the 1982 World Series, Ozzie Smith's playoff home run in 1985, and the McGwire home run that tied Roger Maris's record.[93] When he died on a June night in 2002 at the age of seventy-seven, Joe Buck phoned KMOX to break the news. The station went commercial-free for hours, opening up the phone lines to listeners to share the memories of the man the *Post-Dispatch* called the "soul of the city." A peerless master of ceremonies, a prodigious fundraiser for charitable causes, a father of eight who was inducted into 11 halls of fame, Buck was remembered for so much more than baseball. "There never has been ... a better ambassador for the game of baseball or the city of St. Louis," said Mayor Francis Slay. "One of America's great storytellers," declared the *Post-Dispatch.*

Joe Buck joined his father in the Cardinals broadcast booth in 1991, hearing the same criticisms leveled at Skip Caray when he began his career. "There's 'daddy's boy' and 'coattailer' and his favorite, the 'Lucky Sperm Club,'" Dennis Tuttle wrote in a 2000 story for the *Washington Post*. Joe became the lead baseball broadcaster for Fox in 1996, calling his first World Series that fall. Except for two seasons, he called every one of them through the 2021 season. "If people want to call me 'Jack Buck's kid' for the rest of my life, that's fine by me," he said.[94]

Milo Hamilton spent the last 30 years of his life in Houston, calling Astros games from 1985 until he retired in 2012. He died in 2015 at the age of eighty-eight. His feud with Caray lasted more than a half-century, beginning soon after Milo arrived in St. Louis to the publishing of his autobiography. "That's behind me, and I settled that in my book, Hamilton told the *Chicago Tribune* in 2007. "I felt it was something I had to say, but I haven't said anything about it since."

The year before he passed, Skip Caray drove to Rome, Georgia on a Sunday to call a minor league baseball game with his son Josh. Skip, whose broadcasting work with his kin started with his father in the 1960s and continued with Chip in the 2000s, completed the family circle. "I've got to be able to say I've worked with all of them," he told a reporter before the game. "I just hope I don't cry, to be honest with you."[95] Skip died 15 months later, in August of 2008, nine days short of his 69th birthday.[96]

As for the man who started the family broadcasting dynasty, Harry Caray's career resembled all three of his early partners. Like Hamilton, Caray spent time with multiple teams in different cities. Like Buck, whose statue is located outside Busch Stadium, Caray is now primarily identified with one team. Harry's statue is perched near an entrance to Wrigley Field. And like Garagiola, whose career at NBC spanned more than a quarter-century, Caray would eventually be seen nationwide. But long before he broadcast games on WGN, Harry could be *heard* in much of the country.

Caray got another broadcasting partner in 1955. Unlike Jack, Milo, or Joe, this one didn't demand any time behind the microphone, but instead amplified and spread Caray's voice to new territories. Every night when the sun went down, the signal of KMOX radio boomed from the Rocky Mountains to the Eastern Seaboard. The crackle of AM radio carried the voice of the Cardinals, influencing a generation of fans and journalists.

---

[1] "Banister's first connection with St. Louis was in 1923 when, as athletic director at Country Day School, he set up the school's sports program," wrote Neal Russo. *St. Louis Post-Dispatch*, February 26, 1961.

[2] *St. Petersburg Times*, June 1, 1975.

[3] *Democrat and Chronicle* (Rochester, NY), November 5, 1980.

[4] Ibid. Years later, in his autobiography, Buck wrote that it was Danny Whalen, not his wife, who saved his daughter.

[5] According to Buck, broadcaster Bill Stern also auditioned that same day in New York, accompanied by two spotters. "I knew he wasn't going to get the job if he needed spotters at a baseball game." Buck, *Jack Buck*.

[6] *New York Times*, June 15, 1958. Buck's time broadcasting those games left a lasting impression. When the Yankees were looking for a new broadcaster after the 1964 season, columnist Dick Young wrote that Buck "captivated New York audiences with his candor a few years back when he piped NL games into this one-team town." *Daily News*, October 24, 1964. Filling in for Buck, Garagiola also got his first exposure to the New York market in 1958.

[7] *Sports Illustrated,* September 22, 2014.
[8] Buck, *Jack Buck.*
[9] Ibid.
[10] Walter Armbruster of D'Arcy, the advertising agency representing Anheuser-Busch, listened to tapes of more than 40 announcers. His first choice, a broadcaster for the minor-league Kansas City Blues, turned down the job because he didn't want to leave Kansas City. Buck was his second choice. *St. Louis Post-Dispatch,* July 26, 1987. Because Caray was so associated with Griesedieck Beer, Buck had an advantage. Anheuser-Busch owned the team in Rochester and Buck had experience touting their products. "That's how I got the job, because I had done Budweiser commercials during my stint in Rochester," Jack said.
[11] Buck claimed KMOX executive Robert Hyland was so determined to make the switch in formats, he donated the station's entire music library to a Veteran's Hospital.
[12] Among Buck's many "At Your Service" interviewees was former first lady Eleanor Roosevelt.
[13] The Los Angeles Dodgers defeated the Milwaukee Braves in a playoff series in 1959 to win the National League pennant. "Our sponsor (Falstaff) didn't get the playoff. So the agency for ABC sold it to a cigarette sponsor," (L&M Cigarettes) Blattner recalled. "The sponsor didn't want Diz because of his outspoken dislike for the product. But they wanted me. I got George Kell to go on with me. But Diz got it into his head that somehow I was responsible for it and he told me that if I went on, 'I'll get you.' So I beat him to the punch. I called the agency in New York and dictated my resignation." *Knoxville News-Sentinel,* October 3, 1961. "Oh, he [Dean] never apologized," Blattner told Curt Smith. "His only reaction was utter amazement, as though I had lost my mind."
[14] Blatter started broadcasting in California in 1962. He continued broadcasting St. Louis Hawks basketball for one more season. At halftime of a Hawks game in March 1963, it was announced that Blattner wouldn't be returning. *St. Louis Globe-Democrat,* March 21, 1963. Jerry Gross was his replacement. Buck returned to the air in 1961, joining Caray and Garagiola (who joined NBC for weekend games that year) on the radio broadcasts. Blattner, Garagiola and Gross did the Cardinals telecasts that season on KPLR, Channel 11. *St. Louis Post-Dispatch,* March 5, 1961.
[15] Buck partnered on ABC's baseball broadcasts with former Dodgers pitcher Carl Erskine. "I loved working with Carl Erskine," Buck told Curt Smith, calling him a "lifelong friend."
[16] ABC replaced baseball with "Wide World of Sports" in 1961.
[17] On Sundays in Dallas, Buck would hire an ambulance driver in order to catch a 5:00 p.m. flight back to St. Louis. Buck would lie down in the back and be transported directly to the waiting plane on the tarmac. More than one worried flight attendant would ask if he was ok. "I'm good," Jack would reply. "Please give me a VO [whisky] and water." Buck, *Jack Buck.*

[18] "We've got the Cosell thing where people turn down their TV sound. We have a lot of fun with that," said Buck. *Democrat and Chronicle*, November 5, 1980. "I've known Howard Cosell for an awful long time, and I appreciate his accomplishments," Buck told columnist Gary Deeb. "But I honestly think he's about to run his course, just like 'I Love Lucy,' and 'The Honeymooners.' His day may be just about over." *Chicago Tribune*, September 8, 1978.

[19] "I think it takes talent to do what Harry does," Buck told Ray Holliman, "but I also think it takes talent to do what I do." *Florida Today*, March 30, 1975.

[20] Buck had an opportunity to take another job with the Cardinals. After Branch Rickey returned to St. Louis in the fall of 1962, he pressed Buck to become the team's traveling secretary. (Rickey didn't like Leo Ward.) "I would have left before I changed jobs," said Jack.

[21] Ed Wilks was the writer. *St. Louis Post-Dispatch*, January 23, 1966.

[22] *Sporting News*, December 1, 1962.

[23] *St. Louis Post-Dispatch*, April 8, 1969.

[24] While calling the Bears-49ers football game, Buck "followed the Redbirds' progress by way of an open-line telephone play-by-play delivered by Cardinals publicity director Jim Toomey from the Busch Stadium press box." Ibid, January 23, 1966.

[25] The two men alternated broadcasting games with their Detroit counterparts: Caray with George Kell and Buck with Ernie Harwell.

[26] *Florida Today*, March 30, 1975.

[27] Wolfe, Rich. *Remembering Jack Buck: Wonderful Stories Celebrating the Life of a Broadcasting Legend*. Rich Wolfe. 2002.

[28] *St. Louis Post-Dispatch*, July 26, 1987.

[29] Caray called Missouri football on KMOX in 1954 and Notre Dame football for the station the following year. KMOX began carrying all Missouri football games in 1956 with Caray behind the microphone for 14 straight seasons. He called Tigers games over WIL for three years (1970-1972).

[30] *Post-Tribune*, September 16, 1971. When Caray was injured in the fall of 1968, Buck was the fill-in announcer for Missouri football.

[31] Buck and Shannon started working together in 1972. "Mike's improving, but he could work harder at things like grammar and pitch and diction," Buck told a reporter in 1975. "I would like to see him get some help from teachers in the St. Louis area. It would be good for him." *Columbia Missourian*, May 31, 1975. The two would work together for the rest of Jack's career. Buck worked with more than 35 partners broadcasting football games. "The only football partner with whom I didn't jell was Len Dawson, the former Kansas City quarterback and a Hall of Famer," Buck wrote in his autobiography. "We got along well off the air, but once the game began he tried to be dominating." Former St. Louis Cardinals offensive lineman Dan Dierdorf was among the many Buck worked well with. "He was such a mentor to me," said Dierdorf. "I owe him a debt of gratitude I never was able to fully repay." *St. Louis Post-Dispatch*, December 17, 2021.

[32] Ibid, May 23, 1982.
[33] Kindred grew up in Illinois listening to Buck and Caray. *Atlanta Journal-Constitution*, July 31, 1987. That same year, a Detroit columnist asked Tigers broadcaster Ernie Harwell if Caray had rubbed a lot of people in baseball the wrong way. "I would imagine so," Harwell said. "He's criticized players and managers. I'm sure it got back to them. But that is Harry's style. I'm very fond of Harry Caray." *Detroit Free Press*, April 6, 1987.
[34] *St. Louis Post-Dispatch*, July 26, 1987.
[35] Stan Musial was among those who spoke to the crowd of 2,300 in the Grand Ballroom of Bally's Casino Resort. The hotel had a special Harry Caray mass that afternoon. The evening ended with Harry leading the audience in a rendition of "Take Me Out to the Ball Game." Before beginning, Caray had a request. "All right, everybody, let's speed this along, because I got a date with the tables." *Chicago Tribune*, November 21, 1988.
[36] The plan was for Chip to join his grandfather in the WGN television booth. "It's a wonderful, overwhelming opportunity. He's my hero," said Chip. "Holy Cow! What a Christmas present," said Harry. The announcement came two months before Harry's death. *Chicago Tribune*, December 18, 1997.
[37] Chip Caray graduated from Parkway West High School in suburban St. Louis in 1983. He was living in suburban Atlanta in 1970 when his parents divorced. Chip and his sister returned to Missouri with their mother. "Like most kids who grew up in St. Louis, I went to bed at 9 o'clock at night with my transistor radio tucked under my pillow," said Chip. Wolfe, *Remembering Jack Buck*.
[38] Ibid.
[39] Hamilton had been broadcasting minor league baseball in Davenport, Iowa. He received a call one day from the manager of a local sporting goods store who wanted to know if he would be interested in interviewing two representatives from Rawlings coming to town to show some new baseball equipment. Impressed with Hamilton's interview, the Rawlings folks asked for a copy of it and took it to WTVI. The program director of the TV station liked it, and offered Hamilton a job. Interview with Mark Liptak, February 4, 2006. Originally published *at White Sox Interactive* that same year.
[40] "Game of the Week" broadcasts in 1953 featured just 20 stations over 13 weeks but expanded to 60 stations over 26 weeks a year later. The Cardinals broadcast 77 road games in 1954 over WTVI. *Wall Street Journal*, May 18, 1954.
[41] Hamilton, Milo and Schlossberg, Dan with Bob Ibach. *Making Airwaves: 60+ Years at Milo's Microphone*. Sports Publishing. 2006, 2007, 2011.
[42] Hamilton was famous for bringing a briefcase to the ballpark. "Nobody, I mean *nobody*, does more preparation, keeps more information around than Milo," said Lindsey Nelson. Smith, *Voices of the Game*.
[43] Hamilton, *Making Airwaves*.
[44] Mancuso became a Cardinals scout after the 1953 season.

45 "It was a shock. [Hamilton] getting that job. It was a plum – everybody thought it would go to a bigger name," said Lindsey Nelson. Mel Allen broadcast Milwaukee Braves games in 1965. Smith, *Voices of the Game*.

46 Aaron's home run call that night was described by three broadcasters who all later received the Ford C. Frick Award bestowed by the Hall of Fame. In addition to Hamilton, Curt Gowdy made the call on television. Vin Scully was behind the mic on the Dodgers broadcast.

47 "I wouldn't do what the Braves wanted me to, and it got messy," said Hamilton. The team wasn't good. "People could smell'em all the way to Chattanooga." Smith, *Voices of the Game*.

48 Buck left for *Grandstand* in August of 1975. Lee Leonard and Bryant Gumbel replaced him on the show in March of 1976. "Curiously ill-at-ease in the studio format," wrote Smith. Caray told the *Kansas City Star* he was rooting for Hamilton to replace Buck because it would mean Skip would get the chance to call Braves games. *Kansas City Star*, September 24, 1975.

49 Pirates infielder Gene Freese once bet Prince $20 to dive into the pool at the Chase Hotel in St. Louis. From his third-floor room, Prince made the jump. He had to clear about 12 feet of concrete. "I swear to God I wasn't drinking, and I still cleared the concrete by four or five feet," Prince recalled. "And it's a good thing I bet with Freese – he paid right up. If I'd bet Dick Stuart, that son of a bitch would have never paid me." Ibid.

50 "It was like competing with a ghost," Milo told Curt Smith. "Bob had bad-mouthed me in every bar in Pittsburgh, and he set the entire media against me." Ibid. Prince had been fired by the Pirates the previous year.

51 *Chicago Tribune*, November 17, 1981. "The White Sox were talking about fifty-thousand homes. The Cubs, meanwhile, were already seen in 28 *million* homes," Caray wrote in his autobiography.

52 Ibid. "The location of the conference, though, tipped off the impending news. Caray sleeps at the Ambassador East and receives his mail at the hotel's Pump Room," wrote *Tribune* columnist David Condon. Early in his St. Louis career, Harry enjoyed apartment life with his second wife, Marian. "Nomination for one of the most eye-catching apartments in town: Mr. and Mrs. Harry Caray's two-story beauty at the Embassy. It's a honey." *St. Louis Globe-Democrat*, June 15, 1954.

53 Hamilton and Schlossberg, *Making Airwaves*.

54 The Caray-Hamilton turmoil was noted early on by the Chicago press. Describing chilly and blustery conditions one April afternoon, columnist Steve Daley wrote, "It was so cold Harry Caray and Milo Hamilton were sitting next to each other." *Chicago Tribune*, April 5, 1982.

55 "I got more out of Steve [Stone] than Harry ever did," Milo claimed. "I didn't treat him like a cigar store Indian." Smith, *Voices of the Game*. The Cubs "hired me to keep the two of them from killing each other and at least thirty feet apart," Stone recalled.

Stone, Steve with Barry Rozner. *Where's Harry? Steve Stone Remembers His Years With Harry Caray*. Taylor Publishing. 1999. On a team bus headed for the Astrodome in 1983, Hamilton reportedly lunged at Caray. Harry had been quoted in a Houston newspaper as saying he "never missed an inning of a game, unlike some other broadcasters here." Hamilton had missed several games while undergoing chemotherapy. Milo's swing at Harry was blocked by a Cubs employee. *Chicago Tribune*, June 5, 2007.

[56] With fans chanting "Harry … Harry … Harry" under the broadcast booth near the end of a game in 1984, "Milo, on the radio side, heard the raucous mob and said something to the effect that the gates at Lincoln Park Zoo (near Wrigley Field) obviously hadn't been locked yet because a lot of the animals were still on the loose," wrote Murray Hurt. *The Rock Island Argus,* October 18, 1984. Later, when Hamilton was with the Astros and the Cubs would visit the Astrodome, "Milo would stand up and rock back and forth, pretending to be drunk and singing during the seventh-inning stretch, a completely classless act." Stone, *Where's Harry?*

[57] Hamilton and Schlossberg, *Making Airwaves*.

[58] *Chicago Tribune*, November 8, 1984. Steve Stone agreed. "The Cubs had no burning desire to get rid of Milo, but he couldn't handle Harry. And Harry didn't get him fired." Stone, *Where's Harry?*

[59] *Atlanta Journal-Constitution*, February 21, 1998. "I tried to approach Skip to give him my side of the story, but he wasn't interested," Hamilton wrote in his autobiography. "He waved me away, which didn't surprise me. Skip is much like his father. He treats people around him like crap, a real chip off the old block. Just ask folks at Turner Broadcasting, WSB, or the ballpark in Atlanta: they'll tell you what he's like."

[60] Interview with Mark Liptak.

[61] *Chicago Tribune*, February 14, 2006.

[62] Ibid, August 2, 1992. "I didn't fire him. He left the best job in baseball," Harry told Steve Nidetz. "I'm pleased he's going into the Hall of Fame. I told him so. I congratulated him."

[63] *The Sporting News*, October 12, 1960.

[64] With Garagiola behind the plate and hitting sixth in the lineup, the Cardinals lost to the Dodgers 2-1 at Sportsman's Park on June 14, 1951. The Cardinals scored just one run despite collecting 15 hits. The game ended with Garagiola popping out to the third basemen to finish an 0-5 day. "The next day I was packing for Pittsburgh," Joe said. *The Sporting News*, November 24, 1954.

[65] Renfro told Garagiola a 15-minute radio show might be available for $12,000 a year. "Before the World's Series games last year [1953], I did a TV show for KSD-TV," said Garagiola. "I got $25 for a 15-minute appearance. That made me interested in broadcasting. I got real hopped up about it and went around to find out more about it." *The Sporting News*, April 14, 1954. Columnist Merle Jones wrote that Garagiola "came within an eyelash" of quitting baseball and joining Caray in the Cardinals broadcast booth in 1954. When Cubs director of player personnel Wid Matthews (a former

Cardinals scout) found out about Joe's interest, he voiced his displeasure about it directly to Gussie Busch. The Cardinals backed off and Garagiola signed with the Cubs. *Southern Illinoisan*, February 8, 1954.

[66] Johnson was the father-in-law to future Cardinals general manager Bob Howsam.

[67] James Busch Orthwein worked at D'Arcy, rising to become chairman and chief executive in 1970. Orthwein's mother, Clara, was Gussie Busch's sister.

[68] *New York Times*, April 9, 1954; *The Sporting News*, April 14, 1954.

[69] "I had never met Harry Caray before I went to Missouri, although I never told him that. We did two shows a week during the season for 12 years [starting in 1958] and became very close friends," wrote Devine in his autobiography. "He is my friend, and friends never disappoint you," Garagiola wrote in the Prologue. Devine, Dan with Michael R. Steele. *Simply Devine: Memories of a Hall of Fame Coach*. Sports Publishing, Inc. 2000.

[70] *St. Petersburg Times*, April 1, 1956, Smith, *Voices of the Game*. "I used to take him [Garagiola] out to nightclubs and show him how singers, tiny little gals, could sing up a storm," Caray told Smith. "I was trying to teach him that it came from your belly, your diaphragm." In the summer of 1955, Garagiola admitted, "My natural voice is high, and I'm working, with Harry's help, to bring it down." *The Sporting News*, July 6, 1955. Skip Caray also claimed to play an early role in Garagiola's career. "I had to teach him how to keep a proper box score." *The Columbus (GA) Ledger*, August 10, 1977.

[71] *St. Petersburg Times*, April 1, 1956.

[72] Nelson, Lindsey. *Hello Everybody, I'm Lindsey Nelson*. Beech Tree Books, William Morrow and Company, Inc. 1985.

[73] Garagiola and Nelson were paired together in 1961. From 1962 to 1964, Garagiola did the NBC broadcasts with Bob Wolff. He later worked with Curt Gowdy, Tony Kubek, and Vin Scully.

[74] Ibid.

[75] Patterson, *The Golden Voices of Baseball*. The speaking engagement was in Peoria, Illinois. Laux was one of many to later take some credit for Garagiola's development. So did Buddy Blattner. "I was the first to put Joe on the air to do play-by-play," Blattner claimed. In 1960, Blattner and Garagiola did Cardinals games on television while Caray was on radio. *St. Louis Post-Dispatch*, August 11, 1987. Jack Brickhouse admitted he tried to talk Garagiola out of the media business. "Stay in baseball," Brickhouse told him. "This broadcasting is one tough field." Smith, *Voices of the Game*.

[76] *St. Louis Globe-Democrat,* April 16, 1961.

[77] Broeg claimed he had the chance to write the book with Garagiola but turned it down back when "I was more stupid." Garagiola wrote it with Martin Quigley, who would become an executive with Fleishman-Hillard. *St. Louis Post-Dispatch*, June 9, 1988. Curt Smith later called the Garagiola-Quigley product the "largest-selling baseball book ever."

[78] *The Sporting News*, October 12, 1960.

[79] *St. Louis Post-Dispatch,* May 11, 1989. Garagiola's duties at the network in the 1960s also included a daily radio show. The "Joe Garagiola Sports Show" was the highest-rated program on the NBC Radio Network and the highest-rated of all sports programs on any network. Smith, *Voices of the Game.*

[80] "Joe came to us very raw," said KMOX general manager Robert Hyland in 1991. "He was like Yogi if you know what I mean. He had no presence, but I saw a personality behind it." *New York Times,* April 22, 1991. "Bob Hyland took a chance on me, a *big* chance," said Garagiola. Over the years, Garagiola broadcast everything from *Wrestling at the Chase* to the Westminster Kennel Club Dog Show. He also hosted numerous game shows. His 1973 pregame show on NBC, "The Baseball World of Joe Garagiola," won a Peabody Award.

[81] Ibid, December 19, 1964.

[82] *St. Louis Globe-Democrat,* April 27, 1961.

[83] Network broadcasts in the early 1960s featured games on both Saturday and Sunday. Baseball's policy at the time was to black out all regular season baseball coverage by television networks in major league markets. The policy wasn't changed until 1965. Dizzy Dean, who broadcast games on CBS from 1955 to 1965, became a weekend television sensation in largely rural markets without network executives in New York even realizing he was on the air. "CBS would never stoop to hiring such a clod – ever," a network executive once said in a meeting with the advertising sponsor. "But he's on your network, each Saturday," replied a representative from Falstaff. Smith, *Voices of the Game.*

[84] *St. Louis Globe-Democrat,* April 27, 1961. "One of the wildest pieces of scuttlebutt floating about town last week was the report that Joe was off KMOX because he and Harry Caray had a big brawl and Joe had been let out," wrote Rahn, who stated that Garagiola was "hopping mad" when he heard the story. Rahn believed that media competition played at least a partial role in the reluctance to acknowledge Garagiola's whereabouts. "KMOX radio [a CBS affiliate] just ain't in the habit of plugging a competing medium, tv, and especially a competing tv network, NBC. Can't blame them on that count." But Rahn also believed there were other factors at play. "I suspect that there may be other contributing factors besides Joe's 'onerous' NBC-tv duties. But that's another story. I suppose all healthy families are beset with inter-member rivalry at some point."

[85] Smith, *Voices of the Game.*

[86] Ibid.

[87] "I see him at the World Series walking across the field; he says, 'Hi, how are ya, nice to see ya,' and walks by," Caray recalled. "I thought, 'Is this the Frankenstein monster I created?' The guy I treated better than my own son?" *The Pensacola News,* August 12, 1975.

[88] *Detroit Free Press,* April 6, 1987.

[89] In 1972, Garagiola was asked to name his favorite play-by-play radio announcers. According to columnist James Doussard, Joe put former Cubs broadcaster Jack Quinlan at the top of his list. (Quinlan, who did Cubs games from 1955 to 1964, was killed in an auto accident before the start of the 1965 season.) "I also like Bob Prince and Jack Buck." Caray was not mentioned. *The Courier-Journal* (Louisville, KY), May 5, 1972.

[90] *Tulsa World*, August 5, 1977.

[91] *St. Louis Post-Dispatch,* May 11, 1989.

[92] *Pensacola News Journal,* May 21, 2021.

[93] Joe Buck once picked another moment as his favorite of his father's calls, Bob Gibson's no-hitter against the Pirates in 1971. "It ends on a called third strike. I can hear his voice crack because he 1) loved his job; 2) loved the game; 3) he LOVED Bob. It was emotional for him." Two other highly cited Buck calls don't involve the Cardinals: The Kirk Gibson home run in the first game of the 1988 World Series ("I don't believe what I just saw!") and the Kirby Puckett home run that forced a Game 7 in the 1991 World Series ("And we'll see you tomorrow night!"). ESPN's Chris Berman named it as one of his favorite sports calls. "In one short sentence: excitement, while typical Buck simplicity," he said. "A huge part of sports is anticipation. He captured the homer, the big picture, and what could top it all in one sentence. BRILLIANT." https://www.si.com/extra-mustard/2020/08/06/play-by-play-broadcasters-favorite-sports-call

[94] *Washington Post*, October 15, 2000. The World Series was broadcast on NBC in 1997 and 1999.

[95] *Atlanta Journal Constitution*, May 5, 2007.

[96] Skip's grandsons and Chip's sons, identical twins Chris and Stefan Caray, began broadcasting for the Amarillo Sod Poodles in 2022. "You know, a Caray has been doing baseball since 1945, so we're up to 77 years. We're hoping to make it to 100 while I'm still alive," Chip said. *Atlanta Journal-Constitution*, April 14, 2022.

Listening to Harry

Covering the George McGovern presidential campaign in 1972, Godfrey Sperling Jr. had an edge over his fellow reporters. Sperling discovered that he and McGovern's campaign director, Frank Mankiewicz were both longtime St. Louis Cardinals fans. "Frank and I loved to stump each other with odd bits of knowledge about our team," he recalled.[1] On deadline one day, he needed information about McGovern's plans, information he knew Mankiewicz could supply. But when he called the campaign director's office, Sperling was informed that Mankiewicz was writing a speech and had asked not to be disturbed. The reporter knew exactly what to do.

He quickly dictated a trivia question to Mankiewicz's secretary. Who, Sperling asked, was the Cardinals outfielder of the 1920s and '30s with a connection to Hollywood actor Buster Keaton? Scrawling the question on a piece of paper, the secretary slipped the note under Mankiewicz's door. Sperling hung up and started counting. Before he could get to twenty, the phone rang. "Who was it? Who was it?" Mankiewicz demanded to know. Sperling supplied the answer (Ernie Orsatti) and turned the questions around on Mankiewicz for his deadline story.[2] Both men got the information they wanted.

Politics, Hollywood, and Cardinals baseball defined much of Mankiewicz's life. Before working for McGovern, he served as Robert F. Kennedy's press secretary. It was Mankiewicz who announced to the world on that horrible night in 1968 that Kennedy had died. His father was a Hollywood screenwriter who co-wrote *Citizen Kane,* and his uncle won Academy Awards for writing and directing *All About Eve.*[3] A Cardinals fan since childhood, Mankiewicz would go on to co-found the Stan Musial Society, a group for Redbirds fans in the Washington, D.C. area.

Born in New York in 1924, Mankiewicz grew up in a "Beverly Hills household, regaled by movie stars, famous writers and comedians like the Marx Brothers."[4] He became a St. Louis fan at the age of ten, the year Dizzy Dean and the Cardinals took the country by storm. Nearly two decades later, Mankiewicz's father wrote the screenplay for *The Pride of St. Louis*, the Dean biography. It would be his last. Herman Mankiewicz died the year after the movie was released, just as his son's career was taking off. Frank Mankiewicz became a journalist and lawyer, served as an executive with the Peace Corps before his time in politics, and as president of National Public Radio afterward. In 1989, the year he kickstarted the Cardinals fan club in Washington D.C., the 65-year-old Mankiewicz admitted he had only attended one game in St. Louis, which had occurred just the season before. He followed Cardinals baseball not by watching, but by listening. And thanks to his many years in the Nation's Capital, he knew exactly where to go. "True St. Louis Cardinal fans in Washington know the place to be at night in August when the pennant race is as hot as the weather – on Wisconsin Ave. up by the Cathedral," he once described for a newspaper. "It is the highest point in Washington and therefore the easiest place to listen to the game on KMOX."[5] Mankiewicz wrote those words for the *Washington Post* in 1994, decades after his first trip to the National Cathedral.

Robert Semple Jr. also knew where to go on summer evenings when the sun went down. Born in St. Louis, Semple joined the Washington bureau of *The New York Times* in 1963. He first met Mankiewicz at the Cathedral a year later; both in their cars, radios on, listening to baseball.[6] (Semple later became a charter member of the Stan Musial Society.)[7]

KMOX made those meetings and memories possible. As a 50,000-watt clear-channel radio station, KMOX increases its power at night as other stations on the same frequency power down. The power boost, combined with AM radio's increased ability to travel at night when the sun's rays no longer hit the ionosphere, meant the Cardinals could be heard in places previously not possible. During nocturnal hours, the station's signal blankets forty-four states, north to Canada, south to Mexico, and beyond. A late-night host once took a call from Guam.[8]

It's different today, of course. Cable television brought an explosion of regional sports networks, transforming the vast majority of baseball fans from listeners to viewers. The Internet and satellite radio make static-free listening possible anywhere on the planet. But when KMOX became the flagship station of the Cardinals network, the information superhighway meant twisting the radio dial in your vehicle, stumbling upon a baseball game on a remote road far from cities and crowds.

A reporter once tried to outrun KMOX's signal. Starting at Busch Stadium two-and-a-half hours before a game, David Waldstein began driving south. Several hours and more than three hundred miles later, he was outside a Mississippi restaurant when the ninth inning rolled around. "The reception could not be better. It is crystal clear, as if the station were transmitting from the parking lot," he noted as the game ended.[9]

For fifteen baseball seasons, that crystal clear reception featured a distinctive voice. "You have to understand what Harry Caray was to the Midwest in my childhood," wrote baseball author and statistician Bill James, who grew up in Kansas. "Harry's remarkable talents and enthusiasm ... forged a link between the Cardinals and the Midwest that remains to this day," he stated in 1985. "In the years when baseball stopped at the Mississippi, KMOX radio built a network of stations across the Midwest and into the Far West that brought major league baseball into every little urb across the landscape."

It was 1955 when that landscape suddenly got a whole lot larger.

*****

Part of Robert Hyland Jr.'s early life looked remarkably similar to the man he would later employ. Like Caray, the St. Louis native worked in sales, once drew a paycheck from an Anheuser-Busch competitor, and first got behind a microphone for a radio station in Illinois. Both men played baseball in their youth. Caray's attempt to join the Cardinals organization ended in tryout rejection. Hyland rejected the tryout. The St. Louis University outfielder turned down a minor-league contract from Branch Rickey.[10]

The differences in their origin stories, though, are dramatic. Hyland grew up in a world of wealth and privilege, in a 14-room apartment on Lindell Boulevard, complete with private schools and private boxes at Sportsman's Park. As the son of Cardinals and Browns team physician Dr. Robert Hyland Sr., he had daily access to his heroes in the clubhouse.[11] After graduating college in 1940 and a stint in the Navy, Hyland's early jobs included selling advertising space for a billboard company, working as a distributor for Hyde Park beer, and doing on and off-air work for radio station WTAD in Quincy, Illinois, where according to one account, he did everything "from announcing to nightly janitorial work."[12] He later worked in sales for KXOK radio in St. Louis and then joined WBBM in Chicago as an account executive. He was the eleventh salesman at the station when he started and the number-one performing rep when he left. He joined KMOX in 1951, became assistant general manager in 1954, and was promoted to the top job the next year. He'd retain his general manager perch at the station for the rest of his life.

His return to St. Louis coincided with a radio industry in crisis. The flourishing television business was rapidly eroding the radio audience for staple programming such as daytime soap operas and evening entertainment shows. When "TV erupted on the scene," noted a *Wall Street Journal* account in 1958, "radio lovers in droves snapped off network shows, plunked themselves in front of their television screens, and tuned in shows that wooed both the ear and the eye and were often of much higher quality than anything radio had to offer."[13] Radio pivoted to music and news.

Hyland's formula included dropping the former for the latter while adding huge dollops of sports programming. By the early 1980s, the station was carrying as many as 350 live sporting events a year, a quarter of its programming. Before Hyland's arrival, KMOX carried no sports programming.[14] With Hyland at the helm, the station could legitimately claim the title: "The Sports Voice of St. Louis." There were years in the city when more than one out of every four people with a radio turned on had it tuned to KMOX. People thought of the station as the city's third newspaper.

Hyland got little sleep (two hours a night) and watched even less television. TV was the enemy, while radio was an "obsession" with him, according to a former KMOX employee. "He treats it like you would treat a newborn baby."[15] He'd arrive at the station in the middle of the night ("I used to report to work at 1:30 a.m. But last year I had a cancer operation, so I pushed it back to 2:30," Hyland once told a columnist),[16] stay until late in the day, and never take vacations. He would get straight to the point on the telephone, never saying hello or goodbye. A devout Catholic who celebrated daily mass at the Old Cathedral in downtown St. Louis, Hyland extended his influence with numerous civic commitments. At one point, he belonged to 13 professional organizations, 52 civic groups, two academic societies, and eight social clubs.[17]

His critics loathed him. "He's pretty much a tyrant," said a former KMOX announcer. "He's respected, but not liked. An opportunist, not an innovator." His supporters admired him. "I would walk through the jaws of hell for him," said longtime station host Jack Carney. [18]

When the Cardinals and KMOX announced their deal in February of 1955, Hyland was one of two men instrumental in Caray's career quoted in the press release. "This ... demonstrates radio's flexibility whereby a 50,000-watt network station can broadcast the same splendid CBS radio network programs and still give the fine public service baseball broadcasts provide," Hyland commented. "I'm happy that the Cardinal games this year will be broadcast on a station as powerful as KMOX," said Gussie Busch.[19]

It would be a perfect marriage of content, medium, and messenger: A storied franchise, a booming flagship station, and a legendary voice behind the microphone. "The real activity was done with radio," wrote A. Bartlett Giamatti in his essay celebrating baseball, "in the only place it will last, the enclosed green field of the mind."[20]

*****

They listened where families gathered. "Harry Caray doesn't announce a game. He brings it into your living room," believed a letter writer to the *Post-Dispatch*. "He lives and exults with you when the Cardinals are winning and he dies with you when things are going against the Cardinals."[21]

They listened from the bedroom. "I'm a child of radio who listened to Harry Caray on KMOX in St. Louis in the 1950s," columnist Dave Kindred once explained on the pages of *The Sporting News*. "Every baseball night, I went to my room with a Coke and a Velveeta sandwich, heavy on the mustard. If it got to be the 14th inning and my parents didn't need to know I was awake, I moved the radio under the blankets with my scorebook and flashlight."[22]

They listened from patient rooms, too. In 1960, an Evansville, Indiana priest estimated that at the local St. Mary's Medical Center, there "were at least a hundred hospital radios" tuned in to every Cardinals broadcast.[23]

They tuned in from cars and bars, cafes and kitchen tables; ubiquitous transistor radios conveying Caray's omnipresent voice. "Harry was everywhere – in my room, out in the yard, at the barbershop, in the car. Wherever there was a radio, there was baseball," Harrell Miller informed the California audience of *The Napa Valley Register*.[24]

Columnist Skip Bayless grew up in Oklahoma listening to Caray. "You ate your dinner and did your homework to Harry. You cruised for 'chicks' with Harry on the radio of your '65 Mustang or '67 Camaro. Girls wouldn't go out with you a second time because you wouldn't let them change the station. Who needed the Beatles or Stones when you could listen to Harry rock and fire?"[25]

Caray's descriptions of games proved so vivid and exciting to Bayless, the real thing proved disappointing. "The St. Louis Harry took me out to the ballgame via radio, and I never wanted to miss the eighth and ninth," he recalled. "That Harry was so good he ruined the first big-league game I saw in St. Louis. It didn't quite measure up to the ones Harry had brought to Technicolor life for me as I lie in bed with the lights out."

Broadcaster Dave Niehaus spent more than three decades as the voice of the Seattle Mariners. Growing up in Indiana, he had a similar experience to Bayless. "I was quite disappointed, to tell you the truth," he said about his first trip to a major league park. "I put all these guys on such a pedestal because of what Harry had described them as. They were almost deities to me. When I saw my first game, they were just normal human beings. I was kind of shot down."[26]

Niehaus wasn't the only fan who followed Caray into the business. Longtime Indiana University announcer Don Fischer was once asked about the broadcaster he most admired. "Harry Caray when he was with the Cardinals. I grew up listening to him [in Rochelle, Illinois], and I always thought he made it so exciting. He could make a foul ball sound exciting," Fischer recalled.[27] "He was kind of an inspiration for me. I revered him."[28]

Long before Bob Harlan rose to become president of the NFL's Green Bay Packers, he was a kid in Iowa listening to baseball on the radio. "In Des Moines, I grew up listening to Harry Caray do Cardinals games. You could pick him up at night. I have great feelings for that organization," he said in 1991.[29] Harlan's last career stop before Green Bay was St. Louis. He joined the Cardinals in 1965 as director of community relations, the same year son Kevin turned five. "I used to ride my bike to Grant's Farm, sneak under a fence and fish for catfish," Kevin recalled. "I remember those days more than many of them in Green Bay."[30] Kevin Harlan would go on to break Jack Buck's record for consecutive Super Bowl calls on the radio. (Thirteen years and counting for Harlan as of 2023. The longtime NCAA, NBA, and NFL announcer was named National Sportscaster of the Year by his peers in 2017 and 2019.)

Harry's calls delighted writers, actors, a future President, and a former candidate. Growing up in Arkansas and Mississippi, author John Grisham played Little League baseball and dreamed of playing for his favorite team. "Always in the background, there were two or three radios with Harry Caray bringing us the Cardinals every night."[31]

Actor John Goodman spent his youth in the St. Louis suburb of Affton. "St. Louis was a world of kids. All playing. Playing in the rain," Goodman told *Esquire* magazine. "Playing till after the sun went down and you got called 'Johnnnnnny!' And then you listened to the Cards at night. Jack Buck and Harry Caray."[32]

Future President Bill Clinton listened from rural Arkansas. "I knew from the start my enjoyment was as a spectator. And being a Cardinals fan, how could you not love them on the radio?"[33] That passion was a bipartisan affair. Republican Alf Landon, who opposed FDR in 1936, was a longtime Cardinals fan. Growing up in Kansas, Landon's daughter, former Senator Nancy Kassebaum, remembered listening to Harry and the Cardinals with her father.[34] In 1987, at the age of 100, Landon was still listening to games, thanks to his daughter's purchase of an amplifier he would hold in his lap to better hear the broadcasts.[35]

Future major league owners and players heard Harry, too. As a child in Arkansas and Illinois, Red Sox owner John Henry remembered listening to Cardinals games "every night, every day."[36] Mickey Mantle tuned in to Harry from Commerce, Oklahoma and Lou Brock listened from Collinston, Louisiana.[37] "I was a nine-year-old in a Southern town," Brock told the crowd at his Hall of Fame induction speech. "Jim Crow was king. I was searching the dial of an old

Philco radio and I heard Harry Caray and Jack Buck, and I felt pride in being alive. The baseball field was my fantasy of what life offered."[38]

While Brock felt pride in hearing Harry's voice, some of his teammates had a different reaction. "Most of us liked him personally, because he was a convivial companion," Curt Flood wrote in his autobiography, "but his rabble-rousing descriptions of ballgames made our flesh crawl."[39] At a spring training banquet one year in St. Petersburg with Caray serving as the emcee, Mike Shannon told the crowd, "You only have to listen to him one night. We have to put up with him all year."[40]

A third group of teammates had an entirely different take when listening to Caray. Tim McCarver first met Harry as a 17-year-old rookie. But the Memphis native had been listening to him long before that, often with friends during backyard cork ball games. "It wasn't a matter of who won the game," said McCarver, "but who could do the best imitation of Harry."[41]

*****

In the third inning of Game 5 of the 2011 World Series, television viewers heard the voice of a man whose father started working with Caray in 1954, a former player who first met Caray in 1959, and a pitcher born in 1986 who aspired to sound like Caray. From the Fox broadcast booth, Joe Buck and McCarver were wrapping up an interview with Derek Holland of the Texas Rangers when Buck said he wanted to hear the pitcher's Caray imitation. In the dugout with a headset on, Holland happily accepted the challenge. With Cardinals outfielder Matt Holliday at the plate, Holland launched into a play-by-play description that *Post-Dispatch* media columnist Dan Caesar later called "the exuberant, unmistakable Caray-style voice that [comedian Will] Ferrell has exaggerated in comic bits."[42]

Holland was just 11 years old when Harry died. Long before Ferrell's inflated impersonation of Caray on *Saturday Night Live* introduced the broadcaster's style to a new generation, ballplayers enjoyed mimicking Harry's delivery. McCarver had started decades before. "My imitation was good," he once claimed. "It was very good."

But in 1964, McCarver's imitation may not have even been the best on his own team. Like McCarver, Bob Uecker was a catcher who later became a broadcaster. The two were roommates on a Cardinals team that defeated the Yankees in the World Series. McCarver remembered his friend's celebration after Game 7. "I remember Bob Uecker, without a stitch of clothing on, dancing around to the dumbest song I've ever heard – 'Pass the Biscuits, Mirandy.' He was dancing all by himself, somehow putting modern moves to this idiotic song, that, for some reason, had been the 1946 [sic] Cardinals' rallying song. Uke could dance, too."[43]

A career .200 hitter, Uecker spent a lot of time watching games from the bullpen or the dugout. "He would sit on the bench and announce a game as we were playing," an early teammate recalled. "The only bad thing was nobody was listening to him but us."[44]

"He was someone," author David Halberstam later wrote, "who thought baseball should be fun." Traded to St. Louis five days before the start of the 1964 season, Uecker kept his teammates loose with games of "Ugly" (card game featuring 52 mug shots), practical jokes (once holding hands for a photo with Bob Gibson and playing the tuba before a World Series game), and "devastating" imitations of Caray he wielded everywhere from bar rooms to the banquet circuit.[45] At a dinner at the beginning of the 1965 season, Uecker emulated the Cardinals broadcaster as he and Jack Buck introduced the team to the assembled.

National audiences would later come to know Uecker from his many appearances with Johnny Carson, a starring role on a television series, and multiple spots in movies and beer commercials. Early in his broadcast career, he drew comparisons to two announcers with St. Louis roots. "A Joe Garagiola type who pokes fun at his ragged playing career, Uecker also shares one sterling virtue with ... Harry Caray. He's extremely popular with fans," wrote *Chicago Tribune* columnist Gary Deeb in 1976.

In those days, imitations of Caray were largely a cottage industry, confined to clubhouses, private gatherings, or public saloons. The cast of characters was primarily connected to baseball, but even then, Caray's voice had crossover appeal. "Basketball players say Cazzie Russell's mimicry of announcers Harry Caray and Bob Elson is hilarious," Dick Young once reported for *The Sporting News*.[46]

In St. Louis, Mickey McTague spent decades working in city government and was known for two things: Being a longtime joke-writer for comedian Bob Hope and his ability to crack-up downtown bar patrons with his Caray impression. "Usually, the Caray imitation will include the names of everyone McTague knows in the bar, with batting averages, fictitious play-by-play, commercial breaks for station identification and Caray-like asides," noted a *Post-Dispatch* account in 1978. "It is more entertaining, and a great deal funnier than most things you'll encounter in a St. Louis saloon."[47] McTague's voice, wrote John McGuire, "resonated out of a tilted, empty beer glass and sounded so much like Caray it was eerie."[48]

Decades later, Ferrell's impression of Caray would spawn a legion of imitators, but not everyone liked what they heard from the comedian's hyperbolic performance. "*Saturday Night Live* began doing skits of Harry as a babbling mush-mouthed, talk-show host. To me, this was appalling," said Bayless.[49] Ferrell and his many copycats presented a caricature of Caray at the end of his career, a man in poor health who slurred his words and struggled to pronounce names, forward or backward. In 1994, a writer described Harry as having a "phlegm-covered Brillo pad" in his esophagus. A *Sports Illustrated* piece from a few years earlier called his voice "three-parts gravel and two-parts Budweiser,"[50] while the *Boston Globe* had a different alcohol in mind. A "whiskey baritone" is how a reporter for the paper once described Caray's sound, while the Chicago media noticed his "peculiar" St. Louis accent "in which some *o's* are pronounced as *a's* as in *McCarmick* Place, *shartstop*, Terry *Farster*."[51]

What the later comedians and writers missed was hearing Harry in his prime, the Caray from his years with the Cardinals. "Harry [in St. Louis] was very sharp," said McCarver in 1998. "If you listen to an old broadcast from 30 years ago, he didn't make many mistakes." After the 1964 World Series, KMOX produced a highlight record of the pennant race, featuring many of Caray's memorable calls. "The voice is crisp, staccato-like," remembered sportswriter Neil Hohlfeld. "People don't realize what a great voice Caray had."[52] For a two-two count on the hitter, "Harry hit the 't's' so hard that he made 'two-two' sound more dramatic than 'four score and seven years ago,'" Bayless believed. "Harry didn't just say words; he fired them at you like rising fastballs, emphasizing odd and unpredictable syllables. 'Ho-LEE cow!' he might say."

It was the voice that greeted you daily. "Hal-low everybody..."

An approach that would linger on a particular word. "HEEEERRZZZZ the pitch."

And a style that quickly signaled disapproval when a Cardinal failed to perform. "He paaahped it up."

While millions of people heard Harry's voice over the years, not all ears were equal. One man not only listened, but kept detailed notes. More than once, he assembled this documentation to raise doubts about Caray's future with the Cardinals. This influential executive also had a direct line to the most important person in Harry's professional life. His boss.

*****

Gussie Busch had been running the family-founded brewery for five years when a major strike threatened to undo decades of progress. Anheuser-Busch "was virtually paralyzed" in early October of 1951.[53] The labor dispute idled more than 2,000 employees in the brewery's bottling and canning operations. More than 120 employees in the department handling draught beer joined those workers a few days later. A company vice president claimed that Anheuser-Busch was losing $1.5 million in sales every day.[54]

Speaking to a *Post-Dispatch* reporter, Busch accused striking workers of putting kerosene in the bottle-washing water. He later relayed the conversation to the man in charge of the brewery's public relations. Are you certain that happened? Al Fleishman asked. When Busch said no, a horrified Fleishman quickly phoned an acquaintance at the paper and explained that what Busch had heard was just hearsay, unfounded gossip. The PR executive instinctively knew how rival brewers would spin the story: "Did you taste the kerosene in Budweiser?"

Fleishman succeeded in getting Busch's comments retracted from later editions of the paper. A grateful brewery chief forever changed how he dealt with the media. "Gussie Busch didn't say good morning unless Al Fleishman told him to," Monsignor John Shocklee said years later.[55]

The St. Louis of the middle years of the 20th century was a world of emerging monopolies. Busch's company created the products, Fleishman shaped the message, Hyland supplied the airwaves and Caray dominated the microphone. In this interlocking web of markets, medium, and message, Fleishman held sway over nearly every step of the process. After the brewery purchased the Cardinals, the co-founder of Fleishman-Hillard strategically blended and blurred the lines between beer and baseball. The first bullet point of a 1958 media manual clarified the purpose of any sports broadcast: "To sell more Busch Bavarian Beer."

Fleishman, a St. Louis native who launched his PR firm after World War II, had the respect of Busch and the gratitude of the majority of the Cardinals broadcast booth during this era. Garagiola frequently credited Fleishman with giving his career a boost. "I must have spoken at more temples and synagogue men's clubs than any Catholic ever," he said decades later. When Buck was briefly forced out of the Cardinals booth after the 1959 season, Fleishman was there to line up speaking engagements that supplemented his income. "I didn't get rich making those appearances. Some of them paid $10, others $25 or even $50 if it was a big event," Buck recalled. "I needed the money and appreciated every dollar."

Fleishman's experience with Caray was altogether different. The PR mogul was a disciplined, behind-the-scenes insider who pushed for a consistent corporate message. "The relationship between Anheuser-Busch, which sponsors the game broadcasts, and the Cardinals, is such that they are inseparable," he once wrote. Caray was a free-wheeling extrovert who talked about whatever came to mind. Oil and water started butting heads in 1954, when Anheuser-Busch began sponsoring the team's games.[56] On June 12, the Cardinals lost to the Pirates, dropping their record to 26-28. What concerned Fleishman was Caray's withering criticisms of manager Stanky. "The radio broadcasting situation is becoming increasingly serious," Fleishman noted in the opening sentence of a five-page memo addressed that day to Richard (Dick) Meyer, who then served as both an Anheuser-Busch executive and the Cardinals general manager. "Harry Caray is a vivid and dramatic broadcaster," Fleishman wrote. "Harry Caray is also a baseball fan – and this places limitations, sometimes, on his objectivity. He reacts like the rabid fan; He reacts like the crowd."[57]

Fleishman reminded Meyer that under the previous ownership, Saigh had removed manager Dyer "due in large measure to the sentiment created against Dyer by Harry Caray's broadcasts."

"Harry Caray's accounts of the games have, in some respects, now reached serious proportions and are becoming a serious problem," Fleishman stressed, while adding specific steps Caray could take to bring more context to his critiques (e.g., Caray's habit of second-guessing outcomes that turned out poorly for the Cardinals and rehashing bad plays for days on end). He ended the memo by emphasizing "there is no desire to change the descriptive colorings of Caray's personality or his broadcasts. We are citing the record with the belief that now is the time to call this to the serious attention of all concerned."

The memo reached Caray, who quickly fired back to Fleishman a letter of his own. "May I ask you a single question?" Harry began. "Assuming your analysis is correct, that my broadcasting is responsible for Eddie Stanky's unpopularity, then would you explain why Stanky is so roundly booed in New York, Brooklyn, Phila[delphia], Chicago, Milwaukee, Cinn[cinati], Pittsburgh, Los Angeles, Mesa and Fresno, places where my broadcasts have never been heard?" (The Cardinals were broadcast over KXOK in 1954.) He signed it, "Sincerely, Harry."[58] (Stanky was fired thirty-six games into the 1955 season.)[59]

In the postscript, which consumed three times the space of Harry's single question, an irritated Caray brought up other topics, including Fleishman's mention of Dyer. Caray reminded him that his "contract [with Anheuser-Busch] began in November 1953" and asked him to "please confine your judgments to that date on." The die had been cast. The rocky relationship between the two would continue for much of the next 15 years. "I never walk with my back to him," Caray said in 1968.

Although few and far between, there were some lighter moments in the relationship between the broadcaster and PR executive. Caray went to Bavaria in the fall of 1956 (a year after A-B unveiled Busch Bavarian Beer)[60] and sent a postcard to Fleishman. "All they seem to do here is work – eat – drink beer (where do they put it all) – and [blank line]," wrote Caray, hinting at more intimate activity in the mountains of southern Germany. "The [blank line] seems to be the international sport in all of Europe."

By this time, however, it wasn't just Fleishman who noticed and documented conduct by Caray deemed unprofessional and not becoming of the image Anheuser-Busch was trying to project. Concerned by Caray's on-air response to a female letter-writer, Harry Renfro of D'Arcy Advertising sent a transcription of the broadcaster's words to the company president, a memo that made its way to Fleishman. Mrs. J.W. Wilson, from the St. Louis suburb of Overland, had written Caray to say he failed to mention a Red Schoendienst home run during a broadcast, just days after Red had been traded from the Cardinals to the Giants. Caray wasted no time in responding, bringing it up in the first inning of the next game.

"Boy, I have received some poisonous things in my life, that's part of this business, but I've got one here tonight that I sure want to tell you about," Caray said over the Cardinals radio network. "Mrs. J.W. Wilson you are about as small and about as petty and about as despicable as anybody can be," adding that he didn't find out about the Schoendienst home run until after the Cardinals game was over.[61] He ended his tirade by telling her, "You certainly have a lot of gall, that's all I can say for you."[62]

That same month (June 1956), Caray upset Cardinals public relations man Jim Toomey with his behavior after a game. Taking the elevator down from the press box with Caray, Toomey and a handful of others stopped to pick up additional passengers on the next two floors. But instead of continuing down, the elevator reversed course to drop off a few people. The elevator operator made the special trip at Caray's request. "Caray is out of line in requesting special attention for anyone on the elevator when possible public relations with other elevator riders, including the deluxe box holders and the press, are involved," Toomey explained in a letter to Fleishman.

A minor transgression, perhaps, but three years later, Toomey unloaded on Caray in a three-page memo to Fleishman regarding "some of the items to which the Cardinals object in the baseball broadcasts." Harry was constantly criticizing trades. "In Caray's presentation, one bad deal makes all deals bad," Toomey wrote. He also cited the broadcaster's repeated denunciations of the team's player development, reaching conclusions that "will be drawn only when someone is <u>trying</u> to find fault."

The Cardinals PR man was just warming up. "Anticipating the outcome of the game or anticipating managerial strategy is one of the great faults Caray has," Toomey believed, before ticking off additional sins: [1] Harry put words into people's mouths. In an interview after the game with an ejected player, "The broadcaster … had lost sight of the fact that he was supposed to be on the same side as the Cardinals and Anheuser-Busch." [2] He conducted too many interviews with other sports personalities. "Caray spent practically an entire game interviewing Clyde Lovellette of the Hawks." [3] He inappropriately aired private issues on a public broadcast. After receiving a ticket from the police, Caray "indicated that he should be immune because some policemen had accepted passes from him." (When the Cardinals traded for Julian Javier in 1960, Toomey delivered the news in person to one St. Louis paper and sent an assistant to the other. Caray, who had a radio show before the game, didn't find out about the deal until he was on the way to the ballpark.)[63]

Fleishman preserved Toomey's dispatches and dozens of others that he and others wrote about Caray over the years. The Fleishman files on the broadcaster began shortly after Anheuser-Busch acquired the team. "Harry Caray – Hold Confidential File" read one early memo regarding the broadcaster, which noted his marriage and divorce from his first wife, the names and ages of his children, and details on his second marriage.

Fleishman escalated his concerns to Meyer in a seven-page memo in early 1957, getting his attention with a focus on the brewery's bottom line. "The record does not show that baseball broadcasts have thus far been productive in increased beer sales," Fleishman wrote to the Anheuser-Busch vice president. "A considerable body of research statistics and information exists on this subject." After making the case that any increase in beer sales didn't justify the cost of the broadcasts, he turned his attention to Caray. "Are people tired of the same voice and style?" he asked. "Do they want a change? What kind of change do people want?" Pointing out that Caray's contract was up in a few years and if things didn't change, "serious consideration must be given to Caray's contract for 1959. Discussion on the 1959 situation must take place not later than July 1958."[64]

After the 1957 season, Fleishman and Caray got into such an ugly back-and-forth over speaking appearances to the point that Meyer had to intercede. When Fleishman-Hillard representatives had trouble reaching Caray and eventually responded by sending him a letter, Harry replied with a litany of issues and complaints, many of them focused on a communication breakdown.

It's best to contact him at KMOX in the afternoon, Caray wrote, "rather than entrust messages with colored maids who are gone long before I get home."

That missive got the attention of Fleishman, who pointed out that while Buck and Garagiola had already been booked for sixty-three speeches, Caray had agreed to only four appearances. "We do not want to start another argument, Harry," Fleishman wrote. "This is a fact!"

Never one to let a charge go unanswered, Caray retaliated. "It may come as a great shock to you, but facts are never merely what Al Fleishman chooses to believe," Harry replied to his nemesis. "Please ... do not twist the situation around in your typical style so as to imply how very difficult one Harry Caray is to get along with."

A cease-fire didn't come until late November. "I am terribly distressed that such correspondence should ever develop in an area over which I have jurisdiction," Meyer stated in a letter to both men. "I cannot tolerate a continuance of friction over matters that have, in my opinion, a vital bearing on Anheuser-Busch."

The tensions with Caray shed a different light on the brewery's decision to add Blattner to an already crowded booth after the 1959 season. A later memo would bluntly state what people with knowledge of the situation must have been thinking. "It is our recommendation that it is in the best interests of Anheuser-Busch, as well as the teams sponsored, to dispense with Caray's services at the end of his present contract," the unsigned letter stated. "We would further recommend that the bulk of the broadcasting load be transferred to Joe Garagiola and Bud Blattner, whose experience, versatile skill and complete cooperative attitude, would, we believe, enable us to produce more effective sports programs."[65]

Somehow, Caray survived. He also escaped unscathed after an off-air comment about the owner of the Hawks made the rounds. "I'm the only man Ben Kerner can't buy," was the statement that alienated much of the rest of the St. Louis media. When Bob Broeg heard about it, he phoned Fleishman to tell him the *Post-Dispatch* staff could no longer accept any Christmas gifts, no matter how small.[66] "Our public relations with the press is presently at a very low ebb," Fleishman wrote to Meyer.

The Kerner quote was included in a memo Fleishman sent to another brewery executive, Walter Smith, in the fall of 1959. Other comments (in addition to many already mentioned) that Fleishman documented included Harry's reference to Sandy Koufax as a "member of the Jewish race," and calling pitcher Sam Jones "Sambo." When Caray made the latter comment, the switchboard of the *St. Louis Argus* "lit up like a Christmas tree," according to the paper's editor. Fleishman arranged for the editor and Caray to meet at the ballpark, but the *Argus* executive left after a few minutes, "disgusted" with the conversation. "All Caray wanted to do was lecture him on Negroes," Fleishman reported. "He agreed, however, not to publish the article already written by his reporter."[67]

Caray survived these comments, too, as well as another dustup with Kerner and his team in the fall of 1961. After a preseason game between the Hawks and Boston Celtics in Lexington, Kentucky, Caray included a story from a Lexington paper in his daily *Sports Digest* radio program. The editorial criticized the game's lackluster play. "The gist of it was you saw more action in a University of Kentucky practice session than in an NBA game," Caray recalled.[68]

The critique upset the Hawks and Gardner Advertising, which had recently convinced Kerner to switch sponsors from Falstaff to Busch. Caray was suspended from his *Sports Digest* radio program and speculation ran rampant that Harry may soon lose other roles. The suspension and controversy attracted media attention. "Harry has a faculty for speaking his mind and it often lands him in a hot spot," read an account in the *Globe-Democrat*. "He's got a thin skin," said one of his not-so-ardent admirers. "That's not so," said Harry. "I say what I think should be said and that's it."[69] The story sparked Gardner and Anheuser-Busch to issue an official statement the next day. "Present plans call for Harry to do play-by-play broadcasts of the 1961-1962 Billikens and the 1962 Cardinal baseball games as in the past."

The suspension from his radio show, however, remained in place. It was now public knowledge that not everyone in the Anheuser-Busch universe was a Harry Caray fan. "A 'don't quote me' confidant told this columnist last week that there are some influential ad people who would like to get Harry's scalp," wrote *Globe-Democrat* media reporter Peter Rahn.[70] With Harry still off the air, brewery, advertising and public relations executives gathered to air their Caray grievances. But Harry rode out this controversy, too, thanks to the one man whose vote mattered most of all. "If you think I'm going to fire the greatest broadcaster in baseball just because you people can't get along with him, you're crazy," said Gussie Busch.

But as Caray would later discover, even the brewery president had his limits.

---

[1] *The Belleville News-Democrat*, August 12, 1989. Sperling started at the *Christian Science Monitor* in 1946 and retired in 2005. He covered presidential campaigns from Harry Truman to Bill Clinton. He died in September of 2013 at the age of 97.

[2] In his 1989 story, Sperling wrote that he asked Mankiewicz which Cardinals outfielder was Buster Keaton's nephew. While there's no indication the two were related, Orsatti did double for Keaton in a scene from the 1924 movie *Sherlock Jr.* (Orsatti grew up in Los Angeles and aspired to a career in the movies.) Keaton had an ownership interest in a minor league team in Vernon, California, a club Orsatti played for in 1925. Orsatti joined the Cardinals in 1927 and spent his entire nine-year career in St. Louis, finishing with a lifetime batting average of .306. Orsatti's son, Ernie F. Orsatti, was a veteran Hollywood stuntman best known for taking a fall through a glass skylight in the 1972 movie, *The Poseidon Adventure*. *The Hollywood Reporter*, September 19, 2020.

[3] Herman Mankiewicz co-wrote *Citizen Kane* with Orson Welles. His brother, Joseph, won back-to-back Academy Awards for writing and directing *A Letter To Three Wives* in 1949 and *All About Eve* in 1950. Josh Mankiewicz, Robert's son, is a reporter for *Dateline NBC*. Another son, Ben, is a host for TCM (Turner Classic Movies).

[4] *New York Times,* October 24, 2014.

[5] *Washington Post*, August 21, 1994.

[6] "I've met some good friends and devoted Cardinals fans up there [at the Cathedral], including Bob Semple and Adam Clymer of the *New York Times* over the years, silently in our cars at midnight in a tight pennant year," Mankiewicz wrote in an email to Bernie Miklasz following the death of Jack Buck. *St. Louis Post-Dispatch,* June 22, 2002.

[7] Semple was one of the reporters featured in Timothy Crouse's book, *The Boys on the Bus*, about the 1972 presidential campaign.

[8] Jim White, a.k.a. "The Big Bumper," was the host. "His voice travels to 44 states and, on clear nights, to South America, and countries as far away as Australia, New Zealand, Japan, the Philippines and Finland. Letters have come from all those places and more, but the longest-distance phone call came from Guam late one night." *St. Louis Post-Dispatch,* March 16, 1989. Joe Buck told a reporter his father once received a letter from a missionary who claimed to listen from Tanzania. *New York Times*, October 30, 2013.

[9] Ibid.

[10] *St. Louis Post-Dispatch*, May 13, 1979.

[11] When Anheuser-Busch purchased the Cardinals in 1953, Hyland Jr. sent Gussie Busch a telegram: "Congratulations. Know my father would be very happy." Ibid, February 22, 1953.

[12] *Alton Evening Telegraph*, October 2, 1970.

[13] *Wall Street Journal*, April 7, 1958.

[14] KMOX had last carried Cardinals baseball in 1940. It did carry some Browns games in 1953. "KMOX will carry portions of night games." *The Sporting News*, April 1, 1953.

[15] Hyland once reprimanded some KMOX employees for smuggling a television set into the station to watch the Super Bowl. *St. Louis Post-Dispatch*, May 14, 1979.

[16] "I believe I have found the most extreme workaholic in the United States," wrote Bob Greene. *Chicago Tribune*, May 11, 1987.

[17] *St. Louis Post-Dispatch,* May 14, 1979. Hyland was a Knight of Malta, the Catholic Church's highest honor for a layman.
[18] Ibid.
[19] *St. Louis Globe-Democrat,* February 17, 1955.
[20] *Yale Alumni Magazine and Journal,* November 1977. https://yalealumnimagazine.com/articles/3864
[21] *St. Louis Post-Dispatch,* July 21, 1950.
[22] *The Sporting News,* March 2, 1998.
[23] *Evansville Press,* August 18, 1960.
[24] *The Napa Valley Register,* March 9, 1998.
[25] *Chicago Tribune,* April 2, 1998.
[26] *Daily Press* (Newport News, Virginia), August 3, 2006.
[27] *Indiana Business Journal,* October 6-12, 2014.
[28] Fischer celebrated his fiftieth year at Indiana University in 2023. "I thought a lot about Harry (after getting into broadcasting)," Fischer said. Growing up in Rochelle, about 80 miles outside Chicago, Fischer would listen to Caray broadcasts at night over KMOX. "I listened to Harry after he came to Chicago," he said, "but I never thought he was as good as he was in St. Louis." Interview with author, February 13, 2023.
[29] *St. Louis Post-Dispatch,* June 18, 1991. Harlan left the Cardinals for the Packers in 1971. "It happened because Bing Devine, my boss with the Cardinals, was a very good friend of Dan Devine, who had just left Missouri to become coach and general manager of the Packers." His first job in Green Bay was assistant general manager. He became the team's president in 1989, serving in that role until 2008.
[30] Ibid, March 2, 2018.
[31] *American Profile,* April 2004.
[32] *Esquire,* January 2009.
[33] *Sports Broadcast Journal,* September 20, 2019. https://www.sportsbroadcastjournal.com/president-bill-clinton-grew-up-listening-to-harry-caray-on-cardinals-radio-hillary-loved-the-cubs/
[34] *The Daily Oklahoman,* July 19, 1987.
[35] Harry influenced politicians and political commentators. "I became a Cub fan because I couldn't stand Harry Caray," George Will once admitted. *St. Louis Post-Dispatch*, April 23, 1990.
[36] *USA Today,* October 28, 2004. Henry attended his first game at the original Busch Stadium (Sportsman's Park) in 1959. "To me, this was mecca." Henry was the Red Sox owner when the club clinched its first World Series in 86 years in 2004 at Busch Stadium II, and St. Louis native Jerry Trupiano was the team's radio broadcaster. "I grew up in St. Louis listening to three baseball Hall of Fame broadcasters – Jack Buck, Harry Caray, and Joe Garagiola. I should have learned something." *Boston Globe,* January 13, 1993.
[37] "My first idol was Stan Musial," Mantle said. "I grew up in northeast Oklahoma. I got Harry Caray on the radio." *Boston Globe,* August 2, 1994.

[38] *New York Times*, July 29, 1985. Brock turned nine in 1948. At that age, he was only listening to Caray. Buck didn't join him for another six years.
[39] Flood, *The Way It Is*. Caray once described his relationship with Flood as "very close." Flood, who enjoyed painting, once did an oil portrait of Caray. "I can't say anything bad about Flood," Caray said. *Chicago Tribune,* May 1, 1971.
[40] New York *Daily News*, March 13, 1965.
[41] "Harry was something of a hero in our house," wrote McCarver, "alongside Aaron, Irvin, Mays, Musial and two guys named Jabbo Jablonski and Rip Repulski." McCarver, Tim with Ray Robinson. *Oh, Baby, I Love It!* Villard Books. 1987.
[42] *St. Louis Post-Dispatch*, October 25, 2011.
[43] McCarver, *Oh, Baby, I Love It!* The song originally inspired the *1942* Cardinals.
[44] *Washington Post,* July 27, 2003.
[45] "Except for a devastating imitation of announcer Harry Caray, Uecker has kept his best stuff under wraps," wrote columnist Stan Hochman. *Philadelphia Daily News*, May 6, 1966. "One of the first times I walked into the [Pink] Pony [in Scottsdale, Arizona], Bob Uecker was sitting at the bar doing his devastating imitation of Harry Caray," wrote *Chicago Sun-Times* columnist Ron Rappaport in 2003. "Uecker … does excellent takeoffs on broadcaster Harry Caray," noted the *Post-Dispatch* just a month after he joined the team. *St. Louis Post-Dispatch,* May 9, 1964.
[46] *The Sporting News*, April 26, 1969.
[47] Ibid, January 29, 1978. McTague first met Hope at the Muny in St. Louis in the late 1950s. "He cornered him in an elevator," recalled brother Michael McTague. "Instead of saying, 'Here's my card,' he handed him a script of jokes." McTague submitted material to Hope for the rest of his life. Ibid, December 29, 2001.
[48] Ibid, February 22, 1998. McTague "wrote comedy routines and radio scripts for Caray, even after the latter departed these shores for Chicago," wrote McGuire.
[49] Ferrell did an impression of Caray for his *Saturday Night Live* audition. "Channel surfing one day, I discovered WGN," he told Richard Deitsch. "Having grown up in California, I didn't know who Harry Caray was, but I was like, 'Who is this commentator for the Cubs?' The events on the field were secondary to him describing how nice Bob and Betty Jo Patterson of Waukegan, Illinois, were. '[Impersonating Caray] I just want to say hello to Patterson Hardware. I bought a claw hammer there, and they're great people. By the way, ground ball hit to second and he's out.' I would come home for lunch and try to catch the Cubs games and just enjoy that kind of randomness from him." *Sports Illustrated*, May 16, 2005.
[50] *Sports Illustrated*, April 16, 1990.
[51] *Chicago Tribune*, August 3, 1975.
[52] Ibid, February 27, 1998.
[53] *St. Louis Globe-Democrat*, October 9, 1951. Later stories in the *Post-Dispatch* put the year of the strike as 1950, but database searches of newspaper archives show it happened the following year.

[54] *Washington Post*, October 13, 1951. The dispute centered around the elimination of 47 bottle inspectors. The strike spread to Falstaff, Griesedieck Brothers, and Hyde Park workers. It lasted 24 days.

[55] *St. Louis Post-Dispatch,* February 21, 1993. Fleishman's longtime acquaintance at the paper was Selwyn Pepper. When Pepper removed the quote from the last editions of the paper, "Mr. Busch never forget that, never forget the importance of what he said to newspapers," Fleishman recalled. "Later on, he hardly talked to anybody, except (sports editor) Bob Broeg." Ibid, January 24, 1988.

[56] Although Anheuser-Busch had already purchased the team, Griesedieck's sponsorship of radio broadcasts (and Caray's contract with GB) didn't end until after the 1953 season.

[57] *Alfred Fleishman Papers 1926-2002*. Unless noted otherwise, all Fleishman quotes are from this collection.

[58] Ibid.

[59] The feud between Caray and Stanky would last for years. With the Cardinals battling an early-season slump in 1968, Stanky appeared on a radio show and sarcastically suggested the club consult Caray's keen baseball mind. Caray responded with a wire that read – KEEP UP THE GOOD WORK. Stanky, managing the Chicago White Sox, was fired 79 games into the season. *Sports Illustrated,* October 7, 1968.

[60] Bavarian was dropped from the name in 1979.

[61] While Harry didn't mention the 1956 Schoendienst home run, columnist Bob Burnes wrote about it in a column in the *Globe-Democrat*. Harry got an appointment with the paper's executive editor "during which he criticized Burnes' column and sought redress," Fleishman explained in a memo. "Writers are still mentioning the incident," he wrote three years later.

[62] *Fleishman Papers*.

[63] *The Sporting News*, June 8, 1960. Toomey worked as a sportswriter for the *St. Louis Star-Times* before joining the Cardinals.

[64] Fleishman wasn't alone in raising concerns about Caray's impact on the beer business during this period. "The constant chatter on every subject on earth except baseball and Budweiser is losing advertising value for you," former owner Fred Saigh wrote in a letter to Anheuser-Busch vice president John Wilson in August of 1956. "It's time for a change," Saigh stated. "He is as stale as last week's open Budweiser bottle." *Fleishman Papers*.

[65] The memo, written before the 1961 season, goes on to state, "The use of a third man would be necessary on certain of our broadcasts and for this assignment we would recommend the selection of a young sports announcer who could fill in as a junior member of the team as required. Such a man is available to us at the present time and could be hired for a fraction of what our more experienced broadcasters are receiving." The "available" man is not named.

[66] Over the years, Fleishman supplied Broeg with non-public information about Caray. More than once, the files show, Broeg was listed on Fleishman's memo distribution list that typically included brewery and advertising executives.

[67] In July of 1958, Cardinals business manager Art Routzong sent a note to Fleishman indicating concern that Caray "more or less out of the blue sky" started referring to Ruben Amaro as "Chico." A copy of the memo was passed along to Caray and broadcast partners Buck and Garagiola.

[68] *Sports Illustrated*, October 7, 1968. There were other issues that night in Lexington besides lackluster play. Several black members of the Celtics and Hawks (five from Boston, two from St. Louis) refused to play in the exhibition after they were denied food service at a local hotel. *Lexington Herald*, October 18, 1961.

[69] *St. Louis Globe-Democrat*, November 1, 1961.

[70] Ibid, November 3, 1961. Caray told Myron Cope for the 1968 *Sports Illustrated* story that he thought Kerner was trying to pave the way for Blattner to take his place in the Cardinals' broadcasting booth. "I think it was a squeeze play," said Harry.

Out With Harry

What does it take to be a close friend of Harry? "It's easy," said longtime pal Pete Vonachen. "Unlimited stamina, a cast-iron stomach, keep your bag packed, and your divorce lawyer on retainer."

Delivering one of the speeches at Caray's funeral in 1998, Vonachen spoke in front of packed pews at Holy Name Cathedral in Chicago while television cameras carried the event over WGN. He emphasized that his words were not a eulogy, but a tribute.[1] He called himself "the brother Harry never had." His many Caray stories drew plenty of laughs. ("Harry's funeral hardly funereal," noted the *Chicago Tribune*.) He admitted the Mass of Resurrection had him a bit unnerved. "Please, Father, don't resurrect him," Vonachen implored. "We couldn't go through this again." He also recalled Harry telling him, "When I die, I hope they don't cremate me. I'll burn forever."

Vonachen spoke of late nights on Rush Street when the pair would top off the evening at 4:00 a.m. with a "hotsy-totsy" and a banana daiquiri. "I haven't liked bananas ever since." He remembered the dread of riding in a car with Harry behind the wheel. "He had to be a driver's-ed school dropout," said Vonachen. Caray's wife, Dutchie, would make him ride in the front passenger seat, "the death seat," he called it, while she would curl up on the floor in the back. Once, with Vonachen driving and inching along in traffic, Harry told him, "Just go up on the sidewalk. I know the cops."[2]

While most people knew Harry from baseball, "Our association was different. It was entirely personal," Vonachen explained. "Talking, laughing, traveling together, playing gin rummy or dinner with our wives." Vonachen once asked his wife where she wanted to go for the couple's twenty-fifth wedding anniversary. "Hawaii," she said. "But do we have to take Harry?"

Late in life, all an exhausted Harry wanted to do after a game was go home. But a crowd would begin to form on his way out of the ballpark. People wanted autographs, a request "which turned into 15, 20, 30 minutes," Vonachen remembered. "I thought you wanted to get going," he would say to Caray. "Yes," came the reply, "but how do I turn down those little kids?"

Holy Cow St. Louis!

"Harry never knew a stranger," said Vonachen. Caray's sidekick first received national attention thanks to frequent mentions of his name during Cubs broadcasts. "A hello to my old friend in Peoria," Harry would say on the air.

Peoria, Illinois is where Vonachen became the owner of a minor-league baseball team in 1984. With Harry's help, the franchise became a Cubs affiliate the following season. The Peoria Chiefs have been associated with either the Cubs or Cardinals ever since. In 2011, the Cubs honored Vonachen in a pregame ceremony at Wrigley Field. Their opponent that day was the Cardinals. Chicago won the game in a season in which St. Louis won the World Series.

Peoria, located halfway between Chicago and St. Louis, is often cited as the dividing line between Cubs and Cards fandom. Vonachen called the city home his entire life. It's also the place where he and Harry first met. Like other things that later got larger attention in Chicago, this friendship had its roots in Harry Caray's St. Louis.

*****

Harry spent his winters in the 1950s as the voice of St. Louis University basketball.[3] While broadcasting a Billikens victory one night, an excited Caray announced a street dance after the game at the intersection of Grand and Lindell Boulevards. Some 2,000 students turned out. So did the Billiken pep band. As more than two dozen policemen arrived to keep snarled traffic moving, drivers dodged conga lines and snake dances. A group of students tried to enter the Fox Theater but were blocked by police. They rushed into the Missouri Theater instead, jumped on stage, took over the balcony, sang "When the Saints Go Marching In," and brought the show to a halt.[4]

What had students excited that night was not only the victory, but the chance to win a conference championship. The Billikens competed in the Missouri Valley at the time. One of their conference rivals was Bradley University, located in Peoria. Vonachen graduated from Bradley in 1949 and took a job running concessions at the school's Robertson Fieldhouse. On a Friday before a Saturday Bradley-SLU basketball game in 1950, Vonachen and the university's sports information director went to the airport to pick up a very important guest. And that is how Harry Caray and Pete Vonachen first met.

"What's there to do in this town?" Caray asked on the ride from the airport to his hotel. "Well, Harry, you're talking to the two right people," Vonachen told him. An evening that began at 6:30 didn't end until 4:30 the next morning. On Saturday, Vonachen had to be at the fieldhouse early to get the concessions in order. After an exhausting day and evening, he stopped by press row after the game to tell Harry goodbye. "Wait a minute. Where are you going?" said Caray, who proposed a "short night" and a "quiet drink." Vonachen reluctantly agreed.

Saturday night turned into a repeat of Friday. Arriving back at the hotel once again at 4:30 a.m. Harry needed a ride to the airport in just a few hours. Vonachen slept a few hours on the floor of Caray's room before getting up and dropping him off. That single weekend evolved into a friendship that lasted almost five decades.

"I never thought I'd get to know him the way I did. For forty-eight years we palled around together," Vonachen recalled. "You don't envision those things at the time. I'm just a punk kid who graduated from Bradley, and he's an up-and-coming sportscaster that everybody knows and everybody's getting to know. He was a celebrity – every place we went, they had to come up to Harry, all the Cardinals fans."[5]

The serendipitous friendship also spoke to Caray's attitude while traveling. He was never afraid to venture out in new cities and meet new people. "I think life on the road is anything but boring," he said. Harry's road adventures had another advantage – he didn't need an entourage. Harry "didn't mind being alone when he began the evening," believed Steve Stone, "because it never stayed that way very long."

After a Cubs game in Philadelphia one night, the team took a bus to New York. Leaving Veterans Stadium at 12:30 a.m., it was close to 3:00 a.m. by the time the club arrived in Manhattan. Just five blocks from the Grand Hyatt Hotel, Caray asked Stone to take his bag and requested the bus driver make a stop. Where was Harry going? Only he knew. "Harry happily disappeared down a darkened and deserted street in search of a couple of cocktails and some conversations about baseball," said Stone.[6]

Harry loved his trips to New York City. The night before Game 1 of the 1963 Dodgers-Yankees World Series, broadcaster Ernie Harwell had a bad cold and a burning sore throat. Leaving the Commodore Hotel at 3:00 a.m., he went searching for an all-night drugstore. On the way back to the hotel, he ran into Caray on the sidewalk. "Harry was out tomcatting," Harwell wrote in his autobiography. "He wasn't doing the Series. He was just there to have a good time."[7]

For years, Harry drank his way across Manhattan. But there was a part of the island that remained virgin territory. "Harlem was a place I always wanted to experience," Harry recalled. "Even though this was long after the era of the Cotton Club, Harlem was still celebrated for its jumping night spots. Count Basie still had a place where they played music all night long. Wilt Chamberlain owned a joint called Small's Paradise." (Chamberlain and a partner owned the club in the 1960s. Willie Mays met his second wife there.)[8]

One night, Harry decided the time had come. "If there's someplace I want to go, eventually, I'm going to get there," he said. Caray asked several sportswriters if they wanted to join him. All of them turned him down. He took off by himself and talked a reluctant cab driver into dropping him off at the Baby Grand, a joint *The New York Times* in 1961 called "Harlem's leading nightclub."[9] After a few hours there, he was ready to leave when he struck up a conversation with the manager. "If you really want to see Harlem, I can take you and show it to you," he told Harry. "I'll show you the *real* Harlem." Caray happily agreed. "By dawn, we must have hit six or seven places, and each one was just as much fun as the last."

Harry's favorite place in the city was the Copacabana. Jack Buck remembered a visit with Harry to the famed establishment for a performance by Sammy Davis.[10] Harry called the Copa "the classiest nightclub of them all." He would often stop there to have a drink before dinner and see a gentleman sitting in a back booth. Over time, the men would exchange nods or wave at one another, but that was the extent of their communication. "Never a conversation. Never a hello. Never even a thank you. There was sort of a gentlemen's code of the saloon at work here, and neither of us was inclined to break it," Caray explained. Harry began having the bartender send over a drink to the man. Frequently, the favor was returned. Caray's curiosity finally got the best of him one day, so he asked the bartender if he knew the identity of his mystery drinking partner. "You *really* don't know who that is?" said the stunned barkeep. "That's Frank Costello." Like Caray, the mob boss of the Luciano crime family loved the Copa.[11]

Exchanging drinks with Costello wasn't Caray's only brush with the underworld. According to Stone, Harry also knew Chicago mobster Tony "Big Tuna" Accardo, a man also known as "Joe Batters," a nickname given to him by Al Capone after he killed two men with a baseball bat as Capone looked on.[12] Harry "liked him because he treated Harry nicely," Stone wrote. "He didn't care what else this guy might have done to others. Harry had a simple, if not naïve, way of looking at life. 'I'll treat you the way you treat me,' was pretty much the extent of it."[13]

It was naivete, or perhaps a willingness to turn a blind eye to questionable activity, that landed Harry in hot water one night. It was at a club called the Glenn Rendezvous, just across the Ohio River from Cincinnati, in Newport, Kentucky, "which was one hell of a wide-open town," Caray recalled. "If something was illegal everywhere else, they did it in [Newport]."[14] He went there to see a singer, and later got invited to the gambling club upstairs. He lost $5,480 playing a rigged dice game and wrote a check to satisfy his debt. When two people (one was an anonymous phone caller) later told him to cancel the check, he began having second thoughts. After a conversation with his attorney in St. Louis, Caray did just that. He called his bank and stopped payment. That brought a visitor to Caray's hotel the next day. Meeting a man who identified himself as Tony Baker in the bar at the Hilton Cincinnati Netherland Plaza, Caray wrote a second check, this one for $500. Harry assumed that was the last he would hear of it. He was wrong.

Back in St. Louis at a club one night, a man named Murph – "a gambling czar" and "a heck of a nice guy" according to Caray – asked him about his experience at the Glenn Rendezvous. A startled Caray asked him how he knew about it. Murph told him he was a part-owner of the place and was called about the canceled check. "I told them you're a nice guy and I didn't want to see you get hurt, but I wanted you to pay for the lesson," he told Harry. "I told them to accept five hundred from you."

The exchange with Murph occurred at the Victorian Club, a restaurant and nightclub closed by the Internal Revenue Service in 1960. Owner Salvatore LoPiccolo owed $46,000 in federal taxes. LoPiccolo's home was sold two years later to satisfy $160,000 in claims against him. LoPiccolo was once known as the "Banana King" of St. Louis. His father had emigrated to America from Sicily and founded the Fortuna Banana Supply Co., which sold bananas to area retailers. Salvatore opened the Victorian Club in 1949 and soon began attracting attention and headlines for other reasons.

When a former waiter robbed the place, LoPiccolo originally refused to press charges. After a two-hour conversation with prosecutors, he changed his mind. "We are not going to have hoodlum justice running affairs in St. Louis," First Assistant Circuit Attorney James W. Connors told him. "The State of Missouri is interested in this case and we are going to prosecute whether you are or not."[15] LoPiccolo had angered authorities by telling an eyewitness, one of his employees, not to appear at the circuit attorney's office and that she could best use the time "to catch up on her work." Police also suspected Tommy Whalen, described as a "gambler and hoodlum," was a partner in the club, a charge LoPiccolo denied.[16] Five years later, when a robber held up the Victorian Club bookkeeper with a knife, he ran away with $1,500 in cash.

None of this mattered to Harry. What he cared about was the clientele the club attracted. In the 1950s, "it was *the* place to be seen in St. Louis," he said of the Victorian, "a carriage-trade favorite." Located at 3719 Washington Boulevard, the nightspot once boasted a marble bust of Anheuser-Busch founder Adolphus Busch and his wife, Lilly. The busts "are adding an air of elegance to a mid-town nightclub, much to the embarrassment of the Busch family," stated the *Globe-Democrat* in 1950.[17] Singer Mai Tatum, daughter of legendary jazz pianist Art Tatum, arrived at the club that same year for a three-week engagement. She ended up performing there for ten years, until IRS agents padlocked its doors.[18]

Just a mile or so west of the Victorian, live singing and entertainment flourished during this era in a part of the city known as Gaslight Square. Described by the *Post-Dispatch* as the "most important and single strongest entertainment area in the St. Louis area," Gaslight Square consisted of "Olive Street, from Sarah to Newstead. And don't forget corners at Whittier, Boyle, and Pendleton. There was nothing square about it," the paper once explained. "Mandatory for the in-crowd of the late 1950s and early 1960s."

The Crystal Palace, located on the south side of Olive Street and Boyle, was arguably the area's most famous club. A young Barbra Streisand performed there. So did comedians Lenny Bruce, George Carlin, Phyllis Diller, and Dick Gregory. The Smothers Brothers played and recorded an album there in 1961. Jazz trumpeter Miles Davis wowed audiences at Jorge's; folk singer Judy Collins performed at the Laughing Buddha.

Blues guitarist Billy Peek was playing in Gaslight Square in 1963 when Chuck Berry first saw him. Peek would later backup Berry on a European tour. He also spent years in Rod Stewart's band. (Peek's guitar solos can be heard on "Hot Legs," one of many Stewart songs the musician played on in the late 1970s.)

By the mid-1960s, discotheque go-go clubs dominated the eastern end of the Square. At one club, "the girls dance like trapped birds in a cage." Moe's Bootheel Club, described as "uncomplicated, unsophisticated, and above all, unpretentious," was deemed "the hottest country and western night club in St. Louis." Dixieland jazz could be found in abundance as one walked west. Heading south, the sound of bagpipes could be heard every Saturday night at O'Connell's Irish Pub. Turnover in the area was constant. "Clubs sprout each year like mushrooms after rain," observed William F. Woo.[19] On summer weekends in 1965, the Square attracted between 5,000 and 10,000 people.

All of this activity occurred just minutes from Sportsman's Park/Busch Stadium, meaning Caray would have likely passed close by or through these neighborhoods after Cardinal games. Harry also had many preferred stops in and around the city, including Busch's Grove, near his home in Ladue. There was Nick Carter's, whose namesake saloon keeper was known to be a favorite of President Truman and was once called "our town's Toots Shor" by a St. Louis columnist.[20] "I never miss going to Nick Carter's," Caray said in 1986. "Nick is a real good friend."[21] The Coal Hole, on Lindell Boulevard, described as having the "atmosphere of an Old English drinking tavern," was a popular Harry stop, as were the Stadium Cinema Lounge downtown and Al Baker's, at the corner of Clayton and Brentwood, known as a "popular place to meet, especially when there was live music." Harry once called bartender Lee Jugloff at His Lordship's in downtown St. Louis "the best in the business."[22]

Later, in Chicago, Harry became known as the "Mayor of Rush Street." (*Sports Illustrated* first used the term in 1978.)[23] In a larger city, with more bars and longer hours, Caray's late-night prowess became the stuff of legend. But Harry was fifty-seven when he arrived in the city, and sixty-eight when he started broadcasting Cubs games. At the peak of his fame and just days away from turning seventy-three, he suffered a stroke and missed the beginning of the 1987 season. He changed his diet and slowed his pace. ("Not nearly as rambunctious" is how one writer described the new Harry.) In 1994, suffering from an irregular heartbeat, Harry collapsed on a set of steps at Joe Robbie Stadium in Miami.[24] On the advice of his doctor, Caray stopped drinking altogether. Harry was just thirty-one when he started calling baseball in St. Louis and did his last broadcast for the Cardinals at the age of fifty-five. If Caray was energetic and rambunctious for most of his time in Chicago, can you imagine what a boozy, boisterous, and younger Harry was like during his St. Louis years?

*****

There is no question that Harry loved going out. When business entertainment was tax-deductible, he maintained a diary of his bar visits, tracking receipts, dates, and names of people entertained. The log from 1972 shows he spent 288 consecutive nights out on the town.[25] The list of names Harry dined and drank with that year included Wilt Chamberlain, Don Drysdale, Jack Dempsey, and Jack Benny. But documenting exactly how much Caray himself drank on those nights isn't so clear. Depending on the audience, Harry would either minimize or boast about his alcohol consumption.

"I wasn't drunk every night," he told Stone. "The tales are widely exaggerated. I might go out every night but it doesn't mean I'm drunk every night." When Jack Craig of the *Boston Globe* wrote that Caray drank beer while at the microphone, "thus violating the equivalent of perhaps five of the 10 commandments of broadcasting," Harry downplayed the behavior. "Oh, I just sip. I don't guzzle," he said.[26]

People would assume that Harry had a lot to drink because he could be seen in so many places in a single night. "He was a real people person, just loved to be around people," said longtime Busch's Grove bartender Otis Dunlap. "And he loved to bar-hop." While a restless Caray enjoyed making the rounds, he frequently wouldn't stay in any one location long. "Harry liked to have a drink in a place, check the action, and then move on," explained Buck.[27] Vonachen had similar experiences. "The stories about him being a lush definitely are not true," Vonachen said in 1994. "Harry has left enough full drinks lying on the bar to throw a New Year's Eve party for the entire town of Kenosha."[28]

Where Harry did enjoy his cocktails was at dinner, where he would almost always order Italian food (sausage and peppers was a frequent request) served late at night.[29] According to Stone, Caray didn't even want to see a menu until he and other members of his dinner party were on their fourth martini. "That was the rule, and that's the way it was," he wrote.

Harry described his pre-stroke drinking routine in his autobiography. "I'd have a few Budweisers at the ballpark during the day, then maybe I'd have four to six drinks after the game, then I'd go home and have a few more, and then I'd go out for a late dinner and have a few more. I never got high, it never impaired my judgment, and believe me, in my heavy-drinking days, I took on some big-time thirsts and was able to drink them all under the table. And without getting drunk myself. I never got drunk, I just got happier."

A happy Harry was how Caray was frequently portrayed in the press. But like Babe Ruth, another larger-than-life figure with an unquenchable thirst and a troubled childhood shrouded in mystery, the portrayal of Harry's drinking habits masked more serious issues. According to Vonachen, Caray spent a night in jail after getting pulled over near his winter home in Palm Springs, California. Buck recalled a night out drinking with Harry in Houston. "I was driving. I went through a flashing red light and a cop stopped us. I was getting along OK with the cop and all of a sudden Harry got out of the car and said, 'What's going on here? Break this up.'" When a cop ordered Harry to get back on the sidewalk, "He said, 'I don't have to get back on the sidewalk. This is a free country,'" remembered Buck. "By that time, there were six police cars there. Somebody pointed a finger in his face and said something to him and he finally calmed down. But he was always very feisty," Buck said.

"When Harry was on the warpath, it was like being called on in class when you didn't study the night before," said Stone. "It could be terrifying."

Harry's late-night habits understandably put a strain on his marriages. One time when Vonachen visited Caray in St. Louis, they stopped at a BBQ restaurant and bought some ribs to bring home to Harry's apartment. Caray was married to his second wife, Marian, at the time. "I was out a little late last night and Marian's not too happy with me," Harry told Pete. "In the apartment, if you went through the bedroom window, there was a roof on the apartment below," Vonachen recalled. "So Harry and I crawled out on the roof and ate the ribs out there, so Marian wouldn't be giving us hell all the time. I'll never forget that night."[30]

It took his third wife to get Harry to better understand his relationship with alcohol. "Dutchie mentioned to me that I'd probably been using drinking as a crutch all those years, and she might have had a point. I was probably more nervous than I cared to admit, or at least more wound up, more hyperactive," he acknowledged. "I'd use alcohol to wind down."

Harry's relationship with booze was not just as a consumer, but also as a salesman. Jackie Robinson's debut with the Dodgers in 1947 got the attention of Griesedieck Brothers. The brewery wanted more focus on boosting its sales in black neighborhoods and got Harry involved in the effort. "The way they explained it, they would give me cash and I would go into taverns, buy drinks for the house, drink Griesedieck, and talk sports with the customers," Harry recalled. "There was no way I was going to refuse. I loved the idea." Caray claimed the effort was a success. "We boosted the hell out of Griesedieck sales in black neighborhoods."

He had a similar role with Anheuser-Busch, going into neighborhood taverns – black or white – to tout the virtues of the company's offerings. Harry and Gussie Busch often went into saloons together "and we'd go behind the bar to serve drinks – trying to convince the owner that he should stock his place with Budweiser," Caray recalled.

"Budweiser gave Caray a budget to buy drinks for the entire bar," remembered Buck. "He managed to overspend it."[31]

It was these relationships – with Budweiser, the Anheuser-Busch corporation, and especially its president – that would define Harry's time in St. Louis starting in 1954. The "King of Beers" was ruled like a monarchy, and for sixteen seasons, Harry had the privilege of being one of the knights of Gussie's round table.

---

[1] Vonachen's entire speech can be found on YouTube.
[2] According to Harry's White Sox broadcasting colleague Jimmy Piersall, Caray once drove up on a sidewalk to avoid a milk truck in the intersection.
[3] Jack Buck replaced Caray on Billikens radio broadcasts for the 1962-1963 season.
[4] *St. Louis Post-Dispatch*, February 26, 1956.
[5] *Peoria* magazine, July 2013.
[6] Stone, *Where's Harry?*
[7] Keegan, Tom. *Ernie Harwell: My 60 Years in Baseball.* Triumph Books. 2002.
[8] Chamberlain would park his white convertible Cadillac in front of the establishment. "So valuable was Chamberlain's name now, so incandescent his persona, that a

historical Harlem nightclub, Smalls Paradise, let him buy in as part-owner and put his name first on the marquee in exchange for his presence," wrote *Wilt, 1962* author Gary Pomerantz. Chamberlain "loved Harlem, the neon, the ladies, James Brown, Etta James, Redd Foxx, a lush life with jazz the soundtrack."

[9] Located at 125th street between Eighth and St. Nicholas Avenues, the Baby Grand's inner room held 180 people and had a minimum charge of $4 on Saturdays. The floor show, described as "prolonged and very noisy," began a little after 10 p.m. "It includes an organist, a jazz combo, a girl singer, a boy singer, and an 'exotic' dancer, who does a joyless strip tease. But the chief attraction is Nipsey Russell, a comic who made several recent and successful television appearances under the aegis of Jack Paar." *New York Times,* May 15, 1961.

[10] Also in the audience that night were Elizabeth Taylor and Richard Burton. "They were a better-looking couple than Harry and I." Buck wrote. Buck, *Jack Buck.*

[11] Caray went over to Costello's table and introduced himself. Caray described him as "engaging" and knowledgeable," adding, "I've met a lot of people in the same line of work as Frank Costello, and they always seemed to like me. Which is good. I'd much rather have them like me than dislike me." Caray, *Holy Cow!*

[12] "In a criminal career that lasted over 70 years, he [Accardo] never did any time in jail." Cimino, Al. *The Mafia Files: Case Studies of the World's Most Evil Mobsters.* Arcturus Publishing Limited. 2014.

[13] Stone, *Where's Harry?*

[14] In his biography, Harry identifies the location of the Glenn Rendezvous as Covington, Kentucky. In fact, it was located in nearby Newport.

[15] *St. Louis Post-Dispatch,* December 29, 1949.

[16] "Whalen for a time operated handbooks in Chicago under Murray (The Camel) Humphrey, topflight Capone mobster, who took a liking to the St. Louisan." Ibid.

[17] *St. Louis Globe-Democrat*, December 2, 1950.

[18] *St. Louis Post-Dispatch*, March 16, 1972.

[19] Ibid, May 8, 1966.

[20] Ibid, October 27, 1987.

[21] Carter died in 1987. He was born in Memphis as Nick Clisaris and later changed his last name. He grew up in Athens, Greece. He moved to St. Louis in the 1940s and served as the catering manager at the Jefferson Hotel until the mid-1950s. He operated the Surf 'n' Sirloin Restaurant in the Forest Park Hotel for thirteen years. The establishment "remained a popular oasis and dining room for union bosses, scions of business, entertainers, crime bosses, and others who caused heads to turn." He then opened Nick Carter's restaurant on Lindell Boulevard. Ibid.

[22] Ibid, February 22, 1998. Coal Hole: https://losttables.com/coalhole/coalhole.htm "The Coal Hole's glory years were from 1945 to 1961." Al Baker's: https://www.stlmag.com/dining/memory-lane-al-baker-s/ His Lordship's: *St. Louis* magazine, September 1968. In a story titled "Retired Saint of Bartenders," reporter Jack

Rice introduced readers to Jugloff. At His Lordship's, "He looked like the bartender, and he listened like the bartender, and he never indicated otherwise. In fact of business he was a vice president of the enterprise and general manager." Jugloff was born in Macedonia, to Bulgarian parents, in 1913. His father brought the family to the United States in 1924. *St. Louis Post-Dispatch*, September 20, 1977.

[23] "The Big Wind in Chicago," *Sports Illustrated*, September 18, 1978. "Four in the morning often arrives too soon for 'the Mayor of Rush Street,'" wrote Ron Fimrite. The earliest reference to the term I could find in the *Chicago Tribune* occurred in an October 12, 1979, Gary Deeb column. "As the unofficial mayor of Rush Street, [Caray would] be hard-pressed to find as much fun in any other town." The *Chicago Sun-Times* online archives begin in 1986.

[24] When Harry collapsed in Miami, he was discovered by a Cardinals scout, Jack Hubbard, who saw Caray lying on his side with his head down. Caray's glasses had fallen off and there was blood on the steps from cuts on his chin and mouth. After the incident, Harry began drinking non-alcoholic beer and wine. Two years earlier, Harry had said, "I'd rather die than not have a cocktail." *Chicago Sun-Times,* September 13, 1992.

[25] Ibid, June 2, 2014.

[26] *Boston Globe*, April 25, 1971.

[27] *Tampa Bay Times*, February 19, 1998.

[28] *Des Moines Register*, April 3, 1994.

[29] Even during his Cardinal days, Harry loved Adolph's in Chicago. He started going to the place in the 1950s, frequently with Stan Musial and Red Schoendienst, where he would habitually order sausage and peppers. "But he wants the sausage burned up – cremated," said co-owner Fortune Renucci. "My chef refuses to prepare it that way, so I have to do it myself, and Harry invariably says, 'Man, that's good … just the way I like it,' even though it looks to me like a piece of coal." *Chicago Tribune*, August 13, 1972.

[30] Wolfe and Castle, *I Remember Harry Caray*. In the book, the restaurant is identified as "McQuarry's." It was likely "McCrary's." The original restaurant, McCrary's Pork House, opened in 1948 at Enright and Vandeventer. A second location, McCrary's Original Hickory Bar-B-Q, located at 8611 Olive, opened in 1965.
https://losttables.com/bbq/bbq.htm

[31] *Tampa Bay Times,* February 16, 1998.

Here Comes The King

Caray's image "revolves around late nights, liquor, and ladies," noted a *People* magazine profile of Harry in 1978. The same could be said of the man he once worked for. Commissioned as an officer when he joined the Army, Gussie Busch spent World War II at a desk job in the Pentagon, becoming a full colonel by 1945. Separated from his second wife, he recalled how he and a military buddy "used to smell powder together – that is women's face powder."[1]

In a battle of larger-than-life figures, just about everything Harry could do, Gussie could do bigger, better, or more outrageously. Caray would become a millionaire. Busch was a billionaire (estimated net worth of $1.5 billion at the time of his death). Harry's first two marriages produced five children. Gussie's first three wives gave him eleven offspring. Caray's third and final marriage came at the age of sixty-one. Busch was just days shy of his eighty-second birthday when he married for the fourth time. Harry claimed, without proof, that he was once a Golden Gloves boxing champion. Gussie loved boxing so much that he would engage in bare-knuckle fights in his private boxing ring. Busch would go to neighborhood saloons as a young man and "pick fights over women." That ended one evening when a professional boxer knocked him out cold. The twice-divorced Caray had a sign in his Chicago hotel residence: "Alimony. The High Cost of Living." Busch's $1 million divorce settlement with his second wife in 1952 set a Missouri record.[2]

The broadcaster and beer baron had much in common. For two men who worked directly or indirectly for breweries nearly their entire adult lives, beer wasn't their preferred drink. "Harry's drink was J&B (scotch) and water," remembered longtime bartender Otis Dunlap.[3] "Joseph, the butler, told me Gussie drank enough martinis to fill a lake," said Helen Busch Conway, Gussie's second cousin. A reporter once asked Busch what he drank at night. "Scotch," he replied. "I only drink beer at lunchtime."[4]

Both men called Frank Sinatra a friend. The entertainer once served as honorary chairman of a Caray roast. Harry "met his match when he met Sinatra. Because Sinatra stayed out until the sun came up," said Tom Dreesen, who knew both men.[5] Sinatra was "maybe the only person Harry actually idolized or was in awe of," believed Steve Stone.[6] The first television broadcast Anheuser-

Busch ever sponsored was a Frank Sinatra show. Gussie later awarded Frank a distributorship in Long Beach, California.

In an era when white men dominated nearly every industry in America, Busch and Caray practiced casual bigotry or misogyny while also having moments of racial enlightenment. Aboard his yacht on one of his many trips to the Caribbean, Busch wanted more women to join the party. "I want white bait and some of that brown bait," he radioed to shore.[7] He was also the first Cardinals owner to have a black player on the team and inspired President Johnson's actions on civil rights. LBJ biographer Robert Caro wrote that Johnson began shedding his image as an "anti-civil rights Southerner" after a visit to Grant's Farm.[8]

Harry, the man who once called pitcher Sam Jones "Sambo," was the same person instrumental in breaking down color barriers in the broadcast booth. In his autobiography, former Cardinals first baseman Bill White thanked Caray and KMOX chief Hyland for giving him his start in the business. In 1981, two black broadcasters worked for major league teams: White in New York for the Yankees and Caray's new partner with the White Sox, Lou Brock.[9]

Each of the St. Louis natives had a child involved in a fatal automobile accident. One of the stories has been well documented. The other received only scant coverage.

Busch's eight-year-old daughter Christina died following an automobile accident in December 1974. On her way home from school with her brother, Andrew, in a vehicle driven by their chauffeur, their Volkswagen van ran head-on into a tractor-trailer truck after the big rig blew a tire on Interstate 44. Only Andrew survived. The family chauffeur, Nathanial Mayes, was killed instantly. Christina suffered brain damage and never regained consciousness. She died eleven days later.

Almost eight years earlier, a Caray family member was involved in a fatal accident on a different stretch of the same interstate. In the spring of 1967, Chris Caray, Harry's son, was a pitcher at Southwest Missouri State University (now Missouri State) in Springfield. On a March weekend, Chris and three other students drove to Evansville, Indiana to attend a college basketball game. Returning home on Interstate 44 just five miles outside Springfield, tragedy struck. When Chris fell asleep at the wheel, the car veered into the median and struck a concrete drainage ditch. The 1967 Chevelle spun around, went onto its side, and struck a steel highway marker support. Pronounced dead at a local hospital was 20-year-old Anna Belle Maxwell. Caray injured his right shoulder, suffered head lacerations and body bruises. The other two passengers also had bruises and possible broken bones. The three survivors were all reported to be in satisfactory condition.[10] The story received brief media attention in the following days, but was never mentioned by Harry or his many chroniclers.

Both Harry and Gussie were injured doing what they loved. Caray broke his shoulder and both legs on the way to a late-night drink with a female companion. Busch broke his shoulder during a horse-riding competition. Neither man liked being alone. They drew their energy from being around others. "I've never missed a day," Caray once told David Letterman. "Never missed a night, either."[11] It wasn't squeeze plays or stolen bases that attracted Busch to sports ownership. "Gussie Busch loved baseball because he loved the crowd, he loved going out there and competing," said Fleishman. "He wanted to win if he had horses. He wanted to win if he had the Cardinals."

Despite their wealth and fame, both the baseball announcer and brewery executive had everyman appeal. Caray called his first game from the bleachers in 1958 and always saw himself as just another fan in the stands. When he started singing during the seventh-inning stretch, the voices from the outfield were often the loudest. When Busch would hop aboard a Clydesdale-pulled beer wagon, he generated a similar response. "What was amazing was the reaction in the bleachers, where these guys making six or seven dollars an hour would rush to buy beer to toast Gussie the billionaire," said St. Louis Brewery co-founder Tom Schlafly. "If Diana was the People's Princess, he was the People's King."[12]

The "People's King" ascended to his baseball throne in 1953 almost by accident. But over the coming decades, he would leave an indelible stamp on the game. Once ensconced, it took death to get him out of his seat.

*****

In the early 1960s, Busch had a picnic for the Cardinal players and their families at Grant's Farm. In a generous mood that day and seeing how the children loved interacting with the animals, Gussie decided to give every kid there a pony. It took one of his assistants to point out that not every child lived on a 200-plus-acre estate nor had the money and space to feed and care for such an animal. It was a viewpoint the Cardinals president had not considered. He changed his mind. If Gussie could seem out of touch with the economics of the common man, it came naturally. He knew nothing but a life of wealth and opulence from the moment he was born.

When his grandfather and family patriarch, Adolphus Busch, died in 1913, his estate included ownership in everything from hotels in Chicago, Dallas, and Paris to a German ammunition and weapons factory in Berlin. In total, Adolphus had interests in fifty different companies. With an estimated value of $50 million, it was the largest estate ever probated in Missouri.[13]

Born in 1899, Gussie was a teenager when his grandfather died and his father, August A. Busch Sr. took control of the brewery. His first marriage came in 1918. He was nineteen. His bride was twenty-two. As a wedding gift, his grandmother gave the couple a $10,000 check and a set of silver.[14]

As a young man, Gussie had two employers before joining the brewery: A railroad owned by his father and a bank, where he would arrive in a red, chauffeur-driven roadster. In addition to a driver, Busch and his bride had a butler, upstairs maid, cook, laundress, and yardman by the mid-1920s. Joining the family firm in 1924, Busch would make the journey from his home on Lindell Boulevard to the brewery on Pestalozzi Street in his grandmother's Rolls Royce.

He arrived at the brewery in the middle of Prohibition and a few years before the beginning of the Great Depression. To survive, the company spun off assets, produced non-alcoholic drinks, and sold everything from syrup and corn sugar to yeast and livestock feed. The twin strains of the beer ban and a listless economy combined with poor health were too much for Gussie's father. August Sr. committed suicide in 1934, not long after it again became legal to sell beer. Gussie's turn to run the company came after his brother, Adolphus, died in 1946.

He went to work expanding brewery operations, while pushing out close family relatives and running the company like his own personal fiefdom. He had two yachts and a 41-foot fishing boat, all nominally owned by the company but always under the control of its president. When it came time to purchase the Cardinals, the brewery needed approval from the board of directors. One of those directors, a Busch relative named Adalbert (Adie) von Gontard, was spending the winter in Palm Beach, Florida and had no interest in returning to St. Louis for a vote on a baseball team. When Adie told Gussie he didn't think he had enough time to make plane reservations, Busch had Fleishman contact Eastern Airlines president Eddie Rickenbacker. "Eddie, I need a ticket from Palm Beach," Busch told the former World War I flying ace. "You got it, Gussie," Rickenbacker replied.[15] "What Gussie wants, Gussie most often gets," Broeg once wrote.

In the middle years of the twentieth century, Gussie turned his acquisitive eye to a woman and a major league team. One of the ventures came naturally. He had to be talked into the other one. On an extended trip through Europe in the summer of 1949, he stopped for a meal at the Old Swiss House in Lucerne. He immediately became enthralled with the hostess, the innkeeper's daughter. He proposed to Trudy Buholzer on their first date. Gussie was still married, but separated from his second wife at the time. He soon brought Trudy to Grant's Farm and began showering her with gifts. One month after his divorce from

Elizabeth Busch, Gussie and Trudy married. The couple married a second time in a Roman Catholic ceremony on March 9, 1953, seventeen days after Anheuser-Busch announced the purchase of the Cardinals.

All Gussie knew about Cardinals baseball was that he enjoyed duck hunting with Musial and Schoendienst. "I've been a fan all my life but I've been too busy to get out to the park in recent years, unfortunately," he admitted the day the brewery bought the team. Anheuser-Busch was a late entrant to the field of suitors for the club.[16] With Saigh headed to prison and seriously entertaining offers from out-of-town groups, it took a push from local bankers David Calhoun and James Hickok to get Gussie interested. "They're the ones who should get full credit, principally Hickok," Saigh said years later.[17] "They had to convince him it was good for the city, and a good thing for his beer. And it took some convincing."[18]

"A good thing for his beer" undoubtedly got Gussie's attention. While Busch's knowledge of baseball may have been limited, "he had hops and barley in his veins," believed one-time brewery executive Ed Vogel.[19] Despite what Busch told reporters that first day – "I am going at this from the sports angle and not as a sales weapon for Budweiser beer" – his actions told a different story. He immediately hiked beer prices on all competitor products sold at the ballpark (with no change in cost for Anheuser-Busch offerings). Sportsman's Park became Busch Stadium (the beer by that name came a few years later) when the brewery paid Bill Veeck and the Browns $800,000 for the park and another $300,000 to leave town.[20]

When Colorado Senator Edwin Johnson began loudly complaining that the purchase of the Cardinals was a tax dodge for the brewery, the company hired investigators to understand why.[21] The brewery's agency, D'Arcy Advertising, had announced plans to extend the Cardinals radio network into new places, including several cities with minor league teams. Johnson owned the Denver Bears, a Western League team, and held an executive position on the league's finance committee. Fleishman remembered Busch challenging Johnson, asking what hat he was wearing: "Is it the hat of the president of the Denver Baseball Bears? Or is it the hat of the treasurer of the Western League of minor league baseball?"[22] The senator's push to get Anheuser-Busch and other large corporations out of baseball soon faded.[23]

The growth of Anheuser-Busch's market share over the years (less than 10% of all beer sales in the United States when the brewery bought the team; more than 44% when it sold the team decades later) gave it political clout.[24] The end of Prohibition under FDR made the Busch family loyal Democrats during this era. Gussie would leave passes at the park for former President Truman, raised large amounts of money for Kennedy's campaign, and bonded over beer and barbecue with LBJ. The Johnson administration later dropped an anti-trust lawsuit filed against Anheuser-Busch by the Kennedy Justice Department.

The brewery brought Gussie wealth and access. The Cardinals gave him fame. "As a business tycoon, Busch could go anywhere, say anything, announce any program, and attract two reporters and one paragraph in the business section of some newspapers," wrote Leonard Koppett in *The New York Times*. "As a baseball owner, any casual remark could trigger headlines and columns of any type." The first color telecast to originate in St. Louis took place at Grant's Farm in 1954. *Life* magazine arrived to shoot a layout of the Busch family, while *Time* put Gussie on the cover in 1955. *Ladies' Home Journal* called him the seventh-richest man in America. Shortly after buying the Cardinals, Busch arrived in New York on a business trip. While in the city, "he decided he'd like to meet some of the sportswriters," said Fleishman. "He arranged a little get-together at Toots Shor's – and 350 people showed up. He never got over that."[25]

Busch would later fall out of step with the team and the times. In spring training of 1969, he publicly lectured his club on baseball salaries. Three years later, he exploded when players threatened to walk out. "Let'em strike. I won't give them one more damned cent!" he roared. "God, that [Joe] Torre. How can any man I pay $280,000 over two years vote to go on strike?"[26] (The strike of 1972 lasted 13 days.) That same spring, he traded Steve Carlton over $5,000 in salary and Jerry Reuss because he didn't like his facial hair, dooming the Cardinals of the 1970s to a lost decade. "Gussie Busch never really understood multimillion-dollar player salaries or players' unions," said Fleishman.[27]

To a man born at the end of the nineteenth century, the world of the 1950s and much of the 1960s proved more hospitable, an age where Busch could show off his wealth and play the role of benevolent baron. In spring training, he'd leave his compound at Pass-a-Grill and sail his yacht to the Cardinals' spring training complex in St. Petersburg. In the early days, he'd occasionally suit up and take batting practice.[28] Before air travel eliminated the option, he'd attach his $300,000 private railroad car to the team train.[29] In 1958, he made Musial the first player in National League history to receive a $100,000 salary. A decade later, the 1968 Cardinals had the highest-paid lineup in baseball. On road trips, players had individual hotel rooms – no roommates. Free beer was abundant. Anheuser-Busch required the local distributor to provide it to the team in any city the Cardinals happened to play. "My three years in the Cardinals' organization were the three happiest years of my life," said former shortstop Dick Groat, who joined the team in 1963. "They were first-class every day, in every way."[30] There was glamour in being a St. Louis Cardinal. "I'll never forget the police escorts to the World Series games," said Betty Busch Von Gontard, a daughter of Gussie and third wife Trudy. "Frank Sinatra sang, the corks popped."[31]

The fifties and sixties represented Gussie at his personal and professional peak. After the age of fifty, he fathered seven of his eleven children. The same year the brewery bought the baseball team, Busch set up a horse breeding operation at Grant's Farm, bringing over a dozen one-ton Clydesdales from Scotland.[32] The Scottish draught horses, which made their first appearance for the brewery at the end of Prohibition, became a staple of Anheuser-Busch advertising, appearing in everything from parades to Super Bowl commercials. Seventy years later, Cardinals fans still cheer the Clydesdales and clap their hands whenever the Busch Stadium organist plays the Budweiser jingle, "Here Comes the King."[33]

The Busch legacy is complicated. The performance of the Cardinals during his stewardship was often like the man himself: erratic and inconsistent. A man who loved animals could be incredibly cruel to people. "If he liked you, he called you 'pal.' If he didn't like you, he called you 'thing!'" remembered former brewery executive Dennis Long. Both his brewery and ballclub would sometimes succeed despite him, not because of him.

Gussie's reign over the Cardinals saw two decades of frustration interlaced with two decades of success. The success of his teams in the 1960s – three pennants and two World Series titles in five years – allowed Busch to showcase another talent, one that helped cement the bond between brewer and broadcaster.

"No one threw a party like Gussie," wrote biographers Peter Hernon and Terry Ganey.

*****

Busch loved to party. His family and friends also enjoyed a good food fight. Baseball gatherings gave Gussie's crew an excuse to do both. There was the 1967 World Series celebration in Boston, where the Cardinals defeated the Red Sox in seven games. Setting up shop at the Ritz Carlton, Gussie and Trudy surprised guests emerging from the elevator with a blast from the fire extinguisher. "They were a wild, wild bunch. They were swinging from the chandeliers," Vogel recalled.[34] The tab for damages and cleanup came to $50,000, a bill paid out of the Anheuser-Busch advertising budget. Busch didn't need a victory celebration to party. Following a Game Six 8-4 Cardinals loss, he hosted the Massachusetts Governor and his wife at a banquet. When one of

Gussie's daughters fired a roll at her father that instead hit the governor's wife, the food fight was on.[35]

Every spring training, Gussie gathered with a group of St. Petersburg business and civic leaders who called themselves the "Bat Boys."[36] As dozens gathered for cocktails and dinner one evening, it didn't take long for guests to start tossing water-soaked napkins and dinner rolls. Cardinals general manager Bob Howsam poured a beer on Musial's head. Someone else grabbed a cheese dip bowl and dumped it on Caray. A free-for-all ensued. The next year, the same group gathered at the same place. Gussie missed cocktails and was late for dinner. Suddenly, the door burst open, revealing Busch wearing boots, a hat, and a yellow raincoat. "Let the party begin!" he declared. [37]

"Gussie Busch was my kind of guy, what I call a booze and broads man," Caray remembered. "He liked to have a drink, appreciate the qualities of a beautiful woman, tell a few stories, and play a few hands of cards."

Gin rummy was Busch's game of choice, but whatever was played, Gussie set the ground rules (and was known to cheat frequently). The stakes could be high.[38] Caray was often at the table with his boss. "He [Harry] loved to play cards and Mr. Busch loved to play cards. And Harry would get the biggest kick out of beating Mr. Busch, because Mr. Busch didn't like to lose. And Harry would stick it right to him," recalled Howsam. "One time, he won quite a bit of money. A thousand dollars or something. And boy did he let him have it. He didn't let him forget it."[39]

"Gussie and I rarely talked baseball," said Harry. "Ours was not a business relationship, it was social." But sometimes the lines between business and baseball would blur. At a party one night at his Grant's Farm estate, Busch pressed Caray for his preference – recently fired general manager Frank Lane – or his replacement, Bing Devine? Backed into a corner by his boss, Harry finally gave his answer. "Bing Devine cannot carry Frank Lane's jockstrap!" he said, an answer that shocked some of the guests at the dinner table. "Gussie ought to fire that son of a bitch," the wife of Anheuser-Busch attorney Tony Buford mouthed to Trudy, a comment that didn't sit well with Harry's wife. The dinner proceeded in awkward silence. When it came time to retire to the den for drinks, the Carays got up to leave. Gussie stopped them. "Like hell you're going to leave!" Busch commanded. "You son of a bitch," Gussie told Harry. "If you hadn't answered like that, I would have fired you."

Caray believed the whole thing had been coordinated by his longtime nemesis, Fleishman, who suspected Harry always told his boss what he wanted to hear. Busch, according to Caray, had a different view. "Gussie was out to prove to Al Fleishman that I was my own man – whether my opinions went along with the party lines or not. My response proved him [Fleishman] wrong, even if it did make for an uncomfortable dinner," Caray recalled.

It was that way from the beginning of their relationship. Busch would comment or make a decision, and all Caray could see were Fleishman's fingerprints.

In September of 1953, with Griesedieck's longtime sponsorship of Cardinals broadcasts soon ending, the company announced that Caray and broadcast partner Mancuso would be "free agents" at the end of the baseball season. That same month, Budweiser began sponsoring a daily 15-minute sports show on ABC radio with broadcaster Bill Stern. Speculation ran rampant that Stern or another big-name announcer would replace Caray on the Budweiser-sponsored 1954 broadcasts. "I have no inside information to conclude that Harry is through as the Cardinal announcer. I do think his position is very precarious," believed *Southern Illinoisan* columnist Merle Jones.[40] To Jones and others, Caray had two big strikes against him. "Perhaps the biggest rap against Caray is his tendency to try to run the club," Jones wrote. "From the Budweiser standpoint, there is also the question of whether his name has been associated too long with another brand of beer."

In October, the brewery announced that some forty broadcasters from all over the country had applied to announce Cardinals baseball. Out of that search came Buck and Hamilton, two broadcasters hired not to replace Caray, but to work with him. Whatever doubt there was about Harry's future was removed on November 6 when he signed a two-year contract with the brewery. "You can imagine how happy I am about the fact that I will continue to broadcast the Cardinal games," he wrote in a letter (on Anheuser-Busch stationary) a week later.[41]

While Caray's time in limbo was relatively brief (the Cardinals had played their last game of the season on September 27; he signed his new contract forty days later), he blamed his old enemy for leaving him twisting in the wind. Fleishman, he later wrote, "wanted *anybody* but Harry Caray to broadcast games for the St. Louis Cardinals and sell Anheuser-Busch beer." According to Caray, he and Gussie struck a gentleman's agreement to continue broadcasting games near the end of the 1953 season. But Busch soon started having second thoughts. "It began to eat away at Gussie – fueled, I'm sure, by Al Fleishman," Harry believed. What saved Caray was a survey of distributors conducted by Anheuser-Busch. "When the final accounting was done, the distributors had favored Harry Caray by a margin of ten to one," claimed the broadcaster.

Harry got the job with one caveat. He was to do no commercials for the brewery. (That's what Buck and Hamilton were hired to do.) But a kinship began to develop as the two men bonded over beer, baseball, and late-night card games. "Gussie and I really hit it off," said Caray, who couldn't resist adding a jab at his rival. "I'm sure this provoked a certain amount of jealousy and bad feelings from people who wanted to have – but didn't have – this kind of relationship with him." The relationship between executive and announcer gave Gussie confidence that Harry could pitch his products. "We want you selling our beer!" Busch soon told him, forgetting his earlier dictate. "That's what we hired you for!"

Hired to sell beer and broadcast games, Caray also had other jobs offered to him or foisted on him by his boss. In the summer of 1964, Busch had Caray play middleman in his attempt to hire a new manager. Unhappy with the team's performance under Johnny Keane, Busch heard Caray interview Leo Durocher (a coach with the Dodgers at the time) before a game with the Cardinals. Caray soon got a call from Busch with instructions to deliver Durocher to Grant's Farm the next morning. "This is an order," Busch told him. "That's all there is to it!"

Gussie and Leo had a history. Before the brewery bought the Cardinals, the one-time Gashouse Gang captain was one of the few ballplayers that Busch knew, through a group known as the "Bastard Club."[42] Described by Durocher as "a very small and exclusive club with a membership consisting of perhaps twenty-five of the most distinguished businessmen and bankers of the city and … well, me," the group had one function. "A dinner was given every week, on a rotating basis, with he whose turn it was to be the Bastard taking over one of the better restaurants or private clubs and picking up the tab for a sumptuous meal," Leo wrote in his autobiography. "That was my relationship with Gussie Busch."[43]

A social relationship was about to become a business one, or so Durocher thought. After an hour-long meeting with the Cardinals president, the two men shook hands on a deal to manage the team in 1965. Although he had served as a liaison, Caray claimed he wanted no part of it. "I like Johnny Keane and don't want to get involved," Harry said he told Leo afterward. Durocher told a different story.[44] "Harry was simply overjoyed when I told him what happened," Leo remembered. "He couldn't have been happier." (Caray would later call Durocher his favorite manager. "If I had one game to win and my life depended upon it, I would want Leo as my manager.")[45]

The confidential meeting soon became an open secret. "Durocher refused to talk on the possibility he might become the next manager of the Cardinals. Durocher slammed down the phone and refused to give out any information when contacted by the *Associated Press*," the wire service reported in September. Someone was leaking.

Holy Cow St. Louis!

The Durocher hire never happened because the Cardinals rallied under Keane to win the pennant. When Keane bolted to the Yankees following a victorious World Series (in large part because of the Durocher reports), an embarrassed Busch made a face-saving move by hiring Red Schoendienst to manage the team. (Publicly, Busch conceded nothing. "I think that if I had to do everything over, I'd have done exactly what I did," he said of the 1964 season at the annual Knights of the Cauliflower Ear dinner the following spring.)[46]

It wasn't his only personnel mistake that season. Busch had fired general manager Devine in August when the team was struggling. Caray claimed Busch offered him the position. He turned it down because he'd have to take a cut in pay. There was also a second reason. "I'd wind up getting fired," Harry told Gussie.

By the end of 1964, the thought of Harry losing *any* job with the Cardinals was simply inconceivable. That year, Caray completed his twentieth season calling Cardinals baseball, a team celebrating its first World Series title under Anheuser-Busch. Both the ballclub and the brewery sat at the top of the heap, and Caray was an enthusiastic employee and backer of both. He even defended the decision to fire the man who assembled the championship talent. "The evidence points strongly to the fact that Gussie Busch's dismissal of Devine was the psychological hot-foot that turned a sleeping Redbird into a fighting tiger," he wrote in a column for the *Globe-Democrat* after the World Series.[47]

Caray was a survivor, successfully transitioning from Griesedieck to Anheuser-Busch and withstanding internal challenges from Fleishman, Toomey, and other insiders upset about the broadcaster's behavior. Most importantly, he had the confidence and backing of the man who signed his paychecks. Caray, for his part, had respect, bordering on awe, for his boss. "If there was one man who deserved to live forever," Caray would later say, "it was Gussie Busch."

Under Busch's leadership, the company's market share nearly doubled in the ten years starting in 1958. In the summer of 1968, Anheuser-Busch reported record sales and earnings.[48] Both his brewery and his baseball team had become the 800-pound gorillas of their industry. "Wherever the Cardinals go, the subject of their salaries always arouses a brisk debate. Some highly placed baseball people believe that by paying so well the Cardinals are undermining the very structure of baseball," wrote William Leggett in *Sports Illustrated* the week of the World Series.

On the morning of October 7, 1968, Busch and Caray found themselves yet again up on top of the beer and baseball worlds. The previous day, St. Louis defeated Detroit 10-1 to take a commanding lead in the Fall Classic. Tigers pitcher Denny McLain, baseball's first 30-game winner since Dizzy Dean, didn't make it out of the third inning. Bob Gibson went the distance, allowing just five hits from the mound and hitting a home run at the plate. Lou Brock had three hits: a single, double, and home run, and four RBI. "What Gibson and Brock and the rest of the Cardinals did was leave the Tigers the almost impossible task of coming back from a 3-1 deficit," noted an AP dispatch. Sportswriters declared the Series all but over. "The Humane Society is trying to cancel today's fifth, and no doubt, final game," wrote John Hall in the *Los Angeles Times*. One more victory and the Cardinals would celebrate their third title of the decade and become the first National League team to repeat since John McGraw's New York Giants of the 1920s.

From the television booth, Caray was broadcasting his third World Series to a national audience. While Harry relished the opportunity to do something denied him in the 1940s, his many vociferous critics had other ideas. "Caray talks too much," wrote *Detroit Free Press* media critic Bettelou Peterson. "At one point in the first game, he said, 'I find myself not wanting to say a word.' There was a unanimous shout of 'then shutup' from around our TV set." *Fort Lauderdale News* columnist Bill Bondurant called Caray a "blatant homer" and his commentary "horribly trite and dreary." Home-state critics were just as tough. "Give me Jack Buck. Give me Mel Allen. Even give me [Cincinnati Reds broadcaster] Waite Hoyt. But please spare me any more Harry Caray," said *Springfield News-Leader* sports editor Dave Schultz.

Tough talk from media detractors was nothing new for Caray. He heard it during the previous World Series: "The National League's foremost flag waver," declared *Los Angeles Times* columnist Don Page. He also heard it back in 1964. "Caray was recruited from the radio ranks for the game and kept forgetting he was not on audio," wrote Vince Leonard in the *Pittsburgh Press*.[49]

Harry's unique style ("He's the last of the umpiring broadcasters and the first of the broadcasting managers," noted one writer)[50] had always brought a certain number of complaints, but what began changing was *who* was registering them. As the GI generation faded from baseball rosters, a new wave of talent had no qualms about telling people exactly what it thought of Harry's commentary. "To hell with Tomato-face," wrote one-time Cardinals pitcher Jim Brosnan. "Why is there no way to tell fans about announcers, while they tell everybody about us?" asked Cardinals pitcher Tracy Stallard in 1965. "Caray just doesn't second-guess us. He ridicules us and runs some of us into the ground."[51] Harry's favorite target, many believed, was third baseman Ken Boyer. Both Broeg and Buck thought it all started with Caray broadcasting a game in the Los Angeles Coliseum at field level. When Boyer refused Caray's request for an in-game interview, Harry felt slighted and took his revenge with biting on-air commentary.⁵² Caray's criticism of players, in turn, impacted fan behavior. "Boyer – you remember him, he's the guy the folks boo at Busch Stadium because they think he never hits at the right time," wrote *Post-Dispatch* reporter Ed Wilks in the summer of 1964, the same year the Cardinals third baseman won the National League MVP award.⁵³

"The difference between Harry and I is that where Caray is 'emotionally' critical ... I can be 'coldly' critical," said Broeg. "In other words, I have that X Key on my typewriter and Harry has nothing between the microphone and his feelings of the moment."⁵⁴

This lack of a filter is something else Caray shared with his boss. Both men had risen to the top of their professions with sharp tongues and sharper elbows. Both men jealously guarded their kingdoms. Caray hated sharing a microphone. Busch hated ceding power. "He had a way of throwing tantrums and threatening people when he didn't get what he wanted," a Busch family member once admitted. Both men had large egos. "I'm the best baseball announcer in the country," Harry once told the *Wall Street Journal*.⁵⁵ With Gussie and Trudy prepared for their second wedding ceremony, Busch took instructions in the Catholic faith. "Why?" asked Bob Griesedieck. "Gussie already thinks he's God."⁵⁶

Both men also had their enemies.

During the difficult decade of the 1970s, Gussie's team lost its shine and its president lost his way. "He was never the same," after the passing of his youngest daughter, Fleishman believed. A boardroom coup engineered by his son, August Busch III, came just five months later. Ousted as CEO of Anheuser-Busch, Gussie remained in charge of the ballclub.

For Caray, the downfall would come even sooner. Harry never got another opportunity to celebrate a World Series victory. Just days after the Cardinals took a 3-1 lead against the Tigers, it was Detroit who claimed the championship.

One month later, Harry would be in critical condition in the hospital with two broken legs. One year later, Harry would be out of a job. Something had soured in his most important business relationship.

It turned out Harry didn't have to take the GM position to get fired. What Gussie wants, Gussie most often gets.

---

[1] Hernon and Ganey, *Under The Influence*.

[2] Ibid. Elizabeth Busch received a $450,000 gross alimony payment, a property settlement of $480,000, and the Busch home and furnishings, valued at $100,000, for a total of $1,030,000.

[3] *St. Louis Post-Dispatch*, February 22, 1998.
[4] Hernon and Ganey, *Under The Influence*.
[5] Wolfe and Castle, *I Remember Harry Caray*.
[6] Stone, *Where's Harry?*
[7] Hernon and Ganey, *Under The Influence*.
[8] *St. Louis Post-Dispatch,* June 11, 2012. While LBJ was at Grant's Farm in 1960, Busch called Fleishman, who arranged a Johnson interview with Howard B. Woods, the editor of the *St. Louis Argus*. Woods was the same man who had argued with Caray after his "Sambo" comment. In 1965, President Johnson appointed Woods as associate director of the United States Information Agency. He served two years before returning to St. Louis to launch the *St. Louis Sentinel,* a weekly publication. Woods died of an apparent heart attack in 1976 at the age of 59 while attending a National Urban League convention in Boston. *New York Times*, August 4, 1976. Bob Goddard, who wrote the "In Our Town" column for the *Globe-Democrat*, once profiled Woods for the paper, rare attention given to a black man in 1951 St. Louis. At the time, Woods was city editor of the *Argus*, broadcast nightly news and commentary for radio station WTMV and was a stringer correspondent for *Ebony* magazine. He was also active in several community organizations, including serving as chairman of the board of the Mound City Press Club. *St. Louis Globe-Democrat*, November 20, 1951.
[9] "The only other regular black baseball announcer [beside Brock] is Bill White of the Yankees," wrote columnist Joe LaPointe. "Harry is one of the true pros; he uses the show-biz technique," said Brock. "There is only one Harry." *Detroit Free Press*, August 28, 1981. "I was a broadcaster in St. Louis when Brock played there," Caray told reporters. "He's a good friend." *Chicago Tribune*, June 21, 1981.
[10] *Springfield Leader and Press* and *Kansas City Star*, March 19, 1967.
[11] *Chicago Tribune*, August 1, 1986.
[12] *St. Louis Post-Dispatch*, June 1, 2008.
[13] Hernon and Ganey, *Under The Influence*.
[14] Busch's first wife, Marie, died of pneumonia in 1930.
[15] *St. Louis Post-Dispatch*, January 24, 1988.
[16] Groups from Houston and Milwaukee made bids for the Cardinals. With backing from former Browns owner Don Barnes, Browns vice president Bill DeWitt reportedly tried to buy the team. *Detroit Free Press*, February 22, 1953.
[17] Calhoun, president of the St. Louis Union Trust Co., and Hickok, executive vice president of First National Bank, represented Anheuser-Busch in negotiations with Saigh. Negotiations with the brewery began on February 13, the day Saigh was scheduled to go to New York, reportedly to get league approval to sell the team to a Milwaukee group. *St. Louis Post-Dispatch,* February 20, 1953. Years later, Schoendienst would recall that he and Musial went to Grant's Farm to convince Busch to buy the team.

[18] Ibid, February 21, 1993. Anheuser-Busch paid $2.5 million for the team and assumed $1.25 million in debt. The new owners soon sold off minor-league teams and parks, including flagship properties in Columbus, Houston, and Rochester, generating an estimated $2 million or more in proceeds.

[19] "I'm never two hours away from my business," Busch said in 1970. "My happiness is my business. I eat it, sleep it, dream about it. My family, of course, comes a close second to my love of business." *St. Louis Post-Dispatch*, April 19, 1970.

[20] In a sign of how much had changed in the relationship between the Browns and Cardinals, the brewery negotiated a lease with their new American League tenant at $175,000 a season (an arrangement that wound up only applying to 1953). Four years earlier, the Browns had sued the Cardinals over the previous rental relationship, when the National League tenant was paying $35,000 a year in rent and sharing expenses.

[21] "Busch will be able to write off losses incurred in operating the Cardinals for income-tax purposes in the Anheuser-Busch organization," Johnson believed. "Unless Busch is kicked out of baseball, other breweries are apt to buy clubs." *Wisconsin State Journal*, March 29, 1954.

[22] *St. Louis Post-Dispatch*, February 21, 1993. In 1954, the Cardinals announced plans to broadcast games on radio stations in several minor league cities: Omaha, Houston, Columbus, Wichita, Indianapolis; Burlington, Iowa; Mount Vernon and Paris, Illinois, and Muskogee, Oklahoma. On February 20, Busch announced that those plans had been canceled. Omaha and Wichita were in the Western League. Omaha, Houston, and Columbus all had Cardinal minor-league teams. Johnson was not the only one complaining. Minor league executive George Trautman appeared at a joint meeting of the American and National Leagues to object to the plan. Ibid, February 21, 1954.

[23] Even after the Cardinals dropped the radio plan, Johnson was still pressing ahead with a bill to block large corporations from owning baseball teams or be subject to anti-trust laws. By late May, however, he threw in the towel. "I'm through," he said on May 26. "I closed up shop yesterday." His bill lacked support. "There was some obvious reluctance among [Johnson's] colleagues in the Senate to buy the suggestion that Mr. Busch is a 'menace' to anything," wrote Shirley Povich. *Washington Post,* May 26, 1954.

[24] The expansion and success of Anheuser-Busch "are triumphs of promotion, personality, back-slapping and tail-kicking," wrote Jack Rice. *St. Louis Post-Dispatch*, April 22, 1970.

[25] *New York Times*, April 11, 1965.

[26] *Los Angeles Times*, August 23, 1972.

[27] "I don't understand what's happening all over our great country, on the campuses and everywhere," Busch said in 1970. New York *Daily News,* March 14, 1970.

[28] As a prep school ballplayer, Busch called himself "a terrible second baseman and not much of a hitter, either." In spring training of 1953, "Busch showed up with a retinue that looked like it had been recruited from a P.G. Wodehouse Watch on the Rhine,"

wrote Jack Rice. "Busch wore a baseball uniform and white tennis shoes." *St. Louis Post-Dispatch*, April 20, 1970.

[29] Busch had a variety of uses for his private transportation. "I still remember sitting in the private railroad car carrying birds back to St. Louis from Tampa," Fleishman recalled. The car was "full of vomiting birds." Hernon and Ganey, *Under The Influence*. Time magazine once described Busch's private railroad car as "an 86-ft. stainless-steel, wood-paneled, deep-carpeted, traveling office with a sitting room, four conference rooms, kitchen, bar, an ample supply of Budweiser, and accommodations for eleven." *Time*, July 11, 1955.

[30] *St. Louis Post-Dispatch,* October 27, 1995.

[31] Ibid, November 5, 1995.

[32] Ibid, December 27, 1953.

[33] "The resident Schweitzer at Busch Stadium spurs on the crowd with little more than ceaseless repetitions of a Budweiser jingle," wrote Roger Angell in his book *Season Ticket*. Busch Stadium featured the jingle for many years instead of the traditional "Take Me Out to the Ballgame" during the seventh-inning stretch. It was written by Steve Karmen, described once as "the Don Draper of advertising jingles." The jingle, wrote columnist Benjamin Hochman, is "the unofficial theme song of the Cardinals." *St. Louis Post-Dispatch*, April 11, 2016.

[34] Hernon and Ganey, *Under The Influence.*

[35] Knoedelseder, William. *Bitter Brew: The Rise and Fall of Anheuser-Busch and America's King of Beers*. Harper Business. 2012.

[36] Busch enjoyed a warm relationship with St. Petersburg city leaders, unlike his predecessor. "Saigh did not have a good relationship with the city. In fact, a letter had been drafted by the city inviting the Cardinals to leave," said William Mills Jr., a building consultant and Busch friend. "Then Gussie came down and invited the city leaders to cocktails and lunch with him at the Vinoy [hotel] and every one of them immediately fell in love with the guy." *St. Petersburg Times*, September 30, 1989. That meeting launched the beginning of the Bat Boys Club, a group of St. Petersburg business and civic leaders who would attend a weekend of games in St. Louis every year.

[37] Buck, *Jack Buck.*

[38] Hawks owner Ben Kerner once apologized for making a mistake as Busch's partner in a game of gin-rummy. "Listen, Hawk," Busch told him, "around me, you're allowed no mistakes." *St. Louis Post-Dispatch*, August 28, 1975.

[39] Wolfe and Castle, *I Remember Harry Caray*. As a man who liked cards, guns, and liquor, Gussie was often at odds with old-money St. Louis. Busch was once asked about the scion of another famous St. Louis family. "Those people have become La Dee Da," he replied. La Dee Da to Busch meant "concerned with the arts and other of life's finer things," wrote Bill McClellan, "but La Dee Da was not the way of Gussie Busch." *St. Louis Post-Dispatch*, October 1, 1990.

[40] *Southern Illinoisan,* September 15, 1953.

[41] Fleishman Papers.
[42] "As a free-swinging kid with a salty vocabulary, he [Busch] had known only a few ballplayers, such as Leo Durocher and Frankie Frisch of the Depression-era Gas House Gang," wrote Bob Broeg. *St. Louis Post-Dispatch*, August 28, 1975.
[43] Durocher, Leo with Ed Linn. *Nice Guys Finish Last*. Simon & Schuster. 1975.
[44] Caray waited outside in his car while Durocher and Busch met.
[45] *St. Louis Magazine*, September 1968. Harry counted Durocher, Sinatra and the late Nat King Cole as close friends. "Nat could have been a professional ballplayer and we had a lot to talk about whenever he hit town. He was a great guy."
[46] *St. Louis Post-Dispatch*, April 21, 1965.
[47] *St. Louis Globe-Democrat*, October 21, 1964.
[48] *St. Louis Post-Dispatch,* July 29, 1968.
[49] Near the end of Game 7 against Boston, Red Sox fans in the Fenway Park bleachers began chanting: "Harry Caray is a Bum." *The Wichita Eagle*, October 13, 1967. Caray did have his defenders, none more prominent than *Orlando Star* sports editor Ed Hayes during the 1967 World Series. "Harry Caray is my friend. Even if he were not I would have to speak up. His is a success story. I don't like to see it belittled." *Orlando Star*, October 12, 1967. That same year, Caray served as the voice of a World Series movie. "The film is narrated superbly by Harry Caray," wrote Richard Dozer. *Chicago Tribune*, December 20, 1967. The 1967 World Series was not the first time a Boston sports audience heard Harry describe a local sports team. During the 1964-1965 NBA season, Caray broadcast ten Celtic games over channel 38 in Boston.
[50] Al Dunning was the writer. *Evansville Press,* October 31, 1967.
[51] *Memphis Press-Scimitar*, September 18, 1965.
[52] "That ticked Caray off, and thereafter when Harry got the chance to say something critical about Boyer, he blasted him." Buck, *Jack Buck*.
[53] *St. Louis Post-Dispatch,* July 27, 1964.
[54] *St. Louis Magazine*, September 1968.
[55] *Wall Street Journal*, September 26, 1972.
[56] Hernon and Ganey, *Under The Influence*.

"My Kinda Guy's Gotta Get Fired"

By the fall of 1968, Harry Caray had become a part of the St. Louis establishment. Married to his second wife Marian for sixteen years, the couple's ten-room colonial-style house in the suburb of Ladue featured a heated swimming pool, his haircuts cost $15, and his travel requests always included a hotel suite.[1] In February, the Missouri Society for Crippled Children and Adults named Caray the state's Easter Seal Campaign Chairman, while the National Council on Delinquency and Crime appointed him chairman of the St. Louis Citizens Committee in September. Gone were the days of traveling to broadcast high school football games, judge state fair contests, or serve as the public address announcer for a minor league game or a postseason barnstorming tour. Reunions of the Webster Groves class of 1932 occurred every five years without Caray's presence. "Harry never made himself a part of those celebrations," remembered classmate Chuck Wanner. "I guess when he started to change his age, people got skeptical."[2]

Wrapping up his twenty-fourth season calling Cardinals baseball, Caray was now the dean of National League announcers. Among active broadcasters, only the Chicago White Sox's Bob Elson had been with his team longer.[3] His resume also featured three World Series broadcasts and the 1965 NBA All-Star Game.[4] But a restless Caray was never content to sit idle. His lifetime ambition was "to broadcast a heavyweight title fight," he confessed in the spring of 1968. "I consider myself a better fight announcer than anything else."[5]

It was a year unlike any in the history of St. Louis sports. For the first and only time, the 1967-1968 St. Louis sports calendar featured a local team in each of the four major professional sports leagues. It began with the Cardinals celebrating a seven-game World Series victory over the Red Sox. It ended with the St. Louis Blues in the Stanley Cup finals in their inaugural season. In between, coach Charley Winner's Big Red team finished third in the NFL's Century Division. The football Cardinals won six games, lost seven and tied once in their second season playing in the new downtown Busch Stadium. Richie Guerin's St. Louis Hawks won the NBA's Western Division but were knocked out in the playoffs by the San Francisco Warriors.

The Hawks had started their season by winning 16 of their first 17 games and held first place in their division throughout the season. The quick start didn't translate to increased attendance. "When your team starts with a 16 and 1 record and you have a hard time drawing crowds at home, you have to wonder," said owner Ben Kerner. "It appears the interest is not there."[6] A month after the playoff loss to the Warriors, Kerner sold the team to a group in Atlanta. For the second time in fifteen years, St. Louis had lost a professional sports team.

Average playoff basketball attendance came to roughly 5,000 at Kiel Auditorium around the same time more than 15,000 fans flocked to the Arena to watch Blues hockey. (Kerner turned down the chance to move his basketball team to the larger venue.) The decline in Hawks attendance had started with the arrival of the football Cardinals in 1960, a trend that only accelerated with the arrival of the Blues. "The Hawks, it developed, could stand everything except competition for the sports buck," wrote Broeg.[7]

No professional sports team in America drew more fans than the Cardinals in 1967. Playing their first full season at Busch Stadium II, St. Louis was the only baseball franchise to cross the two-million threshold. Expectations in 1968 ran high – for both attendance and team performance. "Their pitching is impressive, qualitatively and quantitatively; they have power and speed and can't be seriously faulted defensively," wrote Joseph Sheehan in a spring training preview for *The New York Times*. General manager Bing Devine returned for his second stint with a club set on auto-pilot. With the lineup and staff a virtual carbon copy from the previous season, St. Louis led the National League by ten games or more from July 20 to September 21. A 97-win team ended the season nine games ahead of second-place San Francisco. With 22 victories and a 1.12 ERA, Bob Gibson claimed both the Cy Young and National League MVP awards.

In case anyone hadn't gotten the memo, Caray took delight in reminding people that the 1968 Cardinals were good – really good. After the Cardinals beat the Dodgers on July 14 to make it 11 wins in 12 games, Caray announced, "the magic number is 66."

Harry was not alone in his assessment of the club. "This present Cardinal team will mold the greatest dynasty in the club's history," said a former player with firsthand experience in greatness. "I don't ever want to sound like a pop-off just because we are winning and in first place," Stan Musial said that summer, "but this is truly an amazing club."[8]

A dynastic performance brought increased media scrutiny for the Cardinals, and for the first time in a while, for Harry. Master impressionist and Caray friend, Mickey McTague, profiled the broadcaster for the September issue of *St. Louis* magazine. "In sharp contrast to his radio personality, Harry is soft-spoken, somewhat withdrawn, and presents a demeanor that could almost be described by one who doesn't know him that well, as being shy," he wrote.

A more outgoing and assertive Caray presented himself on the pages of *Sports Illustrated* the following month. Writer Myron Cope captured a Harry full of bravado and bluster. Caray revisited his old battles with a former manager. "Stanky was very unpopular with the fans, and the reason he was unpopular was me." He was unapologetic for criticizing players: "I refuse to fool the audience. These ballclub-controlled announcers think they can, but they're crazy." And he defended his many mentions of small-town visitors at the ballpark. "If I got a guy here from Timbuktu, I'll help him be proud of Timbuktu. I told [Al] Fleishman, 'Class, my ass.'"[9]

It would be a story that Caray would come to regret. "I'm convinced that the beginning of the end for me was the *Sports Illustrated* article about me," Harry told the *Post-Dispatch* in 1974. "It showed the close friendship between me and Gussie. And when an employee gets too close to the boss, somebody in the hierarchy gets upset. They go gunning for you." He told a similar story to the *Chicago Tribune* a year later. "Caray says insiders got worried [after the article appeared], and longtime nemesis Al Fleishman, an Anheuser-Busch public relations man, led a movement to kick him off the Budweiser bandwagon," wrote Clifford Terry.[10]

While the *Sports Illustrated* story captured a mischievous and humorous side of the relationship between broadcaster and brewer (Gussie had given Harry a Sicilian donkey, much to Caray's dismay),[11] its larger point dealt with Harry's independent streak ("Harry Has His Own Ways" was the title) and the perception of his influence over the team. "Caray plays cards with Gussie, doesn't he?" one St. Louis sportswriter said to Cope. When Cardinals public relations director Bob Harlan spoke at an event in southern Illinois, a fan asked him if it was Caray who persuaded the team to trade Ray Sadecki to San Francisco for Orlando Cepeda. "Nobody laughed either," Harlan said. But according to the team president, the rhetoric didn't match reality. How much influence did Harry really have? "Not a damn bit," said Busch. If he were to consult Caray on a deal, "Harry probably would blab the trade all over town," Gussie stated.[12]

Nevertheless, the conspiracy theory floated by Caray would be one of many speculations Harry and others offered to explain the broadcaster's departure from St. Louis. Except for a juicy rumor involving Harry and the wife of August Busch III (more on that later), these various explanations have largely been forgotten. Far more illuminating from the standpoint of October of 1968 – *before* twelve of the most tumultuous months of Caray's career – is the insight into Harry's thinking at the time. "I can't tell you how many times I've been this close to getting fired," Caray said while pinching together his thumb and forefinger. "In the baseball business I'm the last of the nonconformists," he told Cope. "I feel that eventually, in this day and age, my kind of guy's gotta get fired."

*****

"There is no tomorrow," Harry told a national television audience on the afternoon of October 10, 1968. Almost one year to the day – October 9, 1969 – others would say the same about Caray and his relationship with the Cardinals.

Harry's comments came late in the seventh game of the World Series after the Detroit Tigers scored three runs and took a lead they would never relinquish. In a stunning turn of events, Detroit won three straight games against St. Louis – the last two in Busch Stadium – to defeat a Cardinals team many believed was invincible. For several Cardinals of the late 1960s, the bitter memories would linger. Decades later, sportswriter Mike Lupica asked Tim McCarver, "How long does it take you to get over something like the '68 World Series?" Smoking a cigar in the press room with his reading glasses on, McCarver paused, removed his glasses, and said quietly, "You never get over it."[13]

Harry turned the page to his fall and winter sports calendar. In several respects, 1968 was remarkably similar to many other years of Caray's St. Louis career. In January, baseball's senior umpire, Albert Barlick, who would later be elected to the Hall of Fame, recalled missing two seasons because of heart trouble. In the hospital, the Springfield, Illinois native listened to Cubs and Cardinals games on the radio. "I had to turn off the Cards games, though, because Harry Caray's umpiring of balls and strikes shook me."[14] In May, Harry claimed a survey showed even Cubs fans preferred his broadcasts. "When the Cubs are playing the Cardinals, 85 percent of the Cubs fans are listening to our broadcast," he boasted.[15] In September, Caray's comments landed him in hot water with organized labor. Broadcasting a Cardinals-Reds game in Cincinnati, an airplane flew over the field with a banner reading, "Don't buy California grapes." Unaware of an ongoing labor boycott of the product, Caray blurted out, "What's wrong with California grapes?" and added, "Right after the game, I'm going out to buy California grapes." The comments sparked an immediate response from the St. Louis president of the local labor council, who wrote letters to both Busch and Bob Hyland at KMOX. "Editorializing on issues doesn't seem to be an imminent part of a baseball broadcast," wrote Oscar Ehrhardt.[16] "I'll never again say anything about grapes," Harry said after being told of Ehrhardt's complaints.[17]

Cantankerous, cocky, and as controversial as ever, Harry remained in St. Louis as the Cardinals took off in late October for a five-week, eighteen-game tour of Japan. Fall Saturdays meant Mizzou Tigers football with Caray behind the microphone for KMOX.

But there was now one glaring hole in his calendar for the upcoming months. For years, Harry had done basketball play-by-play, first for St. Louis University and then for the St. Louis Hawks. His tenure with the Billikens ended in the early 1960s. Harry repeatedly clashed with John Benington, who had replaced longtime Billikens coach Eddie Hickey. Caray found Benington's style of basketball dull. "I told him to his face," Harry recalled. "With a popular pro team in town and a fresh memory of Hickey, I told him his teams should run more. It was Benington who developed the friction between us, not me."[18]

Switching from college to the longer NBA season meant Harry was busier than ever. An example from March of 1968 illustrated his hectic schedule. On a Saturday afternoon, Caray called a Cardinals spring training game in St. Petersburg, flew to Chicago for a Hawks broadcast that evening, and returned to Florida in time for the Sunday Cardinals game.[19] But with the Hawks now in Atlanta, he no longer had those additional responsibilities.

On November 2, with Caray calling the action from the press box at Faurot Field, the Missouri Tigers defeated the Oklahoma State Cowboys 42-7 in Big 8 football action. He didn't know it then, but Harry had just done his last play-by-play broadcast of the year.

Coach Dan Devine's squad would finish the season ranked ninth in the country, capping off an 8-3 campaign with a 35-10 victory over Alabama in the Gator Bowl. At the end-of-season football banquet, lineman Ed Taylor reflected on a year that saw the assassination of Dr. Martin Luther King, race riots and campus unrest across the country. "All blacks are concerned about their situation," he said. "But, black is beautiful here – not because it's feared, because it's loved."[20] Jack Buck emceed the event in Columbia that evening, an assignment Caray would have normally drawn.[21] But Harry was in a St. Louis hospital, where he'd been recovering from a serious accident since early November. "The accident? Harry was drunk at the time," Buck laughingly recalled years later before turning serious. "It damned near killed him. I thought he was dead – damned near everyone did."

*****

Returning to St. Louis from Columbia on November 2, Caray tuned in to KMOX radio to hear the St. Louis Blues hockey game about to begin. He decided to stop by the Arena, watch some hockey, and call a friend to meet for dinner. "We went out to a nice dinner, and afterward decided to go to the Chase-Park

Plaza Hotel for a nightcap," Harry recalled in his autobiography. Years earlier, speaking to a *Chicago Tribune* reporter, Caray had a more detailed and honest answer regarding his activities that evening. Harry and his "friend" were having an affair. "The hotel parking lot was filled and I ended up parking on the far side of Kingshighway across from the hotel. The owner is a good friend of mine and I had the keys to several suites. I would use whichever ones were vacant. This night, however, all were full and I had to pick up keys for a different suite. I told my lady friend to wait in the car for five minutes while I got the keys and then I'd meet her at the elevator. We'd done this a few times before."[22]

With his lady friend watching from the car, Harry started to cross the street to the hotel around 1:30 a.m. on Sunday in conditions he later described as "driving rain." He never made it. In the middle of the northbound lanes of Kingshighway, Caray was struck by a car. The driver, 21-year-old Michael Poliquin, told police he saw Harry but could not stop because of the wet pavement. The collision left Caray with a broken and dislocated shoulder, cuts to his face, and compound fractures to both legs.

"I'm out of the car and it's raining like the devil. I look to my left until I get to the middle of the street. Then I turn my head to pick up the traffic coming the other way ... well, that's the last I remember until five days later," Harry recalled in 1972. "Anyway, a kid 21 years old, driving a 1953 Plymouth, no driver's license, no insurance, who'd just returned from Vietnam that morning, and just got engaged that afternoon, came zipping around the corner and knocked me 40 feet in the air."

He provided additional details to the paper six years later. "I probably would have died, but a guy driving a Goodwill truck had stopped and put blankets over me to protect against the rain," Harry remembered while also supplying fresh information about the driver. "A young kid who'd just gotten back from Vietnam that morning and who'd gotten engaged that noon had been drinking ever since. He was dead drunk, driving without a license, without insurance, in a driving rain, and he hit me head-on."[23]

The item about the driver being "dead drunk" was classic Caray storytelling, an additional detail that makes a good story even better, but without any facts to back it up. An official incident document (obtained by Caray biographer Don Zminda) showed "nothing in the police report to corroborate this." Authorities did issue Poliquin (driving a Chevrolet, not a Plymouth) a citation for failing to produce a driver's license, but he was allowed to drive off after speaking to the police. Caray received a ticket for jaywalking across Kingshighway. While his injuries were serious – the report stated he was "thrown approximately 35 feet" – Harry was conscious and alert by Monday morning. His condition was upgraded from critical to fair a little more than 24 hours after the incident.

Caray spent nearly two months under the care of St. Louis doctors and nurses, first at City Hospital and then at Barnes. As Harry recovered, thousands of letters and cards poured in from across the country and around the world. Caray received mail and gifts from 37 different states and five foreign countries. The more than fifty-thousand well-wishers included a former Cardinals pitcher who once called him "Tomato-Face."[24]

"I got the nicest letter from Jim [Brosnan]," Caray said. "He wrote, 'You perhaps contribute more to keeping baseball alive than anyone else in the business.'" Harry also received a message written in braille that wasn't deciphered for more than a half-century. The letter later hung on a wall next to Caray's Chicago office. Curious about its contents, Grant DePorter, the owner of Harry Caray's restaurant group, posted a picture of it on Facebook in 2021 and asked for help translating the message typically interpreted by sight-impaired people. A reader saw the plea, opened the photo, and submitted it to an online Braille translator. "Dear Mr. Caray," the translation revealed. "I was so sorry to hear about your accident. I hope you get well soon. Your broadcast of the World Series made it more interesting for me," it read in part. It was signed by "Miss Stephanie Gibson" of Talladega, Alabama.[25]

The many visitors to his room at Barnes Hospital's Queeny Towers included Susan Busch.[26] She was the wife of August Busch III, a brewery executive and the son of the Cardinals president. The couple, married since 1963, would divorce a year later.[27] Both Susan and Harry would later face questions from the media about their relationship during this period.

"She was a volunteer in the hospital three days a week, like a lot of society gals are. And because of her troubles with her husband and because he was away so much, she'd prefer to go to the hospital. My family would be there ... my children," Caray said in 1972. "It was just the idea she could play cards with a friend or have somebody to talk to. So people began making something out of her frequent visits."[28]

If the relationship with Susan Busch helped cause Caray's downfall in St. Louis, as he later suspected, there was no immediate indication that it created any issues for her father-in-law. Released from the hospital shortly before Christmas, Caray continued his rehabilitation at Gussie's Florida home, where he had a nurse, a wheelchair, and broadcast equipment that allowed him to resume his daily radio program. He returned to St. Louis in February to have the casts removed, and by the end of spring training, Caray pronounced himself ready for this twenty-fifth baseball season. "The doctors practically had to rebuild my leg bones. They said I'd be in casts for six months. Well, I got out in four, and now I'm off crutches and walking even without a cane. Oh, I carry that cane there, but it's just for protection."[29]

Caray may have been ready for the season to begin. Whether the Cardinals were prepared was a separate issue. The 1968 season had been especially long, even for a World Series team. The Cardinals won 13 and lost 5 in their tour of Japan, playing their last game on November 21. Lineup regulars Curt Flood and Mike Shannon played in every single Asian contest. Pitchers Bob Gibson and Steve Carlton each pitched four times, combining to throw 31 innings. Players had only about 90 days from the time they returned to American soil until they had to be in Florida to prepare for another season.

It was a spring training to forget. In the middle of March, Flood's brother was charged with robbing a jewelry store in St. Louis and stealing a police cruiser. Police arrested Carl Flood and Earl Harris after firing shots at the vehicle, causing it to swerve into a light standard. That same month, manager Red Schoendienst was hospitalized with severe abdominal pain, physical director Walter Eberhardt had a heart attack, traveling secretary Leo Ward suffered a slight stroke, and catcher Dave Ricketts was diagnosed with a hairline fracture of his right thumb. The month was capped off by a lecture on player salaries delivered by Gussie Busch. "The speech demoralized the 1969 Cardinals," believed outfielder Flood. (Flood was injured that spring, resulting from an accidental spiking at second base. With a deep gash in his right thigh, he received a tetanus shot and stitches.)[30]

The Cardinals returned home to St. Louis in early April, playing the first season under new commissioner Bowie Kuhn. The night before the opener, Caray was honored at the Knights of the Cauliflower Banquet. (The same event where Buck said, "Please drive carefully. Harry's walking again.") Gussie introduced the Cardinals broadcaster, telling the crowd, "I like Jack Buck much better, but 25 years is a long time to be with the Browns and Cardinals – here's a Holy Cow for 25 years: a pair of cuff links." A humbled and reflective Harry told the gathering of 600 people, "If it ended right now, I'd be tickled to death."

The bombastic and dramatic Harry resurfaced the next day. The man who admired Walter Winchell, once drank beer at Graceland with Elvis Presley, and always reminded his friend Frank Sinatra that he was the younger of the two, had always considered himself an entertainer. In Chicago, Harry displayed his sense of theater by singing "Take Me Out to the Ballgame." When he started performing it for the White Sox, Jimmy Piersall stood up to join him. "Sit down, kid," Caray told his broadcast partner. "This is my act." With the Cubs, Steve Stone would take Harry's scorebook and phonetically spell out the names of

Cubs players such as Hector Villanueva. Caray ignored the guide and butchered names early and often. "He knew if he stumbled over the names, it was funny," Stone recalled.

This intuitive grasp of what his audience expected and enjoyed was first perfected in St. Louis. Introduced to the opening day crowd of nearly 40,000, Harry walked onto the field with two canes. He quickly cast one aside, much to the delight of the fans. As he made his way to the field microphone, he tossed the other one to the ground. Now the multitudes were on their collective feet, chanting "Har-ree ... Har-ree ..." Caray had turned the results of a nearly-fatal accident into a memorable crowd-pleasing moment.

After the ceremony, a confused Bob Gibson grabbed Caray as he walked off the field. "Harry, what the hell was that all about? You haven't used those canes for weeks now!"

"Hey Gibby, it's like I always told you, pal," Harry replied. "This just isn't baseball, it's show-biz."

A show-biz act that would be his St. Louis curtain call. A season that began with a standing ovation at Busch Stadium would end with a quiet phone call to a downtown bar.

---

[1] *St. Louis Globe-Democrat*, March 3, 1969.

[2] *Rocky Mountain News,* February 21, 1998.

[3] *The Sporting News,* February 3, 1968. In an article on the career of Cleveland Indians broadcaster Jimmy Dudley, the story noted that "only Bob Elson of the White Sox, Russ Hodges of the Giants, and Harry Caray of the Cardinals have been around longer." Hodges left the Yankees for the Giants after the 1948 season. He replaced Frankie Frisch. Jack Brickhouse did some announcing for the Cubs during World War II but only had been doing their broadcasts on a continuous basis since 1948.

[4] The game was played at Kiel Auditorium in St. Louis. Anheuser-Busch had purchased the television and radio rights. Caray and Bill Sharman did the television broadcast. Hawks play-by-play announcer Jerry Gross called the game on radio.

[5] *Alton Evening Telegraph*, April 23, 1968.

[6] *St. Louis Post-Dispatch,* May 4, 1968.

[7] Despite the attendance struggles, the Hawks made Kerner a wealthy man. "He was helped immeasurably ... by a generous radio-television contract from Anheuser-Busch," Broeg wrote. "Gin-rummy partner Gussie Busch leaned over backward to retain a radio-TV package that apparently wasn't justified by either the ratings or by the most painful evidence of diminishing interest..." Kerner sold the team for an estimated $3 million or more. Ibid, May 5, 1968.

[8] *The Sporting News*, July 6, 1968.

[9] Cope wrote that representatives from Fleishman-Hillard "scowl" when Harry mentioned out-of-town visitors, "calculating that for every fan Caray mentions he offends 20 others." *Sports Illustrated*, October 7, 1968.

[10] *Chicago Tribune*, August 3, 1975.

[11] The donkey cost Caray $1,380 for a corral, shed, harness and rig and between $45 and $55 a month to feed. It constantly kicked the shed. Busch was ready to send him a second one as a companion. "Forget it!" said Harry. *Sports Illustrated*, October 7, 1968.

[12] What did Gussie Busch know about baseball? Harry asked in his autobiography (quoting a passage from Murray Polner's biography of Branch Rickey). "For a lot of years, many people asked that same question. Some of them were guys who were jealous of the friendship and rapport that Gussie and I had developed. So, too, often their answer to the question was something like, "He knows what Harry Caray tells him," Caray wrote before adding, "Well, to be frank, that was a lot of bull."

[13] New York *Daily News*, October 19, 1996.

[14] *Herald and Review* (Decatur, IL), January 23, 1968. A 1961 *Sporting News* poll of managers and coaches named Barlick the most respected umpire in the National League. Barlick accompanied the Cardinals on their five-week tour of Japan after the 1968 season.

[15] *The Wichita Eagle*, May 29, 1968.

[16] Grape growers had refused to enter collective bargaining agreements with migratory farm workers. *The Commercial Appeal*, September 6, 1968.

[17] In 1996, Harry had a long conversation on the air with Steve Stone about seedless grapes. "Can you imagine?" said Harry. "Seedless grapes. What a thing."

[18] "I don't understand what happened to Billiken basketball," Harry said in 1969. "It used to be such a big part of the community." *St. Louis Globe-Democrat*, March 3, 1969.

[19] *St. Petersburg Times,* March 10, 1968.

[20] *St. Louis Post-Dispatch*, December 10, 1968.

[21] Until his stroke in 1987, Harry loved telling reporters he had never missed a game. While he hadn't missed a *baseball* game, he was absent from the last three 1968 regular season Mizzou football games and the bowl game.

[22] *Chicago Tribune*, August 18, 1978. The Chase-Park Plaza was owned at the time by Harold Koplar. Koplar's father, Sam, was the designer and builder of the Park Plaza hotel. (It merged with the Chase in 1961.) Harry liked to give Chicago reporters the impression that he was a single man years before his second divorce. "He seems to like the single life," wrote Stephanie Fuller in the *Tribune* in September 1971. Caray wrote in his autobiography that he and his second wife were estranged when he was released from the hospital in December of 1968. But it would be nearly four years later (November of 1972) before Marian Caray filed for divorce.

[23] Ibid. Caray told Ian Thomsen of the *Boston Globe* that doctors contemplated amputating one of his shattered legs. "I would have died had they done that," Caray said. *Boston Globe*, June 22, 1984.

[24] The fifty-thousand figure comes from the *Globe-Democrat* in 1969. In 1972, Harry told a *Chicago Tribune* reporter that the brewery answered more than two-hundred-thousand pieces of mail.

[25] *Loop North News*, June 28, 2021. https://www.loopnorth.com/news/braille0628.htm

[26] Harry wrote in his autobiography that he had so many visitors to his hospital room, "It was like a nightclub in there."

[27] The former Miss Susan Hornibrook was profiled by the *Post-Dispatch* during the 1967 World Series. "Girl Who Knew Little of Baseball Is Now Card's Luck Charm," read the title. She was described as "a former model who joined the clan almost accidentally four years ago." She called Gussie "big brother," and he called her "his good luck charm." A Los Angeles native, she met her future husband when he was in California for a business trip in 1962. *St. Louis Post-Dispatch*, October 8, 1967.

[28] *Chicago Tribune*, August 13, 1972.

[29] *The Gazette* (Cedar Rapids, Iowa), April 9, 1969.

[30] The day after receiving the tetanus shot and stitches, Flood overslept and missed a promotional banquet. He was fined $250. "I protested angrily," he wrote in his autobiography. Flood, *The Way It Is*.

The Summer of '69

The year 1969 saw men from planet Earth walk on the moon, the Beatles give their last performance as a group in London, and the first ATM launch in Rockville Center, New York. Nineteen-sixty-nine was the year of Chappaquiddick and Charles Manson,[1] of long-shot underdogs and improbable upsets. Joe Namath and the New York Jets claimed the first Super Bowl for the upstart American Football League, while the New York Mets, in only their eighth season, won a World Series. The year marked the beginning of Richard Nixon's presidency and the end of Mickey Mantle's career. The same summer Cooperstown saluted Stan Musial, baseball celebrated its 100th anniversary.

A century after the Cincinnati Red Stockings became baseball's first professional team, "the game faced a crossroads," wrote *1969* author Rob Kirkpatrick. "As the decade neared its end, many sports fans felt that football, or even basketball, threatened to replace baseball as America's pastime." Responding to the threat, owners forced out Commissioner William Eckert and replaced him with Kuhn, lowered the pitching mound to resuscitate the game's moribund offense (Bob Gibson, at 1.12, was one of seven pitchers with a sub-2 ERA the previous season), experimented with a "designated pinch-hitter" in spring training (the American League adopted the DH in 1973, nearly a half-century before the National League), expanded to four new cities and added divisions to each league. (St. Lous was one of six teams in the newly formed National League East.)

"We no longer have a monopoly," Cardinals president Busch told his players in spring training. "People are turning out in droves to watch hockey. And millions are packing the football stadiums."[2] In February of 1969, owners averted a potential players' strike by agreeing to increased pension benefits. The agreement called for owners to raise their contribution to the plan from $4.1 million to $5.45 million for the next three years.[3] Strike threats and increased costs were very much on Busch's mind when he spoke to the team. "We are beginning to lose sight of who really has to pay the ultimate bill for your salary and your pension, namely the fan. And when we do that, I think we have a problem," said Gussie.

"Most fans have had a steady diet of strike talk and dollar signs ... too many fans are saying our players are getting fat," Busch told the club. "Fans are telling us now that if we intend to raise prices to pay for the high salaries, they will stop coming to the games." Busch had found particularly galling comments by Gibson regarding a possible strike and Flood's contract demand for the new season: $100,000, "and I don't mean $99,999.99," he stated.[4] (He would settle for $90,000.)

Gussie, who reminded his team that it had "the biggest payroll in the entire history of baseball," had one final warning for his players. "You can bet on one thing: The fans will be looking at you this year more critically than ever before to watch how you perform and to see whether or not you are really giving everything you have."

Busch had other reasons to be in a foul mood in 1969. In May, brewery workers went on strike at all seven Anheuser-Busch plants. The thirty-four-day walkout lasted until late June. When the company reported financial results in July, it announced that second-quarter revenue plunged $37 million compared to the prior-year period. The loss represented an estimated $12 million, or 53 cents a share, in earnings.[5] During the strike, labor leader Robert Lewis blamed August Busch III for the breakdown in labor relations. "Unless young Busch's activities are curbed, there will be nothing left of this great company. He is directly responsible for the conditions that led to this strike."[6]

Like his father, August III had other worries on his mind. He and his wife Susan separated in February and she filed for divorce that summer, a split that was made official in November. Amid marital strife, the brewery labor agreement was reached, a settlement August found so upsetting he walked into his father's office with a resignation letter. Gussie reportedly stared at it for a few moments before looking up to address his son. "I'll give you another chance because you're a Busch, but if you ever do something like this again, I'll see that the *Post-Dispatch* has your resignation letter within five minutes."[7]

Escalating costs. Labor unrest. Management frustration. Spousal spats. This was the atmosphere in the summer of 1969 in the headquarters of the company that would soon decide Harry Caray's fate.

*****

As baseball owners struggled to comprehend the shifting winds of the late 1960s cultural zeitgeist, the new era presented challenges for the men who covered the teams on a daily basis.

"The world was changing because of drugs, civil rights actions, and the anti-war movement, and baseball players were caught up in all those activities just like everybody else from their age group," Jack Buck said of the post-1968 Cardinals. "There were times when I didn't enjoy being around that group of players. Once at O'Hare Airport in Chicago, we got off the plane and walked through the terminal. The players were carrying music boxes, wearing sandals and T-shirts. One of the players was wearing Levi's without undershorts and had a hole in the seat of his pants. I remember thinking, 'These are the Cardinals?' Almost all of them had long hair, some wore earrings. Other ballclubs were just as motley looking, depending on their leadership and the control the manager and owner had over the players."[8]

On the other side of this generational gap, players had objections of their own and grappled with things they couldn't understand. In 1968, most owners refused to "rearrange their schedule for the days of mourning for the Rev. Martin Luther King and Sen. Robert Kennedy," wrote Robert Lipsyte. "Many players resented having to play and this feeling of powerlessness would be translated into a militant guild spirit against the owners for years to come."[9] That same season, Gibson released his book, *From Ghetto to Glory*, in which he compared "Negro riots" to the brushback pitch. "Their intention, like the brushback pitch, is to get people to think," Gibson explained. "Negroes have been mistreated for years. They are getting tired of being mistreated."[10]

Coming off a Cy Young and MVP season, Gibson received a $125,000 salary for 1969. The game's highest-paid pitcher served as the team's player representative. It was in that capacity that Gibson told Johnny Carson on *The Tonight Show* in February that fans should consider ownership greed when weighing their opinions of player-management issues, a stance that drew the ire of the club's president.[11]

If Gibson angered management, the favor was returned in spring training when the team traded first baseman Orlando Cepeda to the Atlanta Braves for Joe Torre. Describing Cepeda as "our spiritual leader" in his autobiography, Gibson believed that "it wasn't the *deal* that jolted us so much, but the very idea that management was messing in a major way with a club that had run away with two straight pennants. Trading Cepeda signaled to us, loud and clear, that things would no longer be the same around the Cardinal clubhouse."[12]

His teammates agreed. "The glue was gone," said Flood. "The great Cardinals were all washed up." Pitcher Nelson Briles remembered a special camaraderie in the club, a certain chemistry that diminished with the absence of Cepeda. "Sometimes you don't realize as a player, and as management, how special it is when you get a unique blend of players together on a team that are not only talented but are dedicated to one another and have that spirit and devotion to one another, and when you get that, you want to ride that as long as you possibly can, and once you start to chip away at that, it's hard to get that back."[13]

As the two-time defending National League champions began the new season full of angst, the rest of the baseball world was oblivious. "If the Cardinals don't clinch the pennant by July," said Royals scouting director Charlie Metro, "there ought to be an investigation."[14] On July 4, St. Louis stood 16 games behind division-leading Chicago. A second-half surge cut the gap to 7.5 games on August 22, but the club would never get any closer.

Other explanations would be offered for the team's disappointing performance. In June, Buck gave a speech to a group in Cincinnati where he wondered if the trip to Japan the previous fall had been a mistake. He also speculated on the lowering of the pitching mound, its impact on Briles, and how an early-season injury to Vada Pinson had affected the new right fielder's performance.[15] (Pinson suffered a hairline fracture to his lower leg bone against the Pirates. Leaving Pittsburgh in early May with a .301 batting average, he finished the season at .255.)

Mathematically still alive in early September, St. Louis dropped two of three games against Montreal, a series in which a few new players were inserted into the lineup. Flood claimed the front office ordered Schoendienst to begin playing some rookies, including first baseman Joe Hague. "With Hague batting third – Lou Brock and I – the first two batters in the order – would not see any decent pitches," he believed. Flood went straight to Schoendienst with his concerns. "If you insist on playing those goddamned kids, at least don't put them in the heart of your lineup," he told his manager. Schoendienst, according to Flood, shrugged his shoulders and replied, "Okay. If you feel that way about it."[16]

"I knew in my bones that the experiment had been suggested by the front office," Flood later wrote, "now the feeling was confirmed."

The outfielder repeated his complaints to St. Louis newspaper reporters, who quoted an anonymous player upset about the lineup changes. "We deserve the right to lose it on our own after winning two straight years, and somebody gave up on us," Flood told beat writers.

Those comments drew an immediate rebuttal from general manager Bing Devine. "I never wrote out a lineup for a manager in my life," he said. "It really shows a lot of guts to make charges anonymously. That shows they're pretty good front runners," an agitated Devine continued. "All those games early in the season counted, too. Now that the shoe is on the other foot, some of the players can't take it."[17]

At the end of the season, the Cardinals likely became the only non-World-Series-winning team in baseball history to have champagne sent to the locker room in back-to-back years. After the loss to Detroit in 1968, the players drank it. The Cardinals had ordered 96 bottles in anticipation of a championship. "The big boss (Busch) said we might as well drink it," said Schoendienst. "It was here. He told us we had a good season." But after a contentious 1969 campaign, in which the team finished in fourth place in the National League East, no one was in the mood for a toast. "Send it back," ordered Devine. Told the champagne was a gift from Harry Caray, someone wondered aloud, "What is it, a farewell gift?"[18]

*****

On the afternoon of April 8, 1969, new commissioner Bowie Kuhn presented the World Series flag to the Detroit Tigers. After the game, he flew to St. Louis and presented the National League flag to the Cardinals that evening. Stopping by the broadcast booth, Kuhn struck up a conversation with Caray in-between innings. The dialogue continued on-air, with the commissioner kidding the broadcaster that he was missing some of the action. That gave Caray an idea. Would the commissioner want to call some play-by-play? Kuhn liked the idea and described a half-inning of the Cardinals' season opener.[19]

The commissioner joined a long line of guests Caray had invited over the years to participate in a Cardinals broadcast. While Harry reluctantly turned over the microphone to various colleagues, he had no issues when it came to VIP guests. Hollywood actor and future President Ronald Reagan called an inning of a game at Caray's invitation in 1951. (Reagan was in St. Louis to address the national Kiwanis convention.)[20] Shooting a movie in Florida, Jimmy Stewart stopped by the press box during spring training of 1954.[21] On an off day in St. Louis in 1955, Brooklyn Dodgers stars Roy Campanella and Don Newcombe spent the evening in the Busch Stadium broadcast booth.[22] Listeners heard Newcombe describe an inning of action between the Cardinals and Pirates. Caray's penchant for guests in the booth and conversation outside of baseball irritated his critics, but the broadcaster did it his entire career. (President Reagan and Caray reunited during a press box visit in 1988. Just as he had done in St. Louis, Reagan described an inning of a contest at Wrigley Field.)[23]

Caray's critics soon had new ammunition in their campaign against the broadcaster. The Cardinals were the opponent when the Montreal Expos made their home franchise debut. The conditions at Jarry Park were less than ideal. "I pray to God that I don't get killed out there tomorrow," Flood said after the first game. "I've played on some bad diamonds, but this is the worst."[24] Caray agreed with the outfielder's assessment and amplified the criticism with comments during the broadcast.

"Picture if you will Fairgrounds Park or Forest Park with tools and equipment all over the place and with stands – open stands at that – and you can get the major league picture here in Montreal," Harry told his radio audience. "I don't know what they thought of when they picked Montreal. There is no question that Montreal is entitled to big-league baseball ... It is a thriving metropolis ... a cosmopolitan city. But, it just doesn't have any major league facilities yet – and we are liable to have a contender here ... and the comparisons which have been made between Milwaukee, which is not in the major leagues, and Montreal which is ... defy any rhyme or reason."[25]

Caray criticized the playing field. "Just a week ago this whole field was a quagmire minus a baseball diamond." He lamented the logistical challenges of broadcasting. "Maybe [KMOX] has got 50,000 watts, but they sure never heard of us up here." And he indirectly took a swipe at baseball owners with the Montreal-Milwaukee comparison. "People in Milwaukee must be crying today," said Harry. "They see the emergency treatment given major league baseball here in Montreal while [at the same] time a town has drawn over two million people, has a great stadium, has been begging to be realigned into major league baseball. Maybe in due time, they will get a major league baseball team." (The expansion Seattle Pilots moved to Milwaukee and became the Brewers in 1970.)

On the occasion of the first major league game outside of the United States, Caray delivered a broadside that got attention from the highest levels of the Cardinals organization. At Gussie Busch's request, Al Fleishman documented Caray's comments in a memo he would later send to the Cardinals president. Whether the comments only drew concern from the Cardinal brass or proved to be a tipping point in a lengthy list of perceived Caray transgressions, a difficult year for the broadcaster and brewery officials was just getting started. The baseball season was barely a week old and the bullseye was squarely on Caray's back.[26]

The Fleishman memo to Busch landed on his desk on May 1, the same month brewery workers went on strike. In July, Caray would later claim to a reporter, he first heard from Oakland A's owner Charlie Finley at the All-Star Game in Washington, D.C. that he wouldn't be returning to the Cardinals.[27] Days earlier, a representative from Gardner Advertising sent Harry a letter asking for an explanation for his many personal phone calls during his rehabilitation time in Florida over the winter. (Caray's request for reimbursement had been rejected.) "I will be curious to see just how detailed his 'explanation' will be," William Fisher of Gardner wrote to Fleishman.[28]

Whispers and rumors became public in August. Susan Busch filed for divorce from her husband on August 15th. A few days later, both *The Pittsburgh Press* and *Pittsburgh Post-Gazette* reported that KMOX had offered Pirates broadcaster Prince a long-term contract and that Busch was planning a shakeup of the Cardinals broadcasting crew. Prince said he had a contract offer, but "it did not have anything to do with the play-by-play of the Cardinals." (Prince's statement could have been factually true while not telling the whole story. Any offer to broadcast the Cardinals would have come from Anheuser-Busch, not KMOX.) While the baseball team and radio station both denied any contract had been offered, KMOX chief Hyland conceded the station had long admired the work of the Pirates broadcaster. "We told Prince in the past that if he would ever like to make a change in location, we would certainly like to talk to him."[29] (The next day, *Pittsburgh Press* columnist Vince Leonard would write that Prince and Hyland were business associates in the clubhouse restaurant planned for Three Rivers Stadium.)[30]

With the Cardinals in Chicago for a doubleheader against the Cubs on September 20, a *Post-Dispatch* reporter asked Caray for comment on a report that he had been fired. "I'd be the last to know that," he said into the microphone. "I really don't know about it, but if the *Post-Dispatch* definitely has that information, then I'd say it's true. So thanks for letting me know I've been fired." He returned to the topic a short time later during the broadcast. "The Cardinals are about to be eliminated, and apparently so am I. When I took this job 25 years ago, they said it would be temporary."[31]

Caray's comments over the air came as Gussie Busch left for a European trip. According to Buck, Caray's words that day were the final straw. "Gussie was on his way to the airport and heard the interview and said, 'that's it.'"[32]

In Caray's defense, the Prince story had opened the floodgates to speculation about his future (chatter about his departure had started even earlier),[33] and no one in the Anheuser-Busch empire was offering any reassurances. "Rumors persist here that Harry Caray will not return to the Cardinals network next season," stated Wilt Browning in *The Atlanta Journal-Constitution* on August 24. "The hottest rumor going around the National League, and the subject of almost universal gossip in the press lounges, has Harry Caray retiring as St. Louis Cardinal announcer after the season," said *Nashville Tennessean* writer F.M. Williams on August 26. "The St. Louis Cardinals without Harry Caray would be like toast without butter, like California without smog, like Joe Namath without girls," wrote Bob Fallstrom in the *Decatur* (IL) *Herald* on September 9, eleven days before Caray's comments in Chicago.

On October 2, riding a Busch Stadium elevator to the press box on the final day of the season, Caray addressed his job status again, telling a reporter, "this is my last season" working for the Cardinals. "Many thanks for your wires ...

they are all appreciated," he said at the end of the broadcast. "Hope to see you again ... somewhere, sometime ... and hopefully, right here. See you somewhere along the line ... so long everybody!"[34] While no official announcement had yet come from the Cardinals, many media outlets took Caray's words at face value. Typical was the headline the next day in the Davenport, Iowa *Quad-City Times*: "Harry Caray Loses Job."

With attendance for the fourth-place Cardinals totaling 1,682,783, a drop of more than 300,000 from the previous year, the club soon announced 50-cent ticket price increases for both box and reserved seats for 1970, the first such jump since 1965. Team executives also explained the franchise would have no off-season speakers bureau and would not send any public relations caravans of representatives to Missouri cities or adjacent states. "That means several Redbirds will have to go out and find their own jobs, instead of collecting $700 or so a month for speaking appearances," noted Neal Russo in the *Post-Dispatch*. "Apparently, the Redbirds front office sees no point in providing cozy off-season jobs for players who might hold out for conditions the owners feel are far from realistic."[35]

Five days after the season ended, the Cardinals traded one of their players most vocal about his salary, Curt Flood, along with Tim McCarver and others to the Philadelphia Phillies, in a multi-player deal that netted the club outfielder Dick Allen. The Cardinals left Caray twisting in the wind a few days longer.[36]

On Sunday, October 5, Bob Hertzel had this note in a story for *The Cincinnati Enquirer*. "They are saying the rumors that had Pittsburgh announcer Bob Prince going to St. Louis are false but Prince was huddling with Schoendienst and Stan Musial in the Atlanta Stadium Club Saturday."

While the Prince rumors did prove false, the speculation about Caray seemingly intensified with each passing day. "Within the past 48 hours at least 50 people, better than one per hour, queried this column's custodian as to Caray's future," wrote Jim Bell in the *Alton Evening Telegraph* on October 7.[37] The next day, Caray told reporters he'd been relieved of his daily 10-minute sports show on KMOX. In New York for the National League playoffs, Caray had received a call just minutes before taping a broadcast that he had been taken off the air. (Anheuser-Busch sponsored the show.) Told it didn't mean he was fired from Cardinals broadcasts, Caray asked, "What does it mean?"

"We really don't know what it means," said Anheuser-Busch advertising executive Don Hamel. Harry flew home to St. Louis and waited for the other shoe to drop. He didn't have long to wait.

*****

Holy Cow St. Louis!

Ron Jacober was a young sports reporter for KSD-TV in the fall of 1969. On Thursday, October 9, the station's main sports anchor, Jay Randolph, received a tip that Anheuser-Busch's marketing committee had a meeting that day. (Randolph also anchored the station's broadcasts of Cardinal games.) "They sent me to the brewery with a camera crew, and I'm waiting outside this room when the door opens eventually, and it's Al Fleishman of Fleishman-Hillard," Jacober recalled.[38]

"What are you doing here?" Fleishman demanded to know. "Well, we were under the understanding that the decision would be made on the future of Harry Caray as a Cardinal announcer," Jacober replied. "He looked at me and said, 'Well, whenever a decision is made on something like that, it'll be announced at the appropriate time,' and invited me to leave." Jacober and his photographer did as they were told.

"Half hour later, it was on KMOX," Jacober remembered. "Al Fleishman and Bob Hyland ... were good friends, so he leaked it to Hyland. KMOX broke the story [that Caray's contract would not be renewed]." Back at the television station, Jacober and cameraman Dick Deeken decided to go in search of Harry. "We knew a few of his watering holes," said Jacober. "We drove around and we went to a few places, and we found him at Busch's Grove on Clayton Road." (The restaurant/bar in Ladue had no connection to Anheuser-Busch.)

"Ron, have a Schlitz!" Caray told Jacober. (The bar didn't stock the beer, a competitor to Anheuser-Busch. Caray sent bartender Otis Dunlap out to buy a six-pack at nearby Ladue Market.)

"No, Harry. I don't want a Schlitz, but will you talk to me?"

"Damn right I will," Caray responded. (This was not Caray's first bar visit of the day. He was at the Cinema Bar in downtown St. Louis when brewery executive Hamel called to tell him his contract would not be renewed.)[39]

Before the interview began, Jacober had a request. "Harry, will you put the [Schlitz] can down?"

"I won't do the goddamn interview if I got to put the Schlitz down," Harry replied. "I said, 'Okay. Okay.' So we did this interview and it was on fire," Jacober recalled. "It was lethal. I don't remember a lot of specifics about it because it was so long ago, but he blasted the Cardinals and the brewery. Gussie. No holds barred at that point."

When the interview finished, Jacober and Deeken now had a new challenge. In 1969, the television station didn't shoot its footage on videotape, but rather on film that needed time to develop. The duo raced back downtown with the newscast fast approaching.

"I'm standing back in projection during the six 'clock news, and they hand me this reel of film that was almost still dripping out of the lab. And I said to the producer in the control booth, 'What do you want to do with it?' And he said, 'Rack it up and roll it from the top,'" Jacober remembered.

When it finished, a triumphant Jacober returned to the newsroom. "I was the only media person that found him. It was highly exclusive. And in those days, Harry was more popular than the team," he said. "They played six, seven minutes of it, I guess, [during the newscast]. By 6:35, I'm back in the sports office and we're kind of beaming because we did this."

Exhilaration was about to be replaced with dread. "The phone rings and it's Al Fleishman, Fleishman-Hillard."

"Son, do you know how much money Anheuser-Busch spends on Channel 5?" Fleishman asked Jacober. "No sir," the television reporter replied. "Well, I suggest you find out and I strongly suggest you don't use that interview again at 10:00," Fleishman instructed.

Jacober hung up and immediately called station general manager Ray Karpowicz at home. "Oh, my God. Oh, my God," Karpowicz said when informed of Fleishman's comments. "Well, you got to do it, but can you cover the Schlitz can?" he asked. "Well, today, electronically, you can make that a Budweiser can in five seconds. But not on film," Jacober explained. "There was nothing we could do with it. And there was no way to edit it," he told his boss.

"Well, I guess you got to play it," said Karpowicz.

"So we used a big chunk again at 10:00 that night, and we had a half-hour newscast at midnight on Channel 5. And they used it again at midnight; they used it again the next day. Well, my name was less than popular at Anheuser-Busch for a number of years, I was told, because I did the Caray interview," Jacober claimed.

And that is how, after 25 years of broadcasting baseball in the city, the last 16 working for Anheuser-Busch, Caray's career with the Cardinals ended: With a strong-arm tactic from Fleishman backfiring and Harry hoisting a can of Schlitz from a suburban St. Louis bar.

---

[1] In his book *Chaos*, author Tom O'Neill claims undercover CIA agent Reeve Whitson had penetrated the Manson family and had them under surveillance. When actress Sharon Tate and four others were murdered in Los Angeles, Whitson claimed to be in the house on Cielo Drive before police arrived. Former NBA player and coach Bill Sharman and his wife Joyce were friends with Whitson. "He told us he was involved in the [Manson] investigation, but gave us no details," Joyce told O'Neill. "Reeve would tell us the most

preposterous things and eventually we'd find out they were true." O'Neill, Tom with Dan Piepenbring. *Chaos: Charles Manson, the CIA, and the Secret History of the Sixties*. Little, Brown and Company. 2019. Bill Sharman and Caray worked together on NBA broadcasts in the 1960s. From Charles Manson to Harry Caray – three degrees of separation.

[2] Busch read a 10-page statement. "The speech was no public relations man's product. It was his," said Al Fleishman. *The Tampa Tribune*, March 27, 1969.

[3] *Chicago Tribune*, February 26, 1969.

[4] *St. Louis Post-Dispatch,* August 29, 1975.

[5] Ibid, July 25, 1969.

[6] Ibid, June 24, 1969.

[7] Hernon and Ganey, *Under The Influence*.

[8] Buck, *Jack Buck*.

[9] Lipsyte, Robert. *Sportsworld: An American Dreamland.* Quadrangle/The New York Times Book Co. 1975.

[10] Gibson, Bob with Phil Pepe. *From Ghetto to Glory: The Story of Bob Gibson*. Popular Library. 1968.

[11] "It was curious to me and the other players that there didn't seem to be much parallel sentiment concerning the greed of the owners," Gibson wrote. "This is what I explained on the Carson show. It is also apparently what ticked off Gussie Busch."

[12] Gibson, *Stranger to the Game.*

[13] Caray agreed with the players. "The Cepeda trade was a funny one to figure out, it was so strange that some people feel the only reason for it was to remove the last vestige of the [GM] Bob Howsam regime," he wrote for his syndicated column in 1970. With a .363 batting average, 24 home runs, and 137 RBI, Joe Torre won the National League MVP Award for the Cardinals in 1971.

[14] *The Sporting News*, April 19, 1969.

[15] *The Cincinnati Post*, June 12, 1969.

[16] Flood, *The Way It Is.*

[17] *St. Louis Post-Dispatch*, September 10, 1969. The Cardinals entered the series against the Expos in fourth place and ten games behind in the standings. After dropping two of three to Montreal, St. Louis remained ten games behind. The Cardinals were officially eliminated on September 21 following a 4-3 loss to the Cubs.

[18] *The Sporting News*, April 11, 1970.

[19] Caray's invitation had a ripple effect. "Some of the people over in Cincinnati heard me," said Kuhn. "One of the stations on the Cardinal network can be picked up there. When I got to Cincinnati the next day, Jim McIntyre (one of the Reds announcers) told me I wasn't going to get out of there without doing some play-by-play. So I did a half-inning." *Los Angeles Times,* April 15, 1969.

[20] *The Sporting News*, June 27, 1951. In his autobiography, Caray claimed Reagan was in town to promote his starring role in the Grover Cleveland Alexander movie, *The*

Winning Team. In fact, the movie was released a year later. The premier took place in Springfield, Missouri. At a celebration breakfast, the head table featured President Truman and future President Reagan. *The Kansas City Star*, June 7, 1952.

[21] *St. Petersburg Times*, March 22, 1954. Stewart was in Florida to shoot scenes for the movie *Strategic Air Command.*

[22] *The Sporting News*, May 25, 1955.

[23] "I'll be out of work in a couple of months," said the President during the telecast, "so I thought I might come up here and audition." Caray would later marvel that Mr. Reagan – "the President of the United States – had broadcast with me not once but *twice* in my career. It was a very special day for Harry Caray, who just happened to be wearing a jacket and tie."

[24] *The Kansas City Star*, April 15, 1969. Flood's comments angered Montreal Expos manager Gene Mauch. "The commissioner should turn Flood upside down and shake a little money out of his pocket," he said. "It's not in the best interests of baseball to say what he did, write it or print it in a newspaper." *The Sporting News*, May 3, 1969.

[25] *Fleishman Papers.*

[26] "The grounds are dry, the dirt 'skin' of the infield is firm and the footing is solid at the plate," wrote Ted Blackman at the beginning of the following season. "All the faults Curt Flood and Harry Caray found in 1969 are gone. Hey and so are Flood and Caray." *The Gazette* (Montreal, Quebec), April 8, 1970.

[27] *Memphis Press-Scimitar*, April 23, 1970.

[28] *Fleishman Papers.* The Fisher letter to Fleishman was dated July 17. The All-Star Game was played on July 23. Prince later claimed he received a "five-year, six-figure" offer from KMOX on July 13. *The Pittsburgh Press*, August 19, 1969. The paper reported that "Caray may soon be unemployed due to a personal conflict with beer and baseball baron Gussie Busch..."

[29] *St. Louis Post-Dispatch*, August 19, 1970.

[30] *The Pittsburgh Press*, August 20, 1969. Prince told Leonard, "As early as last year, Robert Hyland, vice president and general manager of KMOX Radio, talked to me about a job with his station." As for Caray, "The general feeling is that Harry is in trouble," Prince said. "Some unpleasantness has come up." The Prince-to-KMOX story appeared in St. Louis two days before Stix, Baer & Fuller held a Caray autograph party at its downtown store. Caray's "new 45-rpm recording of 'The Cardinals Are Coming Tra-la-tra-la' has just been released," the department store explained in a newspaper advertisement. Caray's saying had caught on during a brief surge by the team in August.

[31] *St. Louis Post-Dispatch*, September 21, 1969. The *Post-Dispatch* story came the same day Louisville *Courier-Journal* columnist Ron Coons called Caray "the greatest comeback" of the year. "Baseball needs knowledgeable and colorful announcers like Caray."

[32] KSD-TV sports reporter Ron Jacober was in Chicago for the September Cardinals-Cubs series doing the pregame and postgame shows for the television station. "I recall sitting

in the back of that booth, and Harry, during the game, was reading a whole stack of letters, telegrams from people, telling him how much they loved him, and please don't leave, and yada, yada," he told the author in a telephone interview. "I'm thinking at the time ... I don't know too much about all this, but I think Harry [is] digging the hole even deeper."

[33] "Rumors of Caray's dismissal have been circulating since before the [Prince] report." *St. Louis Globe-Democrat*, October 10, 1969.

[34] Earlier in the broadcast, Caray said: "UPI says they know definitely that I've been fired. Why would they know first ... why would anybody know first ... that's what is really grinding inside of me after 25 years." *Sun-Democrat* (Paducah, Kentucky), October 3, 1969.

[35] If the Cardinals hoped the tactic would prevent difficult contract negotiation the following season, it backfired. Newly acquired outfielder Dick Allen and pitcher Steve Carlton were notable holdouts in the spring of 1970. Busch was especially frustrated with Carlton. "I don't care if he doesn't pitch another (blankety-blank) ball for us again," he said, foreshadowing a similar situation two years later that would lead to Carlton's departure. *St. Louis Globe-Democrat*, March 13, 1970.

[36] At a University of Missouri football game in the fall of 1969, McCarver stopped by the broadcast booth. Caray introduced him as "a fellow refugee from the Cardinals." *Chicago Tribune,* February 27, 1998.

[37] While the St. Louis print media stayed neutral during this interim period, smaller-market columnists rallied behind Caray. "He has generated more enthusiasm for a sport that has its abundance of dull moments," Bell believed. *Alton Evening Telegraph*, October 7, 1969. "You can have [Bob Prince], Gussie. I'll take Harry Caray," wrote Merle Jones the same day in the *Southern Illinoisan*. "Perhaps we're more forgiving than most or just weren't listening when he tread on our sensitive toe. But we've never heard Harry say anything that we believed was designed to hurt," said Robert Schaub. "Harry projects an aura of goodwill toward all, and we believe he produces a forgiving attitude in those whose feathers an ill-chosen word might otherwise ruffle." *Edwardsville Intelligencer*, October 6, 1969.

[38] Interview with author, September 1, 2020.

[39] "They [Caray and Hamel] were still friends afterwards," said Hamel's son Dan. "I was pretty young at the time, but I remember that he would never talk about it. And when someone asked him about it, he pretty much dodged around it." Hamel was the brand manager for Busch beer. He later left the brewery and purchased Burkett Travel, where he planned corporate trips for Anheuser-Busch, most notably the annual Budweiser Irish Derby in Dublin, Ireland. His obituary noted that, like Caray, Hamel was a regular at Busch's Grove, "where he shared a table with [A-B executive Mike] Roarty, Stan Musial, Red Schoendienst, and the late Jack Buck." *St. Louis Post-Dispatch*, October 15, 2003.

Did He or Didn't He?

The broadcasting world had changed dramatically since the days of Caray calling home games on a small radio network for Griesedieck Brothers Beer. Television growth exploded in the 1950s, first dominating the audience for entertainment and increasingly capturing news viewers. The JFK assassination greatly impacted how people consumed their daily diet of information.[1] Television's impact on the sports world was no less compelling.

Minor league baseball attracted 42 million fans in 1949. By 1960, total attendance across those same leagues had dropped to 10 million. With major-league attendance essentially flat during this same period, owners intensified their focus on television as a source of revenue.[2] "Major league baseball has moved into the television stratosphere with its first complete network program, a 27-game Saturday and Sunday spectacular that bears a $12,200,000 price tag for the 1965 and '66 seasons," *The Sporting News* announced in December of 1964, figures that would grow exponentially over the coming decades.[3]

Owners saw television as a two-edged sword. They loathed it (believing it hurt attendance),[4] but also recognized how much they needed it. Television "can be a matter of life or death financially," declared Dodgers owner Walter O'Malley. Baseball's complicated relationship with the medium also revealed other challenges. Even in the 1960s, people complained about the pace of play. "Games last too long," asserted television critic Lawrence Laurent. "Pitchers dawdle while deciding what to throw next. About the time the pitcher decides, the batter concludes that he needs more dirt on his hands."[5]

The print media had its own issues of cognitive dissonance when it came time to discuss the visual medium. While writers saw its earliest broadcast competitor as yesterday's news ("The Golden Age of St. Louis Radio" read a headline in the *Post-Dispatch* in March of 1969 about the medium's dominance in the 1930s and 1940s),[6] their coverage of television featured a mix of criticism and fascination.

Although the first televised sports broadcasts had taken place in 1939, so much about the industry still seemed new and cutting edge. Live satellite feeds fed the curiosity of a space-age audience. In May of 1969, *Sports Illustrated* had three reporters cover a Saturday NBC broadcast between the Cardinals and Dodgers: One observed from inside the production truck, another watched from the broadcast booth, while a third joined members of the Elks Club in St. Joseph, Missouri. "The city has long been considered a bastion of Cardinals fans," wrote William O. Johnson.

The *Sports Illustrated* writer turned a series of articles on sports television into the book *Super Spectator and the Electric Lilliputians*. What Johnson and others recognized was that television money had changed athletes: "They are now complex financial figures with grand economic equations of their own." And ownership: "The fortunes of our most spectacular sports franchises are soaring toward stratospheric financial success." But found it challenging to define the evolving role of the men who described the action. "The sportscaster is easier to define by what he is not than by what he is. He is not quite a journalist, not quite a carnival barker, not quite an orator or an interlocuter or master of ceremonies or trained seal. Yet he is a little of all of them."

"Sportscasters: Newsman or Not?" asked columnist Ira Berkow around the same time. Seeking to understand the difference between print and electronic journalism, Berkow sought the opinion of a young Brent Musburger, who worked in newspapers before making the jump to radio and TV. "A newspaperman is fairly anonymous, but a sportscaster is a celebrity," he said.[7]

Television personality Tom Snyder would later ask a similar question: Should sportscasters use "we" when broadcasting a game of the team that employs them? Answering in the affirmative on the *Tomorrow* show panel were Caray and Bob Prince. Marv Albert and Dick Enberg took the other side.[8]

The role sportscasters played increasingly put network executives and team owners at odds. "The biggest problem with announcers," said Roone Arledge, "is their paucity of viewpoint. I think we need more people who can do controversy, who bring more definite opinions." Arledge's opinion carried weight. The ABC television executive launched *Monday Night Football* in 1970 with the controversial (and frequent Caray critic) Howard Cosell as one of three men in the broadcast booth.[9]

With an eye toward pleasing fans and placating sponsors, owners had radically different ideas. Washington broadcaster Shelby Whitfield repeatedly clashed with owner Robert Short. The Senators owner instructed his announcer to inflate crowd numbers and to always claim the weather was sunny, even when mother nature had different ideas. The Senators and Whitfield parted ways after the 1970 season. "At least now I know what it's like being a manager in the majors," he later wrote. "You know when you take a job like that, sooner or later, you are going to be fired. A baseball broadcaster has to please the club, the station, the advertising agency, the sponsor, the fans, and the press, not necessarily in that order. There's no way you can please all of them."[10]

When 413 people paid their way into a game in 1966, the smallest attendance in Yankee Stadium history, Red Barber asked the technical crew to pan the crowd. When the production team refused his request, the broadcaster described the scene for his television audience. "This crowd is the story, not the game," he said. Barber's contract was not renewed for the 1967 season.[11]

"The owners came to the strong conclusion they wanted salesmen, propagandists, people who told the half-truth," Barber claimed. "When I got fired by the Yankees, the *New York Post* got hold of Joe Garagiola and asked him what he thought. He said, 'Look, I'm a house man.' I think that sums up everything."[12]

In between Barber's departure and Whitfield's termination, Harry Caray's descriptions of games over the Cardinals network officially ended in the fall of 1969 with a five-paragraph press release from Anheuser-Busch. "Decisions as to our baseball broadcasting ... are always based upon the study and recommendations of the marketing division of Anheuser-Busch, Inc.," the statement from Gussie began. "The marketing division has made its decision. They have decided that Harry Caray's contract will not be renewed for 1970. Caray has been informed accordingly," it stated before ending with news of his successor. "Our broadcasting team will be headed by Jack Buck."

*****

At nine o'clock on Saturday night, October 11, television viewers in St. Louis could enjoy the detective series, *Mannix*, starring Mike Connors, on CBS. Over on NBC, the movie *The Hell With Heroes* was in its second hour, while the *Hollywood Palace* audience on ABC tuned in to see Bing Crosby and Engelbert Humperdinck perform a medley of Beatles hits. Local viewers also had another option. On KPLR, Channel 11, a station not affiliated with the Big Three Networks, the *Bill Fields Show* had a single guest for the 90-minute program, a man whose departure from the Cardinals had the city buzzing.

In the months and years to come, Caray would polish and refine his message about the end of his St. Louis years, delivering ready-made lines anytime a reporter came calling. "After 25 years, I was expecting a gold watch but got a pink slip instead," he would tell interviewers. He would also later insist that he wasn't fired. Anheuser-Busch had just decided not to renew his contract. But appearing on television just two days after the news, Harry's scripted soundbites had yet to emerge. Viewers on that Saturday night saw a different Caray: Raw. Unfiltered. Emotional. "I'm hurt. I'm hurt," he told Fields. "I've never been fired before in my life."[13]

The interview revealed a Harry fatalistic about his future with the Cardinals. "I know I'll never broadcast in St. Louis again."

He reconstructed the events of that fateful day, getting the call from Hamel at 3:25 p.m. Five minutes later, he began hearing the news on the radio. "I haven't seen anybody from the brewery since. I haven't talked to anybody. It was just 'Goodbye boy. Good luck.'"

"You must have some idea of why you got canned, Harry," Fields insisted.[14]

"I have a couple of suspicions but I can't prove it so I'll just have to keep my mouth shut," Harry replied. Fields pressed him for information. "Can you give us a lead to one of those suspicions?"

Caray offered two explanations. He briefly mentioned "scurrilous rumors," which are "false," he maintained (a reference to the alleged Susan Busch affair), but his initial and more detailed response had to do with former brewery executive Ed Vogel. Caray and Vogel's relationship went back to the days when they both worked for Griesedieck Brothers. Vogel was the brewmaster for Griesedieck before joining Anheuser-Busch. He left the company in 1968 after reportedly clashing with August Busch III and began working as a consultant for Schlitz.[15] Vogel also had a liquor distributorship in Florida. Rumors began circulating that Caray was a business partner. (He wasn't, but Harry took the chatter seriously, meeting with Gussie to tell him that Vogel was only a friend.)[16]

The connection to Vogel brought out another issue. Of all the beers Caray could have selected on Thursday at Busch's Grove, why did he choose Schlitz? "I guess it shows I'm a little vindictive," he explained, "but the only thing I could think of to show my protest was to get some other bottle of beer and the first one I thought of was Schlitz because of this little episode I told you about."

Fields brought up Caray's relationship with the man who ran Fleishman-Hillard. "Al Fleishman is a great public relations man," Harry said. "He'll end up being a great man in semantics. I think the first thing he ought to look up is a little bit about human relationships."

Did Fleishman have any influence on Anheuser-Busch's decision? "I'd shudder to think that he would be that important in the makeup of a big organization like Anheuser-Busch," Caray said. "No, I don't think he was important in the decision, but yes, I'm sure he didn't do a thing to help me." ("Maybe the public relations men ought to get fired," he said at a different point in the interview.)[17]

While Caray dismissed Fleishman's role, he did see a conspiracy at work, pointing to the Bob Prince story out of Pittsburgh in August. "I know for a fact that the story actually originated in St. Louis but they used a Cincinnati dateline, and the Pittsburgh paper that wrote the story thought the St. Louis paper really had it," he believed. The story "broke with a purpose," Caray told Fields.

"There's too much behind it all and too much involved and I can't understand why."[18]

He also speculated about a future where he stayed in St. Louis but didn't broadcast baseball, worrying that Anheuser-Busch may pull advertising dollars from any media outlet that employed him. "It's going to be interesting to see what sort of pressures are going to be applied to me from an economic standpoint," he stated. His preference, though, was to stay in the game, telling Fields that while he hadn't been offered a job yet, he had started discussions with other teams.

"You're not going to quit?" Fields asked.

"I love the hustle and bustle of my job," Cary replied. "No, I have no intention of resigning ... retiring, rather," he said, indicating a desire to stay in the Midwest. "I would have to say that it would be a city like Cincinnati or Kansas City or Chicago.[19] Those are all cities within an hour or so [flight time from St. Louis]. I think anything more remote ... I'd have to think about it."

"Are you mad, Harry?" Fields asked him at one point.

"I'm not mad. I'm hurt," Caray replied. "I'm bitter about the way it was done. I don't think I could treat an animal as badly as I've been treated on this thing."

Before opening up the show to telephone callers, Fields had a request. "Mr. Caray has really got everybody pretty emotional so let's not have any long speeches." (One account later described Harry's condition that night as almost tearful.)[20]

Many of the callers – all pro-Caray – brought up various protests, petitions, and boycotts of Anheuser-Busch.[21] While appreciative of the remarks and admitting he was personally boycotting their products, he didn't advocate it for others. "I, myself, am doing it because I am hurt and hurt deeply inside." He also stated he planned to sell all his Anheuser-Busch stock.[22]

Hopeful callers and a gloomy Harry returned more than once to the topic of a potential comeback with the Cardinals. "Maybe I'm a pessimist, but I just have the feeling that this is a final decision," Caray told Fields. "I wish it were possible but I don't think there's a chance."[23]

"You know you sound so pessimistic, Harry. Is there something you're not telling us?" Fields asked. Harry insisted there wasn't, but he would only speak in generalities about why he believed he was out of a job. "I think it's safe to assume there has to be something personal," he said. "There has to have been some very deeply embedded hatred or dislike," Caray maintained. "I think this had to be a matter of long planning."

Holy Cow St. Louis!

As for *who* made the call not to renew his contract, Harry believed it came down to three men: August Busch Jr. (Gussie), August Busch III, or Executive Vice President Dick Meyer. "I am sure that these are the three men who had to make the decision."

Harry conceded that Meyer "has never been a great admirer of mine and he's been very honest about it," while tacitly expressing reservations about August III. "If they put young Busch in charge, God help us," one caller declared. "No comment," Caray replied. But if Harry was certain about anything that night, it was his faith in Gussie. "I can't believe [the decision] came from Mr. Busch. I've been too great an admirer of his," said Caray. "I just can't believe this friendship would have ended so completely that he wouldn't even call me down to tell me personally."[24]

This was Harry's state of mind in the fall of 1969: Emotionally wounded, shocked and in denial. In the year Mario Puzo published *The Godfather*, Caray simply couldn't believe the man in charge of the family operation had ordered the hit.

*****

On the morning of the 12th, readers of the *Post-Dispatch* opened their Sunday papers to read Bob Broeg's first column since the Caray news broke three days earlier. Broeg, chronicler of all things Cardinals since the 1940s, dedicated the entire column to the St. Louis Blues. If Caray's time with Fields likely represented the longest on-the-record interview he ever gave about his departure, the rest of the St. Louis media yawned. The Anheuser-Busch decision did make front-page news the day after the announcement, but scant coverage followed as to the reasons behind it. Much of the local media was either uncurious or unsympathetic.[25] "Caray certainly made a grandstand play the past few months to use his broadcasting means and Busch's money to try to save his job. After all, public pressure is a big thing to beer sales," declared an editorial in the St. Louis *County News*. "So if Busch was not fair to Caray, neither was Caray all that fair to Busch. There were plenty of other means of getting Harry's point across. And we find it hard to believe that he hasn't known about his dismissal for some time, in plenty of time to use them."[26]

"What the full story is few will ever know," the editorial concluded. "I don't know why Caray was fired," the *Globe-Democrat's* Bob Burnes told a Du Quoin, Illinois audience in May of 1970.[27]

Caray's difficulties with the St. Lous print media dated back to his earliest days broadcasting in the city. Newspaper reporters were frequently employed as straw men in Harry's arguments. "It's sure good that the Cardinals are returning Stan Musial to the outfield during their trip to Japan," he said on the radio one evening in the fall of 1958. "If they tried it while the ball club was in St. Louis, the newspapermen would scare them out of the move," a statement which drew a full-column response from Burnes.[28] "I do not want to sound immodest," Caray once said, "but I'm a helluva reporter."[29]

So while professional rivalry or jealousy played a role, other factors were likely even more significant. Anheuser-Busch cast an enormous shadow over the city, as both an employer and advertiser. Does anyone believe Fleishman's call to Jacober was the only instance of the brewery seeking to intimidate the local media?

A final issue behind the media's reluctance to probe into the motivations behind Caray's exit involved the most explosive allegation against the broadcaster: His alleged affair with Susan Busch. The Caray house on Sheraton Drive sat less than two miles away from August III and Susan's home on Fordyce Lane in Ladue, hardly proof of a dalliance, but it is one of many circumstantial points to consider.[30] From November 1968 to November 1969, stories surrounding Caray's troubles and Busch's eventual divorce seemed to move in lockstep (see Appendix).

On November 25, 1969, eleven days after Busch's divorce, Caray mentioned her by name in a speech. "For the first time I am in a position to discuss it openly, for the parties involved are now divorced," he began. "Mrs. August Busch III is the finest of ladies and she also happens to be a true friend of mine. She visited me daily while I was in the hospital, partly in the line of duty as a volunteer nurse and the rest out of unhappiness and loneliness," he told the Peoria, Illinois Ad Club audience. "The young lady now divorced was a constant companion for a long time of my wife's and a dear friend of mine. I hope she still is a good friend of mine, and I have now and have always had nothing but friendly affection and respect for her. If this is having an affair, our society is sick."[31]

But as the years wore on, Caray's firm denials gave way to more subtle responses. He seemed to relish in the attention and ambiguity. "Hell, I wanted them to believe it," when asked about the alleged affair in 1975. "I was so flattered that I preferred to have people believe the rumor than tell the truth. So what if I got fired – I knew I'd get a job somewhere."[32] He gave a similar answer in 1986. "There were a lot of rumors, and frankly, I'd rather have people believe the rumors, because I could always get another job," Harry told the *Post-Dispatch*.[33] "And the rumors made me feel macho. The woman involved was very young, very beautiful, very rich and married to a very, very, very prominent billionaire type."

Holy Cow St. Louis!

A Pittsburgh columnist asked Caray in 1991 if the rumors were true. "I'm not going to tell you they were, and I'm not going tell you they weren't."[34]

He also had more troubling answers that raised eyebrows. When chatter about his alleged affair escalated in the summer of 1969, Harry relayed his concerns to Gussie. "You never raped anybody, right, Harry?" said the Cardinals president. "That's right," Caray replied.

That line from a private conversation was later repeated in public. "At the time, all I said was I never raped anyone in my life," Harry told Bob Rubin for an *Inside Sports* story in 1984.[35] Critics pounced on the statement. "When I read that," said Milo Hamilton, "It made me sick. It was as plain as Harry's face that he was admitting to having an affair."[36]

Reporter Ted Schafers visited Caray during his hospital stay following his accident. "I asked him what about this story that's going around that you had something with the wife of August III," he told authors Peter Hernon and Terry Ganey.

"I never did chase her," Caray replied.[37]

On a book promotion tour in 1991, *Under the Influence* co-author Hernon was asked about the Caray-Busch connection. "The lawyers went over this a whole lot. A *whoooooole* lot," he said. "And some stuff was deleted from the book that cannot be discussed. But Susan, to her credit, she called me up. She wanted to respond. She said they were just rumors."[38]

Jerry Berger of the *Post-Dispatch* interviewed the former Susan Busch in 1995. He asked her if she and Caray "were an item."

"No, we were a friendship item," she replied, "but not a romance by any means."

"A family member and confidante told some friends she tracked telephone calls from your house to Harry," Berger told her.

"Harry was married to Marian and Harry and I used to play gin-rummy," she explained. "I could have made a phone call to Harry, easily, because Harry and August and I and Marian used to get together and play cards. (Asked by Fields in 1969 how he got along with August III, Harry replied, "I don't hardly know him at all.")

"How did this [rumor] start?" Berger wanted to know. "Why do you think people would do this?

"I think people do this because we both have a name," Susan responded. "And we might have been seen out, having dinner, which was probably a situation. Yes, I did join Harry for dinner. August traveled a lot, and I joined a lot of friends for dinner, as I still do to this day. And people would see us, and I guess decided to go for the romance."[39]

Knowingly or unwittingly, Susan touched on the two issues where conjecture and circumstantial evidence spilled over into tangible proof of a potentially more intimate relationship: Phone calls and dinners. We know from a memo sent to Fleishman that people connected to Anheuser-Busch wanted more information about Caray's calls during his rehabilitation time in the winter of 1969. An anonymous source, identified as "a former sidekick," provided additional details to author Curt Smith. "While Harry was convalescing, some members of the Busch family began to notice there were a lot of telephone charges on the bill linking Harry's room to one of the Busch residences. This rang a bell, and after some checking around, some following by a detective of Harry, it was discovered that Caray was apparently having an affair with the wife of young August Busch [III], Gussie's son. Naturally, this isn't the greatest way to keep your job – breaking up the marriage of your boss's son, and as it got more involved, it wasn't long before the situation became impossible. Why the hell else would Harry have been fired? He was tremendously popular, the greatest salesman Anheuser-Busch ever had."[40]

As for their dinners together, St. Louis native and author William Knoedelseder was an eyewitness to one such encounter. "The pair could not have been less discreet when they were seen dining together at St. Louis's only four-star restaurant, Tony's, just a few blocks from Busch Stadium, visibly under the influence and so physically affectionate that owner Vince Bommarito had to instruct his whispering waitstaff to stop staring at them. But it was hard not to," Knoedelseder wrote in *Bitter Brew*.

"The conclusion you would jump to is that there was something going on there. No one on the staff had heard any rumors prior to that, so it wasn't like we were making it up," the author later told *The Riverfront Times*. "So I don't know. Maybe they were trying to make a statement."[41]

*****

If Harry was hurt by the news of his termination, Skip was angry. If the father suspected three men behind his ouster, the son zeroed in on a single culprit. Skip Caray directed his wrath and fury solely at August Busch III. Typing his correspondence on the stationery of his new employer (the Atlanta Hawks), Skip's letter landed on August's desk on October 24.[42]

>Dear August:
>I have finally gotten around to reading the newspaper drivel regarding the firing of my father by your brewery.

My major regret at this point is that I will never have the opportunity of firing your father in return – that is, if the alleged personal problems quoted in the GLOBE-DEMOCRAT are correct.

I do, however, think you ought to know the utter disgust which I have for you personally, and for all the little people who surround you for the manner in which this was handled. Pettiness has never been the hallmark of your great company – but apparently it is now.

As we are both young men – both following in big footsteps – and both, I hope, reasonably intelligent I've got to ask you: Does it make you feel like a big man to stick knives in people's backs?

I pledge to you this: If there is ever a way that I can get even with you personally, I shall.

Two words would have summed all this up a good deal more quickly, but we do have libel laws, don't we?

He signed it "With Contempt," scrawling his signature above his legal name: Harry Christopher Caray Jr.

A copy of the letter was forwarded to Fleishman, who typed out a "suggested response" for Busch. Whether the letter was ever sent is unclear, but its message is revealing. Ignoring the motivations behind Harry's exit, Fleishman focused on how the situation was handled, blaming Caray for forcing the brewery to act in the manner it did.

"I am sure you know that Harry broadcast for a period of approximately six weeks over radio and television, quoting various reports and rumors – none of which emanated from the Cardinals or Anheuser-Busch – to the effect that he was going to be fired," Fleishman wrote.

"The only reason I [Fleishman writing for August] mention this is to point out that the only statement ever made by our company was that Harry's contract did not expire until December 31, 1969, and that the company would not make a decision or an announcement prior to that approximate time," he continued.

"The persistence of the rumors broadcast on time paid for by the company made an orderly procedure or announcement virtually impossible."

Perhaps it should come as no surprise that someone in public relations would focus a reply to an objection around Caray's departure around process. To Fleishman, public perception mattered most of all. In his mind, Caray crossed a line by openly discussing rumors (that turned out to be true). But did publicly speculating about his departure get him fired, or was Harry merely acknowledging something that had already been decided? The timeline and evidence suggest the latter. If that were the case, one is left to wonder what "an orderly procedure or announcement" would have looked like had Harry kept his mouth shut. Maybe the Cardinals planned to give him a gold watch *with* his pink slip?

*****

Harry would later change his mind about disposing of all of his Anheuser-Busch stock. "Let's face it. Budweiser has made me a very wealthy man. I've had their stock for 40 years." Caray said in 1986. "Hell, I'm a millionaire just on Anheuser-Busch stock. How can you feel any bitterness when you look at it in that vein?" But after he left the Cardinals, he explored relationships with various brewers.

In 1972, he claimed to a reporter he owned 3,000 shares of Schlitz.[43] By then, he was broadcasting White Sox baseball in Chicago, where he began touting a beer with a St. Louis history.[44] "The King of Falstaff" is how the *Chicago Tribune's* Gary Deeb described Caray in 1975. Harry once chugged a bottle of Falstaff during a White Sox broadcast as the camera zoomed in for a closeup. "I did it on purpose," Caray admitted, "because I think that's a ridiculous rule against drinking on camera. Anyway, I don't think it's actually a law. What the hell – you don't think a guy sitting up in a booth isn't gonna take a swig of beer every now and then? C'mon..."[45]

Harry later pitched Stroh's beer during White Sox broadcasts. One television ad showed Caray bagging a six-pack of Stroh's with his fish net.

Around this same time, Anheuser-Busch began to struggle in the Chicago market. A brewery workers' strike in 1976 proved costly.[46] Heileman's Old Style began surging in popularity, becoming the best-selling beer in the city. The Wisconsin brewer's aggressive marketing campaign even came to St. Louis. "Hey Bud, there's a new beer in town," the television ad declared.

To combat Old Style in the Windy City, Anheuser-Busch turned to a familiar face to reinvigorate sales. Caray signed a three-year deal with the brewery in the spring of 1980. "Actually, it gives me a lot of satisfaction to start doing the advertisements with Budweiser," Caray said in April before the start of the baseball season. "I don't harbor any bad feelings. I have a contract and I'm going to start doing the ads with the first game on Thursday."[47]

That relationship between brewer and broadcaster continued for the rest of Harry's life. And beyond. Anheuser-Busch honored the broadcaster after the Cubs won the World Series with a Budweiser ad that combined 2016 video footage of people outside Wrigley Field and fans watching the game from bars with audio from Harry's days calling Cubs games. "This is Harry Caray. So long everybody," the ad concluded over a video of celebrating fans.

Holy Cow St. Louis!

None of this would have been possible without the cooperation of August Busch III. Serving as CEO of Anheuser-Busch from 1975 to 2002, his time running the brewery largely overlapped with Harry's time in Chicago. By the early 1980s, the *Post-Dispatch* proclaimed that Chicago had become so important to the brewery that CEO Busch handled the city "personally."[48] Gussie's son famously didn't give a damn about baseball, but was a cutthroat competitor when it came to the beer business.[49] Whatever the source of tension between August and Harry back in 1969 – be it infidelity talk or Skip's threatening letter – was either forgiven or forgotten eleven years later. Busch put his faith in Caray. Harry returned the favor.

Caray's visibility and connections to Budweiser would soar when he jumped to the crosstown rival Cubs in 1982. He'd frequently plug the product on WGN, wear a red Budweiser jacket during broadcasts, and sing and dance during "Cub Fan Bud Man" television ads.

Like so many other things that contributed to the legend of Harry Caray, these magical Chicago moments had their roots in St. Louis.

---

[1] Instant replay made its national debut on CBS when Jack Ruby fatally shot suspected JFK assassin Lee Harvey Oswald on November 24, 1963.

[2] In 1949, the 16 MLB teams drew 20,215,365. In 1960, attendance totaled 19,911,489.

[3] *The Sporting News*, December 26, 1964.

[4] Sportswriter Jimmy Cannon on how baseball fans responded to games on TV: "It looks like a nice day for a baseball game. I think I'll move the TV set on the porch."

[5] *Los Angeles Times*, April 16, 1964. Caray had his own critique of baseball on television. "As a spectacle, baseball suffers on the tube," he wrote. "Football, boxing, basketball, and even hockey all benefit when subjected to television. They are even more exciting on the tube than they are in person. Other than the World Series, televised baseball leaves much to be desired." *The Sporting News*, October 24, 1970.

[6] "Nostalgia is very much in these days," wrote Irving Litvag. "Lots of people (those past 30 or 35) fondly remember radio's golden age." *St. Louis Post-Dispatch*, March 12, 1969.

[7] *San Francisco Examiner*, February 1, 1970.

[8] During the program, Prince asked Albert about the ring he was wearing. Albert replied that it was a New York Knicks souvenir ring. "You won't say 'we' but you wear their ring?" asked Prince. "The ring question obviously frustrated [Albert]," wrote *Dayton Daily News* executive sports editor Ralph Morrow. *Dayton Daily News*, December 12, 1975.

[9] Cosell and Caray traded barbs throughout the 1970s. "There is no excuse for Harry Caray's cheerleading," Cosell said in 1978. "Caray's broadcasts are on the grade-school level." *Chicago Tribune*, April 8, 1978. A year later, Cosell partially blamed Caray for the mob scene at the Comiskey Park "disco demolition" promotion that ended with

thousands of people on the field. The promotion came between games of a White Sox-Tigers doubleheader. The White Sox forfeited the second game. "Who could be phonier?" Caray said of Cosell. "All these years he's talked about how baseball is as exciting as watching the grass grow. Then as soon as his network gets baseball, he miraculously becomes a devotee of the game." Ibid, July 20, 1979.

[10] Whitfield, Shelby. *Kiss It Goodbye*. Abelard-Schuman. 1973. Thanks in part to Whitfield's book, the FCC passed a regulation – since rescinded – requiring announcers to disclose during games whether they were employees of a team, a league or a broadcasting company. *Washington Post*, February 8, 2013.

[11] According to authors Judith Hiltner and James Walker, the decision not to renew Barber's contract was made prior to his request to the production crew. Hiltner, Judith R., and Walker, James R. *Red Barber: The Life and Legacy of a Broadcasting Legend*. University of Nebraska Press. 2022. Barber's partner, Mel Allen, left the Yankees after the 1964 season, a victim of budget cutting by sponsor Ballentine Beer. "They knew they had to cut the budget, and heads started to roll," Allen told Curt Smith. Barber left broadcasting to write books and newspaper columns and appeared regularly on NPR's *Morning Edition*. "The Yankees did the greatest service I can think of. They presented me with my life." Smith, *Voices of the Game*.

[12] *Battle Creek (MI) Enquirer,* June 2, 1973. The syndicated story was part of a five-part series by Mike Roberts of the *Washington Star-News*. "I never talked to a broadcaster who didn't get some pressure from the owner," said Oakland A's broadcaster Monte Moore in the same article.

[13] Television show transcript from *The Fleishman Papers*.

[14] In a 1971 story, Fields was described as "St. Louis's senior black broadcaster." Reporter Olivia Skinner described him as "a small, smiling man whose ability to make people laugh is equaled by his ability to make them think about unpopular issues." *St. Louis Post-Dispatch*, June 14, 1971. He later changed his name to Amen Thoth. "I began to read Egyptian history because it is the foundation of our civilization and blacks played a major role in it." Ibid, December 29, 1975.

[15] "Young Busch disliked Vogel so much that Vogel either was fired or resigned," Caray said in 1972. "But he walked out with something like $4 million worth of Anheuser-Busch stock." *Chicago Tribune,* August 13, 1972. Vogel began his career with Griesedieck in 1934. In 1946, he co-authored a book on the brewing industry, "a book that is still used by beer brewers," the *Post-Dispatch* noted decades later. He joined Anheuser-Busch in 1956. He left Schlitz for Falstaff in January of 1972. Vogel died in 2001 at the age of 90. *St. Louis Post-Dispatch*, December 30, 1971, and March 16, 2001.

[16] "A friend of Gussie's called me for lunch … Over lunch the man told me Gussie had an idea I was in partnership with Vogel. I wasn't, but he told me he thought I better tell Gussie." *Chicago Tribune*, August 13, 1972.

[17] Caray would later change his mind about Fleishman's role, telling reporters he believed his relationship with Gussie sparked jealousy among others connected to Anheuser-Busch.

[18] Caray repeated the allegation to a Peoria, Illinois audience a month later. "Back in July, a story was planted out of St. Louis indicating my contract would not be renewed," Harry told a crowd of nearly 900 at a banquet for the Peoria Ad Club. *Peoria Journal Star*, November 26, 1969.

[19] Buzz concerning Caray's next landing spot started soon after the press release from Anheuser-Busch. "One of the hot rumors in New York during the World Series was the Caray-Blattner trade," wrote Merle Jones. According to gossip, Caray would go to Kansas City to broadcast the Royals and Blattner would return to St. Louis to join Jack Buck in covering the Cardinals. *Southern Illinoisan*, October 22, 1969. Cincinnati was reportedly considered a landing spot for Caray following both the 1969 and 1970 seasons. "Stroh's Beer … is reportedly ready to meet Caray's six-figure contract demands," noted an account in the *Cincinnati Enquirer* (October 6, 1970). A Montreal columnist wrote that Caray was reportedly headed to San Diego. "We wanted Harry badly," said Padres general manager Buzzie Bavasi. "He tries to run your ball club, but I'm used to that." *The Gazette* (Montreal, Quebec), October 13, 1969; *Terre Haute Tribune*, December 24, 1969. At the time, a lightly-sourced and rarely repeated rumor regarding Caray's departure from the Cardinals appeared in print. Pushing to get a multipurpose dome facility built in his hometown, Indianapolis businessman Bill York visited St. Louis. He was asked by columnist Jimmy Claus if he had heard why Caray was released. "Only what the Busch Stadium people told me … that Harry had second-guessed manager Red Schoendienst too many times and that Schoendienst wanted Caray out." Ibid, November 16, 1969.

[20] *Suburban Journals*, October 15, 1969.

[21] One caller announced a planned protest at Busch Stadium for Monday, October 13th. A petition to reinstate Caray had already begun circulating in Jefferson City. A second one in suburban St. Louis had already attracted some 700 signatures. The brewery was also flooded with letters of protest. From the village of La Grange, Illinois (a Chicago suburb), mayor Thomas Brant sent a letter to Gussie on official town hall stationery. Describing himself as a Cub fan and not much of a beer drinker, he praised Caray as "a super-salesman" and wished him well. "I don't believe this decision will benefit either of your organizations," Brant told Busch. "Mr. Caray could be the chief beneficiary, and I for one hope that he is." From the St. Louis suburb of Overland, Merrill and Jeannette Teson mailed in a newspaper article on Jack Buck and his new sidekick, Jim Woods. "WE ARE OUT OF BUD BUT NOT SCHLITZ. WE LOVE HARRY CARAY," they wrote across the article in black ink and block letters. *The Fleishman Papers*.

[22] At the time, Caray held 8,957 shares of Anheuser-Busch stock. At about $65 a share, the value was approximately $582,000. *Globe-Gazette* (Mason City, Iowa), October 21, 1969.

²³ One caller reminded Caray that "Bing Devine got rehired and there's still a chance. Keep your chin up," he told Harry. "The difference about Mr. Devine and me was that [A-B executive] Dick Meyer never did want him to be fired and he always had Meyer in his corner," Caray responded. "I don't think Meyer will be in my corner."

²⁴ "I think Mr. Busch [Gussie] must have felt badly about it," Caray said at one point. Fields later reminded him that surely Gussie had veto power over any such decision. "That's true and that makes me hurt, too," Caray said before quickly directing suspicion elsewhere. "But when you have a son who is being groomed to take over a corporation as big as Anheuser-Busch, you certainly can't overrule on things he wants to do or he's never going to be able to do anything." Less than two years later, in the spring of 1971, Gussie bypassed his son and made Meyer the first non-Busch president in company history. Meyer resigned in 1974.

²⁵ Smaller-market media outlets again rallied behind Caray. "Nobody can match Harry's style ... never, never, never," wrote Jim Kimball. "I'm truly going to miss him." *Journal Gazette* (Mattoon, Illinois), October 11, 1969.

²⁶ *County News*, October 15, 1969.

²⁷ *Southern Illinoisan,* May 8, 1970.

²⁸ *St. Louis Globe-Democrat*, October 26, 1958. "We must remember to ask Gussie Busch to put us on the payroll. If the word of newspapermen is that important to the operation of the Cardinals, maybe something ought to be done about it," wrote Burnes. "Why such a statement [from Caray] was made we'll never know."

²⁹ Others agreed. "Newspapermen, for the most part, consider Caray an excellent reporter with a nose for news," wrote Bill Fleischman of the *St. Louis Globe-Democrat. The Sporting News*, November 15, 1961. That year, Harry's baseball pregame show featured a debate between Cardinals manager Solly Hemus and umpire Frank Dascoli. On a Sunday in Philadelphia, Hemus was ejected from a game. He later told reporters the umpires "blew" every important call of the series. At a luncheon the next day in Pittsburgh he said, "[Umpires] Frank Secory and Dascoli are the most arrogant umpires and they don't give 100 percent." Informed of Hemus's comments at the ballpark later that day, Dascoli responded by saying, "Let's have a press conference." Caray then invited Dascoli and Hemus to go on his program. The manager again called Dascoli "arrogant" and the umpire responded by calling Hemus a "real busher- a busher as a player and a busher as a manager." After the interview, Caray invited the two men to shake hands. They refused. The on-air debate "was such a great idea I wished I'd thought of it myself," wrote Cincinnati columnist Pat Harmon. "I salute Caray for his genius." *Cincinnati Post and Times-Star*, May 18, 1961.

³⁰ The Fordyce Lane home is named in the story announcing August and Susan's divorce. Susan mentioned another home in a later interview. "We lived on August's farm in St. Peters," she told Jerry Berger. *St. Louis Post-Dispatch,* November 14, 1969, and June 13, 1995.

31 *Peoria Journal Star*, November 26, 1969. William Fisher of Gardner Advertising sent a copy of the article to Fleishman. "There seems to be no length to which he [Caray] will go to strike back," Fisher wrote.

32 *Florida Today*, March 30, 1975.

33 In other interviews around this time, Caray didn't sound nearly as confident about his post-Cardinals future. "Caray said the firing crushed him," wrote columnist George Lapides. *Memphis Press-Scimitar*, May 5, 1982.

34 *Pittsburgh Post-Gazette*, July 5, 1991.

35 In his autobiography, Caray indicated that the line about not raping anyone applied to rumors surrounding more than one woman. "For several months, I'd been hearing stories at home and on the road," he wrote. "I was allegedly having an affair with this executive's wife or that executive's wife."

36 Smith, *Voices of the Game*.

37 Hernon and Ganey, *Under the Influence*.

38 *Daily Press* (Newport News, Va.), July 28, 1991. (Syndicated Knight-Ridder story.)

39 *St. Louis Post-Dispatch*, June 13, 1995.

40 Smith, *Voices of the Game*.

41 *The Riverfront Times*, November 8, 2012. "Before I moved away from St. Louis, I worked for eight or nine months at Tony's. I was not the main maître d', but I greeted people at the door in a tux. This was at the old location, where you had the downstairs dining room for those who wanted to be seen and the upstairs for those who wanted privacy. I was working the night when the two came in together and were seated downstairs. Everyone in the restaurant knew who Harry Caray was, and it quickly flashed around to the staff that the beautiful blond woman who was with him – and getting along with very well – was Mrs. Busch. They were openly affectionate." https://www.riverfronttimes.com/news/busch-unbottled-divulging-secrets-from-the-sudsy-to-the-sordid-a-new-book-pops-the-top-off-st-louis-beer-brewing-dynasty-2501601

42 *Fleishman Papers*. Fleishman sent a copy of Skip's letter to Hawks owner Tom Cousins. "I am disappointed that Skip would write such a letter, and secondly, that he would be so foolish as to use Atlanta Hawks' stationery," Cousins replied. "As you can imagine, neither the Hawks organization nor I had any knowledge of this letter."

43 *The Daily Pantagraph* (Bloomington, Illinois), November 22, 1972. Caray said he purchased 1,000 shares of Schlitz in 1969. Thanks to stock splits, he had 3,000 shares three years later. He had sold *some* of his Anheuser-Busch stock. "The other day, I sold 1,000 shares and you know something? It hurt a little," he said.

44 Falstaff acquired Griesedieck Brothers Brewery in 1957.

45 *Chicago Tribune*, April 4, 1976.

46 "It was 1976 and Anheuser-Busch, then the No. 1 beer company in Chicago, suffered a strike, causing the huge brewer to limit its supply and thereby infuriate bar owners and beer retailers. So what did tavern owners and retailers do? They sought more beer

from G. Heileman Brewing Co. and Miller Brewing Co., and St. Louis-based Anheuser has been looking to regain its market share in Chicago ever since." Ibid, August 5, 1997.
[47] *Belleville News-Democrat*, April 10, 1980.
[48] *St. Louis Post-Dispatch*, February 23, 1981. At one point in the early 1980s, Heileman's market share in Chicago was greater than forty-percent. By 1993, its numbers had fallen to 24.3 percent. Anheuser-Busch claimed 16 percent. Both, however, trailed market leader Miller at 45.4 percent. *La Crosse Tribune*, June 30, 1993.
[49] "Busch III wasn't interested in baseball. He saw the team as a drag on the balance sheet." *St. Louis Post-Dispatch*, July 14, 2008. "Baseball had never been fun for him. He was not a fan." Hernon and Ganey, *Under the Influence*.

Welcome Home, Harry

Caray's St. Louis years coincided with the transformation of the country from the atomic age to the space age. His post-Cardinal career featured a more personal trajectory: A popular radio personality to hundreds of thousands would evolve into a familiar television face to tens of millions. The man known for his iconic voice became just as celebrated for his oversized glasses.

The last third of Harry's life can be framed in three distinctive phases: In the years 1970 to 1972, Caray called baseball in other cities but still called St. Louis home; The Caray from 1973 to 1981 represented an unchained, unchecked Harry, at times a bellicose broadcaster emboldened by owners he either battled or befriended; Caray's years from 1982 until his death featured a friendlier Harry at the peak of his popularity.

It all began with a brief West Coast detour.

What had been rumored since the fall of 1969 became official in the winter of 1970. In January, the Oakland A's introduced Caray as their new lead broadcaster. Harry left the Midwest and the National League to join Charlie Finley's American League club on the West Coast. The micro-managing Oakland owner was known to call the booth during broadcasts and discarded announcers like umpires threw out scuffed baseballs. Harry knew from the beginning that the match might not last. "Better get a lot of pictures now," Caray said at the introductory news conference, "Charlie may not be speaking to me in July."

The new league brought new challenges. On the way to his first spring training broadcast, Caray got lost on the drive from Phoenix to Yuma. He had to charter a plane from a rural airfield to make it on time.[1] His departure from the Cardinals had also given him fresh perspective. "I guess I found out that it's the game I love so much and not just one particular team," he said early in the season.[2] He began to realize not every club negotiated contracts like Anheuser-Busch. "The beautiful thing about this contract with Finley is that it doesn't have any restrictions on what I can do outside games," Caray said. In St. Louis, Harry had once turned down the chance to do NFL games on CBS because Falstaff sponsored the broadcasts.[3] "Once you turn down a network, they somehow forget all about you. I've never had another opportunity," he said in the early 1970s. The St. Louis brewery had also hampered Caray's ability to do commercials for non-Anheuser Busch products. "My love for the Cardinals was so great it blinded my business sense."[4]

Caray's new sense of business kept him busy year-round. He began a five-minute daily syndicated radio program, wrote a weekly column carried by Midwest newspapers and launched a home-study course to educate future broadcasters. The Harry Caray School of Broadcasting opened with an office in the Pierre Laclede building in suburban St. Louis. [5]"My advisors tell me it will be a fantastic money maker," he wrote to a newspaper columnist.[6]

Caray also continued calling Mizzou football, jumping from KMOX to WIL (the flagship station for his syndicated show). Outside of baseball, all these ventures – new and old – were based in the St. Louis area. The Harry Caray Sports Institute produced his radio show with Caray's two sons doing much of the heavy lifting. "Skip and Chris help in securing information, writing the show and putting the thing together," said Harry.

Family was top of mind for Caray when *The Sporting News* caught up with him in June. Explaining why he didn't move to Oakland, Harry mentioned his wife and daughters by name. "St. Louis is still my home," he said, "and Marian and I didn't want to take our daughters, Michele (13) and Elizabeth (7), out of school."[7]

Despite being in a new city in a new league with no family present, Harry quickly settled into a routine, one that would become familiar in Chicago. He preferred day games – "more time to prowl the pubs" – and found new drinking partners who had no connections to baseball. (One was a singer and another wrote the entertainment column for the *Oakland Tribune*.) When the A's did play under the lights, Harry would rise around 9:30 a.m., have coffee and read the newspapers. "The first box score I look for every day in the papers is the one involving the Cardinals," he once confessed.[8] By 5:30 p.m., he'd be at the park preparing for another night of baseball. Harry had a new 1970 Dodge to get him around the Bay Area, and Finley had set him up with a "bachelor's apartment" overlooking Lake Merritt. "It's great sleeping here. Blankets most every night," he said.[9]

But Oakland wasn't St. Louis. "The country out here is beautiful," Caray wrote to *Southern Illinoisan* columnist Merle Jones over the summer. "If St. Louis were not so much a part of my life, I'd move out here in a moment." Caray had other issues that gave him pause. He and Finley didn't always see eye-to-eye. The Oakland owner wanted him to change his trademark phrase "Holy Cow!" to "Holy Mule!" (Finley had adopted the Missouri Mule as a mascot when the A's played in Kansas City.) "I think the world of Charlie, but when he made that suggestion, I told him politely what he could do with the mule," Caray recalled with a chuckle.

He also clashed with broadcast partner Monte Moore. Caray didn't endear himself to Moore by making it clear who would be the lead broadcaster. "You're a good announcer," Harry said he told him. "But you're young, and I've been in the business 25 years. I pulled myself up by the bootstraps. I know all the tricks. If you get in a fight with me, I'll knock you off. I'll kill you. But if you go along, who knows how long I'll be here."[10]

"That was the least enjoyable year as far as working with someone," Moore said years later. "But I'll still say to this day that if there were one game left for a championship, I'd like to hear him do it."[11]

By October, Caray was back in Missouri. His one-year contract had expired and wasn't renewed. For the second straight year, he was searching for a new baseball gig. "Did Caray quit the A's or was he pushed?" asked the *San Francisco Examiner* before answering its own question. "Probably he decided to move along." (Not everyone agreed.)[12] Starting with his appearance on the *Bill Fields Show* just days after being let go by the Cardinals, Caray had made his desire to stay in the Midwest clear. As one columnist noted, "Harry Caray is deserting Charlie Finley after one year because he loves his domicile and family in St. Louis too much to remain 1,000 miles away most of the year."[13]

Harry attended World Series games in Cincinnati with no job in hand and more rumors swirling about his future.[14] "If anybody needs a good announcer in St. Louis, I'm available," he told the *Globe-Democrat's* Peter Rahn shortly after the Series ended.

He also reflected on his year in Oakland and his failed goal of attracting one million fans to A's games. "They drew 780,000, which was roughly [123] more than a year ago," Harry said. "Granted, that's not much of an increase, but the other side of the story is that the San Francisco Giants – right across the bay – dropped 140,000 people at the gate. I figure if I hadn't been there, the A's might have lost in attendance."

Caray's comments about an attendance boost – made to reporters at the beginning of the season – caught the attention of the Cardinals. "I know you are interested in attendance at Oakland," front office executive Jim Toomey wrote to Fleishman. "Here is a story about it you may enjoy reading."

Fleishman had kept a file of press clippings on Caray going back to Anheuser-Busch's purchase of the team. When the Cardinals decided not to renew Harry's contract, the public relations executive collected stories about it from all over the country – small-town papers across Missouri and Illinois; Chattanooga, Tennessee; Wheeling, West Virginia; Vincennes, Indiana; Marquette, Michigan;

Shreveport, Louisiana to Sacramento, California. The dozens of clippings were often identical one or two paragraph wire reports differing only in the headline. Fleishman preserved all of them as if he needed to read it – and read it again – to believe it.

When the *Memphis Commercial Appeal* published a profile of Harry a few years later, Fleishman sent copies of it to Gussie Busch and several other brewery and club executives with a note attached. "Harry admits he is great and by-the-by, he has told everyone about his love affairs or the charges which nobody has mentioned but himself," he wrote. "I guess he could be his own best press agent."[15]

In the early 1970s, the Cardinals and Caray circled each other like two heavyweights at the beginning of a boxing match. Across his various platforms, Harry repeatedly turned to his years in St. Louis and offered regular commentary on his former team. "I loved the Cardinals – and I mean I loved them. I sent them a telegram today," he said at the beginning of his time in California. "I wished them good luck, said I hope they win it in the National League – and then lose four straight to Oakland."

While he offered words of support to the team and acknowledged he still kept in communication with players such as Bob Gibson and Mike Shannon, Caray also made clear there was no love lost when it came to front office and brewery executives. "St. Louis is my home. It's where my friends live – and where my enemies live." He repeated charges that the brewery tried to blackball him in his hometown. "I know it happened: Three people told me, although they would deny it to their grave – the station that touches Caray gets no Anheuser-Busch advertising; it also gets nothing from the two biggest ad agencies in St. Louis."[16] But with a daily radio show and a weekly column, Harry declared victory over his tormenters. "They failed," Caray told the *Los Angeles Times*.

The debut of Caray's syndicated radio program demonstrated the lengths Anheuser-Busch executives went to keep tabs on their former employee. Don Hamel obtained a transcript of Caray's first show before it aired and circulated it to various concerned parties.[17] ("Make 3 photo [copies] stat. Send 1 to [Bob] Broeg," someone scrawled over the inter-office correspondence.) "As you can see, this supposed sports show has turned out to be an editorial comment, at least for the first show," Hamel stated. "I know management at WIL has heard the show but I have been unable to determine their reaction. From my past experience, a station normally would reserve the right to cancel any program that would contain adverse material."[18]

Holy Cow St. Louis!

Absent from the local airwaves since broadcasting the Orange Bowl on New Year's Day (a 10-3 Missouri loss to Penn State), Caray returned on April 6 with an editorial on the broadcasting industry. After a few introductory remarks, he got right to the point: "Today, our subject is going to be a few well-chosen jabs at my own profession, which could certainly stand some improvement. We seem to be in a day and age where the opinionated man is in a lot of trouble," Harry said. "More and more announcers are becoming nothing more than shills, men who praise the club for which they work whether or not that club deserves praise," he declared. "I personally don't think it's fair to the fan for the broadcaster to be a shill. Rooting for your team is one thing. Lying for them is something else again."[19]

An editorial two days later created even wider ripples as Harry launched a blistering attack on the statue of Stan Musial. The statue unveiled in August of 1968 outside Busch Stadium II took three years and cost $35,000. To critics like Caray (and others), the statue wasn't an accurate likeness. Sculptor Carl Mose should be a "good sport," Harry insisted, and re-do the piece. "There is no one I admire more than Musial, which is why I am making such a federal case of this monstrosity," he said.

While *Globe-Democrat* columnist Rahn sympathized with Caray's attempt to break through in a crowded radio market, he viewed the critique as a cynical grab for attention. "Caray's stops-out effort to re-establish his new show on St. Louis radio is understandable. It is a tough medium," he wrote. "So it was predictable that Harry would be taking some potshots at some St. Louis memories that peeved him back when he wasn't allowed. But, holy cow, did the first give'em the shaft subject have to be so 'safe?' After all, that statue can't talk back."[20]

Other Caray targets could. In his editorials and columns, Harry expressed regret for the departure of general manager Bob Howsam: "The press-influenced Cardinals have reacted as if Howsam never existed"; bemoaned the loss of Orlando Cepeda: "It isn't any accident wherever Cepeda plays, they win"; and stressed how much the Cardinals missed third-base coach Joe Schultz: "He was important because he could do what the manager, being so nice a guy, couldn't do. Teamed with Schultz, Schoendienst was a far better manager than he is without him." Near the end of a 1970 season that saw the Cardinals finish in fourth place for the second straight season, Caray ended one column with these words: "You really can't run a ballclub like a brewery!"

In January of 1971, Caray got his wish to land a baseball job closer to St. Louis when the White Sox named him their new announcer. (Friend Pete Vonachen had recommended him to Chicago vice president Stu Holcomb.)

Harry once again stressed family and home as part of the decision-making process. "Yes, I could have stayed in Oakland," Harry said. "But, you know St. Louis is my home. It's only 35 minutes by plane from Chicago and four hours by automobile. My family is in St. Louis ... Oakland is a fine city, but the only way I would've stayed would be to have moved my family out there."[21]

Caray's return to the Midwest created additional anxiety for those in St. Louis (and there were many) who followed his every move. When the White Sox added a station in nearby Granite City, Illinois to their radio network, it caught the attention of KMOX. "Bob Hyland of KMOX in St. Louis did his best to get the station off the network but he was unsuccessful," Harry claimed.[22] Although Caray would later go out of his way to praise Hyland in his autobiography, the early 1970s tension between the broadcaster and the brewery extended to the man running St. Louis's most popular radio station. "If the public only knew just how much [time] Caray spent in Hyland's hair and then in Fleishman's, you'd have a bestseller," Joe Melosi of the *Alton Telegraph* told columnist Jim Bell. "There's clearly no love lost between Caray and KMOX's general manager."[23]

Adding White Sox baseball to the list of Caray's media duties meant Harry could now be heard or read year-round practically every day of the week in the St. Louis area. He was gone from Cardinals baseball but hardly forgotten. A lampooning of Harry at the St. Louis Ad Club's annual Gridiron Dinner in 1971 proved to be the highlight of the evening. In a skit mocking radio's rush hour coverage, an imitator proclaimed, "Hello again, everybody. This is Harry Caray and it's a beautiful day for a traffic jam."[24]

This codependent relationship between Harry and the St. Louis establishment continued throughout 1971 and much of the next year. "I still love the Cardinals," Harry admitted in August 1972. "Yes, I suppose if Busch sold the Cardinals and I had a chance to return to St. Louis, I'd go tomorrow. In fact, I'd get there somehow tonight if they asked me to."[25]

But Harry's life took a dramatic turn three months later when second wife Marian filed for divorce, rupturing his relationship with the city. Caray made a permanent move to Chicago's Ambassador East Hotel. His broadcasts of Missouri football games stopped.[26] His syndicated radio and newspaper deals ended. Advertisements for his broadcasting school ceased.

The biggest proof that Harry's relationship with the city had changed can be found in Fleishman's preserved files. The PR mogul's longtime habit of collecting Caray newspaper clippings halted after 1972.

*****

After two years of broadcasting White Sox games on a small network of low-power AM and FM stations (the single Chicago-area AM outlet on the Sox network in 1971 powered down to just 500 watts after dark), Caray began 1973 on clear-channel 50,000-watt WMAQ. The team also announced a new television deal, with Harry now describing six innings on the visual medium with just three on the radio. Caray's transition from distinctive voice to recognizable face had begun.

Appearing nightly on television brought new challenges to the color-blind Caray. One evening, he showed up for the pregame show in a dark red shirt, a red and white striped pair of Bermuda shorts and bright red socks. A few days earlier, he appeared in an all-pink ensemble.[27] "I really don't know what colors I'm wearing," Harry once confessed.[28] (To avoid these fashion faux pas, Caray systematically organized his wardrobe, grouping matching ties, slacks, shirts, and jackets.)

The 1973 schedule also featured an occasional partner whose broadcast history predated Harry's time in the booth. The White Sox announced over the winter that Dizzy Dean would periodically appear on the telecasts. The baseball season marked somewhat of a farewell tour for Dizzy (he died the following year), who also made a memorable appearance on NBC's Monday Night Baseball. In between innings, Dean sang "Wabash Cannonball" on the network and over the stadium's public address system. Launching into the second verse caused a momentary delay in the game between Houston and San Francisco, with the home plate umpire waving his arms in a "cease-and-desist manner."[29]

Dean's reunion with Harry brought back memories of their days in St. Louis when the duo battled for the attention of Cardinal fans and the blessing of Sam Breadon. "That will be something, won't it?" Dean asked. "I'm going to say he slud into second and Harry will give'em holy cow." The sayings and expressions of these two men influenced broadcasters for decades. In 1984, *Sports Illustrated* launched a campaign to find the best announcer in small-town America. They found him in Fergus Falls, Minnesota, where 69-year-old Odis (Oats) LeGrand had broadcast more than 3,500 high school football and basketball games. He described his style as a cross between Dizzy and Harry. "I really murder the language and I scream louder than Caray ever did."[30]

Dizzy and Harry's sentimental journey masked more serious issues in Caray's life. In January of 1973, Harry's soon-to-be ex-wife filed a lawsuit against Caray's soon-to-be third wife. Marian Caray filed the suit against Dolores "Dutchie" Johnson, asking for $200,000 in damages. Harry's second wife alleged "that the defendant intentionally and maliciously gained the affections of Caray."[31]

In this interim phase between marriages, Caray's enthusiastic style would sometimes be replaced by wearier and more worn-out tones.

In June, a reporter asked his thoughts on players for the upcoming All-Star game and whether he preferred to see up-and-coming talent or more familiar faces. "What the hell is the difference?" Caray responded. "I don't care about the game. I don't even go. I take the three days off. It's just a spectacle."[32]

In August of the following year, Caray began boycotting his three-inning play-by-play stint on the radio along with his pregame interview. The dispute originated in WMAQ's decision to end its White Sox broadcasts after the 1974 season. After the announcement, Caray interviewed a part-time producer at WMAQ and got him to agree with him that the station was making a mistake. WMAQ responded by firing the employee, Jim Malia, and placed Caray on a seven-second delay. Harry responded with a boycott. "I couldn't care less whether they carry baseball or not," Harry told the *Post-Dispatch* in the middle of his strike. "I'm doing nine innings of baseball every day. And it gets to be a hell of a drag."[33]

Harry and Marian were officially divorced in April. "I haven't found the right one yet," Caray later told a reporter. "My last one cost me a half-million." Harry's other battles during this era were familiar to anyone who knew his history. He feuded with his manager and bashed underperforming players.

Caray described Chuck Tanner as "Nixon-like" and a "horse-shit manager" during a 1974 season that saw the White Sox finish in fourth place with a .500 record. Tanner responded by calling Caray "scum" and "a front-running, second-guessing liar."[34]

He also had tough words for players such as third baseman Bill Melton. "It's ridiculous how spoiled this guy is," said Caray. "When a guy makes $100,000 a year and is supposed to be the team's leading home run and RBI man, and he's having a lousy year, it's pretty tough not to be critical … especially when he loafs on the job."[35]

Harry's radio strike ended after a couple of weeks and WMAQ – under new management – changed its mind and stuck with the White Sox for 1975.[36] So did Harry, who signed a one-year deal after the season ended for an estimated $100,000, ending months of speculation about his future. At one point, according to *Chicago Tribune* columnist Gary Deeb, Caray's chances of staying in Chicago was "a 50-50 proposition."[37] (While Caray survived, his broadcast partner did not. Tanner "got Caray's equally honest partner Bob Waller fired last fall," Deeb wrote the following summer.)

Kansas City Star reporter William McCorkle found Caray in a better mood in September of 1975 during a visit to the Missouri city. He was joined on the trip by his new wife. Dutchie and Harry were married in May. She was 46 years old. He was 61, but claimed he was 56. "What's the difference?" Harry asked. "Everyone lies a little bit."

The newlyweds still maintained their separate homes. Harry kept his suite at the Ambassador East while Dutchie stayed in suburban St. Louis. The couple united during her occasional visits to Chicago and road trips to Kansas City, while spending the offseason together at their home in California. "Dutchie lives in St. Louis, I live in Chicago, and we have a home together in Palm Springs. Every time we get together, it's a honeymoon," he once said of the union that lasted the rest of his life.

She spoke of his late-night habits – "That's Harry Time," she said of his penchant for hanging out in Chicago bars that stayed open until 4:00 a.m. And his restless nature – "Harry can't sit still," she remarked as her husband wandered around a restaurant waiting for lunch to be served. "He seemed more than a little disappointed when his announcement to a couple of employees that he was 'Harry Caray with the White Sox' drew virtually no response," wrote McCorkle.

Caray told McCorkle he enjoyed playing tennis but no longer golf, saying it took too much time and he didn't have the patience for it. He also acknowledged – "without hesitation," the reporter noted – that the Cardinals were still his favorite team. "Once a Cardinal fan, always a Cardinal fan," Harry said. "I was born and raised on them."[38]

If his 1972 separation and later divorce from his second wife punctured his relationship with St. Louis and ended flirtatious talk of a reunion with the Cardinals, Harry came to another crossroads in 1975. The newly married broadcaster had new choices to consider, a confluence brought about by Caray's relationships with baseball owners and employers – past, present, and future.

*****

One thing Harry never wavered on (in addition to his Cardinal fandom) in his early post-St. Louis years was his respect and admiration for Gussie:

"I loved him then and I love him now although I haven't seen him since we parted company nearly three years ago." (1972)

"The old man loves me." (1975)

"It wasn't Gussie Busch's fault. We were dear friends." (1978)

Stunned and hurt by Busch's verdict in 1969, Caray quickly saw the advantage of telling a tale that cast the spotlight on a "hatchet man" in the organization and away from the ultimate decision-maker.[39] "Someday, I may write a book on the subject," he said just months after being let go by the Cardinals. "It has all the elements of a bestseller – sex, intrigue, everything."[40]

With Jack Buck off to *Grandstand* in August of 1975, Busch had the opportunity to reward his former drinking buddy and card-playing partner. Ousted as CEO of Anheuser-Busch earlier in the year, Busch still chaired the brewery's board of directors and served as president of the Cardinals. He was considering purchasing the team for himself (ultimately deciding against it)[41] and, with Buck headed to New York, had a vacant broadcasting role to fill.

In town because his wife was undergoing surgery at Barnes Hospital, Caray received a message at his hotel to call Busch. The two men met the next day at either Grant's Farm or Busch's shooting lodge in St. Peter's (accounts vary) and discussed a potential Harry return to the Cardinals. "Nobody knows about this but you and me," Gussie told him. The conversation got serious enough for Busch attorney Lou Susman to make an appearance. But when Susman mentioned speaking with Fleishman, the deal was off. "That's it. Meeting over," Caray said upon hearing the name of his nemesis. The last serious attempt to lure Harry back to his hometown fell apart over a long-standing dispute between bitter rivals. "No way I was coming back to St. Louis," said Caray, who later claimed that Cardinal fans preferred his return by a margin of "95-1."[42]

Harry rejected the Cardinals at the same time he was hanging by a thread in Chicago. Caray's feuds with players and manager Chuck Tanner frustrated White Sox owner John Allyn, who believed Harry's words had damaged the franchise. "If I own the club next year, Harry won't be with us," Allyn said in a television interview at the end of the season. Caray responded by calling Allyn a "stupid man" and expressed no regret over his behavior. "I'm the only thing the fans have to talk about. If there are players who don't like me, it's only the ones who had lousy seasons – Bill Melton, Ken Henderson, and maybe Wilbur Wood." [43]

Allyn never got the chance to fire Caray because he announced a sale of the team to a group led by Bill Veeck just days later. An ecstatic Harry welcomed the change. "I know Bill Veeck as being a great baseball man and a colorful man who always tries to please the fans," Caray said. "I feel the same way." The man forced out of St. Louis because of Anheuser-Busch money, kept the White Sox for Chicago, and Caray in the broadcast booth.

In the span of a few months, Caray rejected his former employer, insulted his current owner, and embraced the man who would soon be his new boss in Chicago. What his adopted city gave him (besides a larger population with more plentiful watering holes) was freedom. Caray lived life under a microscope in St. Louis, constantly receiving scrutiny from a coterie of men. There was Hyland at

KMOX and Fisher at Gardner Advertising (the man who demanded more information about Caray's phone calls in Florida). Anheuser-Busch executive Hamel was the marketing manager for Busch, the beer Caray endorsed. Harry negotiated his contracts with Dick Meyer and his every action and utterance was monitored by Toomey or Fleishman. While Harry took delight in singling out Fleishman – whom he called "a real snake in the grass" – it was also these other men who Caray surely had in mind when he rejected the offer to return to the Cardinals. "There would be a lot of people [in St. Louis] who would always be in the way of a guy like me," he said years later.[44]

These restrictor plates didn't exist in Chicago during his White Sox years. In a larger city with a weaker owner (Allyn had to sell because of financial difficulties), Harry did and said as he pleased. He'd roll up to Comiskey Park in the back of a Cadillac limousine, emerging from the vehicle with music blaring and the driver unrolling the red carpet. "Caray's a phenomenon," Bob Rubin once wrote, "both behind the mike and on the streets."[45]

If Caray enjoyed this kind of life under Allyn, imagine the kind of fun that awaited him with Veeck, a man whose antics, stunts and promotions over the years included giving away everything from livestock to 10,000 cupcakes to five thousand silver dollars in a wheelbarrow.[46]

While Veeck and Caray had clashed in St. Louis, the new owner of the White Sox was well aware of Harry's appeal. "Regardless of what I think of him, the man is good at his job. His mail runs 3-1 in favor in the city, 8-1 in favor out of the city ... fantastic odds in favor of anything, because people usually only write negative mail," said Veeck shortly after taking over the team. "If I hadn't hired Caray, I'd have been cutting off my nose to spite my face."[47]

Caray appreciated Veeck's faith in him, even though he didn't like all the new owner's plans, including a lighthearted ribbing of starting one game at 10:30 in the morning. "Well, after all Bill Veeck's good ideas, I guess he's entitled to have one like this," he said on the air one evening. "So, on your way home, friends, stop by the ballpark for breakfast."[48]

Veeck unveiled new uniform designs (including shorts instead of pants that the players wore for a few games),[49] presided over the infamous Disco Demolition Night, got Harry to start singing into the microphone during the seventh-inning stretch and hired one of the game's first female announcers. Mary Shane debuted in 1977, the same year Jimmy Piersall joined Harry full-time in the broadcast booth (after serving as a guest analyst for several games the prior year).[50]

If Harry's harsh words could sometimes land like a torch, the combination of Caray and Piersall represented a full-blown incinerator.[51] "When Harry's moon face shines on Jimmy, Piersall grows fangs and a fur coat and says anything that pops into his head," noted a *Chicago Sun-Times* sportswriter. "When Caray delivers a biting criticism, Piersall tops him."

"Harry was always loyal to me when things got a little sticky," Piersall would later write in his book, *The Truth Hurts*. "And that, of course, happened a lot."[52] It happened frequently because the two men had much in common. Both could be outspoken and critical and suffered from an inability to let bygones be bygones. "Don't keep bringing up a bad play," a television executive once told Piersall. "Once you've said it, let it drop." Easier said than done. "I didn't always follow that advice," Harry's partner admitted. "Piersall," wrote *Boston Globe* columnist Peter Gammons, "makes his living on other people's blood."[53]

A former outfielder, Piersall spent 17 years in the major leagues, including a rookie season in 1952 in which he suffered a nervous breakdown and spent time in a hospital. He chronicled the saga in his book *Fear Strikes Out*. (Anthony Perkins played Piersall in the movie version.) A playing career that featured fistfights, ejections, and suspensions presaged a volatile broadcasting career.

His time with Harry began with happier times. The 1977 White Sox won 90 games and set an attendance record that had stood since 1960. Harry got a raise in 1978 – to $135,000 – but sluggers Richie Zisk and Oscar Gamble (who combined for 61 home runs) departed for even bigger money in free agency. When Zisk returned to town with his new team, the Texas Rangers, Caray endorsed the idea of booing him when he came to the plate and said during the broadcast that Zisk had "quit" on the White Sox near the end of the prior season. Rangers pitcher Jon Matlack heard Harry's comments from the clubhouse. "If Harry Caray said the things about me that he said about Richie on the radio, I'd have to kill the man," he told reporters. "As soon as I saw him tomorrow I'd punch his lights out. I've never heard such a vicious attack. I lost all respect for Caray tonight." Zisk said he was aware of Caray's critical comments, "But that doesn't bother me. I'm a bigger person than he is."[54]

In the laundry list of Harry and Jimmy contretemps during this stormy era, this one barely registered. Caray and Matlack made peace the next day.[55] Other quarrels had longer-ranging ramifications. Thanks to a White Sox team that lost 90 games and finished in fifth place for the first of three straight seasons, the broadcasters had a lot of material to work with. But while the White Sox struggled, Harry and Jimmy flourished from the beginning, attracting a half-million viewers on television and another 100,000 listeners on radio. "I don't always agree with what they say. But they're good," Veeck said after the 1978 season.

Popularity gave Caray and Piersall a lot of leeway. Harry's rants tended to be more in the vein of a frustrated fan – "What are we waiting for?" an impatient Caray said one night demanding the removal of a struggling pitcher – while Piersall's words and actions carried more ominous tones. "We are concerned," a letter from the law firm representing the Umpire's Association to Piersall read in part, "that your comments exceed the limits of fairness."

The White Sox had a fan known as "Drummer Boy" who would bang on a drum while parading through the stands. Parking himself directly below the broadcast booth one night proved too much for Piersall to handle. He ran out of the booth and physically threatened the drum-banging fan. [56]

Other episodes went beyond threats. Acting as a part-time outfield coach for the White Sox, Piersall had his role terminated by manager Tony La Russa in 1980, the same season the broadcaster referred to Veeck's wife – Mary Frances – as "a colossal bore." The manager's decision and the broadcaster's words led to two separate incidents in a single night.

When Bob Gallas, a reporter for the Arlington Heights *Daily Herald*, began questioning players before a game about Piersall's removal from his coach's role, Jimmy overheard the conversation and started yelling at him. The shouting quickly escalated into a physical confrontation. "I couldn't believe it; he was just yelling at me, and then he started strangling me," said Gallas, whose neck was covered with bruises. It took White Sox bullpen coach Art Kusnyer and a locker room security guard to pull Piersall off the sportswriter.[57]

Piersall left the locker room for the broadcast booth when Mike Veeck (the son of Bill and Mary Frances) arrived 30 minutes later. "You can't say things like that about my mother," Piersall recalled Veeck saying. The owner's son grabbed Piersall by the neck and dragged him out of his chair. "I wanted to give him a good look at someone his own size," Veeck later told reporters.

Following the second incident, security guards escorted Piersall to Bill Veeck's office, where he began to cry and complain of pains in his chest and other body parts. The White Sox took Piersall to the Illinois Masonic Hospital, where he spent nearly a week. Piersall admitted to his psychiatrist that he had not been taking his lithium regularly.[58] After the passing of a second week, Piersall was back on the air, much to the relief of his partner ("One night I almost called you in the hospital and asked you to move over," Harry said on the air) and the dismay of his manager.

Harry and Jimmy never got over Veeck's hiring of La Russa, whose managing experience before the White Sox consisted of minor league baseball. Piersall believed Veeck gave him the job for two reasons. "First, he didn't have to pay him much. Second, he felt he could manipulate him easily." Harry criticized La

Russa frequently, even after he left Chicago's South Side. "Well, the White Sox won again. Can't see how they're doing it with that manager of theirs," he said in 1983.[59]

Tensions between the broadcasters and the manager didn't improve when Veeck, in poor health, sold the team to Eddie Einhorn and Jerry Reinsdorf. "La Russa had Reinsdorf wrapped around his little finger," Piersall claimed.

Einhorn and Reinsdorf bought a struggling franchise with declining attendance for three straight seasons. They also inherited two broadcasters with low opinions of the new owners. "With Harry and Jimmy at the mike, listeners soon got the impression that the Einhorn-Reinsdorf partnership might be compared to another team – Abbott and Costello," wrote Bob Logan. "The new owners couldn't win that propaganda war because Harry and Jimmy, neither South Side nor traditional, had every South Side traditionalist on their side."[60]

"We were a freak show," said Einhorn. "The fans thought Harry and Jimmy were the stars. Comiskey Park was an outdoor saloon, and the players didn't matter. Things were insane."[61]

Caray quickly soured on the new owners because of their push into pay television. Einhorn and Reinsdorf soured on Piersall when the broadcaster – yet again – stuck his foot in his mouth. ("Controversy follows [Piersall] the way May follows April," wrote *Chicago Sun-Times* columnist Ron Rapoport.)

Piersall was already on thin ice because of a dust-up with umpires earlier in the season.[62] That controversy led the White Sox to limit Harry and Jimmy's time together to just a few innings of radio. When play resumed in 1981 after a brief player's strike, Harry had a new television partner, Lou Brock. "The reason they gave me was that they felt Harry was getting me wound up, egging me on," Piersall explained.

Jimmy didn't need Harry to get wound up. When the two men appeared on Mike Royko's television show in September, the columnist asked Piersall about his criticisms of players. "How come the ballplayers' wives are always on your case?"

Jimmy didn't hold back. "I think each ballclub should have a clinic once a week for wives on baseball because I don't think they know what the hell baseball is. First of all, they were horny broads that wanted to get married and they wanted a little money, a little security, and a big strong ballplayer," he said.

That comment, according to *Tribune* columnist David Condon, "went virtually unnoticed" until La Russa brought it up on a radio show four days later.[63] When he did, a firestorm of protest erupted, with ownership announcing Piersall would be suspended indefinitely. When Caray left for the Cubs after the season, the curtain had closed on the memorable Harry-Jimmy era. "Only one man ever compared to interest in Piersall, and that was my first partner, the late Gabby Street," said Caray.[64] "A lot of good things come to an end," Jimmy told reporters after Harry's departure. "He's the best."[65]

*****

To understand the bombshell that hit when Caray joined the Cubs for the 1982 season, one has to appreciate geography, history, and decades of competition. Professional baseball teams in Chicago and St. Louis have been facing off against one another for more than a century. National League champion Chicago twice faced American Association champion St. Louis in the 1880s in a precursor to the modern World Series. The intensity of that rivalry never dissipated. By the late 1960s, bleacher fans at Wrigley Field had officially organized with membership cards, a meeting place, and uniforms – yellow jackets and pith helmets. "The philosophy of the Bleacher Bums is very simple," charter member Mick Nelson explained. "We love the Cubs and hate three things: 1. Harry Caray. 2. The St. Louis Cardinals. 3. Harry Caray."[66]

The Cubs and White Sox met in the World Series in 1906 but were largely defined in the twentieth century by scandals, curses, and a lack of stellar results. The 1919 Black Sox scandal eviscerated Chicago's dominant American League club. The Cubs won their last World Series of the century in 1908. In more than 12 decades of baseball, only three times have both teams qualified for the postseason in the same year.[67]

What really separated the two franchises (and perhaps still does) is the style and reputation of their fans. The White Sox attracted blue-collar and urban fans from the city's South Side. Caray's man-of-the-people approach appealed to the lunch-pail crowd. The feeling was mutual. Sportswriter Jerome Holtzman once drew this contrast between Caray and his predecessor with the White Sox, Bob Elson. "When Elson saw the fans lined up, he would run the other way. When Harry Caray sees the fans, he charges right into their midst."[68]

From the perspective of the White Sox faithful, National League games on the other side of town were the very antithesis of the Comiskey Park experience. They saw Wrigley Field as the purview of the city's more upscale North Siders and suburbanites who flocked there on weekends. These fans came to experience the ballpark and the many surrounding bars and restaurants. It was all one big tourist attraction that happened to include a baseball game – and all too much for a diehard South Sider to stomach. "Yuppie scum go back to Wrigley!" was a popular banner seen frequently at Comiskey Park.

In the midst of these historical rivalries and culture clashes, the man who cheered on the Cardinals for 25 years and yelled for the White Sox for 11 more was suddenly singing and root, root, rooting ... for the Cubbies? It was a lot to take in and took everyone – from fans and media to Harry himself – time to adjust.

Early in his career with the Cubs, Harry's drama-filled days showed no signs of abating. Months before the season began, Milo Hamilton was already complaining to anyone who would listen how upset he was over Caray usurping what he expected to be his role. In January of 1982, a reporter asked Harry what he thought of Milo's comments. "I think, and you can quote me on this," Caray told Mary Shane, the now former broadcaster turned sportswriter, "that he should either get another job or keep his mouth shut and act like a thoroughbred."[69]

Harry's hard edge surfaced that season when he returned to St. Louis. "The Cardinals have got so much talent that if they don't win it all this year, Gussie is sure to fire everybody," he loudly announced in the press lounge during his first visit to Busch Stadium in 13 years. During the telecast, he noted the size of the crowd. "Where are all the people? When I was here, on the other side of the fence as it were, this place would be packed whenever the Cardinals and the Cubs would play." With those words, the broadcaster delivered a not-so-subtle message. "When Caray was the Cardinals broadcaster he was credited with stimulating interest in the team and helping attract big crowds," wrote George Lapides in the *Memphis Press-Scimitar*.[70]

During the series, Caray also had harsh words for struggling Cubs shortstop Larry Bowa. "If a rookie came up and was hitting .186 in the 25th game, do you think he'd be playing?" After back-to-back 0-4 nights, the shortstop's batting average had fallen to .174. "We gotta get that Bowa out of the lineup," Harry said after the game.[71]

The broadcaster had struggles of his own. Cub fans didn't immediately embrace Caray's singing of "Take Me Out to the Ballgame" during the seventh-inning stretch. "Harry might as well be singing in the shower," said columnist Bob Verdi. "It's not working out," Caray conceded. "And if we don't do it right, we might as well not do it at all. Either way, it's OK with me."[72]

But like the showman and entertainer he was, Harry persisted, adapted, and fine-tuned his message. Back on the payroll of a large corporate employer, the Tribune Co., a kinder, gentler Caray emerged. Steve Stone pitched for the White Sox when Harry broadcast on the South Side and became Caray's television partner on the North Side in 1983. "Harry understood who the White Sox fans were. A lot of people really disliked Harry because he was one type of broadcaster with the White Sox [and changed]. But that was his fandom, the guys who would go to McCuddy's and have a couple of boilermakers before the game. He'd get on the players and the manager, just like everybody else in the ballpark," Stone recalled. "But Harry was really smart. And when he came to the Cubs, he knew that wasn't the Cubs fandom and he became good old grandfatherly Harry."

"Harry changed but not because he was older," Stone added. "He knew exactly who he was broadcasting to, and he knew the Tribune Co. didn't want to see that [Sox version of him]."[73]

As Caray adjusted to life at Wrigley Field, Cub fans warmed up to Harry's act. After the third out in the top of the seventh, they stood, stirred, and gazed up at the broadcast booth in anticipation. In Caray's early years with the team – the Cubs finished in fifth place, nineteen games behind in both 1982 and 1983 – a singing Harry was often the highlight of the day.

Harry's calls, cable television and a winning club made for a perfect storm in 1984. The Cubs, baseball's "Lovable Losers," stunned fans by winning the National League East. Suddenly, people around the country tuned in to watch Cubs games and hear Harry's descriptions. The man who honed his radio style in St. Louis and experienced the daily television grind with the White Sox now had a national platform. In his fortieth year in the broadcast booth, Caray emerged as a cable TV star. (A Scripps-Howard columnist called Caray "the voice of America.")[74]

"The Cardinals had the largest broadcasting network of any club in baseball when Caray was working in St. Louis. But televised games were few and only went to a limited audience in the club's drawing area. Caray was just a voice on the radio, albeit a very popular one," wrote Ray Holliman in the *St. Petersburg Times*. "Although he did TV with the White Sox, the telecasts still were seen only on the club's regional network. WGN is quite different. When Caray screams, people are watching in every state of the union. His telecasts, combined with the Cubs sudden surge after so many years of losing, have made the club the biggest ongoing sports story of the year."[75]

WGN, the Tribune's cable superstation seen by 14 million U.S. homes outside the Chicago area by 1984, stretched its tentacles from Canada to Latin America. The tiny Central American country of Belize once asked the U.S. State Department to deliver Caray to its annual festival. Cubs outfielder Gary Matthews visited the country before the 1985 season. "They tell me when Harry Caray comes on during the stretch, you can hear everybody up and down the street singing from their homes," said Matthews. "Boy, is Harry Caray ever big over there."[76]

Highly paid (Caray's salary was more than $200,000 annually at the beginning of his time with the Cubs and in the area of $500,000 by the end) and more popular than ever, a relaxed and confident Harry reconnected with his hometown. By the mid-1980s, Caray was both a pitchman for Budweiser beer and a voice on KMOX radio, joining Buck for their weekly radio show. He struck another endorsement deal with a St. Louis company when Vess Beverages introduced their "Holy Cow" soda.[77] When the Cubs opened the 1986 season with the Cardinals, Caray received a compliment from the St. Louis man whose praise and affection he sought the most. The Busch Stadium seventh-inning stretch featured the recorded voice of Gussie Busch, whose rendition of "Take Me Out to the Ballgame" brought "a big smile to Caray's face," the *Post-Dispatch* recorded. Time and money had healed a lot of wounds.

Harry even made amends with a group he had long battled – the St. Louis print media. When the *Post-Dispatch* profiled the broadcaster in 1986, Caray sent the reporters a handwritten note on his Holy Cow stationary. "I must admit that I enjoyed the article," he wrote, "and what surprised me the most was that you were fair."[78]

The reconciliation roster included Bob Broeg, whose feud with Caray stretched back to the 1940s. When Harry suffered a stroke in 1987, the columnist sent Caray a note. "I wrote to him with encouragement, advice and instructions from one who also suffered a stroke," Broeg recalled. "After his remarkable recovery, Caray expressed surprise and thanks."[79]

The hometown healing tour reached its apex during a memorable and emotional dinner one evening in St. Louis. Caray, Buck, Anheuser-Busch executive Mike Roarty and their wives met for a meal at Tony's Restaurant. "Harry and Jack were reminiscing, and the stories were just hilarious," said Roarty. When the meal ended and the couples got up to leave, someone from the back of the dining room shouted, "Welcome home, Harry."

"And you have to appreciate he's just had a stroke, he was coming back, but he was still struggling with it a little bit. And here this guy in St. Louis said, 'Welcome home, Harry,'" Roarty recalled. "And at that point, instantaneously, the whole room stood up and gave him a rousing standing ovation. We all got misty-eyed. Jack shed a tear, all of us were just stricken by this," he continued. "And Harry, he's the only one who took it in stride. 'Thank you very much, thank you.' Waving like some guy campaigning. It didn't faze him one damn bit and we were all crying."[80]

Harry's recovery from his medical maladies sparked national attention and interest. President Reagan telephoned Caray during his first night back on the air, a year before the President joined him in the Wrigley Field broadcast booth.

Holy Cow St. Louis!

In December 1988, Caray was inducted into the National Italian American Hall of Fame. Honors from the Baseball Hall of Fame, American Sportscasters Hall of Fame and the National Association of Broadcasters Hall of Fame followed. Caray's frequent presence at his Chicago restaurant endeared him to locals and tourists alike.

"He's a national landmark," Skip Caray said of his father in 1989. "I'm not being sarcastic. I really mean that. The 'Bloom County' comic strip the other day showed two guys playing baseball and one guy said, 'Well, good luck. I think the Big Guy's looking down on you today.' And then there's a long pause in the second panel. And in the third panel (the other guy) says, 'Oh, you mean Harry Caray's here?'"

"I have never seen a nonplayer receive the adulation that Harry Caray received all the time," said Tim McCarver.

The man who bonded with baseball fans from the bleachers of American ballparks to the streets of Belize had come a long way from the St. Louis kid who couldn't afford white pants for his grammar school graduation.

"My roots are here," Caray told the *Post-Dispatch* in 1994, a year after he was inducted into the St. Louis Walk of Fame. "I grew up here, went to school here. I have so many friends in St. Louis. I was born here and sold newspapers at 18th and Choteau, and played semi-pro ball here. I'll always love St. Louis."

"Did he ever get St. Louis entirely out of his blood?" asked longtime colleague Stone after Harry passed. "I don't think you ever get out of your blood the place where you're brought up and the first team you broadcast for."[81]

---

[1] *The Sporting News*, March 28, 1970.
[2] *Memphis Press-Scimitar*, April 23, 1970.
[3] Falstaff president Joe Griesedieck owned a minority position in the NFL St. Louis Cardinals, paying $250,000 for a ten-percent interest in the team in 1960. *St. Louis Post-Dispatch*, August 8, 1971. When majority owners Charles and Bill Bidwell seriously considered moving to Atlanta in 1964, Griesedieck opposed the move. Ibid, July 18, 1964.
[4] *Decatur Daily Review*, March 24, 1970; *Chicago Tribune*, August 13, 1972.
[5] The broadcasting school's office was at 7750 Clayton Road in Clayton. "You got to have a good address, you know," Caray told columnist Peter Rahn. When the school debuted in the fall of 1970, it placed ads in the St. Louis newspapers and *The Sporting News*. "Now you can learn about Sportscasting from the guy who knows the business," the ad began. *St. Louis Globe-Democrat*, March 4, 1970; *St. Louis Post-Dispatch*, October 18, 1970.

[6] *Southern Illinoisan*, August 3, 1970. Broadcasting schools were common at the time. Bob Elson's Institute of Broadcast Arts had offices in Milwaukee and Phoenix. *The Sporting News*, February 8, 1969.
[7] *The Sporting News,* June 27, 1970.
[8] *Southern Illinoisan*, August 13, 1972.
[9] *The Sporting News*, June 27, 1970.
[10] *San Francisco Examiner*, April 12, 1970.
[11] *Oakland Tribune*, April 6, 1980. Moore spent 16 years broadcasting A's baseball. During that time, he had 14 broadcast partners. Only with Caray was Moore the Number 2 man. Criticized as "bland and inoffensive," Moore didn't drink or smoke and was an elder in the Church of Christ. He was also suspected of feeding information to Finley. "He's renowned for spying on players and doing everything possible to curry the old man's favor," claimed columnist Gary Deeb. *Chicago Tribune*, January 28, 1975. But there was evidence Caray influenced Moore's broadcasts. "Two of the more virulent practitioners of the art of criticism are Monte Moore of the Oakland A's and Harry Caray of the Chicago White Sox," wrote Dave Nightengale in 1973. "They assail players with immaturity; challenge writers with impunity." *Los Angeles Times,* July 26, 1973.
[12] Broadcaster Jim Woods claimed he asked Finley why Caray was let go. "Hell, that line of bullshit Harry put out might have worked in St. Louis, but nobody was buying it here," Finley responded. Smith, *Voices of the Game.* Woods, Caray's replacement in St. Louis, left after the 1971 season to work with Moore. Finley fired him after two seasons.
[13] *The Pantagraph* (Bloomington, Illinois), October 9, 1970.
[14] The rumors largely centered around the Cincinnati Reds. "All the writers (newspaper) up there just seem to take it for granted that I've got the job in my hip pocket. They think I'm lying," Caray told Rahn. "They are wrong about that. But I hope they are right about the job." *St. Louis Globe-Democrat,* October 16, 1970.
[15] *The Fleishman Papers.*
[16] *The Kansas City Star*, April 8, 1970.
[17] Hamel, the brewery executive who informed Caray of his fate in the fall of 1969, had a new job description – according to Harry. "I had been informed by a clerk – that my contract wasn't going to be renewed," Ibid.
[18] *The Fleishman Papers.*
[19] Ibid.
[20] *St. Louis Globe-Democrat*, April 10, 1970.
[21] *Alton Telegraph*, January 19, 1971.
[22] *Southern Illinoisan*, June 6, 1971.
[23] *Alton Telegraph*, July 12, 1973.
[24] *St. Louis Post-Dispatch*, October 27, 1971. Here is how the paper described the male-only event for its audience. "Everyone dresses in a tuxedo, gulps a cocktail or two, and,

with the fairer sex barred from the Gold Room, sits back to watch the bigwigs squirm," wrote Gary Ronberg.
[25] *Southern Illinoisan*, August 13, 1972.
[26] Harry's last year broadcasting Mizzou football saw the team finish with only a 6-6 record but also one memorable victory. In January 1973, columnist Paul Logan asked Caray about his greatest announcing thrill. "To see Notre Dame beaten by Missouri last year," Harry replied. "I never thought I'd live to see it." *Daily Herald* (Arlington Heights, Illinois), January 18, 1973. Skip Caray, who broadcast Missouri football with his father for years, began calling Florida State games in the fall of 1973.
[27] *Belvedere Daily Republican,* September 4, 1973.
[28] *Chicago Tribune*, September 12, 1971.
[29] *The Sporting News*, June 9, 1973.
[30] *Sports Illustrated*, November 18, 1985.
[31] *St. Louis Post-Dispatch*, January 13, 1973.
[32] *Daily Herald*, June 29, 1973.
[33] *St. Louis Post-Dispatch*, August 22, 1974. Caray was also upset about what he saw as a lack of support from White Sox vice president and treasurer Leo Breen. "I'm so goddamn disappointed in Leo. I work way beyond the line of duty. Who the hell else in the world does nine innings every day, 18 innings on doubleheaders, and extra innings – all to help them sell radio and TV? You'd think that Leo would go to bat for me." *Chicago Tribune*, August 21, 1974. The Gary Deeb column was headlined "Harry Caray: Headed For Professional Suicide?"
[34] *Chicago Tribune,* August 3, 1975.
[35] Ibid, July 22, 1975. The White Sox traded Melton to the California Angels after the 1975 season. "I had to get out of Chicago," he said after the deal. "People turned against me because of that man upstairs [Caray]. "If I had to go back, I'd probably have quit baseball." *The Sporting News*, January 3, 1976.
[36] The White Sox left WMAQ for WBBM following the 1979 season. Veeck had been feuding with WMAQ management and terminated the club's agreement with the station a year early. Disagreements with the station also impacted Caray. When general manager Burt Sherwood asked Caray to do some free commercials, Harry refused. Sherwood responded by telling Caray to cease ad-lib mentions of restaurants and taverns he frequented and later blacked out WMAQ's coverage of Caray's singing during the seventh-inning stretch. *Chicago Tribune*, October 12, 1979.
[37] Ibid, October 16, 1975.
[38] *The Kansas City Star*, September 24, 1975. While no longer broadcasting in St. Louis, Caray still found time to do events in Cardinals territory. In the summer of 1975, Caray did the television play-by-play for the National Baseball Congress (NBC) tournament in Wichita, Kansas. In December 1977, Caray called a college basketball game between Southwest Missouri State and Drury in Springfield, Missouri. It came as the Cardinals' popularity was fading in the southwest part of the state. "I think the biggest connection

with the Cardinals was Harry Caray," a Springfield radio man told the *Kansas City Times*. "I think the Cardinals believe the state of Missouri ends in Springfield," said Tom Murray, a sportswriter for the *Joplin Globe*. "They quit coming here with promotion groups four or five years ago," he said. "Now, it's the Royals in Joplin." *Kanas City Times*, January 24, 1973. By 1979, both the Royals and Cincinnati Reds had larger radio networks than the Cardinals. *St. Louis Post-Dispatch*, April 6, 1979.

[39] "Obviously, there was a hatchet-man in the organization who wanted me out because I was on pretty good terms with Mr. Busch." *Memphis Press-Scimitar*, April 23, 1970.

[40] *Long Beach Independent Press*, March 30, 1970.

[41] Anheuser-Busch sought an independent valuation of the ballclub in the fall of 1975. Tasked with coming up with a price were two banks – Chase Manhattan and Merrill Lynch – and former Browns executive/owner Bill DeWitt Sr. The numbers reportedly came back at around $11-$13 million, with DeWitt's estimate as the lowest of the three. (DeWitt had the advantage of being one of Veeck's investors in the purchase of the White Sox.) Those figures were the same as an estimate provided by former team owner Fred Saigh before the appraisers were hired. Saigh, the largest Anheuser-Busch shareholder outside the Busch family, opposed the sale. In 1975, DeWitt Sr., along with son (and future Cardinals owner) Bill DeWitt Jr., owned the Cincinnati Stingers of the World Hockey Association and 40 percent of the Kentucky Colonels in the American Basketball Association. *St. Louis Post-Dispatch*, October 15, 1975; November 2, 1975. Busch weighed his decision to buy the Cardinals at the same time an independent arbitrator awarded pitchers Andy Messersmith and Daven McNally free-agent status, ushering in an era of escalating salaries. "Well, the inmates have taken over the asylum in baseball, too," said Cardinals board of directors member, former Hawks owner and Gussie friend Ben Kerner. Citing uncertainty in the sport, Gussie announced in January of 1976 that he was ending his attempt to buy the team. Ibid, December 28, 1975; January 27, 1976. "Gussie balked at the price. It was far cheaper to keep the title and the perks." Hernon and Ganey, *Under the Influence*. "It was much harder for Busch to tap his own wealth," said Broeg. "If you were with him, he wouldn't mind sticking you for the hot dogs or a bigger check if he thought you had an expense account." *St. Louis Post-Dispatch*, September 30, 1989.

[42] Ibid. Caray mentioned the 95-1 margin to *Kansas City Star* reporter McCorkle. The *Post-Dispatch* asked its readers in the summer of 1977 if they would like to see Caray return as an announcer for the Cardinals. The poll found 75.6 percent in favor of Harry's return. 24.4 percent opposed the idea. Ibid, September 2, 1977.

[43] *Chicago Tribune*, October 2, 1975.

[44] *St. Louis Post-Dispatch*, September 30, 1989.

[45] *Inside Sports*, August 1984.

[46] *Fort-Worth Star-Telegram,* March 6, 1976.

[47] *Detroit Free Press*, January 31, 1976.

[48] *The Times* (Hammond-East Chicago, Indiana), July 2, 1976.

[49] The shorts were designed by Veeck's wife, Mary Frances. The team wore the navy blue shorts for three games in 1976. Mary Frances Veeck died in September 2022 at the age of 102.

[50] The 1977 White Sox radio and television broadcast booths featured Caray, Piersall, Shane and Lorn Brown. "Caray will stay off the air for one inning every third game or so," wrote Gary Deeb. "Harry probably is the only big league baseball announcer who works every minute of every game, so his 1977 schedule is a bit of a landmark for him." *Chicago Tribune*, February 15, 1977.

[51] As a teenager in Missouri in the late 1970s, I would catch Harry and Jimmy describing White Sox games at night, frequently listening with my mouth open, stunned at what they were saying. The difference between their description of games compared to Buck and Shannon on KMOX was dramatic.

[52] Piersall, Jimmy with Richard Whittingham. *The Truth Hurts*. Contemporary Books, Inc. 1984.

[53] *Boston Globe*, July 31, 1982.

[54] *St. Louis Post-Dispatch*, June 15, 1978.

[55] Caray and Matlack spoke on the telephone. "He was just angry because the Rangers had lost and his team had made a couple of bad defensive plays behind him," Harry explained. *Chicago Tribune,* June 16, 1978.

[56] Ibid, September 15, 1978.

[57] Ibid, July 3, 1980. "If I wanted to hurt Gallas, I would have and could have. But I didn't," Piersall later claimed. "I just wanted to shake him up a little. After it, however, he went around telling everybody that I tried to strangle him." Piersall, *The Truth Hurts*.

[58] Ibid.

[59] "I hope people realize what scum they [Caray and Piersall] are," White Sox owner Jerry Reinsdorf said after the White Sox clinched the American League West in 1983, a comment he later regretted. "The word I used wasn't very gentlemanly. I regret it. But it felt good to say it." He had earlier told reporters that "My biggest mistake was not firing Harry Caray and Jimmy Piersall before the 1981 season." *Chicago Tribune*, September 19, 1983.

[60] Logan, Bob. *Miracle on 35th Street: Winnin' Ugly with the 1983 White Sox*. Icarus Press. 1983.

[61] Ibid.

[62] Piersall was accused of giving the finger to home plate umpire Joe Brinkman from the broadcast booth, a charge Piersall denied. "I went like this with my hands," he said, indicating Brinkman had called a strike on a ball he thought was outside. "Then he started giving me the (rolling) hip motion, so I gave him the thumbs-up gesture, not the finger." The Umpires' Union later threatened to take Piersall to court. Umpire Dale Ford, who was at the first base when the incident occurred, claimed Piersall was leaning out of the booth, "trying to incite the crowd against us." *Chicago Tribune*, June 4, 1981.

[63] Ibid, September 16, 1981.

64 "I miss Piersall," Harry said during his first year with the Cubs. "We're a hell of a team." Ibid, September 14, 1982.
65 The White Sox replaced Caray and Piersall with Don Drysdale and Ken Harrelson. Piersall did pregame and postgame shows for the White Sox for a time before getting fired from that role.
66 *The Rock Island Argus*, August 22, 1969.
67 The three years were 1906, 2008, and 2020.
68 *Phoenix New Times*, July 4, 1990.
69 *The Dispatch* (Moline, Illinois), January 12, 1982. Shane lasted one season with the White Sox. After unsuccessfully auditioning for an on-air role for CBS in New York, she taught high school in suburban Milwaukee and later moved back to Illinois to work for *The Dispatch*. After two and a half years in the Quad Cities, she joined the *Worcester Telegram* to cover the Boston Celtics. See "Mary Shane's Rookie Season" at Slate.com.
70 *Memphis Press-Scimitar*, May 5, 1982.
71 *St. Louis Post-Dispatch,* May 23, 1982.
72 *Chicago Tribune*, April 16, 1982.
73 Ibid, June 7, 2022.
74 "The Chicago Cubs have become America's team," wrote Bob Hertzel in a syndicated column that appeared in papers around the country in September 1984. "And if the Cubs are America's team, then Harry Caray is the voice of America, because this is the day and age of the Superstation."
75 *St. Petersburg Times*, September 23, 1984.
76 *Chicago Tribune*, March 4, 1985.
77 *St. Louis Post-Dispatch*, May 2, 1988.
78 Ibid, August 26, 1998.
79 Ibid, February 22, 1998.
80 Wolfe and Castle, *I Remember Harry Caray*. "If it was me who had died," Buck said shortly after Caray passed, "Harry Caray wouldn't be crying now. Not because we weren't pals, but because he always had a way of accepting things." *St. Petersburg Times*, February 19, 1998.
81 *Hello Again, Everybody: The Harry Caray Story*. The documentary can be viewed on YouTube.

Appendix

Timeline of Events – November 1968 to November 1969

Fall 1968

- With the Cardinals in Japan for a postseason tour, Caray is seriously injured attempting to cross Kingshighway in St. Louis on the way to a late-night liaison with an unidentified female companion.
- Susan Busch, the wife of August Busch III and a volunteer at Barnes hospital, visits Caray frequently.

Winter 1969

- Caray convalesces at the Florida home of Gussie Busch. His long-distance phone calls during this period would later draw scrutiny from the highest levels of the organization.
- August and Susan Busch separate in February.
- Gussie Busch delivers a lecture to players on escalating salaries.

Spring 1969

- With the Cardinals in Canada for the first-ever MLB series outside the United States, Caray criticizes the playing conditions at Jarry Park in Montreal and questions why baseball owners didn't select the city of Milwaukee for expansion, instead.
- Al Fleishman documents Caray's comments in a memo sent to Gussie Busch.
- Brewery workers at all Anheuser-Busch plants begin a 34-day strike in May.

Summer 1969

- Strike ends. Revenue drops $37 million compared to the prior-year period.
- August Busch III reportedly tenders his resignation, an offer rejected by his father.

- On July 13, Pittsburgh Pirates broadcaster Bob Prince reportedly receives a "six-figure, five-year" offer to work in St. Louis.
- Four days later, on July 17, Caray's request for long-distance phone call reimbursement while recuperating from his injuries is rejected. Harry is asked to provide additional details. "I will be curious to see just how detailed his 'explanation' will be," William Fisher of Gardner Advertising writes to Fleishman.
- Ten days after the reported offer to Prince and six days after his reimbursement rejection, Caray claims to hear for the first time that his contract won't be renewed.
- Susan Busch files for divorce on August 15.
- Three days later, newspapers in Pittsburgh publish the reported offer to Prince. Both the Cardinals and KMOX radio deny making any offer.
- In September, a *Post-Dispatch* reporter asks Caray to comment on a report that he is being fired. "I'd be the last to know that," Harry responds.

Fall 1969

- "This is my last season," with the Cardinals, Caray tells a reporter on the final day of the baseball season.
- Later that day, Caray sends champagne to the Cardinals' locker room. "Send it back," orders general manager Bing Devine.
- Shortly after the season ends, the Cardinals increase ticket prices for 1970, cancel all public relations caravan tours, eliminate their off-season speakers bureau and trade Curt Flood, Tim McCarver and two other players to the Philadelphia Phillies.
- The day after the trade, Anheuser-Busch cancels Caray's daily 10-minute sports show on KMOX.
- One day after that move, the brewery announces that Caray's contract will not be renewed.
- August and Susan Busch officially divorce in November.
- Giving a speech in Peoria, Illinois eleven days after the divorce, Caray addresses the rumors surrounding him and Susan Busch for the first time. "I have always had nothing but friendly affection and respect for her. If this is having an affair, our society is sick."

Holy Cow St. Louis!

www.ingramcontent.com/pod-product-compliance
Lightning Source LLC
Chambersburg PA
CBHW032031150426
43194CB00006B/228